THE LOEB CLASSICAL LIBRARY

FOUNDED BY JAMES LOEB 1911

EDITED BY

JEFFREY HENDERSON

EDITOR EMERITUS

G. P. GOOLD

EURIPIDES

V

LCL 11

EURIPIDES

HELEN
PHOENICIAN WOMEN
ORESTES

EDITED AND TRANSLATED BY
DAVID KOVACS

HARVARD UNIVERSITY PRESS
CAMBRIDGE, MASSACHUSETTS
LONDON, ENGLAND
2002

Library of Congress Catalog Card Number 2001047078
CIP data available from the Library of Congress

21.50
7/02 M-W
So

ISBN 0-674-99600-3

CONTENTS

For Charles Willink

PREFACE

The Greek text, as in earlier volumes, is my own, and my editorial principles are explained in the introduction in Volume One. I discuss in a forthcoming book called *Euripidea Tertia* some of the readings and translations adopted here. As usual, text enclosed between square brackets is deemed to be spurious, while text enclosed between angle brackets are words thought to have been accidentally omitted from the manuscripts. As in previous volumes, where I have marked a lacuna of a line or more I have usually filled in, purely by way of illustration, what the sense seems to require. Unattributed supplements are my own.

As in Volumes Three and Four I have marked passages written in lyric meters and sung in the original performance by translating them line-for-line to match the Greek. For spoken verse I use the ordinary typography of prose.

It is a pleasure to acknowledge debts of gratitude incurred. A grant from the National Endowment for the Humanities enabled me to devote the academic year 1996–7 to parts of this volume as well as its predecessor. I was also elected, for that year, to a Visiting Fellowship at Balliol College, Oxford. My deepest thanks to both bodies.

Work on parts of this volume and its successor were

PREFACE

aided by a grant from the Earhart Foundation, research leave from the University of Virginia, and a Visiting Fellowship at Trinity College, Cambridge. I am immensely grateful to the Master and Fellows of Trinity for their generosity and especially to Roger Dawe, who kindly discussed textual problems with me. Residence in Cambridge has also allowed me to benefit from the kindness, learning, and acuity of James Diggle. I have profited immensely over the years from discussions with Charles Willink, and it is to him that this volume is dedicated in thanks for his stimulating friendship.

University of Virginia   David Kovacs

ABBREVIATIONS

AJP	*American Journal of Philology*
ASNP	*Annali della Scuola Normale Superiore di Pisa*
CP	*Classical Philology*
CR	*Classical Review*
GRBS	*Greek, Roman, and Byzantine Studies*
HSCP	*Harvard Studies in Classical Philology*
JHS	*Journal of Hellenic Studies*
RhM	*Rheinisches Museum*
SIFC	*Studi Italiani di Filologia Classica*
SO	*Symbolae Osloenses*
TAPA	*Transactions of the American Philological Association*

HELEN

INTRODUCTION

Helen the virtuous and faithful wife, the Helen who never went to Troy but stayed in Egypt, falsely blamed for the actions of her divinely created *Doppelgänger* at Troy—these novel twists to the story of the Trojan War were not new with Euripides. Stesichorus, a lyric poet from Himera in Sicily who lived in the first half of the sixth century, wrote a famous palinode (i.e. a poem of recantation) in which he says, addressing Helen, "The tale is not true: you did not go on the well-benched ships and never reached the citadel of Troy" (*PMG* 192–3; see, in the Loeb series, David A. Campbell, ed., *Greek Lyric III*, pp. 92–7). The poem (or poems: there may have been two) is represented by a few paltry fragments, but according to one ancient report Stesichorus mentioned a phantom Helen. Legend has it that Stesichorus lost his sight after writing an earlier poem vituperating Helen, but that after his recantation the deified Helen restored it.

Euripides' older contemporary Herodotus also mentions a version of the story that put Helen in Egypt, not in Troy, while the Trojan War was being fought. He claims (*Histories* 2.112–20) that priests at Memphis told him the following story: Paris and Helen stopped at Egypt on their way to Troy, Paris' slave let it be known that his master was making off with his host's wife and treasure, and King Proteus made Paris leave both Helen and treasure behind; then when the Greeks arrived at Troy, the Trojans could not persuade them that Paris had done so; only after Troy was sacked was it clear that the Trojans had been telling the truth; Menelaus then returned home by way of Egypt. Herodotus' story is a rationalizing one: there is no supernatural phantom and no evidence of divine intervention in affairs. But it furnished Euripides with the locale of his play.

The plot, as usual, shows evidence of careful construction. Helen speaks the prologue in which she outlines her situation. When the three goddesses, Hera, Athena, and Aphrodite, competed in a beauty contest before the Trojan prince Paris, the prince awarded the prize to Aphrodite, who had bribed him by promising him marriage to Helen of Sparta, the most beautiful woman alive. When it came time for Aphrodite to fulfill her promise, Hera substituted for the real Helen a phantom figure, which Paris took to Troy, and Hermes was despatched to convey the real Helen to safety in Egypt at the court of Proteus, who piously respected the trust made to him of another man's wife. Proteus' son, Theoclymenus, however, is not godfearing like his father, and he wants to marry Helen himself. She has had to take refuge at the tomb of Proteus to escape his advances. All she knows of her husband is that he has mounted an expedition to Troy to recover her. But she has also heard a prophecy that one day she and he are fated to dwell in Sparta again—if she can escape the embraces of another man.

Next a Greek warrior named Teucer arrives, on his way into exile. From him Helen learns that the war is over and that, while sailing home, Menelaus was driven off from the others by a storm and is presumed dead. She also learns from Teucer's reaction to a woman he thinks merely resembles Helen how hated she is because of deeds she never committed. In sung verse she laments her fate, and a Chorus of Greek women join in her lament. After expressing sympathy, the Chorus persuade her not to despair before asking Theoclymenus' prophetic sister Theonoe whether her husband is still alive. They all go in, leaving the stage empty. This allows the audience to see and hear Menelaus before his reunion with his wife.

Menelaus arrives dressed in sailcloth, his clothes having been ruined at sea, and he delivers a sort of second prologue, telling of his shipwreck, which left him, a few comrades, and his wife on an unknown shore. He expresses horror at the shame of begging but means to present himself at the door of this rich house. He rouses the gatekeeper, an old woman with a rough tongue, who tells him to go away. Menelaus can make nothing of her warning that Theoclymenus kills all Greeks because Helen, daughter of Zeus, is in the house.

When Helen and the Chorus return, having heard from Theonoe that Menelaus is still alive, she recognizes her husband, but he, having just left the Helen he brought back from Troy in a cave by the shore, refuses to believe that Helen is his wife and the other woman a phantom. Finally one of his men comes and reports that the phantom Helen has flown off, and this convinces Menelaus that the woman before him is indeed his wife. Husband and wife sing a duet of recognition and reunion.

But after their rejoicing Helen informs her husband of the hopelessness of the situation: he had better run for his life and leave her behind rather than be killed for her sake.

Menelaus refuses to do this, and the two pledge that they will die together if one dies. The biggest obstacle to any possible plan of escape is Theoclymenus' sister Theonoe, who, Helen says, already knows of Menelaus' arrival and might tell her brother. Helen promises to leave no form of entreaty untried to persuade her to keep this a secret.

Theonoe emerges from the palace. She is a slightly mysterious and forbidding figure with her ritual attendants purifying the air with sulphur. After reminding Helen of her accurate prophecy that Menelaus was alive, she describes the situation in heaven. Hera wants Helen to return, while Aphrodite does not, and so all depends on Theonoe. Helen and Menelaus take turns beseeching her to do the right thing and restore Helen to her husband, as her father would have wanted her to. Theonoe agrees to say nothing to her brother and departs.

Now it is time for husband and wife to plot their escape. As usual in Euripides, it is the woman who has the brains. Helen suggests that Menelaus pretend to be the messenger of his own death. Helen will profess grief but agree to marry Theoclymenus after the funeral. This, they will claim, must by Greek custom be conducted at sea. They will ask for a ship to take them out of sight of the shore, then Menelaus' men will overpower the crew and sail away. Theoclymenus, when he has learned of Menelaus' death and Helen's willingness to marry him, is all too happy to give her a ship and lots of precious gifts to be thrown overboard in honor of the deceased. After their departure the king learns from a messenger that Menelaus is alive and has rescued Helen. Just when he had decided to kill his sister for her disloyalty in not telling him of Menelaus' arrival, Castor and Polydeuces appear on the *mechane*. They forbid him to take vengeance on his sister, promise Helen and Menelaus a safe journey home, and predict that Helen will become a goddess and Menelaus live in the islands of the blest. Theoclymenus graciously accepts the *fait accompli*, and the play ends with five choral anapests that Euripides had used in *Alcestis, Andromache,* and (with a small change) in *Medea*, to the effect that with the gods in the picture mortal expectations are defeated.

Helen was produced in 412 B.C. Like the nearly contemporary *Iphigenia among the Taurians* and *Ion* it ends happily. But all three Athenian tragedians wrote such plays, and there is nothing paradoxical, from the ancient point of view, about a *tragoidia* that turns out happily for the principal characters. The similarities in plot between *Helen* and *Iphigenia* are striking. In both a woman finds herself in a foreign land, in one case with disagreeable duties (Iphigenia must participate in human sacrifice) and in the other with a disagreeable suitor (Theoclymenus, the new king of Egypt). In both cases the gods spirited the woman there, and her family does not know where she is. A close male relative arrives (Iphigenia's brother Orestes, Helen's husband Menelaus), and after the man and the woman have established their identities, they plot to rescue themselves from this hostile environment. The main blocking figure in each case is a local barbarian king. The two protagonists prevail over him by a ruse involving a religious ceremony: Iphigenia pretends that the statue of Artemis that Orestes has been instructed by Apollo to steal is in urgent need of cleansing because of contact with a murderer, while Helen pretends that she wants to give her husband a burial at sea. Thus each pair of Greeks manages to

get away, and a god intervenes to see to it that those who
are complicit in the escape are not punished.

Though *Iphigenia* and *Helen* show a striking structural
similarity, there are differences as well, and these are im-
portant for the way the plays affect their audience. In
Iphigenia it is crucial that brother and sister were sepa-
rated when Orestes was a small child and that therefore
brother and sister cannot recognize each other by sight.
The Oedipus theme, that it is impossible to know who
your parents or other relatives really are, and hence that it
is possible under unpropitious circumstances to commit
horrible crimes against one's kin, finds its counterpart in
Iphigenia, for it is Iphigenia's duty to sacrifice all foreign-
ers to Artemis, and she comes very close to assisting in her
brother's sacrifice. In fact, however, both Orestes' capture
and near sacrifice by Iphigenia, and the fact that the sacri-
fice does not take place, are the result of the kind of happy
chance that can only be ascribed to the unseen guidance of
events by the gods. The human perspective is extremely
limited, but behind the phenomena of human life stand
the fixed purposes of heaven.

In *Helen*, by contrast, a different version of the theme
of human fallibility and weakness comes to the fore. The
radical insecurity of a world in which one does not know
who one's close relatives are does not appear here. Instead
of this form of insecurity, the play introduces another,
epistemological, one in which, because of the intervention
of the gods, the real is always shadowed by the unreal. In
the second half of the prologue, for example, Teucer is
convinced that the woman he sees before him is not Helen,
though in fact she is, and he is convinced that the real

Helen is a morally reprobate person whose wantonness has caused immense destruction, when in fact she is not. As he leaves he congratulates his unknown informant on being, despite resemblance to her in looks, a better woman than Helen. When Menelaus comes on in the absence of Helen and is told by the gatekeeper that he'd better run for it since the local king Theoclymenus kills all foreigners because of a woman named Helen, daughter of Zeus, he tries to make sense of this by supposing mere homonymy. But though he tries the supposition that there is a local man called Zeus who fathered a woman called Helen, he knows that this will not cover the facts. When he finally meets his wife, he nearly leaves her behind, convinced that his real wife is the phantom Helen being kept in a cave, not the woman before him.

Contributing to the bewilderment of the situation is the discord among the gods. Theonoe tells Menelaus of a strife between Hera and Aphrodite, a strife that Theonoe will have to decide: it is up to her whether he can return, for if she tells her brother, return is impossible. Only at the end do we learn from Castor that Theonoe's decision to allow his return is also that of the whole assembly of gods.

There is also another mythical pattern that serves as a backdrop to the action, that of Persephone, carried off by Hades to the underworld. Helen sings (244–5) that Hermes carried her off as she was picking flowers, precisely the circumstances of Persephone's abduction. Helen's return from Egypt is thus a kind of return, like the annual return of Persephone that signals the fertile time of the year. The choral ode at 1301–68, often thought of as a pretty irrelevance, serves to underline this mythic pattern.

Mostly, though, the play gives pleasure by its polish and

cleverness, the beauty of its lyrics, its shifts of mood from despair to elation, and the quick wit and presence of mind of the rehabilitated heroine, who fools Theoclymenus while uttering scarcely a single lie.

Within a year (or possibly two) of its first production, an extended parody of *Helen* was prominently featured in Aristophanes' *Women Celebrating the Thesmophoria* (lines 855–923). The premise of this play is that the women of Athens are conspiring at the women's festival of the Thesmophoria to punish Euripides for portraying women in a bad light. Euripides gets wind of the plot and persuades a kinsman to disguise himself as a woman and attend the festival. He is discovered and kept under guard, and his attempts to get Euripides to rescue him take the form of his impersonating Helen and Andromeda, while Euripides plays the role of their rescuers Menelaus and Perseus. It is thanks to this parody that we are able to restore *Helen* 561, omitted from our only manuscript.

SELECT BIBLIOGRAPHY

Editions

A. M. Dale (Oxford, 1967).
R. Kannicht (Heidelberg, 1969).

Literary Criticism

W. G. Arnott, "Euripides' Newfangled *Helen*," *Antichthon* 24 (1990), 1–18.
A. P. Burnett, *Catastrophe Survived: Euripides' Plays of Mixed Reversal* (Oxford, 1971), pp. 76–100.

———— "Euripides' *Helen*, a Comedy of Ideas," *CP* 55 (1960), 151–63.

R. Eisner, "Echoes of the *Odyssey* in Euripides' *Helen*," *Maia* 32 (1980), 31–7.

H. P. Foley, "*Anodos* Drama: Euripides' *Alcestis* and *Helen*," in R. Hexter and D. Selden, edd., *Innovations of Antiquity* (New York, 1992), pp. 133–60.

B. M. W. Knox, "Euripidean Comedy," in *Word and Action: Essays on the Ancient Theater* (Baltimore, 1979), pp. 250–74.

C. P. Segal, "The Two Worlds of Euripides' *Helen*," *TAPA* 102 (1971), 553–614.

F. Solmsen, "Ὄνομα and πρᾶγμα in Euripides' *Helen*," *CR* 48 (1934), 119–21.

C. H. Whitman, *Euripides and the Full Circle of Myth* (Cambridge, Mass., 1974), pp. 35–68.

C. Wolf, "On Euripides' *Helen*," *HSCP* 77 (1973), 61–84.

G. Zuntz, "On Euripides' *Helena*: Theology and Irony," *Entretiens sur l'Antiquité classique, VI: Euripide* (Vandoeuvres and Geneva, 1958), pp. 201–27.

ΕΛΕΝΗ	HELEN, daughter of Zeus and Leda and wife of Menelaus
ΤΕΥΚΡΟΣ	TEUCER, a Greek warrior, brother of Ajax
ΧΟΡΟΣ	CHORUS of captive Greek women living in Egypt
ΜΕΝΕΛΕΩΣ	MENELAUS, husband of Helen
ΓΡΑΥΣ	OLD WOMAN, servant of Theoclymenus
ΘΕΡΑΠΩΝ	SERVANT of Menelaus
ΘΕΟΝΟΗ	THEONOE, sister of Theoclymenus
ΘΕΟΚΛΥΜΕΝΟΣ	THEOCLYMENUS, king of Egypt
ΑΓΓΕΛΟΣ	Servant of Theoclymenus as MESSENGER
ΘΕΡΑΠΩΝ Β	SECOND SERVANT, slave of Theonoe
ΚΑΣΤΩΡ	CASTOR, deified brother of Helen

Nonspeaking role: Polydeuces, twin brother of Castor

A Note On Staging

The *skene* represents the palace of Theoclymenus in Egypt. Before it is the tomb of Theoclymenus' father Proteus. Eisodos A leads to the seashore, Eisodos B to the inland portions of Theoclymenus' kingdom.

11

ΕΛΕΝΗ

Νείλου μὲν αἵδε καλλιπάρθενοι ῥοαί,
ὃς ἀντὶ δίας ψακάδος Αἰγύπτου γύας
λευκῆς τακείσης χιόνος ὑγραίνει δρόσῳ.
Πρωτεὺς δ᾽ ὅτ᾽ ἔζη τῆσδε γῆς τύραννος ἦν,
5 [Φάρον μὲν οἰκῶν νῆσον, Αἰγύπτου δ᾽ ἄναξ,]
ὃς τῶν κατ᾽ οἶδμα παρθένων μίαν γαμεῖ,
Ψαμάθην, ἐπειδὴ λέκτρ᾽ ἀφῆκεν Αἰακοῦ.
τίκτει δὲ τέκνα δισσὰ τοῖσδ᾽ ἐν δώμασιν,
Θεοκλύμενον ἄρσεν᾽ [†ὅτι δὴ† θεοὺς σέβων
10 βίον διήνεγκ᾽] εὐγενῆ τε παρθένον
Εἰδώ, τὸ μητρὸς ἀγλάισμ᾽, ὅτ᾽ ἦν βρέφος·
ἐπεὶ δ᾽ ἐς ἥβην ἦλθεν ὡραίαν γάμων,
καλοῦσιν αὐτὴν Θεονόην· τὰ θεῖα γὰρ
τά τ᾽ ὄντα καὶ μέλλοντα πάντ᾽ ἠπίστατο,
15 προγόνου λαβοῦσα Νηρέως τιμὰς πάρα.

2–3 γύας . . . δρόσῳ Heiland: πέδον . . . γύας L
5 del. Dingelstad   7 Αἰακοῦ Musgrave: αἰόλου L
8 τοῖσδ᾽ ἐν Lenting: τοῖσδε L   9b–10a del. Nauck
11 Εἰδώ Matthiae: εἶδος L
12 ὡραίαν Reiske: -ων L

12

HELEN

Before the skene, *representing the palace of the Egyptian king Theoclymenus, is the tomb of his father Proteus. When the action begins,* HELEN *is sitting at the tomb as a suppliant.*

HELEN

Here flows the Nile with its fair nymphs! Fed by the melting of pale snow it drenches Egypt's fields with moisture in place of rain sent from Zeus. Proteus, while he lived, was king of this land [dwelling in the island of Pharos but lord of Egypt]. He married Psamathe, one of the maids of the water, when she had left the bed of Aeacus. In this house she bore two children, a boy named Theoclymenus [because he honored the gods throughout his life] and a fine maiden called Eido. When she was a babe she was her mother's glory, but when she came to womanhood and was old enough to marry they called her Theonoe: for she knew all that divination can tell, both present and future, receiving this office from her ancestor Nereus.[1]

---

[1] "Theo-noe" indicates someone whose mind (*nous*) is divinely inspired. For her grandfather Nereus as a prophetic figure see Hesiod, *Theogony* 233–6.

ἡμῖν δὲ γῆ μὲν πατρὶς οὐκ ἀνώνυμος
Σπάρτη, πατὴρ δὲ Τυνδάρεως (ἔστιν δὲ δὴ
λόγος τις ὡς Ζεὺς μητέρ' ἔπτατ' εἰς ἐμὴν
Λήδαν κύκνου μορφώματ' ὄρνιθος λαβών
20 [ὃς δόλιον εὐνὴν ἐξέπραξ' ὑπ' αἰετοῦ
δίωγμα φεύγων, εἰ σαφὴς οὗτος λόγος]),
Ἑλένη δ' ἐκλήθην. ἃ δὲ πεπόνθαμεν κακὰ
λέγοιμ' ἄν. ἦλθον τρεῖς θεαὶ κάλλους πέρι
Ἰδαῖον ἐς κευθμῶν' Ἀλέξανδρον πάρα,
25 Ἥρα Κύπρις τε διογενής τε παρθένος,
μορφῆς θέλουσαι διαπεράνασθαι κρίσιν.
τοὐμὸν δὲ κάλλος, εἰ καλὸν τὸ δυστυχές,
Κύπρις προτείνασ' ὡς Ἀλέξανδρος γαμεῖ,
νικᾷ. λιπὼν δὲ βούσταθμ' Ἰδαῖος Πάρις
30 Σπάρτην ἀφίκεθ' ὡς ἐμὸν σχήσων λέχος.
   Ἥρα δὲ μεμφθεῖσ' οὕνεκ' οὐ νικᾷ θεὰς
ἐξηνέμωσε τἄμ' Ἀλεξάνδρῳ λέχη,
δίδωσι δ' οὐκ ἔμ' ἀλλ' ὁμοιώσασ' ἐμοὶ
εἴδωλον ἔμπνουν οὐρανοῦ ξυνθεῖσ' ἄπο
35 Πριάμου τυράννου παιδί· καὶ δοκεῖ μ' ἔχειν,
κενὴν δόκησιν, οὐκ ἔχων. τὰ δ' αὖ Διὸς
βουλεύματ' ἄλλα τοῖσδε συμβαίνει κακοῖς·
πόλεμον γὰρ εἰσήνεγκεν Ἑλλήνων χθονὶ
καὶ Φρυξὶ δυστήνοισιν, ὡς ὄχλου βροτῶν
40 πλήθους τε κουφίσειε μητέρα χθόνα
γνωτόν τε θείη τὸν κράτιστον Ἑλλάδος.

20–1 del. Kovacs   34 ἄπο Reiske: ὕπο L

14

As for me, glorious Sparta is my homeland, Tyndareus is my father (though there is a story that Zeus flew to my mother Leda in the shape of a swan [who was fleeing from an eagle and had his way with her by treachery, if that story is reliable]), and Helen is my name. I will tell you the troubles I have suffered. Three goddesses, Hera, Cypris,[2] and Zeus's maiden daughter,[3] came to a remote vale of Ida to Alexandros, and loveliness was the cause: they wanted to be judged in a beauty contest. Cypris offered marriage to my beautiful self—if what is unfortunate can be called beautiful—to Alexandros and won the contest. So Paris of Ida left his herds[4] and came to Sparta to take me as his wife.

But Hera, annoyed that she did not defeat the other goddesses, made Alexandros' union with me as vain as the wind: she gave to king Priam's son not me but a breathing image she fashioned from the heavens to resemble me. He imagines—vain imagination—that he has me, though he does not. Joined to these woes were further woes in turn, the plan of Zeus. He brought war upon the Greeks and the poor Trojans to relieve Mother Earth of the throng and press of humankind and also make plain who was the most valiant man in Greece.[5] And for the fight against the Tro-

[2] A frequent name for Aphrodite.   [3] Pallas Athena.

[4] Paris, also called Alexandros, though a prince of Troy, was herding cattle on Mt. Ida when he acted as judge of the goddesses.

[5] Here, as at *Orestes* 1639–42 and *Electra* 1281–2, Euripides follows the story of the lost epic *Cypria* (fr. 1) that Zeus fomented the Trojan War in order to relieve the goddess Earth, oppressed by overpopulation.

---

38 γένει Herwerden

Φρυγῶν δ' ἐς ἀλκὴν προυτέθην ἐγὼ μὲν οὔ,
τὸ δ' ὄνομα τοὐμόν, ἆθλον Ἕλλησιν δορός.
 λαβὼν δέ μ' Ἑρμῆς ἐν πτυχαῖσιν αἰθέρος
45 νεφέλῃ καλύψας—οὐ γὰρ ἠμέλησέ μου
Ζεύς—τόνδ' ἐς οἶκον Πρωτέως ἱδρύσατο,
πάντων προκρίνας σωφρονέστατον βροτῶν,
ἀκέραιον ὡς σώσαιμι Μενέλεῳ λέχος.
κἀγὼ μὲν ἐνθάδ' εἴμ', ὁ δ' ἄθλιος πόσις
50 στράτευμ' ἀθροίσας τὰς ἐμὰς ἀναρπαγὰς
θηρᾷ πορευθεὶς Ἰλίου πυργώματα.
ψυχαὶ δὲ πολλαὶ δι' ἔμ' ἐπὶ Σκαμανδρίοις
ῥοαῖσιν ἔθανον· ἡ δὲ πάντα τλᾶσ' ἐγὼ
κατάρατός εἰμι καὶ δοκῶ προδοῦσ' ἐμὸν
55 πόσιν συνάψαι πόλεμον Ἕλλησιν μέγαν.
 τί οὖν ἔτι ζῶ; θεοῦ τόδ' εἰσήκουσ' ἔπος
Ἑρμοῦ, τὸ κλεινὸν ἔτι κατοικήσειν πέδον
Σπάρτης σὺν ἀνδρί, γνόντος ὡς ἐς Ἴλιον
οὐκ ἦλθον, ἢν μὴ λέκτρ' ὑποστρώσω τινί.
60 ἕως μὲν οὖν φῶς ἡλίου τόδ' ἔβλεπεν
Πρωτεύς, ἄσυλος ἦ γάμων· ἐπεὶ δὲ γῆς
σκότῳ κέκρυπται, παῖς ὁ τοῦ τεθνηκότος
θηρᾷ γαμεῖν με. τὸν πάλαι δ' ἐγὼ πόσιν
τιμῶσα Πρωτέως μνῆμα προσπίτνω τόδε
65 ἱκέτις, ἵν' ἀνδρὶ τἀμὰ διασώσῃ λέχη,
ὡς, εἰ καθ' Ἑλλάδ' ὄνομα δυσκλεὲς φέρω,
μή μοι τὸ σῶμά γ' ἐνθάδ' αἰσχύνην ὄφλῃ.

---

42 προυτέθην Musgrave: προὐθέμην L

jans I was put forward for the Greeks as a prize of war
(though it was not me but only my name).

So Hermes took me up within the recesses of the sky,
hiding me in a cloud (for Zeus had not forgotten me), and
put me down at this house of Proteus, whom he judged the
most virtuous man on earth, so that I might keep my bed
unsullied for Menelaus. Here I am, but my poor husband,
gathering an army, went to the towers of Ilium to win me
back by force. Many lives were lost by Scamander's stream
because of me. And I, who have suffered everything, am
cursed by men, and all think that I have abandoned my
husband and brought a great war upon the Greeks.

Why then do I still live? I have heard a prophecy from
the god Hermes that I shall one day live in Sparta's plain
with my husband, who will learn that I did not go to
Ilium—provided I do not share my bed with anyone.
While Proteus still looked on the light of the sun, no mar-
riage threatened me. But now that he lies buried in earth's
darkness, the late king's son wants to marry me. Hence
honoring the husband I once had I have flung myself as a
suppliant upon this tomb of Proteus so that it may keep me
inviolate for him: even if my name is reviled in Greece, my
body shall not here be put to shame.

Enter by Eisodos A TEUCER.

---

56 οὖν t: δῆτ᾽ L
58 γνόντος] fort. γνωτὸν
59 ἦν Dobree: ἵνα L
67 μή μοι] οὐ μὴ Diggle

ΤΕΥΚΡΟΣ

τίς τῶνδ' ἐρυμνῶν δωμάτων ἔχει κράτος;
Πλούτῳ γὰρ οἶκος ἄξιος προσεικάσαι,
70 βασίλειά τ' ἀμφιβλήματ' εὔθριγκοί θ' ἕδραι.
    ἔα·
ὦ θεοί, τίν' εἶδον ὄψιν; ἐχθίστης ὁρῶ
γυναικὸς εἰκὼ φόνιον, ἥ μ' ἀπώλεσεν
πάντας τ' Ἀχαιούς. θεοί σ', ὅσον μίμημ' ἔχεις
75 Ἑλένης, ἀποπτύσειαν. εἰ δὲ μὴ 'ν ξένῃ
γαίᾳ πόδ' εἶχον, τῷδ' ἂν εὐστόχῳ πτερῷ
ἀπόλαυσιν εἰκοῦς ἔθανες ἂν Διὸς κόρης.

ΕΛΕΝΗ

τί δ', ὦ ταλαίπωρ', ὅστις εἶ μ' ἀπεστράφης
καὶ ταῖς ἐκείνης συμφοραῖς ἐμὲ στυγεῖς;

ΤΕΥΚΡΟΣ

80 ἥμαρτον ὀργῇ τ' εἶξα μᾶλλον ἤ μ' ἐχρῆν·
μισεῖ γὰρ Ἑλλὰς πᾶσα τὴν Διὸς κόρην.
σύγγνωθι δ' ἡμῖν τοῖς λελεγμένοις, γύναι.

ΕΛΕΝΗ

τίς δ' εἶ; πόθεν γῆς τῆσδ' ἐπεστράφης πέδον;

ΤΕΥΚΡΟΣ

εἷς τῶν Ἀχαιῶν, ὦ γύναι, τῶν ἀθλίων . . .

ΕΛΕΝΗ

85 οὐ τἄρα σ' Ἑλένην εἰ στυγεῖς θαυμαστέον.

---

69 Πλούτῳ Nauck: -του L
71 ἐχθίστης Dingelstad: -ην L

HELEN

TEUCER

Who is the master of these well fortified halls? The house is
worthy to be compared with that of Plutus[6] himself, so
royal is its circuit and so lovely the coping of its chambers!

Ah! O gods, what sight is this I see? The deadly image
of a woman most hateful, her who ruined me and all
the Greeks! The gods' hatred be yours for being Helen's
double! If I were not standing on foreign soil, this unerring
arrow would have killed you for looking like Zeus's daugh-
ter!

HELEN

Poor man, whoever you are, why do you recoil from me?
Why loathe *me* for the troubles *she* has caused?

TEUCER

It was wrong of me, and I yielded too much to anger. All
Hellas hates Zeus's daughter. Pardon me for what I have
said, lady.

HELEN

Who are you? What has brought you to this land?

TEUCER

I, lady, one of the unlucky Greeks . . .

HELEN

No wonder, then, that you hate Helen! [But who are you

6 God of wealth.

---

77 ἀπόλαυσιν Reiske: ἀπώλλυσ'. ἵν' L
78 εἶ Cobet: ὢν L   80 τ' Kovacs: δ' L
81 suspectum habuit Nauck, del. Behrns
84 τῶν] ὢν Herwerden

[ἀτὰρ τίς εἶ πόθεν; τίνος ἐξαυδᾶν σε χρή;

ΤΕΥΚΡΟΣ

ὄνομα μὲν ἡμῖν Τεῦκρος, ὁ δὲ φύσας πατὴρ
Τελαμών, Σαλαμὶς δὲ πατρὶς ἡ θρέψασά με.

ΕΛΕΝΗ

τί δῆτα Νείλου τούσδ᾽ ἐπιστρέφῃ γύας;]

ΤΕΥΚΡΟΣ

90   . . . φυγὰς πατρῴας ἐξελήλαμαι χθονός.

ΕΛΕΝΗ

τλήμων ἂν εἴης· τίς δέ σ᾽ ἐκβάλλει πάτρας;

ΤΕΥΚΡΟΣ

Τελαμὼν ὁ φύσας. τίν᾽ ἂν ἔχοις μᾶλλον φίλον;

ΕΛΕΝΗ

ἐκ τοῦ; τὸ γάρ τοι πρᾶγμα συμφορὰν ἔχει.

ΤΕΥΚΡΟΣ

Αἴας μ᾽ ἀδελφὸς ὤλεσ᾽ ἐν Τροίᾳ θανών.

ΕΛΕΝΗ

95   πῶς; οὔ τί που σῷ φασγάνῳ βίου στερείς;

ΤΕΥΚΡΟΣ

οἰκεῖον αὐτὸν ὤλεσ᾽ ἅλμ᾽ ἐπὶ ξίφος.

ΕΛΕΝΗ

μανέντ᾽; ἐπεὶ τίς σωφρονῶν τλαίη τόδ᾽ ἄν;

86–9 del. Diggle post Badham, qui 85–8 suspectos habuit
95 βίου Burges: βίον L
97 τόδ᾽ Wecklein: τάδ᾽ L

and where have you come from? Whose son must I call
you?

TEUCER

My name is Teucer, the father who begot me is Telamon,
and Salamis is the land that brought me up.

HELEN

Then why have you come to this land of the Nile?]

TEUCER

. . . have been exiled from my native country.

HELEN

How terrible for you! Who exiled you?

TEUCER

Telamon my father. What closer relative does a man have?

HELEN

But why? There is unhappiness in this story.

TEUCER

My brother Ajax' death at Troy was my undoing.

HELEN

How? Surely it was not by your sword that he died?

TEUCER

It was leaping on his own sword that killed him.

HELEN

Was he mad? No sane man would have done this.

EURIPIDES

ΤΕΥΚΡΟΣ

τὸν Πηλέως τιν' οἶσθ' Ἀχιλλέα γόνον;

ΕΛΕΝΗ

ναί·
μνηστήρ ποθ' Ἑλένης ἦλθεν, ὡς ἀκούομεν.

ΤΕΥΚΡΟΣ

100 θανὼν ὅδ' ὅπλων ἔριν ἔθηκε συμμάχοις.

ΕΛΕΝΗ

καὶ δὴ τί τοῦτ' Αἴαντι γίγνεται κακόν;

ΤΕΥΚΡΟΣ

ἄλλου λαβόντος ὅπλ' ἀπηλλάχθη βίου.

ΕΛΕΝΗ

σὺ τοῖς ἐκείνου δῆτα πήμασιν νοσεῖς;

ΤΕΥΚΡΟΣ

ὁθούνεκ' αὐτῷ γ' οὐ ξυνωλόμην ὁμοῦ.

ΕΛΕΝΗ

105 ἦλθες γάρ, ὦ ξέν', Ἰλίου κλεινὴν πόλιν;

ΤΕΥΚΡΟΣ

καὶ ξύν γε πέρσας αὐτὸς ἀνταπωλόμην.

ΕΛΕΝΗ

ἤδη γὰρ ἧπται καὶ κατείργασται πυρί;

ΤΕΥΚΡΟΣ

ὥστ' οὐδ' ἴχνος γε τειχέων εἶναι σαφές.

ΕΛΕΝΗ

ὦ τλῆμον Ἑλένη, διὰ σ' ἀπόλλυνται Φρύγες.

HELEN

TEUCER
Do you know of a man called Achilles, Peleus' son?

HELEN
Yes: I heard he once came as Helen's suitor.

TEUCER
His death caused his comrades to quarrel for his armor.

HELEN
But how did this bring trouble upon Ajax?

TEUCER
When another man got the armor, he killed himself.

HELEN
And you suffer from his woes?

TEUCER
Yes, because I did not die with him.

HELEN
Did you really go to the renowned city of Ilium, stranger?

TEUCER
Yes: I helped sack it but came to grief myself.

HELEN
What, has it already been destroyed by fire?

TEUCER
Yes: you cannot even see for sure the footprint of its walls.

HELEN
Poor Helen! On your account the Trojans are ruined!

---

99 Ἑλένης ⟨γ'⟩ Willink deleto ναί

23

ΤΕΥΚΡΟΣ

110 καὶ πρός γ᾽ Ἀχαιοί· μεγάλα δ᾽ εἴργασται κακά.

ΕΛΕΝΗ

πόσον χρόνον γὰρ διαπεπόρθηται πόλις;

ΤΕΥΚΡΟΣ

ἑπτὰ σχεδόν τι καρπίμους ἐτῶν κύκλους.

ΕΛΕΝΗ

χρόνον δ᾽ ἐμείνατ᾽ ἄλλον ἐν Τροίᾳ πόσον;

ΤΕΥΚΡΟΣ

πολλὰς σελήνας, δέκα διελθούσας ἔτη.

ΕΛΕΝΗ

115 ἦ καὶ γυναῖκα Σπαρτιᾶτιν εἵλετε;

ΤΕΥΚΡΟΣ

Μενέλαος αὐτὴν ἦγ᾽ ἐπισπάσας κόμης.

ΕΛΕΝΗ

εἶδες σὺ τὴν δύστηνον, ἢ κλυὼν λέγεις;

ΤΕΥΚΡΟΣ

ὥσπερ σέ γ᾽, οὐδὲν ἧσσον, ὀφθαλμοῖς ὁρῶ.

ΕΛΕΝΗ

σκόπει δὲ μὴ δόκησιν εἴχετ᾽ ἐκ θεῶν.

ΤΕΥΚΡΟΣ

120 ἄλλου λόγου μέμνησο, μὴ κείνης ἔτι.

112 καμπίμους Nauck
119 σκόπει δὲ A. Y. Campbell: σκοπεῖτε L

TEUCER

Yes, and the Greeks as well: great woes have been brought
to pass.

HELEN

How long has it been since Troy was destroyed?

TEUCER

Nearly seven cycles of seedtime and harvest have passed.

HELEN

And beyond that how long were you at Troy?

TEUCER

Many months: they made ten years in all.

HELEN

And did you also capture the Spartan woman?

TEUCER

Menelaus dragged her by the hair and led her off.

HELEN

Did you see the poor creature? Or do you speak at second
hand?

TEUCER

I saw her with my eyes no less than I see you.

HELEN

Take care: you might have been under some divinely sent
illusion.

TEUCER

Speak of some other subject: no more of her.

[ΕΛΕΝΗ

οὕτω δοκεῖτε τὴν δόκησιν ἀσφαλῆ;

ΤΕΥΚΡΟΣ

αὐτὸς γὰρ ὄσσοις εἰδόμην· καὶ νοῦς ὁρᾷ.]

ΕΛΕΝΗ

ἤδη δ᾽ ἐν οἴκοις σὺν δάμαρτι Μενέλεως;

ΤΕΥΚΡΟΣ

οὔκουν ἐν Ἄργει ⟨γ᾽⟩ οὐδ᾽ ἐπ᾽ Εὐρώτα ῥοαῖς.

ΕΛΕΝΗ

125   αἰαῖ· κακὸν τόδ᾽ εἶπας οἷς κακὸν λέγεις.

ΤΕΥΚΡΟΣ

ὡς κεῖνος ἀφανὴς σὺν δάμαρτι κλῄζεται.

ΕΛΕΝΗ

οὐ πᾶσι πορθμὸς αὐτὸς Ἀργείοισιν ἦν;

ΤΕΥΚΡΟΣ

ἦν, ἀλλὰ χειμὼν ἄλλοσ᾽ ἄλλον ὥρισεν.

ΕΛΕΝΗ

ποίοισιν ἐν νώτοισι ποντίας ἁλός;

ΤΕΥΚΡΟΣ

130   μέσον περῶντας πέλαγος Αἰγαίου πόρου.

ΕΛΕΝΗ

κἀκ τοῦδε Μενέλαόν τις οἶδ᾽ ἀφιγμένον;

121–2 del. W. Ribbeck
124 ⟨γ᾽⟩ Musgrave
130 περῶντας Reiske: περῶσι L

[HELEN
Are you so convinced that your impression is right?

TEUCER
I saw her with my eyes. And my mind also sees.]

HELEN
So is Menelaus now home with his wife?

TEUCER
No: not in Argos nor on Eurotas' banks.

HELEN
Ah no! How dreadful! I mean for those it touches.

TEUCER
Yes: rumor is that he and his wife have vanished.

HELEN
Didn't all the Argives sail home together?

TEUCER
Yes, but a storm drove them in different directions.

HELEN
Where were they on the sea's broad surface?

TEUCER
They were making their way through the middle of the Aegean.

HELEN
Does anyone know of Menelaus' making land after that?

---

131 Μενέλαόν τις Hermann: -ον οὔτις L: sed fort. Ἀτρείδην ποί τις

ΤΕΥΚΡΟΣ
οὐδείς· θανὼν δὲ κλῄζεται καθ᾿ Ἑλλάδα.

ΕΛΕΝΗ
ἀπωλόμεσθα· Θεστιὰς δ᾿ ἔστιν κόρη;

ΤΕΥΚΡΟΣ
Λήδαν ἔλεξας; οἴχεται θανοῦσα δή.

ΕΛΕΝΗ
135   οὔ πού νιν Ἑλένης αἰσχρὸν ὤλεσεν κλέος;

ΤΕΥΚΡΟΣ
φασίν, βρόχῳ γ᾿ ἅψασαν εὐγενῆ δέρην.

ΕΛΕΝΗ
οἱ Τυνδάρειοι δ᾿ εἰσὶν ἢ οὐκ εἰσὶν κόροι;

ΤΕΥΚΡΟΣ
τεθνᾶσι κοὐ τεθνᾶσι· δύο δ᾿ ἐστὸν λόγω.

ΕΛΕΝΗ
πότερος ὁ κρείσσων; ὦ τάλαιν᾿ ἐγὼ κακῶν.

ΤΕΥΚΡΟΣ
140   ἄστροις σφ᾿ ὁμοιωθέντε φάσ᾿ εἶναι θεώ.

ΕΛΕΝΗ
καλῶς ἔλεξας τοῦτο· θάτερον δὲ τί;

ΤΕΥΚΡΟΣ
σφαγαῖς ἀδελφῆς οὕνεκ᾿ ἐκπνεῦσαι βίον.
ἅλις δὲ μύθων· οὐ διπλᾶ χρῄζω στένειν.
ὧν δ᾿ οὕνεκ᾿ ἦλθον τούσδε βασιλείους δόμους,
145   τὴν θεσπιῳδὸν Θεονόην χρῄζων ἰδεῖν,

TEUCER

No: in Greece he is reported to be dead.

HELEN

I am undone! Is Thestias' daughter alive?

TEUCER

Do you mean Leda? She is dead and gone.

HELEN

What? Killed by Helen's shame?

TEUCER

So they say: she put a noose about her fair neck.

HELEN

Are the sons of Tyndareus alive or not?

TEUCER

Dead, not dead: there are two accounts.

HELEN

Which is the better one? Oh how miserable these woes make me!

TEUCER

That they have been made like stars and are gods.

HELEN

That at least is good news. But what is the other story?

TEUCER

That they killed themselves because of their sister.
But enough of stories: I do not want to double my tears.
I came to this royal house because I wanted to see
Theonoe, chanter of the gods' will. Arrange this visit for

σὺ προξένησον, ὡς τύχω μαντευμάτων
ὅπῃ νεὼς στείλαιμ' ἂν οὔριον πτερὸν
ἐς γῆν ἐναλίαν Κύπρον, οὗ μ' ἐθέσπισεν
οἰκεῖν Ἀπόλλων, ὄνομα νησιωτικὸν
150 Σαλαμῖνα θέμενον τῆς ἐκεῖ χάριν πάτρας.

ΕΛΕΝΗ

πλοῦς, ὦ ξέν', αὐτὸς σημανεῖ· σὺ δ' ἐκλιπὼν
γῆν τήνδε φεῦγε πρίν σε παῖδα Πρωτέως
ἰδεῖν, ὃς ἄρχει τῆσδε γῆς· ἄπεστι δὲ
κυσὶν πεποιθὼς ἐν φοναῖς θηροκτόνοις·
155 κτείνει γὰρ Ἕλλην' ὄντιν' ἂν λάβῃ ξένον.
ὅτου δ' ἕκατι, μήτε σὺ ζήτει μαθεῖν
ἐγώ τε σιγῶ· τί γὰρ ἂν ὠφελοῖμί σε;

ΤΕΥΚΡΟΣ

καλῶς ἔλεξας, ὦ γύναι· θεοὶ δέ σοι
ἐσθλῶν ἀμοιβὰς ἀντιδωρησαίατο.
160 Ἑλένη δ' ὅμοιον σῶμ' ἔχουσ' οὐ τὰς φρένας
ἔχεις ὁμοίας ἀλλὰ διαφόρους πολύ.
κακῶς ὄλοιτο μηδ' ἐπ' Εὐρώτα ῥοὰς
ἔλθοι· σὺ δ' εἴης εὐτυχὴς ἀεί, γύναι.

ΕΛΕΝΗ

ὦ μεγάλων ἀχέων καταβαλλομένα μέγαν οἶκτον
165 ποῖον ἁμιλλαθῶ γόον ἢ τίνα μοῦσαν ἐπέλθω
[δάκρυσιν ἢ θρήνοις ἢ πένθεσιν];
αἰαῖ.

162 κακῶς Wilamowitz: κ- δ' L   166 del. Willink

me so that I can learn by prophecy how I must sail my ship to reach the seagirt land of Cyprus. It is there Apollo prophesied that I must live, calling the place by the island name of Salamis in honor of my far-off native land.

HELEN

The journeying itself will show you the way, stranger.[7] But leave this land quickly before Proteus' son, the country's ruler, sees you! He is away hunting wild beasts with his hounds, but he kills every Greek he catches. Just why, you should not try to learn, and I will not tell you. What good would it do you?

TEUCER

Thanks for your good advice, lady. And may the gods repay you for your kindness! Though you resemble Helen in body, your heart is not the same as hers but far different. May she die a painful death and never come to the streams of the Eurotas! But may your fortune always be good, lady!

Exit TEUCER *by Eisodos A.*

HELEN

Ah, as I begin a long plaint for my long woes
what strenuous keening shall I make, or what Muse shall I
    call to my aid
[with tears or laments or cries of sorrow]?
Ah me!

---

[7] This might mean that Apollo will see to the fulfillment of his prophecy. There might also be an allusion to the belief (see *Bacchae* 402–8) that the Nile flowed under the sea from Egypt to Cyprus.

στρ. α

πτεροφόροι νεάνιδες,
παρθένοι Χθονὸς κόραι
Σειρῆνες, εἴθ' ἐμοῖς
170 ὁμιλοῖτ' ἔχουσαι
Λίβυν λωτὸν ἢ σύ-
ριγγας [ἢ φόρμιγγας] αἰλίνοις κακοῖς·
τοῖς <δ'> ἐμοῖσι σύνοχα δάκρυα,
πάθεσι πάθεα, μέλεσι μέλεα,
μουσεῖα θρηνήμα-
σι ξυνῳδὰ πέμψαιτε,
175 Φερσέφασσα φόνιον ἄχαριν
ἵν' ἐπὶ δάκρυσι παρ' ἐμέθεν ὑπὸ
μέλαθρα νύχια παιᾶνα
νέκυσιν ὀλομένοις λάβῃ.

ἀντ. α

ΧΟΡΟΣ

κυανοειδὲς ἀμφ' ὕδωρ
180 ἔτυχον ἕλικά τ' ἀνὰ χλόαν
φοίνικας ἁλίῳ
πέπλους χρυσέαισιν
<τ' ἐν> αὐγαῖσι θάλπουσ'
ἀμφὶ δόνακος ἔρνεσιν·
ἔνθεν οἰκτρὸν ὅμαδον ἔκλυον,
185 ἄλυρον ἔλεγον, ὅ τι ποτ' ἔλακεν

169 ἐμοῖς Aldina: ἐμοῖς γόοις L
170 ὁμιλοῖτ' Willink: μόλοιτ' L

You winged maids,
virgin daughters of Earth,
you Sirens, O
bring Libyan shawm or shepherd's pipe
[or lyre] and consort with me
in my terrible griefs:
as songsters harmonious
with my lamentations
send forth tears in accord with my tears,
woes with my woes, and songs with my songs,
that Persephone
in her halls of night
may receive from me with my tears a paean,
deathly and joyless, for the dead!

Enter by Eisodos B the CHORUS, *consisting of enslaved Greek women.*

CHORUS

Near waters of deep blue
and shoots of tender green I chanced
to be drying on standing reeds
my deep-dyed
dresses in the sun
⟨and⟩ its golden rays.
There I heard a noise to stir my pity,
a lament not fit for the lyre, uttered

171a ἢ φόρμιγγας del. Tr3   αἰλίνοις] ἐλεϊνοῖς Willink
172 ⟨δ'⟩ Willink   174b πέμψαιτε Bothe: -ψειε L
175 φόνιον ἄχαριν Willink: φονία χάριτας L
176 ἐμέθεν Seidler: ἐμέ θ' L   182 ⟨τ' ἐν⟩ Willink
184 οἰκτρὸν Badham: οἰ- ἀνεβόασεν L

<λαμπροῖσιν> αἰάγμα-
σι στένουσα νύμφα τις,
οἷα Ναῒς ὄρεσι φύγδα
νόμον ἱεῖσα γοερόν, ὑπὸ δὲ
πέτρινα γύαλα κλαγγαῖσι
190 Πανὸς ἀναβοᾷ γάμους.

στρ. β

ΕΛΕΝΗ

ὦ θήραμα βαρβάρου πλάτας,
Ἑλλανίδες κόραι,
ναύτας Ἀχαιῶν τις
195 ἔμολεν ἔμολε δάκρυσί μοι φέρων·
Ἰλίου κατασκαφαὶ
πυρὶ μέλουσι δαΐῳ
δι' ἐμὲ τὰν πολυκτόνον,
δι' ἐμὸν ὄνομα πολύπονον,
200 Λήδα δ' ἐν ἀγχόναις
θάνατον ἔλαβεν αἰσχύ-
νας ἐμᾶς ὑπ' ἀλγέων,
ὁ δ' ἐμὸς ἐν ἁλὶ πολυπλανὴς
πόσις ὀλόμενος οἴχεται,
205 Κάστορός τε συγγόνου τε
διδυμογενὲς ἄγαλμα πατρίδος
ἀφανὲς ἀφανὲς ἱππόκροτα λέ-
λοιπε δάπεδα γυμνάσιά τε
δονακόεντος Εὐρώ-
210 τα, νεανιᾶν πόνον.

34

in ⟨loud⟩ complaint
by some wife:
so would a Naiad in flight
on the mountains utter a woeful plaint
as in some rocky glen
she cries out that she is being ravished by Pan.

HELEN

Spoil a barbarian ship has taken,
you women of Hellas:
a Greek sailor
has come, has come with a message of tears upon tears:
the ruins of Troy
are now consumed by hostile flame
because of me, murderer of many,
because of my name of many woes.
Leda has perished,
hanging herself from pain
at my disgrace;
my husband wandering on the sea
is lost and gone;
and Castor and his brother,
twin glories of their country,
have vanished, vanished, leaving behind the plains
their horses galloped over and the wrestling grounds
by the reedy Eurotas River
where young men toil.

---

186 lac. indic. Badham: ⟨λαμπροῖσιν⟩ Kovacs, ⟨πολλοῖσιν⟩
Lourenço   187 φύγδα Herwerden: φυγάδα L
188 νόμον Matthiae: γάμων L   189 γύαλα Dindorf:
μύχαλα γύαλα L   κλαγγαῖσι Murray: -ὰς L   191 ὦ Wil-
amowitz: ἰὼ ἰὼ L   196 κατασκαφαὶ Murray: -ὰ L

ἀντ. β

ΧΟΡΟΣ

αἰαῖ δαίμονος πολυστόνου
μοίρας τε σᾶς, γύναι.
αἰὼν δυσαίων τις
ἔλαχεν ἔλαχεν, ὅτε σ' ἐτέκετο ματρόθεν
215 χιονόχρῳ κύκνου πτερῷ
Ζεὺς πρέπων δι' αἰθέρος.
τί γὰρ ἄπεστί σοι κακῶν;
τί δ' ἀνὰ βίοτον οὐκ ἔτλας;
μάτηρ μὲν οἴχεται,
220 δίδυμά τε Διὸς οὐκ εὐ-
δαιμονεῖ τέκεα φίλα,
χθόνα δὲ πάτριον οὐχ ὁρᾷς,
διὰ δὲ πόλιας ἔρχεται
βάξις ἅ σε βαρβάροισι,
225 πότνια, παραδίδωσι λέχεσιν,
ὁ δὲ σὸς ἐν ἁλὶ κύμασί τε λέ-
λοιπε βίοτον οὐδέ ποτ' ἔτι
πάτρια μέλαθρα καὶ τὰν
Χαλκίοικον ὀλβιεῖ.

ἐπῳδ.

ΕΛΕΝΗ

φεῦ φεῦ, τίς ἢ Φρυγῶν
230 ἢ τίς Ἑλλανίας ἀπὸ χθονὸς

215 χιονόχρῳ Wecklein: -ως L
218 τί δ' ἀνὰ Bruhn: τίνα δὲ L

36

CHORUS

O what a sorrowful lot,
what sorrowful fortunes are yours, lady!
It was a destiny of woe
that claimed you for its own the day when Zeus,
flashing through the upper air with snowy swan's wing,
sired you upon your mother!
What trouble is not yours?
What have you not suffered in your lifetime?
Your mother is dead,
Zeus's twin sons, whom you loved,
enjoy no good fortune,
you cannot see your native land,
and throughout the cities of Greece
runs the tale that puts you in the bed
of a barbarian, my lady.
And your husband has died
on the deep and shall never
gladden his ancestral halls
or Athena of the Brazen House![8]

HELEN

Ah me, who of the Phrygians[9]
or who from the land of Greece

___

[8] Athena as worshiped in Sparta in a temple with a shrine of bronze.

[9] The Trojans are called Phrygians and Troy Phrygia in Greek poetry.

___

225 πότνια, παραδίδωσι λέχεσιν Nauck: λέχεσι π- παρα-
δίδωσιν L
228 ὀλβιεῖ Bothe: -οῖς L

ἔτεμε τὰν δακρυόεσσαν
Ἰλίῳ πεύκαν;
ἔνθεν ὀλόμενον σκάφος
συναρμόσας ὁ Πριαμίδας
ἔπλευσε βαρβάρῳ πλάτᾳ
235 τὰν ἐμὰν ἐφ' ἑστίαν
[ἐπὶ τὸ δυστυχέστατον
κάλλος ὡς ἕλοι γάμων ἐμῶν]
ἅ τε δόλιος ἁ πολυκτόνος Κύπρις
Δαναΐδαις ἄγουσα θάνατον·
240 ὦ τάλαινα συμφορᾶς.
ἁ δὲ χρυσέοις θρόνοισι
Διὸς ὑπαγκάλισμα σεμνὸν
Ἥρα τὸν ὠκύπουν
ἔπεμψε Μαιάδος γόνον·
ὅς με χλοερὰ δρεπομέναν ἔσω πέπλων
245 ῥόδεα πέταλα Χαλκίοικον
ὡς Ἀθάναν μόλοιμ'
ἀναρπάσας δι' αἰθέρος
τάνδε γαῖαν εἰς ἄνολβον
ἔριν ἔριν τάλαιναν ἔθετο
Πριαμίδαισιν Ἑλλάδος.
250 τὸ δ' ἐμὸν ὄνομα παρὰ Σιμουντίοις ῥοαῖσι
μαψίδιον ἔχει φάτιν.

236-7 del. Dindorf, omnes 229-52 Lourenço
238 ἅ τε Matthiae: ἁ δὲ L

38

cut down the pine
that brought tears to Ilium?
From that pine the son of Priam
fashioned a ruinous ship,
and sailed with barbarian oar
to my hearth
[to the most woeful
beauty so that he might win me as his bride],
and with him came the treacherous, the murderous Cypris
bringing death to the Greeks.
Ah, woe is me!
But she upon the golden throne,
who sleeps in Zeus's arms and is revered,
Hera, sent the swift-footed
son of Maia.[10]
As I gathered fresh within my garment's folds
petals of roses to go to Athena,
her of the Brazen House,
he swooped me up and took me through the heavens
to this unblest land
and made of me a quarrel, quarrel of woe,
Greece's quarrel with the sons of Priam.
And my name beside the streams of Simois
is falsely reviled.

[10] Hermes.

---

239 θάνατον Nauck: θ- Πριαμίδαις L
241 ἁ Dindorf: εἰ L

ΧΟΡΟΣ

ἔχεις μὲν ἀλγεῖν᾿, οἶδα· σύμφορον δέ τοι
ὡς ῥᾷστα τἀναγκαῖα τοῦ βίου φέρειν.

ΕΛΕΝΗ

255 φίλαι γυναῖκες, τίνι πότμῳ συνεζύγην;
257 γυνὴ γὰρ οὔθ᾿ Ἑλληνὶς οὔτε βάρβαρος
     τεῦχος νεοσσῶν λευκὸν ἐκλοχεύεται,
259 ἐν ᾧ με Λήδαν φασὶν ἐκ Διὸς τεκεῖν.
256 ἆρ᾿ ἡ τεκοῦσά μ᾿ ἔτεκεν ἀνθρώποις τέρας;
260 τέρας γὰρ ὁ βίος καὶ τὰ πράγματ᾿ ἐστί μου,
     τὰ μὲν δι᾿ Ἥραν, τὰ δὲ τὸ κάλλος αἴτιον.
     εἴθ᾿ ἐξαλειφθεῖσ᾿ ὡς ἄγαλμ᾿ αὖθις πάλιν
     αἴσχιον εἶδος ἔλαβον ἀντὶ τοῦ καλοῦ,
     καὶ τὰς τύχας μὲν τὰς κακὰς ἃς νῦν ἔχω
265 Ἕλληνες ἐπελάθοντο, τὰς δὲ μὴ κακὰς
     ἔσῳζον ὥσπερ τὰς κακὰς σῴζουσί μου.
        ὅστις μὲν οὖν ἐς μίαν ἀποβλέπων τύχην
     πρὸς θεῶν κακοῦται, βαρὺ μέν, οἰστέον δ᾿ ὅμως·
     ἡμεῖς δὲ πολλαῖς συμφοραῖς ἐγκείμεθα.
270 πρῶτον μὲν οὐκ οὖσ᾿ ἄδικός εἰμι δυσκλεής·
     καὶ τοῦτο μεῖζον τῆς ἀληθείας κακόν,
     ὅστις τὰ μὴ προσόντα κέκτηται κακά.
     ἔπειτα πατρίδος θεοί μ᾿ ἀφιδρύσαντο γῆς
     ἐς βάρβαρ᾿ ἤθη, καὶ φίλων τητωμένη
275 δούλη καθέστηκ᾿ οὖσ᾿ ἐλευθέρων ἄπο·
     τὰ βαρβάρων γὰρ δοῦλα πάντα πλὴν ἑνός.
     ἄγκυρα δ᾿ ἥ μου τὰς τύχας ὤχει μόνη,

40

CHORUS LEADER

Your lot is painful, I admit. But it is best, you know, to bear
life's harsh necessities as lightly as you can.

HELEN

Dear women, to what fate have I been yoked? No woman,
either Greek or barbarian, ever gave birth to a white-
shelled bird's egg, yet it was in this, men say, that Leda bore
me to Zeus. Did my mother bear me as a monstrosity in
men's eyes? My life and fortunes *are* a monstrosity, partly
because of Hera, partly because of my beauty. I wish I had
been wiped clean like a painting and made plain instead of
beautiful, and that the Greeks had forgotten the evil fate
that I now have and remembered what is good, just as they
now remember what is ill!

Now when a man, his eye fixed on one thing, is hurt by
the gods, that, hard though it is, must be endured. I, how-
ever, am beset by many misfortunes. First, though I am in-
nocent, I have an evil reputation: to be reviled for wrongs
one has not done is worse than if the charges were true.
Second, the gods have settled me far from my native soil to
live with barbarians. I am deprived of my near and dear
and have become a slave though I was born of free parents:
in barbarian lands all except one man are slaves. The one
anchor that steadied me in misfortune, that my husband

πόσιν ποθ᾽ ἥξειν καί μ᾽ ἀπαλλάξειν κακῶν,
ἐπεὶ τέθνηκεν οὗτος, οὐκέτ᾽ ἔστι δή.
280 μήτηρ δ᾽ ὄλωλε καὶ φονεὺς αὐτῆς ἐγώ,
ἀδίκως μέν, ἀλλὰ τἄδικον τοῦτ᾽ ἔστ᾽ ἐμόν.
ἡ δ᾽ ἀγλάισμα δωμάτων ἐμόν τ᾽ ἔφυ,
θυγάτηρ ἄνανδρος πολιὰ παρθενεύεται.
τὼ τοῦ Διὸς δὲ λεγομένω Διοσκόρω
285 οὐκ ἐστόν. ἀλλὰ πάντ᾽ ἔχουσα δυστυχῆ
τοῖς πράγμασιν τέθνηκα, τοῖς δ᾽ ἔργοισιν οὔ.
[τὸ δ᾽ ἔσχατον τοῦτ᾽, εἰ μόλοιμεν ἐς πάτραν,
κλήθροις ἂν εἰργοίμεσθα τὴν ὑπ᾽ Ἰλίῳ
δοκοῦντες Ἑλένην Μενελέῳ †μ᾽ ἐλθεῖν† μέτα.
290 εἰ μὲν γὰρ ἔζη πόσις, ἀνεγνώσθημεν ἄν,
ἐς ξύμβολ᾽ ἐλθόνθ᾽ ἃ φανέρ᾽ ἂν μόνοις ἂν ἦν.
νῦν δ᾽ οὔτε τοῦτ᾽ ἔστ᾽ οὔτε μὴ σωθῇ ποτε.]
τί δῆτ᾽ ἔτι ζῶ; τίν᾽ ὑπολείπομαι τύχην;
γάμους ἑλομένη τῶν κακῶν ὑπαλλαγάς,
295 μετ᾽ ἀνδρὸς οἰκεῖν βαρβάρου πρὸς πλουσίαν
τράπεζαν ἵζουσ᾽; ἀλλ᾽ ὅταν πόσις πικρὸς
ξυνῇ γυναικί, καὶ τὸ σῶμ᾽ ἐστιν πικρόν.
θανεῖν κράτιστον· πῶς θάνοιμ᾽ ἂν οὐ καλῶς;
[ἀσχήμονες μὲν ἀγχόναι μετάρσιοι,
300 κἂν τοῖσι δούλοις δυσπρεπὲς νομίζεται·
σφαγαὶ δ᾽ ἔχουσιν εὐγενές τι καὶ καλόν,
σμικρὸν δ᾽ ὁ καιρὸς ἄρθρ᾽ ἀπαλλάξαι βίου.]
ἐς γὰρ τοσοῦτον ἤλθομεν βάθος κακῶν·

279 ἐπεὶ Cobet: οὗτος L

42

would one day come and rescue me from misery, no longer exists since he has perished. My mother is dead, and I am her slayer: that is unfair, but the unfairness belongs to my lot. My daughter, who is our house's glory and mine, has no husband and grows old in maidenhood. The two Dioscuri, said to be the sons of Zeus, are no more. So since all I have is unblest, I am dead in my fortunes if not in deed. [And here is the worst of it: if I should reach home, I would find the gates barred against me since men would suppose that Helen from Troy perished with Menelaus.[11] For if he were alive, we could be recognized by having recourse to tokens known to us alone. But as it is, that is impossible, and he will never return home.]

Why then do I go on living? What fate is left for me? Choose marriage as an escape from trouble and live with a barbarian husband, sitting at his rich table? But when a woman is married to a man she dislikes, even her own body becomes distasteful to her. Death is best. How can it not be right to die? [To hang oneself is unseemly: it does not look good even in a slave. Death by the sword is noble and glorious, but it is hard to find the vital spot that will end the body's life.] That is the depth of misery to which I have

---

[11] I translate Schmidt's θανεῖν for L's nonsensical μ' ἐλθεῖν without any confidence that this is what the interpolator wrote.

---

282 ἦ δ' Diggle: ὅδ' L   ἐμόν Cobet: ἐμοῦ L
287–92 del. Goguel
289 θανεῖν F. W. Schmidt
291 ἐλθόνθ' ἃ φανέρ' ἂν Porson: ἐλθόντες ἃ φανερὰ L
299–302 del. Hartung
302 ἄρθρ' Keil: ἄρτ' L

αἱ μὲν γὰρ ἄλλαι διὰ τὸ κάλλος εὐτυχεῖς
305 γυναῖκες, ἡμᾶς δ᾽ αὐτὸ τοῦτ᾽ ἀπώλεσεν.

ΧΟΡΟΣ

Ἑλένη, τὸν ἐλθόνθ᾽, ὅστις ἐστὶν ὁ ξένος,
μὴ πάντ᾽ ἀληθῆ δοξάσῃς εἰρηκέναι.

ΕΛΕΝΗ

καὶ μὴν σαφῶς γ᾽ ἔλεξ᾽ ὀλωλέναι πόσιν.

ΧΟΡΟΣ

πόλλ᾽ ἂν λέγοιτο καὶ διὰ ψευδῶν σαφῆ.

ΕΛΕΝΗ

310 καὶ τοὔμπαλίν γε τῶνδ᾽, ἀληθείας ἔπι.

ΧΟΡΟΣ

ἐς ξυμφορὰν γὰρ ἀντὶ τἀγαθοῦ φέρῃ.

ΕΛΕΝΗ

φόβος γὰρ ἐς τὸ δεῖμα περιβαλών μ᾽ ἄγει.

ΧΟΡΟΣ

πῶς δ᾽ εὐμενείας τοισίδ᾽ ἐν δόμοις ἔχεις;

ΕΛΕΝΗ

πάντες φίλοι μοι πλὴν ὁ θηρεύων γάμους.

ΧΟΡΟΣ

315 οἶσθ᾽ οὖν ὃ δρᾶσον· μνήματος λιποῦσ᾽ ἕδραν ...

ΕΛΕΝΗ

ἐς ποῖον ἕρπεις μῦθον ἢ παραίνεσιν;

309 λέγοιτο Blaydes: γένοιτο L
309–10 σαφῆ ... ἔπι Jackson: ἔπη ... σαφῆ L

sunk: while other women are made happy by their beauty,
mine is the very thing that has destroyed me.

CHORUS LEADER

Helen, do not assume that the stranger, whoever he is,
spoke the truth on all points.

HELEN

But he said plainly that my husband was dead.

CHORUS LEADER

Many things plainly said may be false.

HELEN

Yes, and conversely, they may be true.

CHORUS LEADER

You say this because you rush toward woe, not blessing.

HELEN

Yes: anxiety surrounds me, drives my thoughts toward fear.

CHORUS LEADER

How much good will do you have from those in the house?

HELEN

All are my friends except for the man who hunts down my
love.

CHORUS LEADER

Here is what you must do: leaving your seat on this
tomb . . .

HELEN

What are you saying? What advice are you giving me?

---

310 τοὔμπαλίν Stephanus: τἄμπαλίν L
312 τὰ δεινὰ Bothe

ΧΟΡΟΣ

. . . ἐλθοῦσ' ἐς οἴκους, ἢ τὰ πάντ' ἐπίσταται
τῆς ποντίας Νηρῇδος ἐκγόνου κόρης
πυθοῦ πόσιν σὸν Θεονόης, εἴτ' ἔστ' ἔτι
320 εἴτ' ἐκλέλοιπε φέγγος· ἐκμαθοῦσα δ' εὖ
πρὸς τὰς τύχας τὸ χάρμα τοὺς γόους τ' ἔχε.
πρὶν δ' οὐδὲν ὀρθῶς εἰδέναι, τί σοι πλέον
λυπουμένη γένοιτ' ἄν; ἀλλ' ἐμοὶ πιθοῦ.
[τάφον λιποῦσα τόνδε σύμμειξον κόρῃ,
325 ὅθενπερ εἴσῃ πάντα· τἀληθῆ φράσαι
ἔχουσ' ἐν οἴκοις τοῖσδε, τί βλέπεις πρόσω;]
θέλω δὲ κἀγώ σοι συνεισελθεῖν δόμους
καὶ συμπυθέσθαι παρθένου θεσπίσματα·
γυναῖκα γὰρ δὴ συμπονεῖν γυναικὶ χρή.

ΕΛΕΝΗ

330 φίλαι, λόγους ἐδεξάμαν·
βᾶτε βᾶτε δ' ἐς δόμους,
ἀγῶνας ἐντὸς οἴκων
ὡς πύθησθε τοὺς ἐμούς.

ΧΟΡΟΣ

θέλουσαν οὔ με δὶς καλεῖς.

ΕΛΕΝΗ

335 ἰὼ μέλεος ἀμέρα.
τίν' ἄρα τάλαινα τίνα λόγον
δακρυόεντ' ἀκούσομαι;

318 del. Goguel: cf. 1647

46

HELEN

CHORUS LEADER

. . . go into the house and ask the Nereid's omniscient
daughter Theonoe whether your husband is alive or dead.
When you have learned the truth, then weep or rejoice ac-
cording to your fate. But before you know for sure, what
good will it do you to grieve? Take my advice! [Leave this
tomb and meet with the maiden: from her you will learn
all. Since you have her to tell you the truth in this house,
why do you look elsewhere?] I too am willing to go in and
hear the maiden's prophecy with you: women must help
one another.

HELEN

My friends, I accept your admonition:
go, go into the house
so that you may learn within
what trials await me.

CHORUS

I do it willingly: you need not ask me twice.

HELEN

O unlucky day!
What story of tears
shall I in my unhappiness hear?

324–6 del. Goguel
326 τήνδε Nauck
333 fort. ante 332 traiciendus
334 οὔ με δὶς Elmsley: οὐ μόλις L
336–7 λόγον δακρυόεντ᾽ Hermann: δακρυόεντα λ- L

ΧΟΡΟΣ

μὴ πρόμαντις ἀλγέων
προλάμβαν', ὦ φίλα, γόους.

ΕΛΕΝΗ

340   τί μοι πόσις μέλεος ἔτλα;
πότερα δέρκεται φάος τέ-
θριππά θ' ἁλίου κέλευθά τ' ἀστέρων
ἢ ⟨'ν⟩ νέκυσι κατὰ χθονὸς
345   τὰν χρόνιον ἔχει τύχαν;

ΧΟΡΟΣ

ἐς τὸ φέρτερον τίθει
τὸ μέλλον, ὅ τι γενήσεται.

ΕΛΕΝΗ

σέ γ' ἀνεκάλεσα, σὲ δὲ κατόμοσα,
τὸν ὑδρόεντι δόνακι χλωρὸν
350   Εὐρώταν· θανόντος
εἰ βάξις ἔτυμος ἀνδρὸς
ἅδε μοι (τί τάδ' ἀσύνετα;),
φόνιον αἰώρημα
διὰ δέρης ὀρέξομαι,
ἢ ξιφοκτόνον διωγμὸν
355   αἱμορρύτου σφαγᾶς
αὐτοσίδαρον ἔσω πελάσω διὰ σαρκὸς ἅμιλλαν,
θῦμα τριζύγοις θεαῖσι

344 ⟨'ν⟩ Jacobs
345 χρόνιον Bothe: χθόνιον L
348 σέ γ' ἀνεκάλεσα Badham: σὲ γὰρ ἐκάλεσα L

48

CHORUS

Do not be prophet of grief, my friend,
or lament before you need to!

HELEN

What has my unhappy husband suffered?
Does he yet look on the light,
the sun's chariot, and the stars in their paths,
or among the dead under the earth
does he suffer that everlasting fate?

CHORUS

Whatever tomorrow shall bring,
set down to the good.

HELEN

I call upon you, I make you my witness,
Eurotas green with water reeds,
that if the tale
of my husband's death
is true (but how is this unclear?),
I shall fasten a deadly noose
about my neck
or thrust the sword
of bloody death
with self-slaughtering force into my flesh,
a sacrifice to the three goddesses

---

349 ὑδρόεντι Reiske: -τα L
352 τί τάδ'] τίνα δ' Willink
354 διωγμὸν Nauck: δίωγμα L
355 αἱμορρύτου Bothe: λαιμορύτου L
356 ἅμιλλαν Musgrave: -α L

τῷ τε σήραγγας Ἴ-
δας ἐνίζοντι Πρια-
μίδᾳ ποτ᾽ ἀμφὶ βουστάθμους.

360 ἄλλοσ᾽ ἀποτροπὰ κακῶν
γένοιτο, τὸ δὲ σὸν εὐτυχές.

ὦ Τροία τάλαινα,
δι᾽ ἔργ᾽ ἄνεργ᾽ ὄλλυσαι μέλεά τ᾽ ἔτλας·
τὰ δ᾽ ἐμὰ δῶρα Κύπριδος ἔτεκε
365 πολὺ μὲν αἷμα, πολὺ δὲ δάκρυ
[ἄχεά τ᾽ ἄχεσι δάκρυα δάκρυσιν ἔλαβε πάθεα]·
ματέρες τε παῖδας ὄλεσαν,
ἀπὸ δὲ παρθένοι κόμας
ἔθεντο σύγγονοι νεκρῶν Σκαμάνδριον
ἀμφὶ Φρύγιον οἶδμα.
370 βοὰν βοὰν δ᾽ Ἑλλὰς ⟨αἶ⟩
ἐκελάδησεν ἀνοτότυξεν,
ἐπὶ δὲ κρατὶ χέρας ἔθηκεν,
ὄνυχι δ᾽ ἀπαλόχροα γένυν
ἔδευσεν φοινίαισι πλαγαῖς.

375 ὦ μάκαρ Ἀρκαδίᾳ ποτὲ παρθένε
Καλλιστοῖ, Διὸς ἃ λεχέων ἀπέ-

357–8 σήραγγας Ἴδας ἐνίζοντι post Badham Diggle:
σύραγγ᾽ ἀοιδαὶ σέβιζον L   362 ὦ Kannicht: ἰὼ L
364 Κύπριδος L. Dindorf: κύπρις L

and to Priam's son who once
sat in the hollow caves
of Ida with his cattle.

CHORUS

May misfortune be turned aside
and go elsewhere! May your luck be good!

HELEN

O unhappy Troy,
you perished, you suffered pitiably, for deeds never done.
It was my allure that brought forth
much blood, many tears
[and grief upon grief and tears upon tears, sorrow it took]:
mothers lost their sons,
and maidens, sisters of the slain,
cast their cut locks of hair
into the Scamander, Troy's stream.
And Greece raised a cry
of grief and pain,
struck her head with her hand,
and with bloodying stroke of nail
made her tender cheek run.

O lucky maid of Arcadia long ago
Callisto,[12] who left the bed of Zeus

[12] Callisto, a beautiful Arcadian girl, beloved of Zeus, was turned into a bear (and eventually into the constellation of the Great Bear) so that she might evade the anger of Hera.

---

365 δάκρυ Kovacs: δάκρυον L   366 del. G. Müller
369a Σκαμάνδριον del. Bothe   370 ⟨αἲ᾽⟩ Paley

βας τετραβάμοσι γυίοις,
ὡς πολὺ κηρὸς ἐμᾶς ἔλαχες πλέον,
ἁ μορφᾷ θηρῶν λαχνογυίων
[ὄμματι λαβρῷ σχῆμα λεαίνης]
380 ἐξαλλάξασ᾽ ἄχθεα λύπας·
ἄν τέ ποτ᾽ Ἄρτεμις ἐξεχορεύσατο
χρυσοκέρατ᾽ ἔλαφον Μέροπος Τιτανίδα κούραν
καλλοσύνας ἕνεκεν· τὸ δ᾽ ἐμὸν δέμας
ὤλεσεν ὤλεσε πέργαμα Δαρδανίας
385 ὀλομένους τ᾽ Ἀχαιούς.

ΜΕΝΕΛΑΟΣ

ὦ τὰς τεθρίππους Οἰνομάῳ Πῖσαν κάτα
Πέλοψ ἁμίλλας ἐξαμιλληθείς ποτε,
εἴθ᾽ ὤφελες τότ᾽ [ἡνίκ᾽ ἔρανον ἐς θεοὺς
πεφθεὶς ἐποίεις] ἥθεος λιπεῖν βίον,
390 πρὶν τὸν ἐμὸν Ἀτρέα πατέρα γεννῆσαί ποτε,
ὃς ἐξέφυσεν Ἀερόπης λέκτρων ἄπο
Ἀγαμέμνον᾽ ἐμέ τε Μενέλεων, κλεινὸν ζυγόν.

376 ἀπέβας apogr. Par., Hartung: ἐπέβας L
377 κηρὸς Diggle: μητρὸς L   379 del. Dingelstad, 378–
80 dubitanter Willink   380 ἄχθεα Hermann: ἄχεα L
388b-9a del. Nauck (τότ᾽ pro τόθ᾽ idem)
389 πεφθεὶς nescioquis apud Beck: πεισθεὶς L   ἥθεος
Grégoire: ἐν θεοῖς L: ἐν δρόμοις Kannicht

13 No other telling of this legend is known. The girl is probably
Cos, who gave her name to the Aegean island.
14 Oenomaus, king of Pisa near Olympia, set the suitors of his

with limbs that go on all four,
how much your lot surpasses mine
since by taking the form of a shaggy beast
[with violent eye, the form of a lioness]
you have put from yourself the burden of pain!
And you too, Titan daughter of Merops, are blest,
you whom Artemis once chased from her band as a golden
    stag
because of her beauty.[13] Yet my loveliness
has ruined, ruined Troy's citadel
and the Greeks, doomed to death.

Exit HELEN *and* CHORUS *into the palace. Enter to the
empty stage* MENELAUS *by Eisodos A. He is dressed in
pieces of torn sail.*

MENELAUS

O Pelops, who once in Pisa competed in the famous char-
iot race against Oenomaus,[14] how I wish that on that day,
[when you were cooked and furnished a feast to the gods,]
when you were still unmarried, you had lost your life be-
fore you had ever begotten my father Atreus! From his
marriage with Aërope Atreus begot Agamemnon and me,

daughter Hippodamia a test: either defeat him in a chariot race
and marry the girl or lose their lives. Pelops won the race and his
bride by bribing Oenomaus' charioteer. Another story, referred to
in the interpolated half lines, was that Pelops' father Tantalus,
who was the favored associate of the gods, killed and cooked
Pelops and fed him to the gods to test their omniscience. All of the
gods recognized the trick at once except Demeter (she wasn't pay-
ing attention and ate some of Pelops' shoulder), and the boy was
restored to life with a new shoulder of ivory.

πλεῖστον γὰρ οἶμαι—καὶ τόδ᾽ οὐ κόμπῳ λέγω—
στράτευμα κώπῃ διορίσαι Τροίαν ἔπι,
395 τύραννος οὐδὲ πρὸς βίαν στρατηλατῶν,
ἑκοῦσι δ᾽ ἄρξας Ἑλλάδος νεανίαις.
καὶ τοὺς μὲν οὐκέτ᾽ ὄντας ἀριθμῆσαι πάρα,
τούς τ᾽ ἐκ θαλάσσης ἀσμένους πεφευγότας,
νεκρῶν φέροντας ὀνόματ᾽ εἰς οἴκους πάλιν.
400 ἐγὼ δ᾽ ἐπ᾽ οἶδμα πόντιον γλαυκῆς ἁλὸς
τλήμων ἀλῶμαι χρόνον ὅσονπερ Ἰλίου
πύργους ἔπερσα, κὰς πάτραν χρῄζων μολεῖν
οὐκ ἀξιοῦμαι τοῦδε πρὸς θεῶν τυχεῖν.
Λιβύης δ᾽ ἐρήμους ἀξένους τ᾽ ἐπιδρομὰς
405 πέπλευκα πάσας· χὤταν ἐγγὺς ὦ πάτρας,
πάλιν μ᾽ ἀπωθεῖ πνεῦμα κοὔποτ᾽ οὔριον
ἐσῆλθε λαῖφος ὥστε μ᾽ ἐς πάτραν μολεῖν.
  καὶ νῦν τάλας ναυαγὸς ἀπολέσας φίλους
ἐξέπεσον ἐς γῆν τήνδε· ναῦς δὲ πρὸς πέτραις
410 πολλοὺς ἀριθμοὺς ἄγνυται ναυαγίων.
τρόπις δ᾽ ἐλείφθη ποικίλων ἁρμοσμάτων,
ἐφ᾽ ἧς ἐσώθην μόλις ἀνελπίστῳ τύχῃ
Ἑλένη τε, Τροίας ἣν ἀποσπάσας ἔχω.
ὄνομα δὲ χώρας ἥτις ἥδε καὶ λεὼ
415 οὐκ οἶδ᾽· ὄχλον γὰρ ἐσπεσεῖν ᾐσχυνόμην,
[ὥσθ᾽ ἱστορῆσαι τὰς ἐμὰς δυσχλαινίας]
κρύπτων ὑπ᾽ αἰδοῦς τὰς τύχας. ὅταν δ᾽ ἀνὴρ

395 οὐδὲ Dobree: οὐδὲν L
397 πάρα] βαρύ Orelli, quo recepto post 399 post Wecklein

Menelaus, a glorious pair. It was, I think—and it is not boasting to say so—the world's greatest army that I took over by ship to Troy, not as a despot or leading my troops by force but commanding the young men of Greece with their consent. We can call the roll of those who perished and those who escaped sea perils and arrived home safely bearing the names of their dead comrades. But I wander in misery over the waves of the gray sea the whole time since I captured the towers of Ilium. Though I long to reach home, the gods do not see fit to grant me this boon. I have sailed to all the deserted and inhospitable landing places of Libya. Whenever I get near my own country, the wind forces me back and never fills my sail favorably so that I can get home.

And now, a poor shipwreck, having lost my companions, I have been cast up on this land. My ship is smashed into countless bits of flotsam. Of all its carefully fitted pieces only the keel remained, and on it, by a fate no one would have expected, I reached land safely, and with me Helen, whom I have taken from Troy by force. I do not know what this land and its people are called: shame kept me from mingling with the throng [and so being questioned about my shabby clothes], and I concealed my fate

---

lac. fort. indicanda, e.g. ⟨σμικρὸν λέγοις ἂν λείψανον στρα-
τεύματος⟩, etiam δ᾽ 398 recepto

398 τ᾽ Rappold: δ᾽ L
404 δ᾽ Hermann: τ᾽ L
409 πέτραις Heiland: -ας L
414 λεὼ Cobet: -ὼς L
416 del. Bothe

πράξῃ κακῶς ὑψηλός, εἰς ἀηθίαν
πίπτει κακίω τοῦ πάλαι δυσδαίμονος.

420 χρεία δὲ τείρει μ'· οὔτε γὰρ σῖτος πάρα
οὔτ' ἀμφὶ χρῶτ' ἐσθῆτες· αὐτὰ δ' εἰκάσαι
πάρεστι ναὸς ἔκβολ' οἷς ἀμπίσχομαι.
πέπλους δὲ τοὺς πρὶν λαμπρά τ' ἀμφιβλήματα
χλιδάς τε πόντος ἥρπασ'· ἐν δ' ἄντρου μυχοῖς

425 κρύψας γυναῖκα τὴν κακῶν πάντων ἐμοὶ
ἄρξασαν ἥκω, τούς γε περιλελειμμένους
φίλων φυλάσσειν τἄμ' ἀναγκάσας λέχη.
μόνος δὲ νοστῶ, τοῖς ἐκεῖ ζητῶν φίλοις
τὰ πρόσφορ' ἤν πως ἐξερευνήσας λάβω.

430 ἰδὼν δὲ δῶμα περιφερὲς θριγκοῖς τόδε
πύλας τε σεμνὰς ἀνδρὸς ὀλβίου τινὸς
προσῆλθον· ἐλπὶς δ' ἔκ γε πλουσίων δόμων
λαβεῖν τι ναύταις· ἐκ δὲ μὴ 'χόντων βίον
οὐδ' εἰ θέλοιεν ὠφελεῖν ἔχοιμεν ἄν.

435 ὠή· τίς ἂν πυλωρὸς ἐκ δόμων μόλοι,
ὅστις διαγγείλειε τἄμ' ἔσω κακά;

ΓΡΑΥΣ

τίς πρὸς πύλαισιν; οὐκ ἀπαλλάξῃ δόμων
καὶ μὴ πρὸς αὐλείοισιν ἑστηκὼς πύλαις
ὄχλον παρέξεις δεσπόταις; ἢ κατθανῇ

440 Ἕλλην πεφυκώς, οἷσιν οὐκ ἐπιστροφαί.

422 ἔκβολ' οἷς Reiske: ἐκβόλοις L
434 ἔχοιμεν Paley: ἔχοιεν L

56

out of embarrassment. When someone of high degree
fares badly, he falls into an unfamiliar state, and this is a far
worse fate than if a man has long been ill-starred. I am hard
pressed by need: I have no food and no clothing about my
body. You can tell from the look of them that it is just cast-
ups from the wreck that I am wearing. My former gar-
ments, fine and luxurious, have been swallowed up by the
sea. I have concealed in a cave the wife who caused me all
this woe and have come here, compelling the last survivors
of my friends to stand guard over her. I come here alone,
trying to obtain for my friends there what they need. Since
I saw this house, a rich man's house, its walls surmounted
by coping all around and its impressive gates, I have ap-
proached. From a rich house there is hope of getting
something for my sailors. From the poor we could get no
benefit even if they wanted to give it.

Ho there! Gatekeeper! Come out of the house so that
you may carry inside the message of my griefs!

Enter from the palace an OLD WOMAN.

OLD WOMAN
Who is at the gate? Leave this house! Do not stand at our
courtyard gate and bother my master! Otherwise you will
be put to death! You are a Greek, and Greeks are not
allowed here!

EURIPIDES

ΜΕΝΕΛΑΟΣ

ὦ γραῖα, ταὐτὰ ταῦτ' ἔπη κάλλως λέγειν
ἔξεστι, πείσομαι γάρ· ἀλλ' ἄνες χόλου.

ΓΡΑΥΣ

ἄπελθ'· ἐμοὶ γὰρ τοῦτο πρόσκειται, ξένε,
μηδένα πελάζειν τοισίδ' Ἑλλήνων δόμοις.

ΜΕΝΕΛΑΟΣ

445 ἇ· μὴ †προσείλει† χεῖρα μηδ' ὤθει βίᾳ.

ΓΡΑΥΣ

πείθῃ γὰρ οὐδὲν ὧν λέγω, σὺ δ' αἴτιος.

ΜΕΝΕΛΑΟΣ

ἄγγειλον εἴσω δεσπόταισι τοῖσι σοῖς. . . .

ΓΡΑΥΣ

πικρῶς ἂν οἶμαι ⟨σοί⟩ γ' ἐσαγγέλλειν λόγους.

ΜΕΝΕΛΑΟΣ

. . . ναυαγὸς ἥκω ξένος, ἀσύλητον γένος.

ΓΡΑΥΣ

450 οἶκον πρὸς ἄλλον νύν τιν' ἀντὶ τοῦδ' ἴθι.

ΜΕΝΕΛΑΟΣ

οὔκ, ἀλλ' ἔσω πάρειμι· καὶ σύ μοι πιθοῦ.

---

441 κάλλως Herwerden: καλῶς L   λέγειν Kirchhoff:
λέγεις L
442 χόλου Clark: λόγον L
445 πρόσειε Blomfield: ἇ· / μή ⟨μοι⟩ προσείλει Willink
447 fort. δεσπόταισι σοῖς ὅτι (vel 449 ναυαγὸν ἥκειν ξένον)

58

HELEN

MENELAUS

Ancient lady, you may say these same words in a different
tone: I will obey. Stop being angry!

OLD WOMAN

Go away! It is my job, stranger, to see that no Greek
approaches this house.

She moves menacingly toward Menelaus.

MENELAUS

Oh, don't lay hands on me! Don't thrust me away by force!

OLD WOMAN

You are to blame: you don't do as I say.

MENELAUS

Take the word inside to your master . . .

OLD WOMAN

You will regret it, I think, if I carry *your* message indoors!

MENELAUS

. . . that I have come as a shipwrecked foreigner, one under
heaven's protection.

OLD WOMAN

So go to some other house, not this one.

MENELAUS

No, I mean to go in: do as I ask.

---

448 ⟨σοί⟩ Kovacs   ἐσαγγέλλειν λόγους Dale: ἀγγελεῖν
τοὺς σοὺς λόγους L

ΓΡΑΥΣ

ὀχληρὸς ἴσθ' ὤν· καὶ τάχ' ὠσθήσῃ βίᾳ.

ΜΕΝΕΛΑΟΣ

αἰαῖ· τὰ κλεινὰ ποῦ 'στί μοι στρατεύματα;

ΓΡΑΥΣ

οὐκοῦν ἐκεῖ που σεμνὸς ἦσθ', οὐκ ἐνθάδε.

ΜΕΝΕΛΑΟΣ

455 ὦ δαῖμον, ὡς ἀνάξι' ἠτιμώμεθα.

ΓΡΑΥΣ

τί βλέφαρα τέγγεις δάκρυσι; πρὸς τίν' οἰκτρὸς εἶ;

ΜΕΝΕΛΑΟΣ

πρὸς τὰς πάροιθε συμφορὰς εὐδαίμονας.

ΓΡΑΥΣ

οὔκουν ἀπελθὼν δάκρυα σοῖς δώσεις φίλοις;

ΜΕΝΕΛΑΟΣ

τίς δ' ἥδε χώρα; τοῦ δὲ βασίλειοι δόμοι;

ΓΡΑΥΣ

460 Πρωτέως τάδ' ἐστὶ δώματ', Αἴγυπτος δὲ γῆ.

ΜΕΝΕΛΑΟΣ

Αἴγυπτος; ὦ δύστηνος, οἷ πέπλευκ' ἄρα.

ΓΡΑΥΣ

τί δὴ τὸ Νείλου μεμπτόν ἐστί σοι γάνος;

460 Πρωτέως . . ἐστὶ Kirchhoff ex t: Πρωτεὺς . . . οἰκεῖ L

OLD WOMAN

I tell you, you are being troublesome. And soon you will be forced to leave.

MENELAUS

Ah me! My famous military campaigns, where are they now?

OLD WOMAN

You were evidently a person of importance somewhere, but not here.

MENELAUS

O fate, what undeserved scorn I suffer!

OLD WOMAN

Why drench your face with tears? In whose eyes do you deserve pity?

MENELAUS

In the eyes of my former blessed state.

OLD WOMAN

So go away and bestow your tears on your friends!

MENELAUS

What is this land? To whom does this palace belong?

OLD WOMAN

This is the house of Proteus, and the land is Egypt.

MENELAUS

Egypt? O misery! What a long way I have sailed!

OLD WOMAN

And why find fault with the Nile's gleaming water?

ΜΕΝΕΛΑΟΣ

οὐ τοῦτ᾽ ἐμέμφθην· τὰς ἐμὰς στένω τύχας.

ΓΡΑΥΣ

πολλοὶ κακῶς πράσσουσιν, οὐ σὺ δὴ μόνος.

ΜΕΝΕΛΑΟΣ

465 ἔστ᾽ οὖν ἐν οἴκοις ὄντιν᾽ ὀνομάζεις ἄναξ;

ΓΡΑΥΣ

τόδ᾽ ἐστὶν αὐτοῦ μνῆμα, παῖς δ᾽ ἄρχει χθονός.

ΜΕΝΕΛΑΟΣ

ποῦ δῆτ᾽ ἂν εἴη; πότερον ἐκτὸς ἢ 'ν δόμοις;

ΓΡΑΥΣ

οὐκ ἔνδον· Ἕλλησιν δὲ πολεμιώτατος.

ΜΕΝΕΛΑΟΣ

τίν᾽ αἰτίαν σχὼν ἧς ἐπηυρόμην ἐγώ;

ΓΡΑΥΣ

470 Ἑλένη κατ᾽ οἴκους ἐστὶ τοῦσδ᾽ ἡ τοῦ Διός.

ΜΕΝΕΛΑΟΣ

πῶς φής; τίν᾽ εἶπας μῦθον; αὖθίς μοι φράσον.

ΓΡΑΥΣ

ἡ Τυνδαρὶς παῖς, ἣ κατὰ Σπάρτην ποτ᾽ ἦν.

ΜΕΝΕΛΑΟΣ

πόθεν μολοῦσα; τίνα τὸ πρᾶγμ᾽ ἔχει λόγον;

ΓΡΑΥΣ

Λακεδαίμονος γῆς δεῦρο νοστήσασ᾽ ἄπο.

MENELAUS
I wasn't: it was my fate I was lamenting.

OLD WOMAN
Many people have troubles: you are not the only one.

MENELAUS
The king you spoke of: is he in the house?

OLD WOMAN
This is his tomb. His son is the land's king.

MENELAUS
Where might he be? At home or out of doors?

OLD WOMAN
He's out, and he's most hostile to the Greeks.

MENELAUS
Why does he blame them—to *my* cost?

OLD WOMAN
Helen is in this palace, Zeus's daughter.

MENELAUS
What's this? What are you saying? Tell me again.

OLD WOMAN
Tyndareus' daughter, who was once in Sparta.

MENELAUS
Where did she come from? What is the explanation?

OLD WOMAN
She came here from Lacedaemon.

ΜΕΝΕΛΑΟΣ

475 πότ'; οὔ τί που λελήσμεθ' ἐξ ἄντρων λέχος;

ΓΡΑΥΣ

πρὶν τοὺς Ἀχαιούς, ὦ ξέν', ἐς Τροίαν μολεῖν.
ἀλλ' ἕρπ' ἀπ' οἴκων· ἔστι γάρ τις ἐν δόμοις
τύχη, τύραννος ᾗ ταράσσεται δόμος.
καιρὸν γὰρ οὐδέν' ἦλθες· ἢν δὲ δεσπότης
480 λάβῃ σε, θάνατος ξένιά σοι γενήσεται.
[εὔνους γάρ εἰμ' Ἕλλησιν, οὐχ ὅσον πικροὺς
λόγους ἔδωκα δεσπότην φοβουμένη.]

ΜΕΝΕΛΑΟΣ

τί φῶ; τί λέξω; συμφορὰς γὰρ ἀθλίας
ἐκ τῶν πάροιθε τὰς παρεστώσας κλύω,
485 εἰ τὴν μὲν αἱρεθεῖσαν ἐκ Τροίας ἄγων
ἥκω δάμαρτα καὶ κατ' ἄντρα σῴζεται,
ὄνομα δὲ ταὐτὸν τῆς ἐμῆς ἔχουσά τις
δάμαρτος ἄλλη τοισίδ' ἐνναίει δόμοις.
Διὸς δ' ἔλεξε παῖδά νιν πεφυκέναι.
490 ἀλλ' ἦ τις ἔστι Ζηνὸς ὄνομ' ἔχων ἀνὴρ
Νείλου παρ' ὄχθας; εἷς γὰρ ὅ γε κατ' οὐρανόν.
Σπάρτη δὲ ποῦ γῆς ἐστι πλὴν ἵνα ῥοαὶ
τοῦ καλλιδόνακός εἰσιν Εὐρώτα μόνον;
ἁπλοῦν δὲ Τυνδάρειον ὄνομα κλῄζεται.
495 Λακεδαίμονος δὲ γαῖα τίς ξυνώνυμος
Τροίας τ'; ἐγὼ μὲν οὐκ ἔχω τί χρὴ λέγειν.
[πολλοὶ γάρ, ὡς εἴξασιν, ἐν πολλῇ χθονὶ
ὀνόματα ταῦτ' ἔχουσι καὶ πόλις πόλει

MENELAUS

When? Has my wife been stolen from the cave?

OLD WOMAN

She came, stranger, before the Achaeans sailed to Troy.
But leave this house. Something has happened here to
throw all into confusion. You arrive at a bad time. If the
master catches you, death will be the only hospitality you
get. [I am well disposed toward the Greeks, to an extent
not to be measured by the bitter words I spoke to you from
fear of my master.]

Exit OLD WOMAN into the palace.

MENELAUS

What am I to make of this? I hear of new troubles on the
heels of old ones: I come bringing the wife I took from
Troy, and she is being kept in a cave, and yet there's an-
other woman, with the same name as my wife, living in this
house. She said the woman was Zeus's daughter. Is there
some man called Zeus by the banks of the Nile? No, there's
only one, the one in heaven. And where on earth is there a
Sparta except where the Eurotas flows past banks of lovely
reeds? Tyndareus is the name of one man, not two. What
other lands are called Lacedaemon and Troy? I do not
know what to make of it. [Many men in the wide earth, it
seems, have the same names as other men, and the same is

---

475 λέχος Heath: -ους L
481–2 del. Kovacs
486 σῴζομαι Badham
497–9 del. Badham, post 488 trai. Pearson

γυνὴ γυναικί τ'· οὐδὲν οὖν θαυμαστέον.]

500 οὐδ' αὖ τὸ δεινὸν προσπόλου φευξούμεθα·
ἀνὴρ γὰρ οὐδεὶς ὧδε βάρβαρος φρένας
ὃς ὄνομ' ἀκούσας τοὐμὸν οὐ δώσει βοράν.
[κλεινὸν τὸ Τροίας πῦρ ἐγώ θ' ὃς ἧψά νιν,
Μενέλαος, οὐκ ἄγνωστος ἐν πάσῃ χθονί.

505 δόμων ἄνακτα προσμενῶ· δισσὰς δέ μοι
ἔχει φυλάξεις· ἢν μὲν ὠμόφρων τις ᾖ,
κρύψας ἐμαυτὸν εἶμι πρὸς ναυάγια·
ἢν δ' ἐνδιδῷ τι μαλθακόν, τὰ πρόσφορα
τῆς νῦν παρούσης συμφορᾶς αἰτήσομαι.]

510 κακῶν δ' ἐν ἡμῖν ἔσχατον τῶν ἀθλίων,
ἄλλους τυράννους αὐτὸν ὄντα βασιλέα
βίον προσαιτεῖν· ἀλλ' ἀναγκαίως ἔχει.
λόγος γάρ ἐστιν οὐκ ἐμός, σοφῶν δέ του,
δεινῆς ἀνάγκης οὐδὲν ἰσχύειν πλέον.

ΧΟΡΟΣ

515 ἤκουσα τᾶς θεσπιῳδοῦ κόρας
ἃ χρῄζουσ' ἐπλάθην τυράννοις δόμοισιν,
ὡς Μενέλαος οὔ-
πω μελαμφαὲς οἴχεται
δι' ἔρεβος χθονὶ κρυφθείς,

520 ἀλλ' ἔτι κατ' οἶδμ' ἅλιον
τρυχόμενος οὔπω λιμένων
ψαύσειεν πατρίας γᾶς,

503–9 del. Willink

66

true of women and cities. So there is nothing to wonder at.]

Yet I will not run away from the danger the servant mentioned. No man has so uncivilized a heart that he will not give me food once he has heard my name. [The fire of Troy is famous, and so am I who lit it, Menelaus, well known throughout the whole world. I shall await the master of the house. He gives me two ways of guarding against him. If he proves to be a cruel fellow, I shall conceal myself and go back to the shipwreck. But if he shows some sign of kindness, I shall ask him for what my present misfortunes require.]

One thing caps all my other miserable woes, that I, myself a king, must beg my livelihood from other kings. But it can't be helped. It was some wise man who said it, not I: nothing has more power than cruel necessity.

Enter CHORUS *from the palace.*

CHORUS

I have heard from the prophetic maiden
what I entered the palace to hear,
that Menelaus has not yet
been covered by earth
and gone down through the dark-shining gloom:
still buffeted by the sea wave
he has yet to grasp
the harbors of his native land,

---

509 τῇ νῦν παρούσῃ συμφορᾷ σφ' Hermann   510 δ' ἐν
Nauck: δέ θ' L   τῶν ἀθλίων Kovacs: τοῖς ἀθλίοις L
513 δέ του Dobree: δ' ἔπος L
516 ἐπλάθην Diggle: ἐφάνη L

ἀλατείᾳ βιότου
ταλαίφρων, ἄφιλος φίλων,
525 παντοδαπᾶς ἐπὶ γᾶς πέδον
χριμπτόμενος εἰναλίῳ
κώπᾳ Τρῳάδος ἐκ γᾶς.

ΕΛΕΝΗ

ἥδ᾽ αὖ τάφου τοῦδ᾽ εἰς ἕδρας ἐγὼ πάλιν
στείχω, μαθοῦσα Θεονόης φίλους λόγους.
530 [ἣ πάντ᾽ ἀληθῶς οἶδε· φησὶ δ᾽ ἐν φάει
πόσιν τὸν ἁμὸν ζῶντα φέγγος εἰσορᾶν,
πορθμοὺς δ᾽ ἀλᾶσθαι μυρίους πεπλωκότα
ἐκεῖσε κἀκεῖσ᾽, οὐδ᾽ ἀγύμναστον πλάνοις
ἥξειν ὅταν δὴ πημάτων λάβῃ τέλος.
535 ἓν δ᾽ οὐκ ἔλεξεν, εἰ μολὼν σωθήσεται.
ἐγὼ δ᾽ ἀπέστην τοῦτ᾽ ἐρωτῆσαι σαφῶς,
ἡσθεῖσ᾽ ἐπεί νιν εἶπέ μοι σεσωμένον.
ἐγγὺς δέ νίν που τῆσδ᾽ ἔφασκ᾽ εἶναι χθονός,
ναυαγὸν ἐκπεσόντα σὺν παύροις φίλοις.
540 ὤμοι, πόθ᾽ ἥξεις; ὡς ποθεινὸς ἂν μόλοις.]
    ἔα, τίς οὗτος; οὔ τί που κρυπτεύομαι
Πρωτέως ἀσέπτου παιδὸς ἐκ βουλευμάτων;
οὐχ ὡς δρομαία πῶλος ἢ Βάκχη θεοῦ
τάφῳ ξυνάψω κῶλον; ἄγριος δέ τις
545 μορφὴν ὅδ᾽ ἐστὶν ὅς με θηρᾶται λαβεῖν.

525 πέδον Blaydes: πόδα L
530-40 del. Willink

68

but spends his life wandering,
poor man, bereft of friends,
going to lands of every sort
with his seagoing ship
since setting sail from Troy.

Enter HELEN *from the palace.*

HELEN

I too am now returning to my seat upon the tomb, having
had good news from Theonoe. [She knows the truth about
everything. She says that my husband lives in the light and
looks upon the daylight, but that he crisscrosses the sea
endlessly, now here now there, and that he will come
home, much worn out with wandering, when he has
reached the end of his troubles. One thing she did not say:
whether he will live once he reaches home. I did not ask
her explicitly since I was so glad that she reported him safe.
She also says he is somewhere near this land, cast up as a
shipwreck with only a few of his companions. Ah, when will
you come? You will be a welcome sight when you arrive!]

   (*Catching sight of Menelaus*) Oh, oh, who is this? Can it
be that I am being ambushed at the bidding of Proteus'
godless son? Quick, to the tomb, run like a galloping colt or
one of the god's bacchants! He's a savage, by the look of
him, the man who hunts me!

*Helen runs toward the tomb, but Menelaus cuts off her
retreat.*

ΜΕΝΕΛΑΟΣ

σὲ τὴν ὄρεγμα δεινὸν ἠμιλλημένην
τύμβου 'πὶ κρηπῖδ' ἐμπύρους τ' ὀρθοστάτας,
μεῖνον· τί φεύγεις; ὡς δέμας δείξασα σὸν
ἔκπληξιν ἡμῖν ἀφασίαν τε προστίθης.

ΕΛΕΝΗ

550   ἀδικούμεθ', ὦ γυναῖκες· εἰργόμεσθα γὰρ
τάφου πρὸς ἀνδρὸς τοῦδε, καί μ' ἑλὼν θέλει
δοῦναι τυράννοις ὧν ἐφεύγομεν γάμους.

ΜΕΝΕΛΑΟΣ

οὐ κλῶπές ἐσμεν οὐδ' ὑπηρέται κακῶν.

ΕΛΕΝΗ

καὶ μὴν στολήν γ' ἄμορφον ἀμφὶ σῶμ' ἔχεις.

ΜΕΝΕΛΑΟΣ

555   στῆσον, φόβον μεθεῖσα, λαιψηρὸν πόδα.

ΕΛΕΝΗ

ἵστημ', ἐπεί γε τοῦδ' ἐφάπτομαι τάφου.

ΜΕΝΕΛΑΟΣ

τίς εἶ; τίν' ὄψιν σήν, γύναι, προσδέρκομαι;

ΕΛΕΝΗ

σὺ δ' εἶ τίς; αὐτὸς γὰρ σὲ κἄμ' ἔχει λόγος.

ΜΕΝΕΛΑΟΣ

οὐπώποτ' εἶδον προσφερέστερον δέμας.

553 οὐδ' Hermann: οὐχ L
555 φόβον Valckenaer: -ου L

MENELAUS

You, the one trying so desperately to get to the steps of the tomb and the pillars where burnt offering is made, stay! Why do you run? By showing me yourself you have astonished me, made me speechless!

HELEN

Violence, women! This man is cutting me off from the tomb! He wants to take me and give me to the king I don't want to marry!

MENELAUS

I am no thief, and no doer of base services either.

HELEN

Well you are most villainously dressed.

MENELAUS

Don't be afraid! Halt where you are!

HELEN

(*reaching the tomb*) See, I am halting, now that I have my hand on the tomb.

MENELAUS

Who are you, lady? In you what sight do I see?

HELEN

And you, who are you? You and I both have the same question.

MENELAUS

Never have I seen a greater resemblance!

---

556 τάφου Elmsley: τόπου L
559 προσφερεστέραν Aldina

ΕΛΕΝΗ

560 ὦ θεοί· θεὸς γὰρ καὶ τὸ γιγνώσκειν φίλους.

⟨ΜΕΝΕΛΑΟΣ

Ἑλληνὶς εἶ τις ἢ ᾿πιχωρία γυνή;⟩

ΕΛΕΝΗ

Ἑλληνίς· ἀλλὰ καὶ τὸ σὸν θέλω μαθεῖν.

ΜΕΝΕΛΑΟΣ

Ἑλένῃ σ᾿ ὁμοίαν δὴ μάλιστ᾿ εἶδον, γύναι.

ΕΛΕΝΗ

ἐγὼ δὲ Μενελέῳ γε σ᾿· οὐδ᾿ ἔχω τί φῶ.

ΜΕΝΕΛΑΟΣ

565 ἔγνως ἄρ᾿ ὀρθῶς ἄνδρα δυστυχέστατον.

ΕΛΕΝΗ

ὦ χρόνιος ἐλθὼν σῆς δάμαρτος ἐς χέρας.

ΜΕΝΕΛΑΟΣ

ποίας δάμαρτος; μὴ θίγῃς ἐμῶν πέπλων.

ΕΛΕΝΗ

ἥν σοι δίδωσι Τυνδάρεως, ἐμὸς πατήρ.

ΜΕΝΕΛΑΟΣ

ὦ φωσφόρ᾿ Ἑκάτη, πέμπε φάσματ᾿ εὐμενῆ.

ΕΛΕΝΗ

570 οὐ νυκτίφαντον πρόπολον Ἐνοδίας μ᾿ ὁρᾷς.

---

561 ex t rest. Markland: om. L
565 ἄρ᾿ t: γὰρ L

HELEN

O gods! To recognize your own is also something divine!

‹**MENELAUS**

Are you a Greek or a native here?›

HELEN

A Greek. But I too would know about you.

MENELAUS

You are more like Helen than any woman I have seen.

HELEN

So are you like Menelaus. I do not know what to say.

MENELAUS

So you recognize me, man of great misery that I am.

HELEN

(*trying to embrace him*) How long you have taken to come to your wife's arms!

MENELAUS

Wife? What wife? Do not touch my garments!

HELEN

The wife my father Tyndareus gave you.

MENELAUS

O Hecate with your torches,[15] send me kindly visions!

HELEN

It is no phantom attendant of Enodia that you see here.

[15] Hecate, also called Enodia, is the goddess of crossroads and goes about attended by ghostly apparitions.

ΜΕΝΕΛΑΟΣ

οὐ μὴν γυναικῶν γ᾽ εἷς δυοῖν ἔφυν πόσις.

ΕΛΕΝΗ

ποίων δὲ λέκτρων δεσπότης ἄλλων ἔφυς;

ΜΕΝΕΛΑΟΣ

ἣν ἄντρα κεύθει κἀκ Φρυγῶν κομίζομαι.

ΕΛΕΝΗ

οὐκ ἔστιν ἄλλη σοί τις ἀντ᾽ ἐμοῦ γυνή.

ΜΕΝΕΛΑΟΣ

575 οὐ που φρονῶ μὲν εὖ, τὸ δ᾽ ὄμμα μου νοσεῖ;

ΕΛΕΝΗ

οὐ γάρ με λεύσσων σὴν δάμαρθ᾽ ὁρᾶν δοκεῖς;

ΜΕΝΕΛΑΟΣ

τὸ σῶμ᾽ ὅμοιον, τὸ δὲ σαφές γ᾽ ἀποστατεῖ.

ΕΛΕΝΗ

σκέψαι· τί σοι δεῖ πίστεως σαφεστέρας;

ΜΕΝΕΛΑΟΣ

ἔοικας· οὔτοι τοῦτό γ᾽ ἐξαρνήσομαι.

ΕΛΕΝΗ

580 τίς οὖν διδάξει σ᾽ ἄλλος ἢ τὰ σ᾽ ὄμματα;

ΜΕΝΕΛΑΟΣ

ἐκεῖ νοσοῦμεν, ὅτι δάμαρτ᾽ ἄλλην ἔχω.

ΕΛΕΝΗ

οὐκ ἦλθον ἐς γῆν Τρῳάδ᾽, ἀλλ᾽ εἴδωλον ἦν.

MENELAUS
But I am one man: I cannot have two wives.

HELEN
Of what other woman are you lord and master?

MENELAUS
Her in the cave, the one I brought from Troy.

HELEN
You have no other wife but me.

MENELAUS
Can it be that my mind is sound but my eyes are bad?

HELEN
In seeing me aren't you convinced you see your wife?

MENELAUS
You look like her, but certainty eludes me.

HELEN
Just look! Why do you need clearer proof than that?

MENELAUS
You look like her: that I shall not deny.

HELEN
Who but your eyes should be your teacher?

MENELAUS
My trouble is this: I have another wife.

HELEN
That was an image: I never went to Troy.

---

⁵⁷⁴ σοί Lightfoot: σή L   ⁵⁷⁷ γ᾽ ἀποστατεῖ Paley: μ᾽
ἀποστερεῖ L   ⁵⁷⁸ τί σοι δεῖ πίστεως σαφεστέρας Bad-
ham: τί σου δεῖ; τίς ἔστι σοῦ σοφώτερος; L

ΜΕΝΕΛΑΟΣ

καὶ τίς βλέποντα σώματ' ἐξεργάζεται;

ΕΛΕΝΗ

αἰθήρ, ὅθεν σὺ θεοπόνητ' ἔχεις λέχη.

ΜΕΝΕΛΑΟΣ

585   τίνος πλάσαντος θεῶν; ἄελπτα γὰρ λέγεις.

ΕΛΕΝΗ

Ἥρας, διάλλαγμ', ὡς Πάρις με μὴ λάβοι.

ΜΕΝΕΛΑΟΣ

πῶς οὖν; ἅμ' ἐνθάδ' ἦσθ' ⟨ἄρ'⟩ ἐν Τροίᾳ θ' ἅμα;

ΕΛΕΝΗ

τοὔνομα γένοιτ' ἂν πολλαχοῦ, τὸ σῶμα δ' οὔ.

ΜΕΝΕΛΑΟΣ

μέθες με· λύπης ἅλις ἔχων ἐλήλυθα.

ΕΛΕΝΗ

590   λείψεις γὰρ ἡμᾶς, τὰ δὲ κέν' ἐξάξεις λέχη;

ΜΕΝΕΛΑΟΣ

καὶ χαῖρέ γ', Ἑλένῃ προσφερὴς ὁθούνεκ' εἶ.

ΕΛΕΝΗ

ἀπωλόμην· λαβοῦσά σ' οὐχ ἕξω πόσιν.

ΜΕΝΕΛΑΟΣ

τοὐκεῖ με μέγεθος τῶν πόνων πείθει, σὺ δ' οὔ.

587 dist. A. Y. Campbell   ἅμ' . . . ἦσθ' ⟨ἄρ'⟩ anonymus: ἂν
. . . ἦσθ' L

MENELAUS

And what craftsman can fashion a living body?

HELEN

The upper air: it was from there that you got this god-fashioned bride.

MENELAUS

Which of the gods made her? What you say is astonishing.

HELEN

Hera, as a substitute so that Paris would not get me.

MENELAUS

What? Were you at the same time both here and at Troy?

HELEN

A name may be in many places, though a body in only one.

MENELAUS

Let me go! I had enough grief when I came here!

HELEN

What? Will you leave me and take your phantom wife away?

MENELAUS

I wish you joy for so resembling Helen!

HELEN

O the misery! I have found you, husband, but may not keep you!

MENELAUS

I trust my many labors at Troy, not you.

ΕΛΕΝΗ

οἲ 'γώ· τίς ἡμῶν ἐγένετ' ἀθλιωτέρα;
595 οἱ φίλτατοι λείπουσί μ' οὐδ' ἀφίξομαι
Ἕλληνας οὐδὲ πατρίδα τὴν ἐμήν ποτε.

ΘΕΡΑΠΩΝ

Μενέλαε, μαστεύων σε κιγχάνω μόλις,
πᾶσαν πλανηθεὶς τήνδε βάρβαρον χθόνα,
πεμφθεὶς ἑταίρων τῶν λελειμμένων ὕπο.

ΜΕΝΕΛΑΟΣ

600 τί δ' ἔστιν; οὔ που βαρβάρων συλᾶσθ' ὕπο;

ΘΕΡΑΠΩΝ

θαῦμ' ἔστ', ἔλασσον τοὔνομ' ἢ τὸ πρᾶγμ' ἔχον.

ΜΕΝΕΛΑΟΣ

λέγ'· ὡς φέρεις τι τῇδε τῇ σπουδῇ νέον.

ΘΕΡΑΠΩΝ

λέγω πόνους σε μυρίους τλῆναι μάτην.

ΜΕΝΕΛΑΟΣ

παλαιὰ θρηνεῖς πήματ'· ἀγγέλλεις δὲ τί;

ΘΕΡΑΠΩΝ

605 βέβηκεν ἄλοχος σὴ πρὸς αἰθέρος πτυχὰς
ἀρθεῖσ' ἄφαντος· οὐρανῷ δὲ κρύπτεται
λιποῦσα σεμνὸν ἄντρον οὗ σφ' ἐσῴζομεν,
τοσόνδε λέξασ'· Ὦ ταλαίπωροι Φρύγες

597n Θεράπων Kannicht: Ἄγγελος L
601 θαῦμ' ἔστ' Scaliger: θαυμάστ' L
607 λιποῦσ' ἐρεμνὸν Schneidewin

78

HELEN

Ah, ah! Who is more ill-starred than I am? My dear husband deserts me, and I shall never reach Greece or my native city!

Enter by Eisidos A a SERVANT *of Menelaus.*

SERVANT

Menelaus, what trouble it has been to find you! I have been up and down this entire barbarian land looking for you, sent by the comrades you left behind.

MENELAUS

What is it? You aren't being plundered by the barbarians, I trust.

SERVANT

A strange thing has happened, stranger in fact than in the telling of it.

MENELAUS

Tell me: in your haste you must be bringing me something unusual.

SERVANT

My tale: your countless labors have been in vain.

MENELAUS

An old story, this lament of yours. What is your news?

SERVANT

Your wife has disappeared, swept out of sight into the sky's recesses, vanished into the heavens! She has left the holy cave where we were guarding her, having said only this: "You poor Phrygians and all you Greeks, day after day you

πάντες τ' Ἀχαιοί, δι' ἔμ' ἐπὶ Σκαμανδρίοις
610 ἀκταῖσιν Ἥρας μηχαναῖς ἐθνῄσκετε,
δοκοῦντες Ἑλένην οὐκ ἔχοντ' ἔχειν Πάριν.
ἐγὼ δ', ἐπειδὴ χρόνον ἔμειν' ὅσον μ' ἐχρῆν,
τὸ μόρσιμον σώσασα πατέρ' ἐς οὐρανὸν
ἄπειμι· φήμας δ' ἡ τάλαινα Τυνδαρὶς
615 ἄλλως κακὰς ἤκουσεν οὐδὲν αἰτία.

ὦ χαῖρε, Λήδας θύγατερ, ἐνθάδ' ἦσθ' ἄρα.
ἐγὼ δέ σ' ἄστρων ὡς βεβηκυῖαν μυχοὺς
ἤγγελλον εἰδὼς οὐδὲν ὡς ὑπόπτερον
δέμας φοροίης. οὐκ ἐῶ σε κερτομεῖν
620 ἡμᾶς τόδ' αὖθις· ὡς ἅδην ἐν Ἰλίῳ
πόνους παρεῖχες σῷ πόσει καὶ συμμάχοις.

ΜΕΝΕΛΑΟΣ
τοῦτ' ἔστ' ἐκεῖνο· ξυμβεβᾶσί μοι λόγοι
οἱ τῆσδ' ἀληθεῖς. ὦ ποθεινὸς ἡμέρα,
ἥ σ' εἰς ἐμὰς ἔδωκεν ὠλένας λαβεῖν.

ΕΛΕΝΗ
625 ὦ φίλτατ' ἀνδρῶν Μενέλεως, ὁ μὲν χρόνος
παλαιός, ἡ δὲ τέρψις ἀρτίως πάρα.
ἔλαβον ἀσμένα πόσιν ἐμόν, φίλαι,
περί τ' ἐπέτασα χέρα φίλιον ἐν μακρᾷ
φλογὶ φαεσφόρῳ.

ΜΕΝΕΛΑΟΣ
630 κἀγὼ σέ· πολλοὺς δ' ἐν μέσῳ λόγους ἔχων

perished for my sake on the banks of the Scamander by
Hera's contrivance, thinking that Paris had Helen, which
he never did! I have completed my allotted task and tarried
here as long as I was meant to, and now I am departing for
the heaven that begot me. The ill-starred daughter of
Tyndareus has been falsely vilified: she is not to blame."

(*catching sight of Helen*) O hello, daughter of Leda! So
this is where you were hiding! I was just bringing the news
that you had left for the starry heaven. I did not know that
you had wings. I'll not have you mocking us like this again.
The troubles you gave your husband and his comrades in
Troy are enough.

MENELAUS

Why, this is just what she said! Her words turn out to be
true! O day of love-longing fulfilled, that has brought you
to my arms!

Menelaus and Helen embrace.

HELEN

O Menelaus, man I love best, the time
has been long delayed, but now my joy is come!
My friends, with what gladness do I greet my husband
and put my arms about him
after all the days that have dawned!

MENELAUS

And I, how glad I am to have you! There is much I would
  speak of,

---

⁶⁰⁹ πάντες] τάλανές Hermann   ⁶²² ξυμβεβᾶσί μοι
Willink: -σιν οἱ L   ⁶²⁴ ἤ σ᾽ Canter: ὡς L
  ⁶²⁸ περί τ᾽ ἐπέτασα Hermann: περιπετάσασα L

οὐκ οἶδ᾽ ὁποίου πρῶτον ἄρξωμαι τὰ νῦν.
γέγηθα, κρατὶ δ᾽ ὀρθίους ἐθείρας
ἀνεπτέρωσα καὶ δάκρυ σταλάσσω,
περὶ δὲ γυῖα χέρας ἔβαλον, ἡδονᾷ
635 ⟨νέᾳ⟩ σ᾽ ὡς λάβω.

ΕΛΕΝΗ

ὦ πόσις·
ὦ φιλτάτα πρόσοψις.

ΜΕΝΕΛΑΟΣ
οὐκ ἐμέμφθην·
†ἔχω τὰ τοῦ Διὸς λέκτρα Λήδας τε†.

⟨ΕΛΕΝΗ⟩

ἅ γ᾽ ὑπὸ λαμπάδων κόροι λεύκιπποι
640 ξυννομαίμονες ὤλβισαν ὤλβισαν οὐ μάταν
τὸ πρόσθεν.

ΜΕΝΕΛΑΟΣ
⟨τὸ πρόσθε⟩ν; πρὸς ἄλλαν γ᾽ ἐλαύνει
θεὸς συμφορὰν τᾶσδε κρείσσω.

ΕΛΕΝΗ

τὸ κακὸν δ᾽ ἀγαθὸν σέ τε κἀμὲ συνάγαγεν, πόσι,

632–5 Menelao contin. Willink: Ἐλ. L
634–7 χέρας Π, coni. Elmsley: χεῖρ᾽ L   ἡδονᾷ / ⟨νέᾳ⟩ σ᾽ ὡς
λάβω / ὦ πόσις / ὦ φιλτάτα Willink: ηδονη / [3–4?]c ωc λάβω /
[c. 6?] ω φιλτατα Π: ἡδονὰν / ὡς λάβω ὦ πόσις / ὦ φιλτάτη L
637b Menelao trib. L et u. v. Π
638 fort. ἔχω τὰν Διὸς Λήδας τ᾽ ἔκγονον
639n ⟨Ἐλ.⟩ Zuntz

but for the moment I know not where to begin!
My heart exults, the hair of my head
stands on end, tears stream from my eyes!
I throw my arms about you
with pleasure <fresh>
to receive you!

HELEN

O husband!
O sight I look on with greatest joy!

MENELAUS

                I am content!
I have my wife, daughter of Zeus and Leda!

<HELEN>

Yes, her whom by bridal torch light the lads of the white horses,
my brothers, called blessed, blessed: their words were not false
in time past.

MENELAUS

      <In time past>? But it is to another fate,
a better one than this, that heaven is leading you.

HELEN

Yes, it was fortunate misfortune that brought you and me together, husband,

---

639 ἅ γ' Willink: ἂν L

640 οὐ μάταν Willink: εμε σε τε ματαν Π: om. L

641 <τὸ πρόσθε>ν. Με. <τὸ πρόσθε>ν; Willink: [8–9]ν / [8–9]ν
Π, altero versu Menelao tributo u. v.: τὸ πρόσθεν ἐκ δόμων δ'
ἐνόσφισαν θεοί σ' ὁμοῦ L   γ' Π: δ' L

645 χρόνιον, ἀλλ᾽ ὅμως· ὀναίμαν τύχας.

ΜΕΝΕΛΑΟΣ

ὄναιο δῆτα. ταὐτὰ δὲ ξυνεύχομαι·
δυοῖν γὰρ ὄντοιν οὐχ ὁ μὲν τλήμων, ὁ δ᾽ οὔ.

ΕΛΕΝΗ

φίλαι φίλαι·
τὰ πάρος οὐκέτι στένομεν οὐδ᾽ ἀλγῶ.
650 πόσιν ⟨γ᾽⟩ ἁμὸν ἔχομεν ἔχομεν ὃν ἔμενον
ἔμενον ἐκ Τροίας πολυετῆ μολεῖν.

ΜΕΝΕΛΑΟΣ

ἔχεις, ἐγώ τε σ᾽· ἡλίους δὲ μυρίους
μόλις διελθὼν ᾐσθόμην τὰ τοῦ θεοῦ.
ἐμὰ δὲ χαρμονᾶς δάκρυα· πλέον ἔχει
655 χάριτος ἢ λύπας.

ΕΛΕΝΗ

τί φῶ; τίς ἂν τάδ᾽ ἤλπισεν βροτῶν ποτε;
ἀδόκητον ἔχω σε πρὸς στέρνοις.

ΜΕΝΕΛΑΟΣ

κἀγὼ σὲ τὴν δοκοῦσαν Ἰδαίαν πόλιν
μολεῖν Ἰλίου τε μελέους πύργους.
660 πρὸς θεῶν, δόμων πῶς τῶν ἐμῶν ἀπεστάλης;

ΕΛΕΝΗ

ἒ ἔ· πικρὰς ἐς ἀρχὰς βαίνεις,
ἒ ἔ· πικρὰν δ᾽ ἐρευνᾷς φάτιν.

645 dist. Kannicht   650 ⟨γ᾽⟩ ἁμὸν Willink: ἐμὸν L
653 τοῦ Kovacs: τῆς L

however long it took: may I enjoy its blessing!

MENELAUS

Yes, may you enjoy it! That is the prayer I too make,
for of a pair one cannot be in misery and the other happy.

HELEN

My friends, my friends:
no longer do I mourn or grieve for the past.
I have my husband, for whose return from Troy I waited,
waited so many years!

MENELAUS

Yes, you have me, and I have you! It was hard to live
    through
so many days, but now I recognize heaven's hand.
My tears are those of joy: they have more in them
of gratefulness than grief.

HELEN

What am I to say? What mortal ever expected this?
I hold you all unlooked for to my breast!

MENELAUS

And I as well hold you, who I thought had gone
to the city near Ida and the ill-starred towers of Ilium.

Menelaus and Helen separate.

In the gods' name, how were you taken from my house?

HELEN

Ah me, painful is the cause you seek!
Ah me, painful the story you would hear!

---

654 χαρμονᾶς Reiske: -ὰ L

85

ΜΕΝΕΛΑΟΣ

λέγ᾽· ὡς ἀκουστὰ πάντα δῶρα δαιμόνων.

ΕΛΕΝΗ

ἀπέπτυσα μὲν λόγον, οἷον
οἷον ἐσοισόμεθα.

ΜΕΝΕΛΑΟΣ

665   ὅμως δὲ λέξον· ἡδύ τοι μόχθων κλύειν.

ΕΛΕΝΗ

οὐκ ἐπὶ βαρβάρου λέκτρα νεανία
πετομένας κώπας ἔποχον οὐδ᾽ ἔρω-
τος ἀδίκων γάμων . . .

ΜΕΝΕΛΑΟΣ

τίς <δή> σε δαίμων ἢ πότμος συλᾷ πάτρας;

ΕΛΕΝΗ

670   ὁ Διὸς ὁ Διὸς ὦ πόσι με παῖς <Μαίας τ᾽>
ἐπέλασεν Νείλῳ.

ΜΕΝΕΛΑΟΣ

θαυμαστά· τοῦ πέμψαντος; ὦ δεινοὶ λόγοι.

ΕΛΕΝΗ

κατὰ δ᾽ ἔκλαυσα καὶ βλέφαρον ὑγραίνω
δάκρυσιν· ἁ Διός μ᾽ ἄλοχος ὤλεσεν.

ΜΕΝΕΛΑΟΣ

675   Ἥρα; τί νῶν χρήζουσα προσθεῖναι κακόν;

664 ἐσοισόμεθα Willink: ἐσοίσομαι L
666 βαρβάρου λ- Kluge: λ- βαρβάρου L

MENELAUS

Tell me: all that the gods give can be listened to.

HELEN

I feel revulsion at the tale,
the tale I now utter.

MENELAUS

Yet tell me: to hear of trouble past is a pleasure.

HELEN

Not to the bed of a young barbarian prince,
borne on his flying oar, borne on the wings of desire
for an unholy marriage . . .

MENELAUS

What power divine, what fate stole you from your country?

HELEN

It was Zeus's son, Zeus's ⟨and Maia's⟩
that brought me to the Nile.

MENELAUS

What a strange and terrible tale! At whose behest?

HELEN

I weep, I wet my eyes
with tears: it was Zeus's wife who destroyed me.

MENELAUS

Hera? Why did she wish to cause us bane?

---

667 ἔποχον οὐδ᾽ post Reiske Willink: πετομένου δ᾽ L
669 ⟨δή⟩ Zuntz
670 με παῖς ⟨Μαίας τ᾽⟩ Hermann: παῖς μ᾽ L
673 κατὰ δ᾽ ἔκλαυσα Willink: κατέδακρυσα L

ΕΛΕΝΗ

ὤμοι ἐγὼ κείνων λουτρῶν καὶ κρηνᾶν,
ἵνα θεαὶ μορφὰν ἐφαίδρυναν, εὖτ᾽
ἔμολον ἐς κρίσιν.

ΜΕΝΕΛΑΟΣ

†τὰ δ᾽ ἐς κρίσιν σοι τῶνδ᾽ ἔθηχ᾽ Ἥρα κακῶν;†

ΕΛΕΝΗ

680 Πάριν ὡς ἀφέλοιτο . . .

ΜΕΝΕΛΑΟΣ

πῶς; αὔδα.

ΕΛΕΝΗ

. . . Κύπρις ᾧ μ᾽ ἐπένευσεν . . .

ΜΕΝΕΛΑΟΣ

ὦ τλᾶμον.

ΕΛΕΝΗ

. . . τλάμονα τλάμον᾽ ὧδ᾽ ἐπέλασ᾽ Αἰγύπτῳ.

ΜΕΝΕΛΑΟΣ

εἶτ᾽ ἀντέδωκ᾽ εἴδωλον, ὡς σέθεν κλύω.

ΕΛΕΝΗ

τὰ δὲ ⟨σὰ⟩ κατὰ μέλαθρα πάθεα πάθεα, μᾶ-
685 τερ, οἲ ᾽γώ.

676 ἐγὼ Badham: ἐμῶν L   κείνων Dale: δεινῶν L
677 εὖτ᾽ Diggle: ἔνθεν L
678 ἔμολον ἐς κρίσιν Willink: ἔμολε κρίσις L
679 fort. πόθεν ἔθηχ᾽ Ἥρα κακόν;
680–1 Πάριν . . . Κύπρις Reiske: Κύπριν . . . Πάριν L

HELEN

Ah, alas for those gushing springs, that bath
where the goddesses made themselves beautiful
when they came to be judged!

MENELAUS

Why did Hera make from the judgment a woe for you?

HELEN

So that she could take me from Paris . . .

MENELAUS

Tell me what you mean.

HELEN

. . . to whom Aphrodite had given me . . .

MENELAUS

O poor woman!

HELEN

. . . she sent me in misery, misery thus to Egypt!

MENELAUS

Then she gave him a phantom to replace you, I heard you
say.

HELEN

But at home what sorrows, sorrows were ⟨yours⟩, mother:
ah woe is me!

---

680 ὥς ⟨μ'⟩ Bothe
682 τλάμονα τλάμον' Hermann: -μων -μων L
684 ⟨σὰ⟩ Hermann

ΜΕΝΕΛΑΟΣ

τί φῄς;

ΕΛΕΝΗ

οὐκ ἔστι μάτηρ· ἀγχόνιον δὲ βρόχον
δι᾽ ἐμὰν κατεδήσατο δύσγαμον αἰσχύναν.

ΜΕΝΕΛΑΟΣ

ὤμοι· θυγατρὸς Ἑρμιόνης δὲ τίς βίος;

ΕΛΕΝΗ

ἄγαμος ἄτεκνος, ὦ πόσι, καταστένει
690 γάμον ἄγαμον ⟨ἐμόν⟩.

ΜΕΝΕΛΑΟΣ

ὦ πᾶν κατ᾽ ἄκρας δῶμ᾽ ἐμὸν πέρσας Πάρις.

ΕΛΕΝΗ

τάδε καὶ σὲ διώλεσε μυριάδας τε
χαλκεόπλων Δαναῶν.
ἐμὲ δὲ πατρίδος ἀπο⟨πρὸ⟩ κακόποτμον ἀραι-
695 ον ἔβαλε θεὸς ἀπὸ πόλεος ἀπό τε σέθεν,
ὅτι μέλαθρα λέχεά τ᾽ ἔλιπον οὐ λιποῦσ᾽
ἐπ᾽ αἰσχροῖς γάμοις.

ΧΟΡΟΣ

εἰ καὶ τὰ λοιπὰ τῆς τύχης εὐδαίμονος
τύχοιτε, πρὸς τὰ πρόσθεν ἀρκέσειεν ἄν.

688 θυγατρὸς Ἑρμιόνης δὲ τίς βίος Willink: θ- Ἑρ- ἔστι L
690 ἄγαμον ⟨ἐμόν⟩ Hermann: ἄγαμον αἰσχύνα L
694 ἀπο⟨πρὸ⟩ Diggle   ἀραῖον Diggle: ἀραίαν L
696 ὅτε Barnes

90

MENELAUS
What do you mean?

HELEN
My mother is dead: she tied a noose
about her neck for shame at my foul union.

MENELAUS
Ah me! And what is our daughter Hermione's life?

HELEN
Without husband or child she grieves, dear husband,
for ⟨my⟩ disastrous marriage.

MENELAUS
O Paris, how thoroughly you have pillaged my house!

HELEN
Yes, this has been your death and that of countless others
among the bronze-armored Danaans.
But I was sent by heaven far from my country,
far from my city and from you. I was ill-starred and cursed
  by men
for leaving (though I did not leave) your house and your
  bed
for a marriage of shame.

CHORUS LEADER
If you get good fortune in the future, it will be sufficient
solace for all that is past.

---

698 εἰ καὶ] ἀλλ᾽ εἰ Rauchenstein

ΘΕΡΑΠΩΝ

700 Μενέλαε, κἀμοὶ πρόσδοτον τῆς ἡδονῆς,
    ἣν μανθάνω μὲν καὐτός, οὐ σαφῶς δ' ἔχω.

ΜΕΝΕΛΑΟΣ

ἀλλ', ὦ γεραιέ, καὶ σὺ κοινώνει λόγων.

ΘΕΡΑΠΩΝ

οὐχ ἥδε μόχθων τῶν ἐν Ἰλίῳ βραβεύς;

ΜΕΝΕΛΑΟΣ

οὐχ ἥδε, πρὸς θεῶν δ' ἦμεν ἠπατημένοι
705 [νεφέλης ἄγαλμ' ἔχοντες ἐν χεροῖν λυγρόν].

ΘΕΡΑΠΩΝ

[τί φῄς;]
νεφέλης ἄρ' ἄλλως εἴχομεν πόνους πέρι;

ΜΕΝΕΛΑΟΣ

Ἥρας τάδ' ἔργα καὶ θεῶν τρισσῶν ἔρις.

ΘΕΡΑΠΩΝ

τί δ'; ὡς ἀληθῶς ἐστιν ἥδε σὴ δάμαρ;

ΜΕΝΕΛΑΟΣ

710 αὕτη· λόγοις ἐμοῖσι πίστευσον τάδε.

ΘΕΡΑΠΩΝ

ὦ θύγατερ, ὁ θεὸς ὡς ἔφυ τι ποικίλον
    καὶ δυστέκμαρτον. εὖ δέ πως πάντα στρέφει
    ἐκεῖσε κἀκεῖσ' ἀναφέρων· ὁ μὲν πονεῖ,

---

700 πρόσδοτον Cobet: -δοτε L   705 del. Kirchhoff
706 del. Matthiae

SERVANT

Menelaus, share your pleasure with me also. I have heard it myself, but I don't fully understand.

MENELAUS

Well, old man, take part in our conversation.

SERVANT

Was this woman not the author of all our toils in Troy?

MENELAUS

No, not this one: the gods had deceived us. [We had in our embrace a baleful image made of cloud.]

SERVANT

[What do you mean?] Do you mean we toiled in vain for a cloud?

MENELAUS

This was the doing of Hera and of the three goddesses' strife.

SERVANT

But then is this really your wife?

MENELAUS

Yes: you may take my word for that.

SERVANT

My daughter, how changeable and inscrutable is the divine! How thoroughly does it turn everything now this way, now that! One man has trouble ‹but afterwards finds hap-

---

709 τί δ’; ὡς F. W. Schmidt: ἡ δ’ οὖσ’ L

710 λόγοις Paley: λ- δ’ L

712 πάντα στρέφει Herwerden: ἀναστρέφει L

<ὄλβου δ' ἔπειτα κευμενῶν θεῶν κυρεῖ,>
ὁ δ' οὐ πονήσας αὖθις ὄλλυται κακῶς,
715 βέβαιον οὐδὲν τῆς ἀεὶ τύχης ἔχων.
σὺ γὰρ πόσις τε σὸς πόνων μετέσχετε,
σὺ μὲν λόγοισιν, ὁ δὲ δορὸς προθυμίᾳ.
σπεύδων δ' ὅτ' ἔσπευδ' οὐδὲν εἶχε· νῦν δ' ἔχει
αὐτόματα πράξας τἀγάθ' εὐτυχέστατα.
720   οὐκ ἄρα γέροντα πατέρα καὶ Διοσκόρω
ᾔσχυνας οὐδ' ἔδρασας οἷα κλήζεται.
νῦν ἀνανεοῦμαι τὸν σὸν ὑμέναιον πάλιν
καὶ λαμπάδων μεμνήμεθ' ἃς τετραόροις
ἵπποις τροχάζων παρέφερον· σὺ δ' ἐν δίφροις
725 ξὺν τῷδε νύμφη δῶμ' ἔλειπες ὄλβιον.
κακὸς γὰρ ὅστις μὴ σέβει τὰ δεσποτῶν
καὶ ξυγγέγηθε καὶ συνωδίνει κακοῖς.
[ἐγὼ μὲν εἴην, κεἰ πέφυχ' ὅμως λάτρις,
ἐν τοῖσι γενναίοισιν ἠριθμημένος
730 δούλοισι, τοὔνομ' οὐκ ἔχων ἐλεύθερον,
τὸν νοῦν δέ· κρεῖσσον γὰρ τόδ' ἢ δυοῖν κακοῖν
ἕν' ὄντα χρῆσθαι, τὰς φρένας τ' ἔχειν κακὰς
ἄλλων τ' ἀκούειν δοῦλον ὄντα τῶν πέλας.]

ΜΕΝΕΛΑΟΣ
ἄγ', ὦ γεραιέ, πολλὰ μὲν παρ' ἀσπίδα
735 μοχθήματ' ἐξέπλησας ἐκπονῶν ἐμοί,
καὶ νῦν μετασχὼν τῆς ἐμῆς εὐπραξίας
ἄγγειλον ἐλθὼν τοῖς λελειμμένοις φίλοις
τάδ' ὡς ἔχονθ' ηὕρηκας οὗ τ' ἐσμὲν τύχης,

piness and heaven's blessing⟩, while another, who has had
no trouble, dies a painful death, since nothing in the fate
he enjoys can be relied on. You and your husband had your
share of troubles, you in your reputation, he in the toils of
war. For all his efforts he got nothing at the time. But now
he gets blessing without exertion, by a great stroke of luck.

So you did not bring shame on your old father or the
Dioscuri nor did you do the things that rumor speaks of.
Now I sing your marriage song once more. Now I think of
the torches I carried beside you in your chariot. It was a
house of blessedness you left in that chariot with him be-
side you. Base is the man who does not revere his master,
rejoice at his joys, and grieve at his sorrows. [Even if I am a
slave, may I be one of the good slaves, one with a free man's
heart even if he lacks a free man's name. Better that than to
join two misfortunes in a single person: having a base heart
and hearing yourself called another man's slave.]

MENELAUS

Old man, you have done me much service in battle. Now
share in my good fortune: go and tell my friends who are
left how you have found things and where our fortunes

---

713 post h. v. lac. indic. Holzner (713–9 del. Diggle)
717 ψόγοισιν F. W. Schmidt
728–33 suspectos habuit Dale, del. Willink
738 οὖ Tyrwhitt: οἶ L

μένειν τ᾽ ἐπ᾽ ἀκταῖς τούς τ᾽ ἐμοὺς καραδοκεῖν
740 ἀγῶνας οἳ μένουσί μ᾽, ὡς ἐλπίζομεν,
καὶ τήνδ᾽ [πῶς δυναίμεθ᾽ ἐκκλέψαι χθονὸς
φρουρεῖν] ὅπως ἂν εἰς ἓν ἐλθόντες τύχης
ἐκ βαρβάρων σωθῶμεν, ἢν δυνώμεθα.

ΘΕΡΑΠΩΝ

ἔσται τάδ᾽, ὦναξ. ἀλλά τοι τὰ μάντεων
745 ἐσεῖδον ὡς φαῦλ᾽ ἐστὶ καὶ ψευδῶν πλέα.
[οὐδ᾽ ἦν ἄρ᾽ ὑγιὲς οὐδὲν ἐμπύρου φλογὸς
οὐδὲ πτερωτῶν φθέγματ᾽· εὔηθες δέ τοι
τὸ καὶ δοκεῖν ὄρνιθας ὠφελεῖν βροτούς.]
Κάλχας γὰρ οὐκ εἶπ᾽ οὐδ᾽ ἐσήμηνε στρατῷ
750 νεφέλης ὑπερθνῄσκοντας εἰσορῶν φίλους
οὐδ᾽ Ἕλενος, ἀλλὰ πόλις ἀνηρπάσθη μάτην.
[εἴποις ἄν, οὕνεχ᾽ ὁ θεὸς οὐκ ἠβούλετο.
τί δῆτα μαντευόμεθα; τοῖσι θεοῖσι χρὴ
θύοντας αἰτεῖν ἀγαθά, μαντείας δ᾽ ἐᾶν·
755 βίου γὰρ ἄλλως δέλεαρ ηὑρέθη τόδε,
κοὐδεὶς ἐπλούτησ᾽ ἐμπύροισιν ἀργὸς ὤν·
γνώμη δ᾽ ἀρίστη μάντις ἥ τ᾽ εὐβουλία.]

ΧΟΡΟΣ

ἐς ταὐτὸ κἀμοὶ δόξα μάντεων πέρι
χωρεῖ γέροντι· τοὺς θεοὺς ἔχων τις ἂν
760 φίλους ἀρίστην μαντικὴν ἔχοι δόμοις.

---

740 μένουσί μ᾽, ὡς Musgrave: μένουσιν οὓς L
741–2 πῶς . . . φρουρεῖν del. Jackson
746–8 del. Wecklein (744–60 iam Hartung)

stand. Tell them to stay on the beach and watch for the outcome of the trials that I fear will be mine and hers, [and if I can somehow manage to steal her from this land, they should be ready and waiting] so that joining our fortunes together we may, if possible, escape this barbarian land.

SERVANT

I will do it, my lord. But now I know about prophets: how worthless they are, what liars! [There's no truth in the flame of sacrifice or in the cries of birds. How foolish even to imagine that birds are mortals' benefactors!] Calchas said not a word to the army, nor did Helenus,[16] though they saw that their comrades were dying for a mere cloud. Instead, a city was sacked for nothing. [You might reply, "That was because the god did not wish the truth known." Well, then, why do we consult prophets? No, one should sacrifice to the gods and ask for blessings but leave prophecy alone. That invention is one of life's foolish traps. No idle man ever got rich by looking at burnt offerings. The best way to tell the future is to be intelligent and plan ahead.]

Exit SERVANT *by Eisodos A.*

CHORUS LEADER

My opinion of prophecy is the same as this old man's. If a man has the gods' friendship, that is the best prophecy his house can have.

---

16 Trojan seer, son of Priam.

---

751 οὐδ᾽ Ἕλενος Porson: οὐδέν γε L   752–7 del. Willink
757 ἄριστος Dobree

ΕΛΕΝΗ

εἰέν· τὰ μὲν δὴ δεῦρ᾽ ἀεὶ καλῶς ἔχει.
ὅπως δ᾽ ἐσώθης, ὦ τάλας, Τροίας ἄπο
κέρδος μὲν οὐδὲν εἰδέναι, πόθος δέ τις
τὰ τῶν φίλων φίλοισιν αἰσθέσθαι κακά.

ΜΕΝΕΛΑΟΣ

765 ἦ πόλλ᾽ ἀνήρου μ᾽ ἑνὶ λόγῳ μιᾷ θ᾽ ὁδῷ.
τί σοι λέγοιμ᾽ ἂν τὰς ἐν Αἰγαίῳ φθορὰς
τὰ Ναυπλίου τ᾽ Εὐβοικὰ πυρπολήματα
Κρήτης τε Λιβύης θ᾽ ἃς ἐπεστράφην πόλεις,
σκοπιάς τε Περσέως; εἰ γὰρ ἐμπλήσαιμί σε
770 μύθοις, λέγων τ᾽ ἄν σοι κάκ᾽ ἀλγοίην ἔτι
πάσχων τ᾽ ἔκαμνον· δὶς δὲ λυπηθεῖμεν ἄν.

ΕΛΕΝΗ

καὶ πλείον᾽ εἶπας ἤ σ᾽ ἀνηρόμην ἐγώ.
ἓν δ᾽ εἰπὲ τἄλλα παραλιπών, πόσον χρόνον
πόντου 'πὶ νώτοις ἅλιον ἐφθείρου πλάνον;

ΜΕΝΕΛΑΟΣ

775 ἐν ναυσὶν ὢν πρὸς τοῖσιν ἐν Τροίᾳ δέκα
ἔτεσι διῆλθον ἑπτὰ περιδρομὰς ἐτῶν.

763 δέ τοι Kannicht
768 Κρήτης Kirchhoff: -ην L   Λιβύης Reiske: -ην L
769 εἰ Pearson: οὐ L
770 μύθοις Diggle: -ων L
772 καὶ πλείον᾽ Nauck: κάλλιον L
773 τἄλλα Herwerden: πάντα L
775 ἐν ναυσὶν ὢν Palmer: ἐνιαύσιον L

HELEN

So: up to this point all is well. But, poor man, though it
does me no good to know how you got safely away from
Troy, still we somehow long to hear of the troubles that
befall our dearest kin.

MENELAUS

By your single question you ask much. Why should I tell
you of the many shipwrecks on the Aegean, the false bea-
cons set by Nauplius on Euboea,[17] all the cities in Crete
and Libya I visited, and the lookout place of Perseus? If I
should give you your fill of my tale, I would be suffering
still more in the telling of it, just as I suffered in the actual
experience, and would be twice grieved.

HELEN

Your answer gives more than I asked for. But tell me one
thing and leave out the rest: how long did your miserable
wandering over the sea last?

MENELAUS

It was seven circling years I passed on shipboard, over and
above the ten at Troy.

---

[17] Nauplius set false beacons to wreck the Greek fleet in re-
venge for the unjust death of his son Palamedes, who was falsely
accused of treason. His trial was the subject of Euripides'
Palamedes, put on in 415 together with *Alexandros* and *Trojan
Women*.

ΕΛΕΝΗ

φεῦ φεῦ· μακρόν γ' ἔλεξας, ὦ τάλας, χρόνον.
σωθεὶς δ' ἐκεῖθεν ἐνθάδ' ἦλθες ἐς σφαγάς.

ΜΕΝΕΛΑΟΣ

πῶς φῄς; τί λέξεις; ὥς μ' ἀπώλεσας, γύναι.

ΕΛΕΝΗ

780 [φεῦγ' ὡς τάχιστα τῆσδ' ἀπαλλαχθεὶς χθονός.]
θανῇ πρὸς ἀνδρὸς οὗ τάδ' ἐστὶ δώματα.

ΜΕΝΕΛΑΟΣ

τί χρῆμα δράσας ἄξιον τῆς συμφορᾶς;

ΕΛΕΝΗ

ἥκεις ἄελπτος ἐμποδὼν ἐμοῖς γάμοις.

ΜΕΝΕΛΑΟΣ

ἦ γὰρ γαμεῖν τις τἄμ' ἐβουλήθη λέχη;

ΕΛΕΝΗ

785 ὕβριν γ' ὑβρίζων ἐς τὰ σ', ἣν ἔτλην ἐγώ.

ΜΕΝΕΛΑΟΣ

ἰδίᾳ σθένων τις ἢ τυραννεύων χθονός;

ΕΛΕΝΗ

ὃς γῆς ἀνάσσει τῆσδε Πρωτέως γόνος.

ΜΕΝΕΛΑΟΣ

τόδ' ἔστ' ἐκεῖν' αἴνιγμ' ὃ προσπόλου κλύω.

---

780 del. Valckenaer
783 ἐμποδὼν Badham: ἐμποδών τ' L   785 γ' ὑβρίζων
Kirchhoff: τ' ὑβρίζειν L   ἐς τὰ σ' Kovacs: εἰς ἔμ' L

HELEN

Oh my! Poor man, what a long time! But you got safely away from those troubles only to be slaughtered here.

MENELAUS

What's this? What do you mean? Your words are the death of me, dear wife!

HELEN

[Flee with all speed from this land!] You will be killed by the master of this house.

MENELAUS

What have I done to deserve such a fate?

HELEN

Your unexpected arrival is a hindrance to my marriage.

MENELAUS

What? Does someone want to marry my wife?

HELEN

Yes, committing an outrage against your rights, an outrage directed against me.

MENELAUS

Is he a king or someone with private might?

HELEN

It is Proteus' son, this land's ruler.

MENELAUS

So that is the meaning of the gatekeeper's riddling words.

ΕΛΕΝΗ

ποίοις ἐπιστὰς βαρβάροις πυλώμασιν;

ΜΕΝΕΛΑΟΣ

790   τοῖσδ', ἔνθεν ὥσπερ πτωχὸς ἐξηλαυνόμην.

ΕΛΕΝΗ

οὔ που προσῄτεις βίοτον; ὦ τάλαιν' ἐγώ.

ΜΕΝΕΛΑΟΣ

τοὔργον μὲν ἦν τοῦτ', ὄνομα δ' οὐκ εἶχεν τόδε.

ΕΛΕΝΗ

πάντ' οἶσθ' ἄρ', ὡς ἔοικας, ἀμφ' ἐμῶν γάμων.

ΜΕΝΕΛΑΟΣ

οἶδ'· εἰ δὲ λέκτρα διέφυγες, τόδ' οὐκ ἔχω.

ΕΛΕΝΗ

795   ἄθικτον εὐνὴν ἴσθι σοι σεσωμένην.

ΜΕΝΕΛΑΟΣ

τίς τοῦδε πειθώ; φίλα γάρ, εἰ σαφῆ λέγεις.

ΕΛΕΝΗ

ὁρᾷς τάφου τοῦδ' ἀθλίους ἕδρας ἐμάς;

ΜΕΝΕΛΑΟΣ

ὁρῶ ταλαίνας στιβάδας· ὧν τί σοὶ μέτα;

ΕΛΕΝΗ

ἐνταῦθα λέκτρων ἱκετεύομεν φυγάς.

---

792 εἶχεν Wecklein: εἶχον L
794 τόδ' Reeve: τάδ' L
798 ταλαίνας P²: τάλαινα L

HELEN

At what barbarian gates were you standing?

MENELAUS

These, and was driven from them like a beggar.

HELEN

You weren't asking for food, were you? How dreadful for me!

MENELAUS

That was what I was doing, but it was not called by that name.

HELEN

Well, you know the whole story, I think, concerning my marriage.

MENELAUS

I know it, but I am not clear whether you have escaped his embraces.

HELEN

You can rest assured: my bed has been kept inviolate for you.

MENELAUS

How can I believe this? It's welcome news if true.

HELEN

Do you see this tomb, the joyless place where I sit?

MENELAUS

I see a miserable couch of leaves. What does it have to do with you?

HELEN

That is where I sit as suppliant to avoid marriage.

ΜΕΝΕΛΑΟΣ

800 βωμοῦ σπανίζουσ᾽ ἢ νόμοισι βαρβάροις;

ΕΛΕΝΗ

ἐρρύεθ᾽ ἡμᾶς τοῦτ᾽ ἴσον ναοῖς θεῶν.

ΜΕΝΕΛΑΟΣ

οὐδ᾽ ἄρα πρὸς οἴκους ναυστολεῖν <σ᾽> ἔξεστί μοι;

ΕΛΕΝΗ

ξίφος μένει σε μᾶλλον ἢ τοὐμὸν λέχος.

ΜΕΝΕΛΑΟΣ

οὕτως ἂν εἴην ἀθλιώτατος βροτῶν.

ΕΛΕΝΗ

805 μή νυν καταιδοῦ, φεῦγε δ᾽ ἐκ τῆσδε χθονός.

ΜΕΝΕΛΑΟΣ

λιπὼν σέ; Τροίαν ἐξέπερσα σὴν χάριν.

ΕΛΕΝΗ

κρεῖσσον γὰρ ἤ σε τἄμ᾽ ἀποκτεῖναι λέχη.

ΜΕΝΕΛΑΟΣ

ἄνανδρά γ᾽ εἶπας Ἰλίου τ᾽ οὐκ ἄξια.

ΕΛΕΝΗ

οὐκ ἂν κτάνοις τύραννον, ὃ σπεύδεις ἴσως.

ΜΕΝΕΛΑΟΣ

810 οὕτω σιδήρῳ τρωτὸν οὐκ ἔχει δέμας;

ΕΛΕΝΗ

εἴσῃ· τὸ τολμᾶν δ᾽ ἀδύνατ᾽ ἀνδρὸς οὐ σοφοῦ.

MENELAUS

Don't you have an altar? Or is this the local custom?

HELEN

This tomb protected me just like a temple.

MENELAUS

So I am not allowed to take ⟨you⟩ home by ship.

HELEN

A sword awaits you, not my bed.

MENELAUS

That would make me the most miserable of mortals.

HELEN

Don't let shame prevent you: flee this land!

MENELAUS

And leave you behind? I sacked Troy for your sake.

HELEN

Yes, leave me: far worse to be killed because of your wife.

MENELAUS

You make me out to be a coward, unworthy of Troy.

HELEN

Perhaps you want to kill the king. That is impossible.

MENELAUS

Is his body invulnerable to the sword, then?

HELEN

You'll find out. But a wise man does not undertake the impossible.

---

802 ⟨σ'⟩ Reiske

ΜΕΝΕΛΑΟΣ

σιγῇ παράσχω δῆτ᾽ ἐμὰς δῆσαι χέρας;

ΕΛΕΝΗ

ἐς ἄπορον ἥκεις· δεῖ δὲ μηχανῆς τινος.

ΜΕΝΕΛΑΟΣ

δρῶντας γὰρ ἢ μὴ δρῶντας ἥδιον θανεῖν.

ΕΛΕΝΗ

815   μί᾽ ἔστιν ἐλπὶς ᾗ μόνῃ σωθεῖμεν ἄν.

ΜΕΝΕΛΑΟΣ

ὠνητὸς ἢ τολμητὸς ἢ λόγων ὕπο;

ΕΛΕΝΗ

εἰ μὴ τύραννός ⟨σ᾽⟩ ἐκπύθοιτ᾽ ἀφιγμένον.

ΜΕΝΕΛΑΟΣ

οὐ γνώσεταί μ᾽ ὅς εἰμ᾽, ἐγῷδ᾽· ἐρεῖ δὲ τίς;

ΕΛΕΝΗ

ἔστ᾽ ἔνδον αὐτῷ ξύμμαχος θεοῖς ἴση.

ΜΕΝΕΛΑΟΣ

820   φήμη τις οἴκων ἐν μυχοῖς ἱδρυμένη;

ΕΛΕΝΗ

οὔκ, ἀλλ᾽ ἀδελφή· Θεονόην καλοῦσί νιν.

ΜΕΝΕΛΑΟΣ

χρηστήριον μὲν τοὔνομ᾽· ὅ τι δὲ δρᾷ φράσον.

817 ⟨σ᾽⟩ Schaefer
818 sic Diggle: ἐρεῖ δὲ τίς μ᾽; οὐ γνώσεταί γ᾽ ὃς εἰμ᾽ ἐγώ L

HELEN

MENELAUS

Shall I quietly hold out my hands for the shackles?

HELEN

Your situation is desperate: you need a clever ruse.

MENELAUS

Yes, better to die doing than not doing.

HELEN

There is one hope, our only salvation.

MENELAUS

Does it lie in bribery, or daring deeds, or argument?

HELEN

If only the king can be unaware of your arrival.

MENELAUS

I am sure he will not know who I am. And who will tell him?

HELEN

He has indoors an ally powerful as the gods.

MENELAUS

Some voice dwelling in the house's inmost recesses?

HELEN

No, his sister: she is called Theonoe.

MENELAUS

The name has a prophetic ring to it.[18] Tell me what she does.

18 See note on line 15.

ΕΛΕΝΗ

πάντ' οἶδ' ἐρεῖ τε συγγόνῳ παρόντα σε.

ΜΕΝΕΛΑΟΣ

θνήσκοιμεν ἄν· λαθεῖν γὰρ οὐχ οἷόν τέ μοι.

ΕΛΕΝΗ

825 ἴσως ἂν ἀναπείσαιμεν ἱκετεύοντέ νιν . . .

ΜΕΝΕΛΑΟΣ

τί χρῆμα δρᾶσαι; τίν' ὑπάγεις μ' ἐς ἐλπίδα;

ΕΛΕΝΗ

. . . παρόντα γαίᾳ μὴ φράσαι σε συγγόνῳ.

ΜΕΝΕΛΑΟΣ

πείσαντε δ' ἐκ γῆς διορίσαιμεν ἂν πόδα;

ΕΛΕΝΗ

κοινῇ γ' ἐκείνῃ ῥᾳδίως, λάθρᾳ δ' ἂν οὔ.

ΜΕΝΕΛΑΟΣ

830 σὸν ἔργον, ὡς γυναικὶ πρόσφορον γυνή.

ΕΛΕΝΗ

ὡς οὐκ ἄχρωστα γόνατ' ἐμῶν ἕξει χερῶν.

ΜΕΝΕΛΑΟΣ

φέρ', ἢν δὲ δὴ νῷν μὴ ἀποδέξηται λόγους;

ΕΛΕΝΗ

θανῇ· γαμοῦμαι δ' ἡ τάλαιν' ἐγὼ βίᾳ.

825 ἴσως Kirchhoff: εἴ πως L
829 γ' Reiske: τ' L   ἂν οὔ L. Dindorf: ὁμοῦ L

HELEN

HELEN
She knows everything and will tell her brother you are here.

MENELAUS
Then I'm dead. I cannot escape detection.

HELEN
Perhaps we could persuade her by entreaty . . .

MENELAUS
To do what? What hope do you raise in me?

HELEN
. . . not to tell her brother you are in the country.

MENELAUS
And once we have persuaded her, we could escape?

HELEN
With her help, easily. Without her knowledge, never.

MENELAUS
This is your task: nothing like a woman to deal with a woman.

HELEN
I will surely grasp her knees in supplication.

MENELAUS
Tell me, what if she is not won over?

HELEN
Then you will be killed. And I, to my sorrow, will be forcibly married.

ΜΕΝΕΛΑΟΣ

προδότις ἂν εἴης· τὴν βίαν σκήψασ᾽ ἔχεις.

ΕΛΕΝΗ

835 ἀλλ᾽ ἁγνὸν ὅρκον σὸν κάρα κατώμοσα ...

ΜΕΝΕΛΑΟΣ

τί φής; θανεῖσθαι κοὔποτ᾽ ἀλλάξειν λέχη;

ΕΛΕΝΗ

ταὐτῷ ξίφει γε· κείσομαι δὲ σοῦ πέλας.

ΜΕΝΕΛΑΟΣ

ἐπὶ τοῖσδε τοίνυν δεξιᾶς ἐμῆς θίγε.

ΕΛΕΝΗ

ψαύω, θανόντος σοῦ τόδ᾽ ἐκλείψειν φάος.

ΜΕΝΕΛΑΟΣ

840 κἀγὼ στερηθεὶς σοῦ τελευτήσειν βίον.

ΕΛΕΝΗ

πῶς οὖν θανούμεθ᾽ ὥστε καὶ δόξαν λαβεῖν;

ΜΕΝΕΛΑΟΣ

τύμβου 'πὶ νώτοις σὲ κτανὼν ἐμὲ κτενῶ.
πρῶτον δ᾽ ἀγῶνα μέγαν ἀγωνιούμεθα
λέκτρων ὑπὲρ σῶν· ὁ δὲ θέλων ἴτω πέλας.
845 τὸ Τρωικὸν γὰρ οὐ καταισχυνῶ κλέος
οὐδ᾽ Ἑλλάδ᾽ ἐλθὼν λήψομαι πολὺν ψόγον,
ὅστις Θέτιν μὲν ἐστέρησ᾽ Ἀχιλλέως,
Τελαμωνίου δ᾽ Αἴαντος εἰσεῖδον σφαγὰς
τὸν Νηλέως τ᾽ ἄπαιδα· διὰ δὲ τὴν ἐμὴν
850 οὐκ ἀξιώσω κατθανεῖν δάμαρτ᾽ ἐγώ;

MENELAUS

That would be betrayal. Mentioning force is only an excuse.

HELEN

I swear by your head a sacred oath . . .

MENELAUS

What's this? That you will die? Never take a new husband?

HELEN

Yes, die, and by the same sword. I shall lie next to you.

MENELAUS

Grasp my hand and swear to this.

HELEN

I grasp it: if you are killed I shall die as well.

MENELAUS

And if I am deprived of you, I will end my life.

HELEN

How then shall we die so as to win glory?

MENELAUS

On top of the tomb I will kill you and then myself. But first I shall fight a great fight for your love. I'll take on all comers! I shall never disgrace my Trojan reputation or bring shame on myself by returning to Greece! I am the man who deprived Thetis of Achilles, who saw the suicide of Telamonian Ajax, and saw Neleus' son Nestor bereft of his son. Shall I not think it right to die for my own wife? Most

---

840 τελευτήσειν Musgrave: -σω L
842 νώτοις Herwerden cl. 984: -ῳ L
849 Νηλέως Musgrave: Θησέως L

μάλιστά γ᾽· εἰ γάρ εἰσιν οἱ θεοὶ σοφοί,
εὔψυχον ἄνδρα πολεμίων θανόνθ᾽ ὕπο
κούφῃ καταμπίσχουσιν ἐν τύμβῳ χθονί,
κακοὺς δ᾽ ἐφ᾽ ἕρμα στερεὸν ἐκβάλλουσι γῆς.

ΧΟΡΟΣ

855 ὦ θεοί, γενέσθω δή ποτ᾽ εὐτυχὲς γένος
τὸ Ταντάλειον καὶ μεταστήτω κακῶν.

ΕΛΕΝΗ

οἲ 'γὼ τάλαινα· τῆς τύχης γὰρ ὧδ᾽ ἔχω·
Μενέλαε, διαπεπράγμεθ᾽· ἐκβαίνει δόμων
ἡ θεσπιῳδὸς Θεονόη· κτυπεῖ δόμος
860 κλήθρων λυθέντων. φεῦγ᾽· ἀτὰρ τί φευκτέον;
ἀποῦσα γάρ σε καὶ παροῦσ᾽ ἀφιγμένον
δεῦρ᾽ οἶδεν· ὦ δύστηνος, ὡς ἀπωλόμην.
Τροίας δὲ σωθεὶς κἀπὸ βαρβάρου χθονὸς
ἐς βάρβαρ᾽ ἐλθὼν φάσγαν᾽ αὖθις ἐμπεσῇ.

ΘΕΟΝΟΗ

865 ἡγοῦ σύ μοι φέρουσα λαμπτήρων σέλας
θείου τε σεμνὸν θεσμὸν αἰθέρος μυχούς,
ὡς πνεῦμα καθαρὸν οὐρανοῦ δεξώμεθα·
σὺ δ᾽ αὖ κέλευθον εἴ τις ἔβλαψεν ποδὶ
στείβων ἀνοσίῳ, δὸς καθαρσίῳ φλογί,
870 κροῦσόν τε πεύκην, ἵνα διεξέλθω, πάρος.
πόνον δὲ νόμιμον θεοῖσιν ἀποδοῦναι πάλιν

854 ὑφ᾽ . . . ἐμβάλλουσι Scaliger   857 del. Willink
866 τε Reiske: δὲ L   σεμνὸν Hermann: -οῦ L   μυχούς
Wecklein: -ῶν L

112

certainly. If the gods are wise, they cover the brave man, killed by the enemy, with earth that lies light upon him. But they cast out cowards on ridges of hard earth.

CHORUS LEADER
Gods, let the race of Tantalus be someday blessed and escape from misery!

A sound is heard of the palace door being unbarred.

HELEN
Oh, woe is me: that is what my fate is like! Menelaus, we are ruined! The prophet Theonoe is coming out of the house: the bolt is being drawn back and the house resounds. Run! But why should you run? Whether she is here or elsewhere she knows of your arrival. Oh, I am lost! And you, having escaped the barbarian land of Troy, shall now run once more into barbarian swords!

Enter from the skene THEONOE *accompanied by two servants.*

THEONOE
Go on before me with torch gleam and, as holy ordinance decrees, cleanse the sky's recesses with sulfur so that I may breathe heaven's pure air! And you, in case anyone has harmed the path by treading with unholy foot, apply to it the purifying flame and strike the torch against it so that I may pass through. When you have given the gods the ser-

---

867 δεξώμεθα Schaefer: -αίμεθα L
870 τε Reiske: δὲ L   πάρος Reiske: πυρός L
871 πόνον δὲ νόμιμον Kirchhoff: νόμον δὲ τὸν ἐμὸν L

ἐφέστιον φλόγ᾽ ἐς δόμους κομίζετε.

Ἑλένη, τί τἀμὰ—πῶς ἔχει;—θεσπίσματα;
ἥκει πόσις σοι Μενέλεως ὅδ᾽ ἐμφανής,
875 νεῶν στερηθεὶς τοῦ τε σοῦ μιμήματος.

ὦ τλῆμον, οἵους διαφυγὼν ἦλθες πόνους,
οὐδ᾽ οἶσθα νόστον οἴκαδ᾽ εἴτ᾽ αὐτοῦ μενεῖς·
ἔρις γὰρ ἐν θεοῖς σύλλογός τε σοῦ πέρι
ἔσται πάρεδρος Ζηνὶ τῷδ᾽ ἐν ἤματι.
880 Ἥρα μέν, ἥ σοι δυσμενὴς πάροιθεν ἦν,
νῦν ἐστιν εὔνους κἀς πάτραν σῶσαι θέλει
ξὺν τῇδ᾽, ἵν᾽ Ἑλλὰς τοὺς Ἀλεξάνδρου γάμους
δώρημα Κύπριδος ψευδονύμφευτον μάθῃ·
Κύπρις δὲ νόστον σὸν διαφθεῖραι θέλει,
885 ὡς μὴ ᾽ξελεγχθῇ μηδὲ πριαμένη φανῇ
τὸ κάλλος Ἑλένης οὐκ ἀνυστοῖσιν γάμοις.
τέλος δ᾽ ἐφ᾽ ἡμῖν εἴθ᾽, ἃ βούλεται Κύπρις,
λέξασ᾽ ἀδελφῷ σ᾽ ἐνθάδ᾽ ὄντα διολέσω
εἴτ᾽ αὖ μεθ᾽ Ἥρας στᾶσα σὸν σώσω βίον,
890 κρύψασ᾽ ὁμαίμον᾽, ὅς με προστάσσει τάδε
εἰπεῖν, ὅταν γῆν τήνδε νοστήσας τύχῃς.
[τίς εἶσ᾽ ἀδελφῷ τόνδε σημανῶν ἐμῷ
παρόνθ᾽, ὅπως ἂν τοὐμὸν ἀσφαλῶς ἔχῃ;]

ΕΛΕΝΗ

ὦ παρθέν᾽, ἱκέτις ἀμφὶ σὸν πίτνω γόνυ
895 καὶ προσκαθίζω θᾶκον οὐκ εὐδαίμονα

---

877 νόστον (vel potius νόστος) οἴκαδ᾽ εἴ σ᾽ αὐτοῦ μένει Herwerden   879 παρέδροις Dawe

114

vice custom ordains, take the hearth fire back into the house.

The servants perform the purification and exit into the skene.

Helen, what about my prophecies? How are they faring? Your husband has come—here he is, plain to see—deprived of his ships and of your counterfeit image.

Poor man, what troubles you have escaped! Yet you do not know whether you will return home or remain here! There is strife this very day among the gods about you as they gather in Zeus's court. Hera, who previously was your enemy, is now your friend and wants to bring you and Helen safely home so that Greece may learn that Alexandros' marriage, the gift of Cypris, was no marriage at all. But Cypris wants to prevent your coming home. She does not want to be disgraced when it is known that she has bought the beauty prize with false coin, a marriage to Helen that could not be fulfilled. The outcome lies with me: shall I, as Cypris prefers, tell my brother of your arrival and end your life? Or shall I stand with Hera and save you by concealing it from my brother, who ordered me to tell him when you arrived? [Who will go and tell my brother that this man is here so that my welfare may be safeguarded?]

HELEN

(*kneeling before Theonoe*) Maiden, I fall as a suppliant at your knees for myself and for this man, sitting before you

883 ψευδονύμφευτον Hermann: -φεύτου L   886 οὐκ ἀνυστοῖσιν Kovacs: οὕνεκ' ὠνητοῖς L   892–3 del. Hartung

ὑπέρ τ' ἐμαυτῆς τοῦδέ θ', ὃν μόλις ποτὲ
λαβοῦσ' ἐπ' ἀκμῆς εἰμι κατθανόντ' ἰδεῖν·
μή μοι κατείπῃς σῷ κασιγνήτῳ πόσιν
τόνδ' εἰς ἐμὰς ἥκοντα φίλτατον χέρας,

900 σῶσον δέ, λίσσομαί σε· συγγόνῳ δὲ σῷ
τὴν εὐσέβειαν μὴ προδῷς τὴν σήν ποτε,
χάριτας πονηρὰς κἀδίκους ὠνουμένη.
μισεῖ γὰρ ὁ θεὸς τὴν βίαν, τὰ κτητὰ δὲ
κτᾶσθαι κελεύει πάντας οὐκ ἐς ἁρπαγάς.

905 [ἐατέος δ' ὁ πλοῦτος †ἄδικός τις ὤν†.
κοινὸς γάρ ἐστιν οὐρανὸς πᾶσιν βροτοῖς
καὶ γαῖ', ἐν ᾗ χρὴ δώματ' ἀναπληρουμένους
τἀλλότρια μὴ σχεῖν μηδ' ἀφαιρεῖσθαι βίᾳ.]
ἡμᾶς δὲ καιρίως μέν, ἀθλίως δ' ἐμοί,

910 Ἑρμῆς ἔδωκε πατρὶ σῷ σῴζειν πόσει
τῷδ' ὃς πάρεστι κἀπολάζυσθαι θέλει.
[πῶς οὖν θανὼν ἂν ἀπολάβοι; κεῖνος δὲ πῶς
τὰ ζῶντα τοῖς θανοῦσιν ἀποδοίη ποτ' ἄν;
ἤδη τὰ τοῦ θεοῦ καὶ τὰ τοῦ πατρὸς σκόπει.]

915 πότερόν <σ'> ὁ δαίμων χὠ θανὼν τὰ τῶν πέλας
βούλοιντ' ἂν ἢ οὐ βούλοιντ' ἂν ἀποδοῦναι πάλιν;
δοκῶ μέν. οὔκουν χρή σε συγγόνῳ πλέον
νέμειν ματαίῳ μᾶλλον ἢ χρηστῷ πατρί.
εἰ δ' οὖσα μάντις καὶ τὰ θεῖ' ἡγουμένη

920 τὸ μὲν δίκαιον τοῦ πατρὸς διαφθερεῖς,
τῷ δ' οὐ δικαίῳ συγγόνῳ δώσεις χάριν,
αἰσχρὸν τὰ μέν σε θεῖα πάντ' ἐξειδέναι
τά τ' ὄντα καὶ μέλλοντα, τὰ δὲ δίκαια μή.

116

in an attitude of misery. I have barely got him back, and
now I am in danger of seeing him perish. Please do not tell
your brother that my dear husband has come to my arms!
Save him, I beg you! Do not sacrifice your own godliness
for your brother's sake, buying with it tokens of gratitude
that are wicked and unjust. God hates violence, and he
bids all men acquire their goods without stealing. [Unjust
wealth must be left alone. The sky is the common posses-
sion of all mortals, and so is the earth, on which men
should not hold other men's property or take it by force as
they fill their houses.] It was timely, though it meant mis-
ery for me, that Hermes gave me to your father to keep
safe for my husband. Now he is here and wants to take me
back. [How can he receive me if he is killed? And how can
your brother give back the living to the dead? It is time
to consider what belongs to the god and to your father.]
Would the god and your dead father wish ⟨you⟩ to give
back their neighbors' goods or not? I think they would. So
you should not regard your foolish brother more highly
than your good father. If you are a prophet and believe in
the gods but yet corrupt your father's justice by doing your
unjust brother a favor, it is a disgrace that you know from
the gods the present and the future but not what is just.

---

898 μοι Lenting: μου L   899 φίλτατον Cobet: -τάτας L
905–8 (una cum 903–4) del. Hartung
908 σχεῖν Headlam: ῎χειν L
909 καιρίως Badham: μακαρίως L
912–4 del. Schenkl
913 ἀπ- ποτ' ἄν Porson: ἂν ἀπ- ποτέ L
915 ⟨σ'⟩ Kovacs
921 χάριν Reiske: δίκην L

τὴν δ᾽ ἀθλίαν ἔμ᾽, οἷσιν ἔγκειμαι κακοῖς,
925 ῥῦσαι, πάρεργον δοῦσα τοῦτο τῆς δίκης·
Ἑλένην γὰρ οὐδεὶς ὅστις οὐ στυγεῖ βροτῶν·
ἢ κλῄζομαι καθ᾽ Ἑλλάδ᾽ ὡς προδοῦσ᾽ ἐμὸν
πόσιν Φρυγῶν ᾤκησα πολυχρύσους δόμους.
ἢν δ᾽ Ἑλλάδ᾽ ἔλθω κἀπιβῶ Σπάρτης πάλιν,
930 κλύοντες εἰσιδόντες ὡς τέχναις θεῶν
ὤλοντ᾽, ἐγὼ δὲ προδότις οὐκ ἄρ᾽ ἦ φίλων,
πάλιν μ᾽ ἀνάξουσ᾽ ἐς τὸ σῶφρον αὖθις αὖ,
ἑδνώσομαί τε θυγατέρ᾽, ἣν οὐδεὶς γαμεῖ,
τὴν δ᾽ ἐνθάδ᾽ ἐκλιποῦσ᾽ ἀλητείαν πικρὰν
935 ὄντων ἐν οἴκοις χρημάτων ὀνήσομαι.
κεἰ μὲν θανὼν ὅδ᾽ ἐν πυρᾷ κατεφθάρη,
πρόσω σφ᾽ ἀπόντα δακρύοις ἂν ἠγάπων·
νῦν δ᾽ ὄντα καὶ σωθέντ᾽ ἀφαιρεθήσομαι;
μὴ δῆτα, παρθέν᾽, ἀλλά σ᾽ ἱκετεύω τόδε·
940 δὸς τὴν χάριν μοι τήνδε καὶ μιμοῦ τρόπους
πατρὸς δικαίου· παισὶ γὰρ κλέος τόδε
κάλλιστον, ὅστις ἐκ πατρὸς χρηστοῦ γεγὼς
ἐς ταὐτὸν ἦλθε τοῖς τεκοῦσι τοὺς τρόπους.

ΧΟΡΟΣ
οἰκτρὸν μὲν οἱ παρόντες ἐν μέσῳ λόγοι,
945 οἰκτρὰ δὲ καὶ σύ. τοὺς δὲ Μενέλεω ποθῶ
λόγους ἀκοῦσαι τίνας ἐρεῖ ψυχῆς πέρι.

ΜΕΝΕΛΑΟΣ
ἐγὼ σὸν οὔτ᾽ ἂν προσπεσεῖν τλαίην γόνυ
οὔτ᾽ ἂν δακρῦσαι βλέφαρα· τὴν Τροίαν γὰρ ἂν

I am in misery from the troubles that surround me: rescue me, performing this as an extra to your deed of justice. All men hate Helen, every single one. It is reported throughout Hellas that I abandoned my husband and went to live in the Phrygians' gilded halls. But if I reach Greece and walk once more in Sparta, men will hear and see that they were ruined by the gods' contrivances and that I was not after all a traitor to my family. They will restore my virtue to me once more, and I shall betroth my unmarried daughter to a husband. Leaving behind this galling life of beggary here I shall have the enjoyment of what belongs to me at home.

If my husband here had been killed and consumed on a pyre, I would be honoring him with my tears though far away. But he is alive and safely returned to me: shall I then be robbed of him? Not so, maiden! I beg of you, grant me this favor and imitate the ways of your righteous father. For children the fairest renown is this, to be born of a noble father and to take after him in character.

CHORUS LEADER
The pleas you make evoke pity, and so likewise do you yourself. But I want to hear what Menelaus will say in defense of his life.

MENELAUS
For my part, I could not bring myself to fall at your knees or shed tears. Such cowardly behavior would bring the

---

925 δίκης Wecklein: τύχης L
932 ἐς] ἐπὶ Diggle, casu felici u. v.: cf. Or. 617
936 κατεφθάρη Schenkl: κατεσφάγη L
944n Χο. L. Dindorf: Θε. L

δειλοὶ γενόμενοι πλεῖστον αἰσχύνοιμεν ἄν.
950 καίτοι λέγουσιν ὡς πρὸς ἀνδρὸς εὐγενοῦς
ἐν ξυμφοραῖσι δάκρυ᾽ ἀπ᾽ ὀφθαλμῶν βαλεῖν.
ἀλλ᾽ οὐχὶ τοῦτο τὸ καλόν, εἰ καλὸν τόδε,
αἱρήσομαι ᾽γὼ πρόσθε τῆς εὐψυχίας.
ἀλλ᾽, εἰ μὲν ἄνδρα σοι δοκεῖ σῶσαι ξένον
955 ζητοῦντά γ᾽ ὀρθῶς ἀπολαβεῖν δάμαρτ᾽ ἐμήν,
ἀπόδος τε καὶ πρὸς σῶσον· εἰ δὲ μὴ δοκεῖ,
ἐγὼ μὲν οὐ νῦν πρῶτον ἀλλὰ πολλάκις
ἄθλιος ἂν εἴην, σὺ δὲ γυνὴ κακὴ φανῇ.

ἃ δ᾽ ἄξι᾽ ἡμῶν καὶ δίκαι᾽ ἡγούμεθα
960 καὶ σῆς μάλιστα καρδίας ἀνθάψεται,
λέξω τάδ᾽ ἀμφὶ μνῆμα σοῦ πατρὸς πεσών·
Ὦ γέρον, ὃς οἰκεῖς τόνδε λάινον τάφον,
ἀπόδος, ἀπαιτῶ τὴν ἐμὴν δάμαρτά σε,
ἣν Ζεὺς ἔπεμψε δεῦρό σοι σῴζειν ἐμοί.
965 οἶδ᾽ οὕνεκ᾽ ἡμῖν οὔποτ᾽ ἀποδώσεις θανών·
ἀλλ᾽ ἥδε πατέρα νέρθεν ἀνακαλούμενον
οὐκ ἀξιώσει τὸν πρὶν εὐκλεέστατον
κακῶς ἀκοῦσαι· κυρία γάρ ἐστι νῦν.

ὦ νέρτερ᾽ Ἅιδη, καὶ σὲ σύμμαχον καλῶ,
970 ὃς πόλλ᾽ ἐδέξω τῆσδ᾽ ἕκατι σώματα
πεσόντα τὠμῷ φασγάνῳ, μισθὸν δ᾽ ἔχεις·
ἢ νυν ἐκείνους ἀπόδος ἐμψύχους πάλιν,
ἢ τήνδ᾽ ἀνάγκασόν γε ⟨μὴ⟩ εὐσεβοῦς πατρὸς
χείρω φανεῖσαν τἀμά μοι δοῦναι λέχη.

953 εὐψυχίας Heath: εὐδαιμονίας L

120

greatest disrepute on what befell at Troy, though they do say that it belongs to a nobleman to weep in an hour of disaster. But I shall not choose such noble behavior—if noble it is—in preference to acting bravely. Well, if you think it best to save the life of a stranger properly trying to recover his wife, give her back and save my life in addition. But if not, I will be unfortunate not for the first time— I have been so many times before—whereas you will be shown to be a base woman.

But the words I think are worthy of me and fair and will touch your heart most closely—these I will say, falling at the tomb of your father. Old sir, who dwell in this monument of stone, I ask you for the return of my wife, whom Zeus sent to you to keep safe for me. Give her back! Since you are dead, you cannot give her back to me, I know. But this woman will not deem it right that her father, whom I invoke from the dead, should have a bad name when before it was good. That is now in her power.

Hades under the earth, on you too I call for help! You have received, as the price of this woman, many bodies slain by my sword, payment in full. Either therefore give these men back alive or compel this woman to show herself equal to her godly father by giving me my wife back![19]

[19] That is, since you have received payment for Helen (in the form of the lives expended to get her back), either produce Helen or return the payment.

---

961 πεσών Badham: πόθῳ L

973 γε ⟨μὴ⟩ Hermann: γε L: γ᾽ Tr2

974 χείρω Nauck post Hermann (ἥσσω): κρείσσω L   τἀμά μοι δοῦναι Wecklein: τἄμ᾽ ἀποδοῦναι L

975　εἰ δ' ἐμὲ γυναῖκα τὴν ἐμὴν συλήσετε,
　　ἅ σοι παρέλιπεν ἥδε τῶν λόγων φράσω.
　　ὅρκοις κεκλήμεθ', ὡς μάθῃς, ὦ παρθένε,
　　πρῶτον μὲν ἐλθεῖν διὰ μάχης σῷ συγγόνῳ,
　　κἀκεῖνον ἢ 'μὲ δεῖ θανεῖν· ἁπλοῦς λόγος.
980　ἢν δ' ἐς μὲν ἀλκὴν μὴ πόδ' ἀντιθῇ ποδί,
　　λιμῷ δὲ θηρᾷ τύμβον ἱκετεύοντε νώ,
　　κτανεῖν δέδοκται τήνδε μοι κἄπειτ' ἐμὸν
　　πρὸς ἧπαρ ὦσαι δίστομον ξίφος τόδε
　　τύμβου 'πὶ νώτοις τοῦδ', ἵν' αἵματος ῥοαὶ
985　τάφου καταστάζωσι· κεισόμεσθα δὲ
　　νεκρὼ δύ' ἑξῆς τῷδ' ἐπὶ ξεστῷ τάφῳ,
　　ἀθάνατον ἄλγος σοί, ψόγον δὲ σῷ πατρί.
　　οὐ γὰρ γαμεῖ τήνδ' οὔτε σύγγονος σέθεν
　　οὔτ' ἄλλος οὐδείς· ἀλλ' ἐγὼ σφ' ἀπάξομαι,
990　εἰ μὴ πρὸς οἴκους δυνάμεθ' ἀλλὰ πρὸς νεκρούς.
　　[τί ταῦτα; δακρύοις ἐς τὸ θῆλυ τρεπόμενος
　　ἐλεινὸς ἦν ἂν μᾶλλον ἢ δραστήριος.
　　κτεῖν', εἰ δοκεῖ σοι· δυσκλεᾶς γὰρ οὐ κτενεῖς·
　　μᾶλλόν γε μέντοι τοῖς ἐμοῖς πείθου λόγοις,
995　ἵν' ᾖς δικαία καὶ δάμαρτ' ἐγὼ λάβω.]

　　　　　　ΧΟΡΟΣ
　　ἐν σοὶ βραβεύειν, ὦ νεᾶνι, τοὺς λόγους·
　　οὕτω δὲ κρῖνον, ὡς ἅπασιν ἀνδάνῃς.

　　　　　　ΘΕΟΝΟΗ
　　ἐγὼ πέφυκά τ' εὐσεβεῖν καὶ βούλομαι
　　φιλῶ τ' ἐμαυτήν, καὶ κλέος τοὐμοῦ πατρὸς

But if you are going to rob me of my wife, I will tell you what she has left unsaid. You should know that we have bound ourselves by an oath, maiden, first that I should fight your brother: the simple truth is that either he or I must die. But if he refuses to meet me in battle and tries to capture us by starving suppliants at the tomb, I am resolved to kill her and then to thrust this two-edged sword through my own heart on top of this tomb, so that streams of blood will seep down into the grave. We shall lie here as two corpses upon this monument of dressed stone, an immortal grief to you and a reproach to your father. Neither your brother nor any other man shall ever marry her: I shall take her away, if not home then at least to the grave. [What is going on? If I incline to the womanish side with my tears, I will be pitiful rather than a man of action. Kill, if that is what you think best! You will not kill a man who has disgraced himself. But rather, do as I ask, so that you may be righteous and I may get my wife!]

CHORUS LEADER
It is up to you, maiden, to be judge of what has been said. Render a judgment that will please everyone!

THEONOE
As for me, both my nature and my will tend toward piety. I love my own self and will not stain the good reputation of

---

980 πόδ' Badham: ποτ' L
987 ψόγον Diggle: -ος L
991–5 del. Schenkl
993 δυσκλεᾶς Wilamowitz: -εῶς L

123

1000 οὐκ ἂν μιάναιμ᾽, οὐδὲ συγγόνῳ χάριν
δοίην ἂν ἐξ ἧς δυσκλεὴς φανήσομαι.
ἔνεστι δ᾽ ἱερὸν τῆς δίκης ἐμοὶ μέγα
ἐν τῇ φύσει· καὶ τοῦτο Νηρέως πάρα
ἔχουσα σῴζειν, Μενέλεως, πειράσομαι.

1005 Ἥρᾳ δ᾽, ἐπείπερ βούλεταί σ᾽ εὐεργετεῖν,
ἐς ταὐτὸν οἴσω ψῆφον· ἡ Κύπρις δέ μοι
ἵλεως μὲν εἴη, ξυμβέβηκε δ᾽ οὐδαμοῦ.
[πειράσομαι δὲ παρθένος μένειν ἀεί.]

ἃ δ᾽ ἀμφὶ τύμβῳ τῷδ᾽ ὀνειδίζεις πατρός,
1010 ἡμῖν ὅδ᾽ αὐτὸς μῦθος· ἀδικοίημεν ἄν,
εἰ μὴ ἀποδώσω· καὶ γὰρ ἂν κεῖνος βλέπων
ἀπέδωκεν ἂν σοὶ τήνδ᾽ ἔχειν, ταύτῃ δὲ σέ.
[καὶ γὰρ τίσις τῶνδ᾽ ἐστὶ τοῖς τε νερτέροις
καὶ τοῖς ἄνωθεν πᾶσιν ἀνθρώποις· ὁ νοῦς
1015 τῶν κατθανόντων ζῇ μὲν οὔ, γνώμην δ᾽ ἔχει
ἀθάνατον εἰς ἀθάνατον αἰθέρ᾽ ἐμπεσών.]

ὡς οὖν περαίνω μὴ μακράν, σιγήσομαι
ἅ μου καθικετεύσατ᾽ οὐδὲ μωρίᾳ
ξύμβουλος ἔσομαι τῇ κασιγνήτου ποτέ.
1020 εὐεργετῶ γὰρ κεῖνον οὐ δοκοῦσ᾽ ὅμως,
ἐκ δυσσεβείας ὅσιον εἰ τίθημί νιν.
αὐτοὶ μὲν οὖν εὑρίσκετ᾽ ἔξοδόν τινα,
ἐγὼ δ᾽ ἀποστᾶσ᾽ ἐκποδὼν σιγήσομαι.
ἐκ τῶν θεῶν δ᾽ ἄρχεσθε χἰκετεύετε
1025 τὴν μέν σ᾽ ἐᾶσαι πατρίδα νοστῆσαι Κύπριν,
Ἥρας δὲ τὴν ἔννοιαν ἐν ταὐτῷ μένειν
ἣν ἐς σὲ καὶ σὸν πόσιν ἔχει σωτηρίας.

my father. I shall not do a kindness to my brother that will bring me a bad name. I have in my nature a great temple to Justice. This, Menelaus, is my inheritance from Nereus, and I shall attempt to keep it intact. Since Hera wants to do you good, I shall cast my vote with her. May Cypris be propitious to me, though she does not suit me! [I shall attempt to remain a virgin forever.]

As for the reproaches you uttered around the tomb of my father, I take the same view: I would be doing wrong if I did not return your wife. If my father were alive, he would have given her to you and you to her. [In fact punishment for these deeds comes to those below and to all men above. For though the mind of dead men does not live, it has eternal sensation once it has been hurled into the eternal upper air.]

To make my tale brief: I shall keep silent, as you have begged me to do, and never help my brother's folly with my counsel. I am doing him a good turn (though he might not think so) if I cause him to be god-fearing instead of impious. So you yourselves find some way of escape: I shall stand out of the way and hold my peace. But begin by entreating the gods: pray to Cypris to allow you to reach home and to Hera that the thought she has of saving you

<hr />

1006 Κύπρις Canter: χάρις L
1008 del. Badham
1009 πατρός Wecklein: -τρί L
1010 ἀδικοίην νιν ἄν Porson
1013-6 del. Hartung
1019 τῇ Dobree: τοῦ L
1022 εὑρίσκετ᾽ ἔξοδόν τινα Hermann: τὴν ἔξοδόν γ᾽ εὑρί-σκετε L

σὺ δ᾽, ὦ θανών μοι πάτερ, ὅσον γ᾽ ἐγὼ σθένω,
οὔποτε κεκλήσῃ δυσσεβὴς ἀντ᾽ εὐσεβοῦς.

ΧΟΡΟΣ

1030 οὐδείς ποτ᾽ ηὐτύχησεν ἔκδικος γεγώς,
ἐν τῷ δικαίῳ δ᾽ ἐλπίδες σωτηρίας.

ΕΛΕΝΗ

Μενέλαε, πρὸς μὲν παρθένου σεσώμεθα·
τοὐνθένδε δ᾽ εἰς ἓν τοὺς λόγους φέροντε χρὴ
κοινὴν ξυνάπτειν μηχανὴν σωτηρίας.

ΜΕΝΕΛΑΟΣ

1035 ἄκουε δή νυν· χρόνιος εἶ κατὰ στέγας
καὶ συντέθραψαι προσπόλοισι βασιλέως.

ΕΛΕΝΗ

τί τοῦτ᾽ ἔλεξας; ἐσφέρεις γὰρ ἐλπίδας
ὡς δή τι δράσων χρηστὸν ἐς κοινόν γε νῷν.

ΜΕΝΕΛΑΟΣ

πείσειας ἄν τιν᾽ οἵτινες τετραζύγων
1040 ὄχων ἀνάσσουσ᾽ ὥστε νῷν δοῦναι δίφρους;

ΕΛΕΝΗ

πείσαιμ᾽ ἄν· ἀλλὰ τίνα φυγὴν φευξούμεθα
πεδίων ἄπειροι βαρβάρου γ᾽ ὄντες χθονός;

ΜΕΝΕΛΑΟΣ

ἀδύνατον εἶπας. φέρε, τί δ᾽ εἰ κρυφθεὶς δόμοις
κτάνοιμ᾽ ἄνακτα τῷδε διστόμῳ ξίφει;

1033 δ᾽ εἰς ἓν . . . φέροντε Jackson: δή σε . . . φέροντα L

126

and your husband may last. My departed father, as far as in me lies you shall never be called impious instead of godly.

Exit THEONOE *into the* skene.

CHORUS LEADER

No unjust man has ever enjoyed good fortune. But in righteousness there is hope of rescue.

HELEN

Menelaus, our lives have been spared by the maiden. From here on we two must take common counsel and devise a way for us both to reach home safely.

MENELAUS

Listen, then. You have been in this house a long time and have shared meals with the king's servants.

HELEN

What is your drift? You raise hopes that you will benefit both of us.

MENELAUS

Could you persuade one of the chariot keepers to give us a chariot?

HELEN

I could. But what kind of escape could we make? We are on foreign soil and do not know our way.

MENELAUS

Impossible: you are right. Well then, what if I hid in the palace and killed the king with this two-edged sword?

1042 γ' Reiske: τ' L

ΕΛΕΝΗ

1045 οὐκ ἄν σ᾽ ἀνάσχοιτ᾽ οὐδὲ σιγήσειεν ἂν
μέλλοντ᾽ ἀδελφὴ σύγγονον κατακτανεῖν.

ΜΕΝΕΛΑΟΣ

ἀλλ᾽ οὐδὲ μὴν ναῦς ἔστιν ᾗ σωθεῖμεν ἂν
φεύγοντες· ἣν γὰρ εἴχομεν θάλασσ᾽ ἔχει.

ΕΛΕΝΗ

ἄκουσον, ἤν τι καὶ γυνὴ λέξῃ σοφόν.
1050 βούλῃ λέγεσθαι μὴ θανὼν λόγῳ θανεῖν;

ΜΕΝΕΛΑΟΣ

κακὸς μὲν ὄρνις· εἰ δὲ κερδανῶ, λέγε·
ἕτοιμός εἰμι μὴ θανὼν λόγῳ θανεῖν.

ΕΛΕΝΗ

καὶ μὴν γυναικείοις ⟨σ᾽⟩ ἂν οἰκτισαίμεθα
κουραῖσι καὶ θρήνοισι πρὸς τὸν ἀνόσιον.

ΜΕΝΕΛΑΟΣ

1055 σωτηρίας δὲ τοῦτ᾽ ἔχει τί νῷν ἄκος;
ματαιότης γὰρ τῷ λόγῳ γ᾽ ἔνεστί τις.

ΕΛΕΝΗ

ὡς δὴ θανόντα σ᾽ ἐνάλιον κενῷ τάφῳ
θάψαι τύραννον τῆσδε γῆς αἰτήσομαι.

ΜΕΝΕΛΑΟΣ

καὶ δὴ παρεῖκεν· εἶτα πῶς ἄνευ νεὼς
1060 σωθησόμεσθα κενοταφοῦντ᾽ ἐμὸν δέμας;

1050 λόγῳ θανεῖν] τεθνηκέναι Cobet

128

HELEN

His sister would never allow you: she would tell him that
you intended to kill him.

MENELAUS

Well, we have no ship to escape on either. The one we had
is at the bottom of the sea.

HELEN

Listen and see whether a woman too might say something
clever. Are you willing, though alive, to be reported dead?

MENELAUS

It is a bad omen. But if I am going to profit by the tale, tell
it: I am willing, though alive, to die in report.

HELEN

Then I would mourn ⟨you⟩ before the godless man, crop-
ping my hair and wailing as women do.

MENELAUS

But how does that help us to escape with our lives? Your
story seems a bit pointless.

HELEN

Since you died at sea I shall ask the king's permission to
bury you in a cenotaph.

MENELAUS

Well, suppose he agrees: how can giving me a cenotaph
win our escape if we don't have a ship?

1051 λέγε Seidler: -ειν L
1053 ⟨σ'⟩ Hermann
1056 ματαιότης Cobet: παλαιότης L

ΕΛΕΝΗ

δοῦναι κελεύσω πορθμίδ᾽, ᾗ καθήσομεν
κόσμον τάφῳ σῷ πελαγίους ἐς ἀγκάλας.

ΜΕΝΕΛΑΟΣ

ὡς εὖ τόδ᾽ εἶπας πλὴν ἕν· εἰ χέρσῳ ταφὰς
θεῖναι κελεύσει σ᾽, οὐδὲν ἡ σκῆψις φέρει.

ΕΛΕΝΗ

1065 ἀλλ᾽ οὐ νομίζειν φήσομεν καθ᾽ Ἑλλάδα
χέρσῳ καλύπτειν τοὺς θανόντας ἐναλίους.

ΜΕΝΕΛΑΟΣ

τοῦτ᾽ αὖ κατορθοῖς· εἶτ᾽ ἐγὼ συμπλεύσομαι
καὶ συγκαθήσω κόσμον ἐν ταὐτῷ σκάφει.

ΕΛΕΝΗ

σὲ καὶ παρεῖναι δεῖ μάλιστα τούς τε σοὺς
1070 πλωτῆρας οἵπερ ἔφυγον ἐκ ναυαγίας.

ΜΕΝΕΛΑΟΣ

καὶ μὴν ἐάνπερ ναῦν ἐπ᾽ ἀγκύρας λάβω,
ἀνὴρ παρ᾽ ἄνδρα στήσεται ξιφηφόρος.

ΕΛΕΝΗ

σὲ χρὴ βραβεύειν πάντα· πόμπιμοι μόνον
λαίφει πνοαὶ γένοιντο καὶ νεὼς δρόμος.

ΜΕΝΕΛΑΟΣ

1075 ἔσται· πόνους γὰρ δαίμονες παύσουσί μου.
ἀτὰρ θανόντα τοῦ μ᾽ ἐρεῖς πεπυσμένη;

1061 καθήσομεν Heath: -σομαι L

HELEN

I shall ask him to provide a vessel so that we may throw overboard adornment for your grave in the arms of the deep.

MENELAUS

What a good idea—except for one thing: if he tells us to perform the funeral on land, the pretext does us no good.

HELEN

Well, we will say that it is not our custom in Greece to give land burial to those who die at sea.

MENELAUS

Another good suggestion! Then I shall sail along on the same ship and help throw the adornment overboard.

HELEN

Yes, it is most important that you be there, and also those of your sailors who have escaped from the shipwreck.

MENELAUS

If I am provided with a ship at anchor, my men will stand by each other with ready swords.

HELEN

You must be in charge of everything. Now if only the winds will fill our sails and the ship run swiftly!

MENELAUS

It will be so: the gods are putting an end to my troubles. But who will you say told you of my death?

1064 κελεύσει L. Dindorf: -εύει L
1073 ταῦτα Kirchhoff
1074 καὶ νεὼς] χίλεως Jackson   δρόμῳ H. Cron

ΕΛΕΝΗ

σοῦ· καὶ μόνος γε φάσκε διαφυγεῖν μόρον
Ἀτρέως πλέων σὺν παιδὶ καὶ θανόνθ᾽ ὁρᾶν.

ΜΕΝΕΛΑΟΣ

καὶ μὴν τάδ᾽ ἀμφίβληστρα σώματος ῥάκη
1080 ξυμμάρτυρές σοι ναυτικῶν ἐρειπίων.

ΕΛΕΝΗ

ἐς καιρὸν ἦλθε, τότε δ᾽ ἄκαιρ᾽ ἀπώλλυτο·
τὸ δ᾽ ἄθλιον κεῖν᾽ εὐτυχὲς τάχ᾽ ἂν πέσοι.

ΜΕΝΕΛΑΟΣ

πότερα δ᾽ ἐς οἴκους σοι συνεισελθεῖν με χρὴ
ἢ πρὸς τάφῳ τῷδ᾽ ἥσυχοι καθώμεθα;

ΕΛΕΝΗ

1085 αὐτοῦ μέν· ἢν γὰρ καί τι πλημμελές σε δρᾷ,
τάφος σ᾽ ὅδ᾽ ἂν ῥύσαιτο φάσγανόν τε σόν.
ἐγὼ δ᾽ ἐς οἴκους βᾶσα βοστρύχους τεμῶ
πέπλων τε λευκῶν μέλανας ἀνταλλάξομαι
παρῇδί τ᾽ ὄνυχα φόνιον ἐμβαλῶ †χροός†.
1090 μέγας γὰρ ἀγὼν καὶ βλέπω δύο ῥοπάς·
ἢ γὰρ θανεῖν δεῖ μ᾽, ἢν ἁλῶ τεχνωμένη,
ἢ πατρίδα τ᾽ ἐλθεῖν καὶ σὸν ἐκσῶσαι δέμας.
ὦ πότνι᾽ ἢ Δίοισιν ἐν λέκτροις πίτνεις
Ἥρα, δύ᾽ οἰκτρὼ φῶτ᾽ ἀνάψυχον πόνων,
1095 αἰτούμεθ᾽ ὀρθὰς ὠλένας πρὸς οὐρανὸν
ῥίπτονθ᾽, ἵν᾽ οἰκεῖς ἀστέρων ποικίλματα.
σύ θ᾽, ἢ 'πὶ τὠμῷ κάλλος ἐκτήσω γάμῳ,
κόρη Διώνης Κύπρι, μή μ᾽ ἐξεργάσῃ.

HELEN

You: you will claim that you sailed with the son of Atreus,
saw him perish, and were the only one to survive.

MENELAUS

Well, these rags I have cast about my body will second your
story of my wreck at sea.

HELEN

The loss of your clothes was timely, though when it hap-
pened it seemed untimely. That misfortune may prove to
be a blessing.

MENELAUS

Shall I go into the house with you or sit quietly here near
the tomb?

HELEN

Stay here. If he acts violently against you, this tomb—
and your own sword—will protect you. I shall go into the
house, cut my hair, change my white robe for a black one,
and bloody my cheeks with my nails. The contest before us
is a great one, and I see two outcomes. Either I must die if
my tricks are discovered, or return to my fatherland and
save your life.

O lady Hera, sharer of Zeus's bed, relieve two pitiable
creatures of their troubles! We entreat you, casting our
hands straight up to heaven, where you dwell among the
stars' splendor! And you, Cypris, daughter of Dione, who
won the prize of beauty by the bribe of marriage with me,

1079 ἀμφιβλητὰ Boissonade   1080 ξυμμάρτυρές σοι
Pearson: ξυμμαρτυρήσει L: -μάρτυρές μοι Willink
1089 χερός Jacobs

EURIPIDES

ἅλις δὲ λύμης ἥν μ' ἐλυμήνω πάρος
1100 τοὔνομα παρασχοῦσ', οὐ τὸ σῶμ', ἐν βαρβάροις.
θανεῖν δ' ἔασόν μ', εἰ κατακτεῖναι θέλεις,
ἐν γῇ πατρῴᾳ. τί ποτ' ἄπληστος εἶ κακῶν,
ἔρωτας ἀπάτας δόλιά τ' ἐξευρήματα
ἀσκοῦσα φίλτρα θ' αἱματηρὰ δωμάτων;
1105 εἰ δ' ἦσθα μετρία, τἄλλα γ' ἡδίστη θεῶν
πέφυκας ἀνθρώποισιν· οὐκ ἄλλως λέγω.

ΧΟΡΟΣ

στρ. α

σὲ τὰν ἐναύλοις ὑπὸ δενδροκόμοις
μουσεῖα καὶ θάκους ἐνί-
ζουσαν ἀναβοάσω,
σὲ τὰν ἀοιδοτάταν
1110 ὄρνιθα μελῳδὸν ἀηδόνα δακρυόεσσαν,
ἔλθ' ὦ διὰ ξουθᾶν γενύων ἐλελιζομένα
θρήνων ἐμοὶ ξυνεργός,
Ἑλένας μελέους πόνους
τὸν Ἰλιάδων τ' ἀει-
1115 δούσᾳ δακρυόεντα πότμον
Ἀχαιῶν ὑπὸ λόγχαις,
ὅτ' ἔδραμε ῥόθια πολιὰ βαρβάρῳ πλάτᾳ
ὃς ἔμολεν ἔμολε μέλεα Πριαμίδαις ἄγων

1111 ἔλθ' ὦ Musgrave ἐλθὲ L
1112 θρήνων ἐμοὶ Wilamowitz: θρήνοις ἐμῶν L
1113 μελέους Hermann: -ας L
1114-5 ἀειδούσᾳ Lachmann: ἀείδουσα L

134

do not destroy me! You have already treated me spitefully
enough when you gave my name, though not my person, to
the barbarians. But if you mean to kill me, at least let me
die in my own country! Why is your appetite for mischief
so insatiable? Why bring about passions, deceits, treacher-
ous devices, and loves that bring blood upon houses? If you
were moderate, you would otherwise be—I admit it—the
pleasantest of gods for mortals.

Exit HELEN *into the* skene.

CHORUS

You that in your steading among the leaves
keep your house of song,
I call aloud to you,
most gifted in music,
bird of song, nightingale of tears:
come, you that through tawny throat trill your lay of woe,
share in my lamentation
as I sing of Helen's grievous troubles
and the sorrowful fate
of the daughters of Troy
at the hands of Greek spearmen:
sing how he ran swiftly over the gray sea with barbarian
 oar,
the man who came, who came bringing to the sons of
 Priam

1115 πότμον Badham: πόνον L

1117–8 π- βαρβάρῳ πλάτᾳ . . . μέλεα Πριαμίδαις ἄγων O.
Schultze: μ- Π- ἄ- . . . π- β- π- L

1117 πολιὰ Herwerden: πέδια L

Λακεδαίμονος ἄπο λέχεα
1120 σέθεν, ὦ Ἑλένα, Πάρις αἰνόγαμος
πομπαῖσιν Ἀφροδίτας.

ἀντ. α

πολλοὶ δ' Ἀχαιῶν δορὶ καὶ πετρίναις
ῥιπαῖσιν ἐκπνεύσαντες Ἅι-
δαν μέλεον ἔχουσιν,
ταλαινᾶν ἀλόχων
1125 κείραντες ἔθειραν· ἄνυμφα δὲ μέλαθρα κεῖται·
πολλοὺς δὲ πυρσεύσας φλογερὸν σέλας ἀμφιρύταν
Εὔβοιαν εἷλ' Ἀχαιῶν
μονόκωπος ἀνὴρ πέτραις
Καφηρίσιν ἐμβαλών,
1130 Αἰγαίαις ἐνάλοις δόλιον
ἄκραις ἀστέρα λάμψας.
ἀλίμενα δ' ὅρια μέλεα βαρβάρου στολᾶς
τότ' ἔσυτο πατρίδος ἀποπρὸ χειμάτων πνοᾷ
γέρας οὐ γέρας ἀλλ' ἔριν
1135 Δαναῶν Μενέλας ἐπὶ ναυσὶν ἄγων,
εἴδωλον ἱερὸν Ἥρας.

στρ. β

ὅ τι θεὸς ἢ μὴ θεὸς ἢ τὸ μέσον

1130 Αἰγαίαις Herwerden: Αἰ- τ' L   ἐνάλοις Musgrave: -
λίοις L   1130–1 δόλιον ἄ- Hermann: ἄ- δ- L
1131 ἄκραις Bothe: ἀκταῖς L
1133 τότ' ἔσυτο Diggle: ὅτε σὺ τὸ L: ὅτ' ἔσυτο Musgrave
1134 γέρας οὐ γέρας Badham: τέρας οὐ τέρας L
1135 Μενέλας Wilamowitz: νεφέλαν L

you, Helen, as his bride from Lacedaemon,
Paris the grimly wedded,
by the sending of Aphrodite.

Many Greeks died by the sword
and from great boulders hurled at them:
they have grim death as their companion.
In sorrow for them their luckless wives
cut off their long hair, and from their houses bridal love is
    gone.
Many too were killed by an Achaean, who sent forth his
    bright gleam
about seagirt Euboea,
a solitary oarsman
dashing them on the Capherean rocks,
flashing his treacherous star
on the Aegean headlands.[20]
It was then that to lands harborless and cruel, where men
    dress outlandishly,
Menelaus was driven far from his home by storm winds,
bringing on his ship
his prize, no prize, but strife for the Greeks,
Hera's divine phantom.

What mortal can search out and tell

[20] See note to line 767. Nauplius rowed out alone in a boat at
night and lit a beacon near some rocks. A beacon, unlike the mod-
ern lighthouse which warns against dangerous coast, marked a
harbor.

τίς φησ’ ἐρευνάσας βροτῶν;
1140 μακρότατον πέρας ηὗρεν ὃς τὰ θεῶν ἐσορᾷ
δεῦρο καὶ αὖθις ἐκεῖσε καὶ πάλιν ἀμφιλόγοις
πηδῶντ’ ἀνελπίστοις τύχαις.
σὺ Διὸς ἔφυς, ὦ Ἑλένα, θυγάτηρ·
1145 πτανὸς γὰρ ἐν κόλποις σε Λή-
δας ἐτέκνωσε πατήρ·
κακὰ δ’ ἰαχῇ καθ’ Ἑλλανίαν
προδότις ἄπιστος ἄδικος ἄθεος· οὐδ’ ἔχω
ὅ τι σαφές, ὅ τι ποτ’ ἐν βροτοῖς τῶν θεῶν
1150 ἔπος ἀλαθὲς εὕρω.
ἀντ. β

ἄφρονες ὅσοι τὰς ἀρετὰς πολέμῳ
λόγχαισί τ’ ἀλκαίου δορὸς
κτᾶσθ’, ἀμαθῶς θανάτῳ πόνους καταλυόμενοι.
1155 εἰ γὰρ ἅμιλλα κρινεῖ νιν αἵματος, οὔποτ’ ἔρις
λείψει κατ’ ἀνθρώπων πόλεις·
ἃ Πριαμίδος γᾶς ἔλιπ’ ἂν θαλάμους,
ἐξὸν διορθῶσαι λόγοις
1160 σὰν ἔριν, ὦ Ἑλένα.
νῦν δ’ οἱ μὲν Ἅιδα μέλονται κάτω
τείχεα δὲ †φλογερὸς† ὥστε Διὸς ἐπέσυτο φλόξ,

1138 τίς φησ’ Bothe: τί φῂς L
1140 ηὗρεν Dindorf: εὑρεῖν L
1141–2 δεῦρο Bothe: δεινὰ L   ἀμφιλόγοις Dobree: ἀντι- L
1147 κακὰ δ’ ἰαχῇ Willink: καὶ ἰαχὴ σὴ L
1148 προδότις Hermann: ἀδίκως προδότης L
1149 ὅ τι (prius) Schenkel: τί τὸ L   τῶν Willink: τὸ τῶν L

what is god, what is not god, and what lies between?
The farthest bourne is reached by him who sees that what
   the gods send
veers first this way, then that, and once more this way,
with outcomes wavering and unexpected.
You, Helen, are Zeus's daughter:
your father came on wing to Leda
and in her embrace sired you.
Yet you are reviled throughout Greece
as traitor, faithless, lawless, and godless: and I do not know
what reliable, what true word about the gods
I can find among mortals.

All men are fools who by war
and the spear of stout-heart battle
acquire renown for valor, foolishly winning release from
   toil in death.
If contests of blood shall always decide, never will strife
cease among the cities of men.
Strife would have spared the bedchambers of Priam's land
had it been possible, Helen, to end
with words the quarrel you caused.
But now the men are in Hades' care below,
their walls are overrun by violent flame, like Zeus's light-
   ning,

1150 εὕρω Willink: εὗρον L

1153–4 ἀ- θανάτῳ πόνους κατα- Willink: κατα- πόνους θνατῶν ἀ- L   καταλυόμενοι Herwerden: -παυόμενοι L

1158 ἃ Willink: αἱ L   ἔλιπ᾽ ἂν Willink: ἔλιπον L

1162 φόνιος Herwerden: μαλερὸς Kannicht

ἐπὶ δὲ πάθεα πάθεσι φέρεις ἀθλία
συμφοραῖς ἐλεινοῖς.

ΘΕΟΚΛΥΜΕΝΟΣ

1165 ὦ χαῖρε, πατρὸς μνῆμ'· ἐπ' ἐξόδοισι γὰρ
ἔθαψα Πρωτεῦ σ' ἕνεκ' ἐμῆς προσρήσεως·
ἀεὶ δέ σ' ἐξιών τε κἀσιὼν δόμους
Θεοκλύμενος παῖς ὅδε προσεννέπω, πάτερ.
ὑμεῖς μὲν οὖν κύνας τε καὶ θηρῶν βρόχους,
1170 δμῶες, κομίζετ' ἐς δόμους τυραννικούς·
ἐγὼ δ' ἐμαυτὸν πόλλ' ἐλοιδόρησα δή·
οὐ γάρ τι θανάτῳ τοὺς κακοὺς κολάζομεν.
καὶ νῦν πέπυσμαι φανερὸν Ἑλλήνων τινὰ
ἐς γῆν ἀφῖχθαι καὶ λεληθέναι σκοπούς,
1175 ἤτοι κατόπτην ἢ κλοπαῖς θηρώμενον
Ἑλένην· θανεῖται δ', ἤν γε δὴ ληφθῇ μόνον.
ἔα·
ἀλλ', ὡς ἔοικε, πάντα διαπεπραγμένα
ηὕρηκα· τύμβου γὰρ κενὰς λιποῦσ' ἕδρας
ἡ Τυνδαρὶς παῖς ἐκπεπόρθμευται χθονός.
1180 ὠή, χαλᾶτε κλῇθρα· λύεθ' ἱππικὰς
φάτνας, ὀπαδοί, κἀκκομίζεθ' ἅρματα,
ὡς ἂν πόνου γ' ἕκατι μὴ λάθῃ με γῆς
τῆσδ' ἐκκομισθεῖσ' ἄλοχος ἧς ἐφίεμαι.
ἐπίσχετ'· εἰσορῶ γὰρ οὓς διώκομεν
1185 παρόντας ἐν δόμοισι κοὐ πεφευγότας.
αὕτη, τί πέπλους μέλανας ἐξήψω χροὸς

1164 ἀθλία Dale: -ίοις L   ἐλεινοῖς Nauck: αἰλίνοις L

and you endure grief upon grief,
made luckless by pitiable woes.

Enter by Eisodos B THEOCLYMENUS *with servants carrying nets and leading dogs.*

THEOCLYMENUS

Tomb of my father, greeting! I have buried you near my gates, father Proteus, so that I may greet you: I, Theoclymenus, always have a word for you as I go in and out of my house! You servants, take the dogs and the hunting nets into the palace! (*Exit the servants into the* skene.)

I have often criticized myself: we are not putting the evildoers to death. And now I learn that a Greek has slipped by the guards and showed his face here. He is either a spy or has come to steal Helen away. He will be killed if only he is caught.

But what is this? I have come too late, it seems, and the whole business has already been carried out! Tyndareus' daughter has left her seat on the tomb and been spirited away! Ho, there, servants, unbar the gates, open the stables, and bring the chariots out! If my efforts can stop her, the wife I desire will not be carried secretly from this country!

Enter HELEN *from the* skene.

But wait! My quarry, I see, is at home, not fled. You, why have you changed your white clothes for black? Why

---

1168 προσεννέπω Lenting: -ει L
1172 θανάτῳ] πάντας Herwerden
1173 φανερὸν] φλαῦρον Reiske

λευκῶν ἀμείψασ᾽ ἔκ τε κρατὸς εὐγενοῦς
κόμας σίδηρον ἐμβαλοῦσ᾽ ἀπέθρισας
χλωροῖς τε τέγγεις δάκρυσι σὴν παρηίδα
1190 κλαίουσα; πότερον ἐννύχοις πεπεισμένη
στένεις ὀνείροις; ἢ φάτιν τιν᾽ οἴκοθεν
κλυοῦσα λύπη σὰς διέφθαρσαι φρένας;

ΕΛΕΝΗ
ὦ δέσποτ᾽—ἤδη γὰρ τόδ᾽ ὀνομάζω σ᾽ ἔπος—
ὄλωλα· φροῦδα τἀμὰ κοὐδέν εἰμ᾽ ἔτι.

ΘΕΟΚΛΥΜΕΝΟΣ
1195 ἐν τῷ δὲ κεῖσαι συμφορᾶς; τίς ἡ τύχη;

ΕΛΕΝΗ
Μενέλαος—οἴμοι, πῶς φράσω;—τέθνηκέ μοι.

ΘΕΟΚΛΥΜΕΝΟΣ
[οὐδέν τι χαίρω σοῖς λόγοις, τὰ δ᾽ εὐτυχῶ.]
πῶς οἶσθα; μῶν σοι Θεονόη λέγει τάδε;

ΕΛΕΝΗ
κείνη τε φησὶν ὅ τε παρὼν ὅτ᾽ ὤλλυτο.

ΘΕΟΚΛΥΜΕΝΟΣ
1200 ἥκει γὰρ ὅστις καὶ τάδ᾽ ἀγγέλλει σαφῆ;

ΕΛΕΝΗ
ἥκει· μόλοι γὰρ οἷ σφ᾽ ἐγὼ χρῄζω μολεῖν.

1197 del. Hartung
1201 δ᾽ ἄρ᾽ Dobree   οἷ σφ᾽ Lenting: ὡς L

142

did you take the knife and cut the hair from your noble head? Why are you weeping, moistening your cheek with pale tears? Has a persuasive dream in the night made you weep? Or have you heard a report from home that rends your heart with grief?

HELEN

Master—for that is the name I will call you from now on— I am undone! My fortunes are ruined, and I am dead!

THEOCLYMENUS

What has happened? What is the trouble that besets you?

HELEN

My Menelaus—ah, how can I say it?—is dead!

THEOCLYMENUS

[Not at all do I rejoice at your words, though my fortune is good.] How do you know? Do you have this from Theonoe?

HELEN

Yes, and from one who was there when he died.

THEOCLYMENUS

What? Is someone here who can confirm the truth of this?

HELEN

Yes. And I wish he would go to a place I have in mind![21]

---

[21] Helen pretends to wish him, as the bearer of bad news, an evil destination. (In tragedy bearers of good news are treated as deserving reward and bearers of bad as deserving punishment.) To herself, of course, her words mean "May he get home safely."

ΘΕΟΚΛΥΜΕΝΟΣ
τίς ἐστι; ποῦ 'στιν; ἵνα σαφέστερον μάθω.

ΕΛΕΝΗ
ὅδ' ὃς κάθηται τῷδ' ὑποπτήξας τάφῳ.

ΘΕΟΚΛΥΜΕΝΟΣ
Ἄπολλον, ὡς ἐσθῆτι δυσμόρφῳ πρέπει.

ΕΛΕΝΗ
1205 οἴμοι, δοκῶ μὲν κἀμὸν ὧδ' ἔχειν πόσιν.

ΘΕΟΚΛΥΜΕΝΟΣ
ποδαπὸς δ' ὅδ' ἀνὴρ καὶ πόθεν κατέσχε γῆν;

ΕΛΕΝΗ
Ἕλλην, Ἀχαιῶν εἷς ἐμῷ σύμπλους πόσει.

ΘΕΟΚΛΥΜΕΝΟΣ
θανάτῳ δὲ ποίῳ φησὶ Μενέλεων θανεῖν;

ΕΛΕΝΗ
οἰκτρόταθ', ὑγροῖσιν ἐν κλυδωνίοις ἁλός.

ΘΕΟΚΛΥΜΕΝΟΣ
1210 ποῦ βαρβάροισι πελάγεσιν ναυσθλούμενον;

ΕΛΕΝΗ
Λιβύης ἀλιμένοις ἐκπεσόντα πρὸς πέτραις.

ΘΕΟΚΛΥΜΕΝΟΣ
καὶ πῶς ὅδ' οὐκ ὄλωλε κοινωνῶν πλάτης;

1207 Ἕλλην abundat: fort. ἐς Φρύγας

144

THEOCLYMENUS

Who is he? Where is he? Let me get a clearer report.

HELEN

That man there, who sits cowering at the foot of the tomb.

THEOCLYMENUS

Apollo! How ugly his clothing is!

HELEN

Ah me! I think my husband must be dressed like him.

THEOCLYMENUS

What is his nation? From where did he arrive at our shores?

HELEN

He is Greek, one of the Achaeans who sailed with my husband.

THEOCLYMENUS

What kind of death does he say your husband died?

HELEN

A most miserable one, death at sea.

THEOCLYMENUS

Where was he sailing in barbarian waters?

HELEN

He was cast out upon Libya's harborless cliffs.

THEOCLYMENUS

How did this man survive? He shared the same ship.

ΕΛΕΝΗ

ἐσθλῶν κακίους ἐνίοτ᾽ εὐτυχέστεροι.

ΘΕΟΚΛΥΜΕΝΟΣ

λιπὼν δὲ ναὸς ποῦ πάρεστιν ἔκβολα;

ΕΛΕΝΗ

1215 ὅπου κακῶς ὄλοιτο, Μενέλεως δὲ μή.

ΘΕΟΚΛΥΜΕΝΟΣ

ὄλωλ᾽ ἐκεῖνος. ἦλθε δ᾽ ἐν ποίῳ σκάφει;

ΕΛΕΝΗ

ναῦταί σφ᾽ ἀνείλοντ᾽ ἐντυχόντες, ὡς λέγει.

ΘΕΟΚΛΥΜΕΝΟΣ

ποῦ δὴ τὸ πεμφθὲν ἀντὶ σοῦ Τροίᾳ κακόν;

ΕΛΕΝΗ

νεφέλης λέγεις ἄγαλμ᾽; ἐς αἰθέρ᾽ οἴχεται.

ΘΕΟΚΛΥΜΕΝΟΣ

1220 ὦ Πρίαμε καὶ γῆ Τρῳάς, ⟨ὡς⟩ ἔρρεις μάτην.

ΕΛΕΝΗ

κἀγὼ μετέσχον Πριαμίδαις δυσπραξίας.

ΘΕΟΚΛΥΜΕΝΟΣ

πόσιν δ᾽ ἄθαπτον ἔλιπεν ἢ κρύπτει χθονί;

ΕΛΕΝΗ

ἄθαπτον· οἲ ᾽γὼ τῶν ἐμῶν τλήμων κακῶν.

ΘΕΟΚΛΥΜΕΝΟΣ

τῶνδ᾽ οὕνεκ᾽ ἔτεμες βοστρύχους ξανθῆς κόμης;

HELEN
The lowly are often luckier than their betters.

THEOCLYMENUS
Where has he left the remnants of his ship?

HELEN
Where I pray it may be cursed! But not Menelaus!

THEOCLYMENUS
Menelaus is dead. But on what ship did this man come here?

HELEN
Sailors, he says, found and rescued him.

THEOCLYMENUS
Where then is that curse sent in your place to Troy?

HELEN
You mean that image made of cloud? Gone up into the sky.

THEOCLYMENUS
O Priam and Troy, how pointless was your death!

HELEN
I too shared in misfortune with the sons of Priam.

THEOCLYMENUS
Did he bury your husband or leave him unburied?

HELEN
Unburied. Oh what woe is mine!

THEOCLYMENUS
So that is why you have cut your blond locks?

1217 ἀνείλοντ’ Cobet: ἀνεῖλον L
1220 ⟨ὡς⟩ Scaliger

ΕΛΕΝΗ

1225 φίλος γάρ †ἐστιν ὅς ποτ᾽ ἐστὶν ἐνθάδ᾽ ὤν†.

ΘΕΟΚΛΥΜΕΝΟΣ

ὀρθῶς μὲν ἥδε συμφορὰ δακρύεται.

< ΕΛΕΝΗ

ὄλωλ᾽ ἐγὼ τάλαινα κοὐδὲν εἴμ᾽ ἔτι.

ΘΕΟΚΛΥΜΕΝΟΣ

ὅρα δὲ μὴ τάδ᾽ οὐ σαφῶς ἠγγελμέν᾽ ᾖ.>

ΕΛΕΝΗ

ἐν εὐμαρεῖ γοῦν σὴν κασιγνήτην λαθεῖν.

ΘΕΟΚΛΥΜΕΝΟΣ

οὐ δῆτα. πῶς οὖν; τόνδ᾽ ἔτ᾽ οἰκήσεις τάφον;

< ΕΛΕΝΗ

θανὼν ἔτ᾽ ἔστ᾽ ἐκεῖνος· οὐ τιμητέος;>

ΘΕΟΚΛΥΜΕΝΟΣ

τί κερτομεῖς με, τὸν θανόντα δ᾽ οὐκ ἐᾷς;

< ΕΛΕΝΗ

οὗ πόσις, ἐκεῖ γυναῖκα συνναίειν χρεών.>

ΘΕΟΚΛΥΜΕΝΟΣ

1230 πιστὴ γὰρ εἶ σὺ σῷ πόσει φεύγουσά με;

ΕΛΕΝΗ

ἀλλ᾽ οὐκέτ᾽· ἤδη δ᾽ ἄρχε τῶν ἐμῶν γάμων.

1225 ἐστ᾽ ἔθ᾽ ὅσπερ (melius ὥσπερ) ἦν ποτ᾽ ἐνθάδ᾽ ὤν A. Y. Campbell
1226 post h. v. lac. indic. Dale

148

HELEN

Yes: he is still dear to me as he was in life.

THEOCLYMENUS

This is indeed cause for tears.

⟨HELEN

I am undone: my life is over!

THEOCLYMENUS

But take care: the tale of his death may be false.⟩

HELEN

Is it so easy then to fool your sister?

THEOCLYMENUS

No indeed! But what follows? Will you still make this tomb your home?

⟨HELEN

Though dead, he lives still: should he not be honored?⟩

THEOCLYMENUS

Why do you provoke me? Why not let the dead be?

⟨HELEN

Where a husband is, there must his wife dwell with him.⟩

THEOCLYMENUS

Are you being faithful to your husband in running from me?

HELEN

I will be so no more: begin the wedding arrangements.

1227 λαθεῖν Jacobs: θανεῖν L
1229, 1230 ante hos vv. lacc. indic. Willink
1230 εἶ σὺ Elmsley: ἐσσὶ L

149

ΘΕΟΚΛΥΜΕΝΟΣ

χρόνια μὲν ἦλθεν, ἀλλ' ὅμως αἰνῶ τάδε.

ΕΛΕΝΗ

οἶσθ' οὖν ὃ δρᾶσον· τῶν πάρος λαθώμεθα.

ΘΕΟΚΛΥΜΕΝΟΣ

ἐπὶ τῷ; χάρις γὰρ ἀντὶ χάριτος ἐλθέτω.

ΕΛΕΝΗ

1235   σπονδὰς τέμωμεν καὶ διαλλάχθητί μοι.

ΘΕΟΚΛΥΜΕΝΟΣ

μεθίημι νεῖκος τὸ σόν, ἴτω δ' ὑπόπτερον.

ΕΛΕΝΗ

πρός νύν σε γονάτων τῶνδ', ἐπείπερ εἶ φίλος . . .

ΘΕΟΚΛΥΜΕΝΟΣ

τί χρῆμα θηρῶσ' ἱκέτις ὠρέχθης ἐμοῦ;

ΕΛΕΝΗ

τὸν κατθανόντα πόσιν ἐμὸν θάψαι θέλω.

ΘΕΟΚΛΥΜΕΝΟΣ

1240   τί δ'; ἔστ' ἀπόντων τύμβος; ἢ θάψεις σκιάν;

ΕΛΕΝΗ

Ἕλλησίν ἐστι νόμος, ὃς ἂν πόντῳ θάνῃ . . .

ΘΕΟΚΛΥΜΕΝΟΣ

τί δρᾶν; σοφοί τοι Πελοπίδαι τὰ τοιάδε.

1232 ἦλθεν Musgrave: -ες L

150

THEOCLYMENUS

This has been long in coming, but I thank you for it!

HELEN

Here is what you must do: let us forget what is past.

THEOCLYMENUS

On what terms? Favor must answer favor.

HELEN

Let's make a truce. Be reconciled with me.

THEOCLYMENUS

I renounce my quarrel with you: let it take wing and vanish!

HELEN

(*kneeling and grasping Theoclymenus' knees*) By your knees, then, if you are my friend . . .

THEOCLYMENUS

What does your suppliant grasp aim to gain?

HELEN

I want to give my dead husband a burial.

THEOCLYMENUS

How? Can you bury a man who is missing? Will you inter his shade?

HELEN

The Greeks have a custom: whenever someone dies at sea . . .

THEOCLYMENUS

What do you do? The descendants of Pelops are skilled in such things.

ΕΛΕΝΗ

. . . κενοῖσι θάπτειν ἐν πέπλων ὑφάσμασιν.

ΘΕΟΚΛΥΜΕΝΟΣ

κτέριζ'· ἀνίστη τύμβον οὗ χρῄζεις χθονός.

ΕΛΕΝΗ

1245 οὐχ ὧδε ναύτας ὀλομένους τυμβεύομεν.

ΘΕΟΚΛΥΜΕΝΟΣ

πῶς δαί; λέλειμμαι τῶν ἐν Ἕλλησιν νόμων.

ΕΛΕΝΗ

ἐς πόντον ὅσα χρὴ νέκυσιν ἐξορμίζομεν.

ΘΕΟΚΛΥΜΕΝΟΣ

τί σοι παράσχω δῆτα τῷ τεθνηκότι;

ΕΛΕΝΗ

ὅδ' οἶδ', ἐγὼ δ' ἄπειρος, εὐτυχοῦσα πρίν.

ΘΕΟΚΛΥΜΕΝΟΣ

1250 ὦ ξένε, λόγων μὲν κληδόν' ἤνεγκας φίλην.

ΜΕΝΕΛΑΟΣ

οὔκουν ἐμαυτῷ γ' οὐδὲ τῷ τεθνηκότι.

ΘΕΟΚΛΥΜΕΝΟΣ

πῶς τοὺς θανόντας θάπτετ' ἐν πόντῳ νεκρούς;

ΜΕΝΕΛΑΟΣ

ὡς ἂν παρούσης οὐσίας ἕκαστος ᾖ.

ΘΕΟΚΛΥΜΕΝΟΣ

πλούτου λάβ' οὕνεχ' ὅ τι θέλεις ταύτης χάριν.

HELEN

. . . we bury the body in effigy with fine robes.

THEOCLYMENUS

Bury him! Raise a funeral mound wherever you like in the land!

HELEN

That is not the way we bury sailors who have died.

THEOCLYMENUS

How then? I am ignorant of Greek custom.

HELEN

We take out to sea all that the dead require.

THEOCLYMENUS

What shall I provide then for your dead husband?

HELEN

This man knows: I have no experience, being fortunate until now.

THEOCLYMENUS

Stranger, you have brought us welcome news.

MENELAUS

Not welcome to me or to him who died.

THEOCLYMENUS

How do you bury those who die at sea?

MENELAUS

As well as each man's wealth allows.

THEOCLYMENUS

Take what you want for her sake: spare no expense.

1254 λάβ' Kovacs: λέγ' L

ΜΕΝΕΛΑΟΣ

1255 προσφάζεται μὲν αἷμα πρῶτα νερτέροις.

ΘΕΟΚΛΥΜΕΝΟΣ

τίνος; σύ μοι σήμαινε, πείσομαι δ' ἐγώ.

ΜΕΝΕΛΑΟΣ

αὐτὸς σὺ γίγνωσκ'· ἀρκέσει γὰρ ἂν διδῷς.

ΘΕΟΚΛΥΜΕΝΟΣ

ἐν βαρβάροις μὲν ἵππον ἢ ταῦρον νόμος.

ΜΕΝΕΛΑΟΣ

διδούς γε μὲν δὴ δυσγενὲς μηδὲν δίδου.

ΘΕΟΚΛΥΜΕΝΟΣ

1260 οὐ τῶνδ' ἐν ἀγέλαις ὀλβίαις σπανίζομεν.

ΜΕΝΕΛΑΟΣ

καὶ στρωτὰ φέρεται λέκτρα σώματος κενά.

ΘΕΟΚΛΥΜΕΝΟΣ

ἔσται· τί δ' ἄλλο προσφέρειν νομίζεται;

ΜΕΝΕΛΑΟΣ

χαλκήλαθ' ὅπλα (καὶ γὰρ ἦν φίλος δορί) ...

ΘΕΟΚΛΥΜΕΝΟΣ

ἄξια τάδ' ἔσται Πελοπιδῶν ἃ δώσομεν.

ΜΕΝΕΛΑΟΣ

1265 ... καὶ τἄλλ' ὅσα χθὼν καλὰ φέρει βλαστήματα.

1260 οὐχ ὧδ' Bruhn

154

MENELAUS

The blood of an animal is the first offering to the dead.

THEOCLYMENUS

What animal? Say, and I shall do as you ask.

MENELAUS

You decide yourself: whatever you give will be sufficient.

THEOCLYMENUS

Among the barbarians, a horse or a bullock is customary.

MENELAUS

If you are giving one, make sure it is in no way malformed.

THEOCLYMENUS

Our rich herds do not lack for proper victims.

MENELAUS

Bedding—with no body therein—is also offered.

THEOCLYMENUS

You shall have it. What other offering does custom ordain?

MENELAUS

Armor of bronze, since Menelaus loved the spear . . .

THEOCLYMENUS

What we will provide will be worthy of Pelops' descendants.

MENELAUS

. . . and other good fruits the earth brings forth.

ΘΕΟΚΛΥΜΕΝΟΣ

πῶς οὖν; ἐς οἶδμα τίνι τρόπῳ καθίετε;

ΜΕΝΕΛΑΟΣ

ναῦν δεῖ παρεῖναι κἀρετμῶν ἐπιστάτας.

ΘΕΟΚΛΥΜΕΝΟΣ

πόσον δ᾽ ἀπείργειν μῆκος ἐκ γαίας δόρυ;

ΜΕΝΕΛΑΟΣ

ὥστ᾽ ἐξορᾶσθαι ῥόθια χερσόθεν μόλις.

ΘΕΟΚΛΥΜΕΝΟΣ

1270   τί δή; τόδ᾽ Ἑλλὰς νόμιμον ἐκ τίνος σέβει;

ΜΕΝΕΛΑΟΣ

ὡς μὴ πάλιν γῇ λύματ᾽ ἐκβάλῃ κλύδων.

ΘΕΟΚΛΥΜΕΝΟΣ

Φοίνισσα κώπη ταχύπορος γενήσεται.

ΜΕΝΕΛΑΟΣ

καλῶς ἂν εἴη Μενέλεῳ τε πρὸς χάριν.

ΘΕΟΚΛΥΜΕΝΟΣ

οὔκουν σὺ χωρὶς τῆσδε δρῶν ἀρκεῖς τάδε;

ΜΕΝΕΛΑΟΣ

1275   μητρὸς τόδ᾽ ἔργον ἢ γυναικὸς ἢ τέκνων.

ΘΕΟΚΛΥΜΕΝΟΣ

ταύτης ὁ μόχθος, ὡς λέγεις, θάπτειν πόσιν.

ΜΕΝΕΛΑΟΣ

ἐν εὐσεβεῖ γοῦν νόμιμα μὴ κλέπτειν νεκρῶν.

THEOCLYMENUS
What then? How will you commit these thing to the deep?

MENELAUS
We must have a ship and skilled rowers.

THEOCLYMENUS
To take the ship how far out from the land?

MENELAUS
To where you can barely see the waves beating on the shore.

THEOCLYMENUS
Why does Greece observe this custom?

MENELAUS
So that the tide may not wash pollution back to the land.

THEOCLYMENUS
A speedy Phoenician ship will be provided.

MENELAUS
That will be good—and gratifying to Menelaus.

THEOCLYMENUS
Will it not be enough if you perform this task without her?

MENELAUS
It must be done by mother, wife, or children.

THEOCLYMENUS
You mean it is her job to bury her husband.

MENELAUS
It is a pious thing not to cheat the dead of their due.

1268 ἀπείργειν Matthiae: -ει L
1271 θύματ᾽ Hermann

ΘΕΟΚΛΥΜΕΝΟΣ

ἴτω· πρὸς ἡμῶν ἄλοχον εὐσεβῆ τρέφειν.
ἐλθὼν δ' ἐς οἴκους ἐξελοῦ κόσμον νεκρῷ·
1280 καὶ σ' οὐ κεναῖσι χερσὶ γῆς ἀποστελῶ,
δράσαντα τῇδε πρὸς χάριν· φήμας δ' ἐμοὶ
ἐσθλὰς ἐνεγκὼν ἀντὶ τῆς ἀχλαινίας
ἐσθῆτα λήψῃ σῖτά θ', ὥστε σ' ἐς πάτραν
ἐλθεῖν, ἐπεὶ νῦν γ' ἀθλίως <σ'> ἔχονθ' ὁρῶ.
1285   σὺ δ', ὦ τάλαινα, μὴ 'πὶ τοῖς ἀνηνύτοις
τρύχουσα σαυτὴν <Μενέλεων ἄγαν στένε·
σὺ μὲν βλέπεις φῶς,> Μενέλεως δ' ἔχει πότμον,
κοὐκ ἂν δύναιτο ζῆν ὁ κατθανὼν γόοις.

ΜΕΝΕΛΑΟΣ

σὸν ἔργον, ὦ νεᾶνι· τὸν παρόντα μὲν
στέργειν πόσιν χρή, τὸν δὲ μηκέτ' ὄντ' ἐᾶν·
1290 ἄριστα γάρ σοι ταῦτα πρὸς τὸ τυγχάνον.
ἢν δ' Ἑλλάδ' ἔλθω καὶ τύχω σωτηρίας,
1293 παύσω ψόγου σε τοῦ πρίν, ἢν γυνὴ γένῃ
1292 οἵαν γενέσθαι χρή σε σῷ ξυνευνέτῃ.

ΕΛΕΝΗ

ἔσται τάδ'· οὐδὲ μέμψεται πόσις ποτὲ
1295 ἡμῖν· σὺ δ' αὐτὸς ἐγγὺς ὢν εἴσῃ τάδε.
ἀλλ', ὦ τάλας, εἴσελθε καὶ λουτρῶν τύχε
ἐσθῆτά τ' ἐξάλλαξον· οὐκ ἐς ἀμβολὰς
εὐεργετήσω σ'· εὐμενέστερον γὰρ ἂν
τῷ φιλτάτῳ μοι Μενέλεῳ τὰ πρόσφορα
1300 δρῴης ἄν, ἡμῶν τυγχάνων οἵων σε χρή.

HELEN

THEOCLYMENUS

She may go: it is to my advantage to encourage my wife's piety. Go into the house and choose adornment for the dead man. You also will not be sent away empty-handed once you have performed this service for her. Since you brought good news to me, you will receive clothing to replace your rags, and also food, so that you can return to your own land. Your present state, I see, is a sorry one.

And you, poor lady, do not wear yourself down to no purpose ⟨or grieve excessively for Menelaus: you look on the light,⟩ but he has met his fate, and weeping can never bring him back.

MENELAUS

Now you know your task, young lady. You must be content with the husband you have and pay no attention to him who is no more. That is the best you can do in the present circumstances. If I reach Greece safely, I will free you from the old slander, provided you prove to be a good wife to your husband.

HELEN

It shall be so: my husband shall have nothing to complain of in me. You yourself shall stand by and be my witness. So, poor man, go in, bathe yourself, and put on fresh clothes. My benefactions to you will begin at once. You will perform the rites for my dear Menelaus in a kindlier spirit if you receive proper treatment from me.

1279 ἐξελοῦ Cobet: -ῶ L   post h. v. lac. indic. Diggle
1284 ⟨σ'⟩ Lenting   1286 post σαυτὴν lac. indic. Badham,
suppl. Diggle   1287 γόοις Jackson: πόσις L: πάλιν Reiske
1293 ante 1292 trai. Canter

ΧΟΡΟΣ

στρ. α

ὀρεία ποτὲ δρομάδι κώ-
λῳ Μάτηρ ἐσύθη θεῶν
ἀν᾽ ὑλᾶντα νάπη
ποτάμιόν τε χεῦμ᾽ ὑδάτων
1305 βαρύβρομόν τε κῦμ᾽ ἅλιον
πόθῳ τᾶς ἀποιχομένας
ἀρρήτου κούρας.
κρόταλα δὲ βρόμια διαπρύσιον
ἱέντα κέλαδον ἀνεβόα,
1310 θηρῶν ὅτε ζυγίους
ζεύξασα θεὰ σατίνας
τὰν ἁρπασθεῖσαν κυκλίων
χορῶν ἔξω παρθενίων
κούραν ⟨ὦρμα σωσομένα⟩
μετὰ δ᾽ ⟨ἦξαν⟩ ἀελλόποδες,
1315 ἁ μὲν τόξοις Ἄρτεμις, ἁ δ᾽
ἔγχει Γοργῶπις πάνοπλος,
αὐγάζων δ᾽ ἐξ οὐρανίων
⟨Ζεὺς ὁ παντάρχας ἑδράνων⟩

1302 ἐσύθη θεῶν Diggle: θ- ἐ- L
1311 σατίνας Musgrave: -αν L
1314–14a post κούραν et μετὰ δ᾽ lacunas indic. Maas: μετὰ
κούραν δ᾽ ἀελλόποδες L   1314a ⟨ἦξαν⟩ Maas
1316 Γοργῶπις Heath: Γοργὼ L
1317 post h. v. lac. indic. L. Dindorf in qua Ζεὺς et ἑδράνων
desiderabat, suppl. Wilamowitz

HELEN

Exit into the skene MENELAUS, HELEN, *and* THEOCLY-
MENUS.

CHORUS[22]

Once upon a time the mountain-dwelling
Mother of the Gods rushed on swift feet
along the wooded glens
and the gushing streams of water
and the deep-thundering breakers of the sea
in longing for her vanished
daughter whose name is never spoken.[23]
The roaring cymbals, their sharp note uttering,
cried aloud
when she yoked her chariot
with its team of wild beasts
and ‹darted off to find› her daughter
snatched away from the circling
dances of maidens;
after her ‹there darted› on feet like the wind storm
Artemis with her bow
and the Grim-eyed One[24] in full armor.
But looking down from his heavenly ‹abode
Zeus the all-ruler›

---

[22] The Mother of the Gods, whose worship was imported
into Greece from Asia Minor, is often called Rhea or Cybele or
the Mountain Mother. In this lovely ode she is identified with
Demeter, who grieves for her daughter Persephone, abducted by
Hades. The ode is only lightly attached to its context, and the idea
(1335–7) that Helen is in trouble because of neglect of the god-
dess is without answering echo elsewhere in the play.
[23] The Athenians avoided calling Persephone by her name,
calling her "the Maiden" instead.   [24] Athena.

ἄλλαν μοῖραν ἔκραινεν.

ἀντ. α

δρομαῖον τότε πολυπλάνη-
1320 τον μάτηρ ἔπαυσε πόνον,
ματεύουσα φίλας
θυγατρὸς ἁρπαγὰς δολίους,
χιονοθρέμμονάς τ’ ἐπέρασ’
Ἰδαιᾶν Νυμφᾶν σκοπιὰς
1325 ῥίπτει τ’ ἐν πένθει
πέτρινα κατὰ δρία πολυνιφέα.
βροτοῖσι δ’ ἄχλοα πεδία γᾶς
⟨ἔθηκε, πυροφόρους⟩
οὐ καρπίζουσ’ ἀρότους
λαῶν δὲ φθείρει γενεάν·
1330 ποίμναις δ’ οὐχ ἵει θαλερὰς
βοσκὰς εὐφύλλων ἑλίκων·
πόλεων δ’ ἀπέλειπε βίος,
οὐδ’ ἦσαν θεῶν θυσίαι,
βωμοῖς δ’ ἄφλεκτοι πελανοί·
1335 παγὰς δ’ ἀμπαύει δροσερὰς
λευκῶν ἐκβάλλειν ὑδάτων
πένθει παιδὸς ἀλάστῳ.

στρ. β

ἐπεὶ δ’ ἔπαυσ’ εἰλαπίνας

1319–20 δρομαῖον . . . πολυπλάνητον . . . πόνον Murray
(δρομαῖον iam Herwerden, πόνον Nauck): -αίων . . . -ήτων . . .
-ων L   1319 τότε Diggle: δ’ ὅτε L

brought a different fate to fulfillment.

Then her labor of aimless rushing about
the mother brought to an end,
the search for her dear
daughter, craftily taken away.
As she passed through the snow-nurturing
peaks where the nymphs of Ida keep watch,
she hurled herself in grief
down the stony copses filled with snow.
For mortals all grassless the fields
‹she rendered and›
did not make fertile their ‹grain-bearing› lands:
she was destroying the human race.
For the herds she did not send
the increase of their fodder in shoot and leaf;
the cities' food was running out,
the gods had no sacrifices,
and on their altars no cakes flamed;
the dewy springs of clear water
she ceased to pour forth
in grief unassuageable for her daughter.

When she had stopped all feasting

1321 φίλας Nauck: πόνους L   1323 τ' Elmsley: δ' L
1325 τ' Elmsley: δ' L   1327 post h. v. lac. indic. Maas
1328 ἀρότους Maas: -οις L
1329 γενεάν Seidler: γένναν L
1334 δ' Murray: τ' L
1335 δ' Hartung: τ' L
1336b ἀλάστῳ L. Dindorf: -τωρ L

θεοῖς βροτείῳ τε γένει,
Ζεὺς μειλίσσων στυγίους
1340 Ματρὸς ὀργὰς ἐνέπει·
Βᾶτε, σεμναὶ Χάριτες,
ἴτε, τᾷ περὶ παρθένῳ
Δηοῖ θυμωσαμένᾳ
λύπαν ἐξαιρεῖτ᾽ ἀλαλᾷ,
1345 Μοῦσαί θ᾽ ὕμνοισι χορῶν.
χαλκοῦ δ᾽ αὐδὰν χθονίαν
τύπανά τ᾽ ἔλαβε βυρσοτενῆ
καλλίστα τότε πρῶτα μακά-
ρων Κύπρις· γέλασεν δὲ θεὰ
1350 δέξατό τ᾽ ἐς χέρα
βαρύβρομον αὐ-
λὸν τερφθεῖσ᾽ ἀλαλαγμῷ.

ἀντ. β

†ὧν οὐ θέμις οὔθ᾽ ὅσια
ἐπύρωσας ἐν θαλάμοις,†
1355 μῆνιν δ᾽ ἔσχες μεγάλας
Ματρός, ὦ παῖ, θυσίας
οὐ σεβίζουσα θεᾶς.
μέγα τοι δύναται νεβρῶν

1342–3 τᾷ . . . Δηοῖ Musgrave: τὰν . . . Δηίω L
1344 ἐξαιρεῖτ᾽ Willink: ἐξαλλάξατ᾽ L
1345 χορῶν Matthiae: -ὸν L
1347 τ᾽ ἔλαβε Hermann: τε λάβετε L
1349 δὲ Seidler: τε L
1350 χέρα Hermann: -ας L

by gods and mortal men,
Zeus trying to soften the grim
wrath of the Mother said,
"Go, you august Graces,
go and from the heart
of Deo[25] angered for her daughter
drive the grief by loud cries,
and you, Muses, by dance and song."
It was then that Cypris, loveliest of the blessed ones,
first took up the rumbling voice of bronze
and the drums of stretched hide.
The goddess laughed
and took into her hand
the deep-sounding pipe,
delighting in its loud cry.

Right and holiness neglecting,
you tarried nightlong in your chamber[26]
and have incurred the wrath of the Great
Mother, my child, by not honoring
the goddess' sacrifices.
Great is the power of the dappled

---

[25] Another name for Demeter.
[26] These two lines, together with the last three of this stanza,
are desperately corrupt, and not even their approximate sense is
known.

1353–4 fort. ὃ δ' οὐ θέμις ⟨σ'⟩ οὔθ' ὁσία / νύχευσας ἐν ⟨σοῖς⟩
θαλάμοις (⟨σ'⟩ iam Heinisch, ⟨σοῖς⟩ Hermann)
1355 ἔσχες Hermann: ἔχεις L
1358 δύναται Musgrave: -νται L

παμποίκιλοι στολίδες
1360 κισσοῦ τε στεφθεῖσα χλόα
νάρθηκας εἰς ἱεροὺς
ῥόμβου θ᾽ εἱλισσομένα
κύκλιος ἔνοσις αἰθερία
βακχεύουσά τ᾽ ἔθειρα Βρομί-
1365 ῳ καὶ παννυχίδες θεᾶς,
†εὖ δέ νιν ἅμασιν
ὑπέρβαλε σελάνα
μορφᾷ μόνον ηὔχεις.†

ΕΛΕΝΗ

τὰ μὲν κατ᾽ οἴκους εὐτυχοῦμεν, ὦ φίλαι·
1370 ἡ γὰρ συνεκκλέπτουσα Πρωτέως κόρη
πόσιν παρόντα τὸν ἐμὸν ἱστορουμένη
οὐκ εἶπ᾽ ἀδελφῷ· κατθανόντα δ᾽ ἡλίου
οὔ φησιν αὐγὰς εἰσορᾶν ἐμὴν χάριν.
κάλλιστα δ᾽ αὖ τήνδ᾽ ἥρπασεν τύχην πόσις·
1375 ἃ γὰρ καθήσειν ὅπλ᾽ ἔμελλεν εἰς ἅλα,
ταῦτ᾽ ἐμβαλὼν πόρπακι γενναίαν χέρα
αὐτὸς κομίζει δόρυ τε δεξιᾷ λαβών,
ὡς τῷ θανόντι χάριτα δὴ συνεκπονῶν.
προύργου δ᾽ ἐς ἀλκὴν σῶμ᾽ ὅπλοις ἠσκήσατο,
1380 ὡς βαρβάρων τροπαῖα μυρίων χερὶ
θήσων, ὅταν κωπῆρες ἐσβῶμεν σκάφος.

1360 κισσοῦ Musgrave: -ῷ L   1366–8 fort. εὖτε σὺν
ἅρμασι / πρέπῃ σελά- / να ᾽ν ὄρφνᾳ μελαναυγεῖ (εὖτε et
ἅρμασι Heath, ὄρφνᾳ μελαναυγεῖ Hermann)

garb of deerskin,
the ivy shoots wound about
the sanctified hollow reed,
the din in the air
of the bull-roarer whirled in a circle,
the long hair leaping in bacchic joy
for Bromius, and the goddess' nightlong feasts[27]
when the moon
with her chariot shines forth
in the dark gloom of night.

Enter from the palace HELEN.

HELEN

My friends, events in the house have gone well for us.
Proteus' daughter, who joins in concealing my husband's
arrival, did not tell her brother, but when questioned said
for my sake that he was dead and no longer saw the light of
the sun. My husband for his part has snagged a fine bit of
luck here: the armor he was to sink into the sea he is bring-
ing himself, and he has his noble arm through the shield
strap and the spear in his right hand, pretending to join in
pleasing the dead man. And most conveniently for battle
he wears the defensive panoply, meaning to make count-
less barbarians turn tail and run when we board the vessel.

[27] The cult of Rhea is here assimilated to the cult of Dionysus.
For a similar mixture see *Bacchae* 78–134.

1372 ἡλίου Wecklein: ἐν χθονὶ L
1374 δ' αὖ τήνδ' ἥρπασεν τύχην Willink (δ' αὖ) et Wecklein:
δῆτ' ἀνήρπασ' ἐν τύχῃ L

πέπλους δ' ἀμείψασ' ἀντὶ ναυφθόρου στολῆς
ἐγώ νιν ἐξήσκησα καὶ λουτροῖς χρόα
ἔδωκα, χρόνια νίπτρα ποταμίας δρόσου.

1385　ἀλλ', ἐκπερᾷ γὰρ δωμάτων ὁ τοὺς ἐμοὺς
γάμους ἑτοίμους ἐν χεροῖν ἔχειν δοκῶν,
σιγητέον μοι· καὶ σὲ προσποιούμεθα
⟨δόλου συνεργὸν τοῦδέ μοι· μένειν δὲ χρὴ⟩
εὔνουν κρατεῖν τε στόματος, ἢν δυνώμεθα
σωθέντες αὐτοὶ καὶ σὲ συσσῶσαί ποτε.

ΘΕΟΚΛΥΜΕΝΟΣ

1390　χωρεῖτ' ἐφεξῆς, ὡς ἔταξεν ὁ ξένος,
δμῶες, φέροντες ἐνάλια κτερίσματα.

Ἑλένη, σὺ δ', ἤν σοι μὴ κακῶς δόξω λέγειν,
πείθου, μέν' αὐτοῦ· ταὐτὰ γὰρ παροῦσά τε
πράξεις τὸν ἄνδρα τὸν σὸν ἤν τε μὴ παρῇς.

1395　δέδοικα γάρ σε μή τις ἐμπεσὼν πόθος
πείσῃ μεθεῖναι σῶμ' ἐς οἶδμα πόντιον
τοῦ πρόσθεν ἀνδρὸς χάρισιν ἐκπεπληγμένην·
ἄγαν γὰρ αὐτὸν οὐ παρόνθ' ὅμως στένεις.

ΕΛΕΝΗ

ὦ καινὸς ἡμῖν πόσις, ἀναγκαίως ἔχει
1400　τὰ πρῶτα λέκτρα νυμφικάς θ' ὁμιλίας
τιμᾶν· ἐγὼ δὲ διὰ τὸ μὲν στέργειν πόσιν
καὶ ξυνθάνοιμ' ἄν· ἀλλὰ τίς κείνῳ χάρις
ξὺν κατθανόντι κατθανεῖν ⟨μ'⟩; ἔα δέ με
αὐτὴν μολοῦσαν ἐντάφια δοῦναι νεκρῷ.

I took off his shipwrecked clothes and gave him fine new ones, and bathed him, fresh water at last from a stream.

But since he is coming out, the man who thinks he has me safely in his possession, I must say nothing. I call on you ‹to help in this deception: you must remain› well-disposed toward me and hold your tongue. It may be that when we ourselves have escaped we will be able to rescue you as well.

Enter from the palace THEOCLYMENUS *followed by* MENELAUS, *now dressed in new clothes and armor, who heads the party of servants bringing offerings.*

THEOCLYMENUS

Servants, you are to go in good order and carry these offerings for a sea funeral according to the foreigner's instructions!

Helen, if you think my advice is not bad, do as I say and stay here. Whether you are present or not you will do the same service to your husband. I am afraid that you will be seized by a desire to throw yourself into the waves, overcome by the memory of the joy you had in him. Though he is gone, you still mourn him too much.

HELEN

My new husband, it is inevitable that I honor my first marriage and the love I gave him as his bride. For the love of my husband I would even die. But what favor is it to him to join him in death? Let me go and give funeral honors to the

---

1387 post h. v. lac. indic. Hartung, suppl. Diggle
1399 καινὸς Reiske: κλεινὸς L
1403 ‹μ᾽› Lenting

1405 θεοὶ δὲ σοί τε δοῖεν οἷ᾿ ἐγὼ θέλω,
καὶ τῷ ξένῳ τῷδ᾿, ὅτι συνεκπονεῖ τάδε.
ἕξεις δέ μ᾿ οἵαν χρή σ᾿ ἔχειν ἐν δώμασιν
γυναῖκ᾿, ἐπειδὴ Μενέλεων εὐεργετεῖς
κἄμ᾿· ἔρχεται γὰρ δή τιν᾿ ἐς τύχην τάδε.
1410 ὅστις δὲ δώσει ναῦν ἐν ᾗ τάδ᾿ ἄξομεν,
πρόσταξον, ὡς ἂν τὴν χάριν πλήρη λάβω.

ΘΕΟΚΛΥΜΕΝΟΣ

χώρει σὺ καὶ ναῦν τοῖσδε πεντηκόντερον
Σιδωνίαν δὸς κἀρετμῶν ἐπιστάτας.

ΕΛΕΝΗ

οὔκουν ὅδ᾿ ἄρξει ναὸς ὃς κοσμεῖ τάφον;

ΘΕΟΚΛΥΜΕΝΟΣ

1415 μάλιστ᾿· ἀκούειν τοῦδε χρὴ ναύτας ἐμούς.

ΕΛΕΝΗ

αὖθις κέλευσον, ἵνα σαφῶς μάθωσί σου.

ΘΕΟΚΛΥΜΕΝΟΣ

αὖθις κελεύω καὶ τρίτον γ᾿, εἴ σοι φίλον.

ΕΛΕΝΗ

ὄναιο· κἀγὼ τῶν ἐμῶν βουλευμάτων.

ΘΕΟΚΛΥΜΕΝΟΣ

μή νυν ἄγαν σὸν δάκρυσιν ἐκτήξῃς χρόα.

ΕΛΕΝΗ

1420 ἥδ᾿ ἡμέρα σοι τὴν ἐμὴν δείξει χάριν.

dead man myself. May the gods grant you the blessings I wish you, and likewise this stranger here, for helping us in the task! You will find me to be the kind of wife you ought to have in your house since you are benefitting Menelaus and me. Things are working out for the best. But just tell someone to give us a ship to carry these offerings, and my pleasure will be full.

THEOCLYMENUS

(*to a servant*) Go and give them a Sidonian penteconter and rowers.

HELEN

Shouldn't the one conducting the funeral command the ship?

THEOCLYMENUS

Of course: my sailors must obey his orders.

HELEN

Tell him again, so that they may get your instructions clear.

THEOCLYMENUS

I give the order again and three times, if you like.

HELEN

Blessings on you! And may the task I have in mind bring me blessing!

THEOCLYMENUS

So do not waste your cheeks with too much weeping.

HELEN

This day will show you how grateful I am!

1407 χρή σ' Matthiae: χρῆν L
1415 χρὴ Reiske: χρῆν L

ΘΕΟΚΛΥΜΕΝΟΣ

τὰ τῶν θανόντων οὐδὲν ἀλλ᾽ ἄλλως πόνος.

ΕΛΕΝΗ

†ἔστιν τι κἀκεῖ κἀνθάδ᾽ ὧν ἐγὼ λέγω.†

ΘΕΟΚΛΥΜΕΝΟΣ

οὐδὲν κακίω Μενέλεω μ᾽ ἕξεις πόσιν.

ΕΛΕΝΗ

οὐδὲν σὺ μεμπτός· τῆς τύχης με δεῖ μόνον.

ΘΕΟΚΛΥΜΕΝΟΣ

1425 ἐν σοὶ τόδ᾽, ἢν σὴν εἰς ἔμ᾽ εὔνοιαν διδῷς.

ΕΛΕΝΗ

οὐ νῦν διδαξόμεσθα τοὺς φίλους φιλεῖν.

ΘΕΟΚΛΥΜΕΝΟΣ

βούλῃ ξυνεργῶν αὐτὸς ἐκπέμψω στόλον;

ΕΛΕΝΗ

ἥκιστα· μὴ δούλευε σοῖς δούλοις, ἄναξ.

ΘΕΟΚΛΥΜΕΝΟΣ

ἀλλ᾽ εἶα· τοὺς μὲν Πελοπιδῶν ἐῶ νόμους·
1430 καθαρὰ γὰρ ἡμῖν δώματ᾽· οὐ γὰρ ἐνθάδε
ψυχὴν ἀφῆκε Μενέλεως· ἴτω δέ τις
φράσων ὑπάρχοις τοῖς ἐμοῖς φέρειν γάμων
ἀγάλματ᾽ οἴκους εἰς ἐμούς· πᾶσαν δὲ χρὴ
γαῖαν βοᾶσθαι μακαρίαις ὑμνῳδίαις,
1435 ὑμέναιος Ἑλένης κἀμὸς ὡς ζηλωτὸς ᾖ.

1422 κἀκεῖ τἀνθάδ᾽, ὡς Herwerden

HELEN

THEOCLYMENUS
Care for the dead is labor wasted.

HELEN
What we do here has some effect, I think, on the other world.

THEOCLYMENUS
You will find me no worse a husband than Menelaus.

HELEN
I find no fault with you. All I need now is fortune's blessing.

THEOCLYMENUS
That lies in your own hands: just show your good will toward me.

HELEN
I do not have to be taught at this point to love my friends.

THEOCLYMENUS
Do you want me to conduct this expedition myself and help you?

HELEN
Certainly not! No need to serve your own slaves, my lord!

THEOCLYMENUS
Very well, then. The rituals of the sons of Pelops I shall leave to you: my own house is free of stain since Menelaus did not die here. But let someone go and tell my subjects to bring wedding decorations into the house! All the land must be filled with the sound of happy singing so that Helen's marriage and mine may be truly enviable.

1424 με δεῖ Musgrave: μέλει L   1433 χρὴ Matthiae:
χρῆν L   1435 ὑμέναιος . . . κἀμὸς Paley: -ον . . . -ὸν L

σὺ δ᾽, ὦ ξέν᾽, ἐλθὼν πελαγίους ἐς ἀγκάλας
τῷ τῆσδε πρίν ποτ᾽ ὄντι δοὺς πόσει τάδε
πάλιν πρὸς οἴκους σπεῦδ᾽ ἐμὴν δάμαρτ᾽ ἔχων,
ὡς τοὺς γάμους τοὺς τῆσδε συνδαίσας ἐμοὶ
1440 στέλλῃ πρὸς οἴκους ἢ μένων εὐδαιμονῇς.

ΜΕΝΕΛΑΟΣ

ὦ Ζεῦ, πατήρ τε καὶ σοφὸς κλῄζῃ θεός,
βλέψον πρὸς ἡμᾶς καὶ μετάστησον κακῶν.
ἕλκουσι δ᾽ ἡμῖν πρὸς λέπας τὰς συμφορὰς
σπουδῇ σύναψαι· κἂν ἄκρᾳ θίγῃς χερί,
1445 ἥξομεν ἵν᾽ ἐλθεῖν βουλόμεσθα τῆς τύχης.
ἅλις δὲ μόχθων οὓς ἐμοχθοῦμεν πάρος.
κέκλησθέ μοι, θεοί, πόλλ᾽ ἄχρηστά που κλύειν
καὶ λύπρ᾽· ὀφείλω δ᾽ οὐκ ἀεὶ πράσσειν κακῶς,
ὀρθῷ δὲ βῆναι ποδί· μίαν δέ μοι χάριν
1450 δόντες τὸ λοιπὸν εὐτυχῆ με θήσετε.

ΧΟΡΟΣ

στρ. α

Φοίνισσα Σιδωνιὰς ὦ
ταχεῖα κώπα, ῥοθίοισι Νηρέως
εἰρεσία φίλα,
χοραγὲ τῶν καλλιχόρων
1455 δελφίνων, ὅταν αὔρας

1441 τε] γὰρ Kirchhoff
1443 λέπας Musgrave: λύπας L
1447 πόλλ᾽ ἄχρηστά που Willink: πολλὰ χρήστ᾽ ἐμοῦ L

174

Exit a servant by Eisodos B.

You, stranger, go and deliver these offerings into the arms of the sea to her former husband, then hurry back to the house again with my wife. You will be my guest at the marriage feast and then set out for home, or else stay here and have a happy life.

Exit THEOCLYMENUS into the skene.

MENELAUS

O Zeus, since you are called father and wise god, look on us and rescue us from trouble. As we pull our misfortunes up the steep cliff, help us with your good will! If you touch us with just the tip of your finger, we will arrive at the good fortune we desire. We have suffered enough in the past! You gods, I have called you many hard and unpleasant names. But I should not always be unfortunate but should be allowed to walk erect. If you grant me this one favor, you will make me blessed for all time to come.

Exit MENELAUS and HELEN with servants by Eisodos A.

CHORUS

O swift ship
of Sidon in Phoenicia, oared vessel
dear to Nereus' waves,
you lead in their lovely dances
the graceful dolphins when the sea

1452 Νηρέως Badham cl. *IT* 425–6: μ$\overline{ηρ}$ (h. e. μήτηρ) L
1455 αὔρας Badham: -αις L

πέλαγος ἀνήνεμον ἦ,
γλαυκὰ δὲ Πόντου θυγάτηρ
Γαλάνεια τάδ᾽ εἴπῃ·
Κατὰ μὲν ἱστία πετάσετ᾽ αὔ-
1460 ραις πλέοντες εἰναλίαις,
λάβετε δ᾽ εἰλατίνας πλάτας,
ὦ ναῦται ⟨ἴτε⟩ ναῦται,
πέμποντες εὐλιμένους
Περσείων οἴκων Ἑλέναν ἐπ᾽ ἀκτάς.

ἀντ. α
1465 ἦ που κόρας ἂν ποταμοῦ
παρ᾽ οἶδμα Λευκιππίδας ἢ πρὸ ναοῦ
Παλλάδος ἂν λάβοι,
χρόνῳ ξυνελθοῦσα χοροῖς
ἢ κώμοις Ὑακίνθου
1470 νύχιον ἐς εὐφροσύναν,
ὃν ἐξαμιλλασάμενος
τροχὸν ἀτέρμονα δίσκου
ἔκανε Φοῖβος, εἶτα Λακαί-
νᾳ γᾷ βούθυτον ἀμέραν
1475 ὁ Διὸς εἶπε σέβειν γόνος·
μόσχον θ᾽ ἂν λίπετ᾽ οἴκοις
⟨δέρκοιτ᾽ ἂν Ἑρμιόναν,⟩
ἃς οὔπω πεῦκαι πρὸ γάμων ἔλαμψαν.

1456 ἀνήνεμον Murray: νήνεμον L
1459 πετάσετ᾽ Willink: -σατ᾽ L
1460 πλέοντες Willink: λιπόντες L
1462 ⟨ἴτε⟩ Jackson cl. Ba. 83   1467 λάβοι Pflugk: -οις L

is calm and windless
and the Sea's gray-eyed daughter
Galeneia[28] says:
"You will spread your sails
and run before the sea breezes,
but take now your oars of pine,
O sailors, ⟨go⟩ sailors,
as you bring Helen home to the fair-harbored strand
settled by Perseus."

I think she will find the daughters
of Leucippus by the river or before
the temple of Pallas,
as she arrives home at the time of the dances
or revels of Hyacinth
and their nightlong feasting,
Hyacinth, whom Phoebus,
trying to hurl far the round discus,
killed, and thereafter to the land
of Lacedaemon the son of Zeus
gave order to keep a day of sacrifice.
And ⟨she may see⟩ the calf she left
in the house, ⟨Hermione,⟩
whose marriage torches have not yet gleamed.

[28] Goddess of windless calm.

1470 εὐφροσύναν Matthiae: -φρόναν L
1472 τροχὸν ἀτέρμονα Willink: τροχῷ τέρμονι L
1473 εἶτα Willink: τᾷ L: ὅθεν Hermann
1475 Διὸς Heath: Δ- δ' L
1476 λίπετ' Jackson: λίποιτ' L   post h. v. lac. indic. Heath

στρ. β

δι᾽ αἰθέρος εἴθε ποτανοὶ
γενοίμεθ᾽ ὅπᾳ Λιβύας
1480 οἰωνῶν στιχάδες
ὄμβρον χειμέριον λιποῦ-
σαι νίσονται πρεσβυτάτου
σύριγγι πειθόμεναι
1485 ποιμένος, ὃς ἄβροχα πεδία καρποφόρα τε γᾶς
ἐπιπετόμενος ἰαχεῖ.
ὦ πταναὶ δολιχαύχενες,
σύννομοι νεφέων δρόμου,
βᾶτε Πλειάδας ὑπὸ μέσας
1490 Ὠρίωνά τ᾽ ἐννύχιον,
καρύξατ᾽ ἀγγελίαν,
Εὐρώταν ἐφεζόμεναι,
Μενέλεως ὅτι Δαρδάνου
πόλιν ἑλὼν δόμον ἥξει.

ἀντ. β

1495 μόλοιτέ ποθ᾽ ἵππιον οἶμον
δι᾽ αἰθέρος ἱέμενοι
παῖδες Τυνδαρίδαι,
λαμπρῶν ἀστέρων ὑπ᾽ ἀέλ-
λαις οἳ ναίετ᾽ οὐράνιοι,
1500 σωτῆρε τᾶς Ἑλένας
ἅλιον ἐπ᾽ οἶδμα κυανόχροά τε κυμάτων

1478 αἰθέρος J. H. H. Schmidt: ἀέρος L   1479 γενοίμεθ᾽
ὅπᾳ Pearson: -μεθα L   Λιβύας Hartung: Λίβνες L

178

Could I but wing through the firmament
to where the Libyan
birds, rank on rank,
fleeing the wintry weather,
fly obedient
to the piping of their eldest,
their shepherd, who flies to the rainless and fruitful lands
and shrills as he goes!
O winging long-necks,
consorts of the racing clouds,
pass beneath the Pleiades in mid sky
and Orion aloft in the night
and speak out your news,
as you settle on the Eurotas,
that Menelaus, having taken Dardanus' city,
will be coming home.

On the path your horses make
go winging through the heavens,
you sons of Tyndareus,
who dwell above under the whirling
of the bright stars:
go as Helen's saviors
over the salty billows and the dark

1480 οἰωνῶν Bothe: -οὶ L   στιχάδες Burges: στολάδες L
1481 ὄμβρον χειμέρον λιποῦσαι Hermann: ὄ- λ- χ- L
1482 πρεσβυτάτου Paley: -τάτᾳ L
1495 οἶμον Blaydes: οἶμα L
1500 σωτῆρε Musgrave: -ες L   τᾶς] βᾶθ' Kannicht
1501 ἅλιον ἐπ' οἶδμα Fritzsche: γλαυκὸν ἐπ' οἶδμ' ἅλιον L

ῥόθια πολιὰ θαλάσσας,
ναύταις εὐαεῖς ἀνέμων
1505 πέμποντες Διόθεν πνοάς,
δύσκλειαν δ' ἀπὸ συγγόνου
βάλετε βαρβάρων λεχέων,
ἃν Ἰδαιᾶν ἐρίδων
ποιναθεῖσ' ἐκτήσατ' ἄγαν,
1510 οὐκ ἐλθοῦσά ποτ' Ἰλίου
Φοιβείους ἐπὶ πύργους.

ΑΓΓΕΛΟΣ
†ἄναξ, τὰ κάκιστ' ἐν δόμοις εὑρήκαμεν·†
ὡς καίν' ἀκούσῃ πήματ' ἐξ ἐμοῦ τάχα.

ΘΕΟΚΛΥΜΕΝΟΣ
τί δ' ἔστιν;

ΑΓΓΕΛΟΣ
ἄλλης ἐκπόνει μνηστεύματα
1515 γυναικός· Ἑλένη γὰρ βέβηκ' ἔξω χθονός.

ΘΕΟΚΛΥΜΕΝΟΣ
πτεροῖσιν ἀρθεῖσ' ἢ πεδοστιβεῖ ποδί;

1508 Ἰδαιᾶν Diggle: -δαίων L
1509 ἐκτήσατ' ἄγαν Willink: -σατο τὰν L
1510 ἐλθοῦσά ποτ' Bothe: -σαν ἐς L
1512 del. Dindorf ut lacunae resarciendae gratia confictum

gray waves of the sea,
bringing the sailors
fair breezes from Zeus.
Strike from your sister's name
the reproach of a barbarian marriage,
reproach she had to bear in full measure,
punishment for the strife on Ida,
though she never went to the towers
of Troy built by Phoebus.

Enter from the skene THEOCLYMENUS. *Enter by Eisodos
A a servant of Theoclymenus as* MESSENGER.

MESSENGER
[My lord, we have found things very ill in the house.]²⁹ So
strange is the trouble you will soon hear from me.

THEOCLYMENUS
What is it?

MESSENGER
Arrange for a marriage with someone else: Helen has left
the country!

THEOCLYMENUS
Flying on wings, or walking on the earth?

²⁹ This line, which is deficient both in meter and in sense, was
doubtless intended as a stopgap replacement for several lines lost
accidentally. We would expect the entrance of Theoclymenus to
be handled roughly thus: ‹MESS: Where's the king? I must speak
with him. CHO. LEADER: Here, he's just coming out. MESS: My
lord, I have just come from the seashore with news. THEO: News
of the funeral rites of Menelaus? MESS: News to astonish you,› so
strange is the trouble you will soon hear from me.

EURIPIDES

ΑΓΓΕΛΟΣ

Μενέλαος αὐτὴν ἐκπεπόρθμευται χθονός,
ὃς αὐτὸς αὑτὸν ἦλθεν ἀγγέλλων θανεῖν.

ΘΕΟΚΛΥΜΕΝΟΣ

ὦ δεινὰ λέξας· τίς δέ νιν ναυκληρία
1520 ἐκ τῆσδ᾽ ἀπῆρε χθονός; ἄπιστα γὰρ λέγεις.

ΑΓΓΕΛΟΣ

ἥν γε ξένῳ δίδως σύ· τοὺς δὲ σοὺς ἑλὼν
ναύτας βέβηκεν, ὡς ἂν ἐν βραχεῖ μάθῃς.

ΘΕΟΚΛΥΜΕΝΟΣ

πῶς; εἰδέναι πρόθυμος· οὐ γὰρ ἐλπίδων
ἔσω βέβηκε μίαν ὑπερδραμεῖν χέρα
1525 τοσούσδε ναύτας ὧν ἀπεστάλης μέτα.

ΑΓΓΕΛΟΣ

ἐπεὶ λιποῦσα τούσδε βασιλείους δόμους
ἡ τοῦ Διὸς παῖς πρὸς θάλασσαν ἐστάλη,
σοφώταθ᾽ ἁβρὸν πόδα τιθεῖσ᾽ ἀνέστενεν
πόσιν πέλας παρόντα κοὐ τεθνηκότα.
1530 ὡς δ᾽ ἤλθομεν σῶν περίβολον νεωρίων,
Σιδωνίαν ναῦν πρωτόπλουν καθείλκομεν
ζυγῶν τε πεντήκοντα κἀρετμῶν μέτρα
ἔχουσαν. ἔργου δ᾽ ἔργον ἐξημείβετο·
ὁ μὲν γὰρ ἱστόν, ὁ δὲ πλάτην καθίστατο
1535 †ταρσόν τε χειρὶ† λευκά θ᾽ ἱστί᾽ †εἰς ἓν ἦν†
πηδάλιά τε ζεύγλαισι παρακαθίετο.
    κἀν τῷδε μόχθῳ, τοῦτ᾽ ἄρα σκοπούμενοι,
Ἕλληνες ἄνδρες Μενέλεῳ ξυνέμποροι

182

MESSENGER

Menelaus has ferried her out of the land, Menelaus who came bearing the news of his own death!

THEOCLYMENUS

This is dreadful! What ship carried them from here? Your report is incredible.

MESSENGER

The ship you gave the foreigner. He took your sailors captive and has gone. That is the story in brief.

THEOCLYMENUS

How? I must know. It is beyond all reckoning that one man should overcome so many sailors, the whole crew that went with you.

MESSENGER

Zeus's daughter left the palace and set off for the sea, and as she walked delicately along she cleverly lamented for her husband—who was not dead but nearby. When we reached your dockyard walls, we launched a new Sidonian vessel fitted for fifty rowers. And now one task succeeded another. One man put on board the mast, and another the oars; the white sails were put in place, and the rudders were let down into the sea on their crossbars.

While the men were performing these tasks, some Greeks, Menelaus' crew, who it seems had been waiting

---

1521 δὲ Kirchhoff: τε L   ἑλὼν Schenkl: ἔχων L
1524 βέβηκε Murray: -κα L
1534–5 πλάτης . . . ταρσὸν κατήρη Wecklein

προσῆλθον ἀκτὰς ναυφθόροις ἠσκημένοι
1540 πέπλοισιν, εὐειδεῖς μέν, αὐχμηροὶ δ' ὁρᾶν.
ἰδὼν δέ νιν παρόντας Ἀτρέως γόνος
προσεῖπε δόλιον οἶκτον ἐς μέσον φέρων·
Ὦ τλήμονες, πῶς ἐκ τίνος νεώς ποτε
Ἀχαιίδος θραύσαντες ἥκετε σκάφος;
1545 ἀλλ' Ἀτρέως παῖδ' ὀλόμενον συνθάπτετε,
ὃν Τυνδαρὶς παῖς ἥδ' ἀπόντα κενοταφεῖ.
οἱ δ' ἐκβαλόντες δάκρυα ποιητῷ τρόπῳ
ἐς ναῦν ἐχώρουν Μενέλεῳ ποντίσματα
φέροντες. ἡμῖν δ' ἦν μὲν ἥδ' ὑποψία
1550 λόγος τ' ἐν ἀλλήλοισι, τῶν ἐπεσβατῶν
ὡς πλῆθος εἴη· διεσιωπῶμεν δ' ὅμως
τοὺς σοὺς λόγους σῴζοντες· ἄρχειν γὰρ νεὼς
ξένον κελεύσας πάντα συνέχεας τάδε.
καὶ τἄλλα μὲν δὴ ῥᾳδίως ἔσω νεὼς
1555 ἐθέμεθα κουφίζοντα· ταύρειος δὲ ποὺς
οὐκ ἤθελ' ὀρθὸς σανίδα προσβῆναι κάτα,
ἀλλ' ἐξεβρυχᾶτ' ὄμμ' ἀναστρέφων κύκλῳ,
κυρτῶν τε νῶτα κὰς κέρας παρεμβλέπων
μὴ θιγγάνειν ἀπεῖργεν. ὁ δ' Ἑλένης πόσις
1560 ἐκάλεσεν· Ὦ πέρσαντες Ἰλίου πόλιν,
οὐχ εἶ' ἀναρπάσαντες Ἑλλήνων νόμῳ
νεανίαις ὤμοισι ταύρειον δέμας
ἐς πρῷραν ἐμβαλεῖτε (φάσγανον δ' ἅμα
πρόχειρον αἴρει) σφάγια τῷ τεθνηκότι;
1565 οἱ δ' ἐς κέλευσμ' ἐλθόντες ἐξανήρπασαν
ταῦρον φέροντές τ' εἰσέθεντο σέλματα.

for this moment, came to the beach. Their clothes had
been ruined by shipwreck, and although they were hand-
some, their appearance was squalid. Atreus' son saw them
arrive and called to them, producing a deceptive display of
pity: "Poor men, from what Greek vessel were you ship-
wrecked? But help me bury the son of Atreus, who has
died. Tyndareus' daughter here is giving him a funeral in
effigy."

The men shed feigned tears and embarked, bringing
offerings to throw overboard for Menelaus. We began to
be suspicious and noted to each other the large number of
passengers we had taken on. But with your commands in
mind we raised no objection: it was you who ruined it all by
putting the foreigner in charge of the ship.

All the other things, which were light, we easily brought
on board. But the bull refused to walk straight up the
plank. He bellowed, rolling his eyes and arching his back.
He looked fiercely through his horns, warning us not to
touch him. But Helen's husband called out, "Come, sack-
ers of Ilium, pick up the bull, Greek fashion, on your young
shoulders and put him in the prow," and here he raised his
drawn sword, "as an offering to the dead man."

They obeyed his order, picked up the bull, and set
it amid the rowing benches. As for the horse, Menelaus

1539 ἀκτὰς Heiland: -αῖς L   ἠσκημένοι Porson: ἠσθ- L
1543 νεώς] fort. πόλεως
1545 ἀλλ' Zuntz: ἆρ' L
1550 τ' L. Dindorf: δ' L
1563 δ' Diggle: τ' L
1564 αἴρει Hartung: ὤσει L

μονάμπυκος δὲ Μενέλεως ψήχων δέρην
μέτωπά τ᾽ ἐξέπεισεν ἐσβῆναι δόρυ.
τέλος δ᾽, ἐπειδὴ ναῦς τὰ πάντ᾽ ἐδέξατο,
1570 πλήσασα κλιμακτῆρας εὐσφύρῳ ποδὶ
Ἑλένη καθέζετ᾽ ἐν μέσοις ἐδωλίοις
ὅ τ᾽ οὐκέτ᾽ ὢν λόγοισι Μενέλεως πέλας·
ἄλλοι δὲ τοίχους δεξιοὺς λαιούς τ᾽ ἴσοι
ἀνὴρ παρ᾽ ἄνδρ᾽ ἕζονθ᾽, ὑφ᾽ εἵμασι ξίφη
1575 λαθραῖ᾽ ἔχοντες, ῥόθιά τ᾽ ἐξεπίμπλατο
βοῆς, κελευστοῦ φθέγμαθ᾽ ὡς ἠκούσαμεν.
    ἐπεὶ δὲ γαίας ἦμεν οὔτ᾽ ἄγαν πρόσω
οὔτ᾽ ἐγγύς, οὕτως ἦρετ᾽ οἰάκων φύλαξ·
Ἔτ᾽, ὦ ξέν᾽, ἐς τὸ πρόσθεν—ἢ καλῶς ἔχει;—
1580 πλεύσωμεν; ἀρχαὶ γὰρ νεὼς μέλουσι σοί.
ὁ δ᾽ εἶφ᾽· Ἅλις μοι. δεξιᾷ δ᾽ ἑλὼν ξίφος
ἐς πρῷραν εἶρπε κἀπὶ ταυρείῳ σφαγῇ
σταθεὶς νεκρῶν μὲν οὐδενὸς μνήμην ἔχει,
τέμνων δὲ λαιμὸν ηὔχετ᾽· Ὦ ναίων ἅλα
1585 πόντιε Πόσειδον Νηρέως θ᾽ ἁγναὶ κόραι,
σώσατέ μ᾽ ἐπ᾽ ἀκτὰς Ναυπλίας δάμαρτά τε
ἄσυλον ἐκ γῆς. αἵματος δ᾽ ἀπορροαὶ
ἐς οἶδμ᾽ ἐσηκόντιζον οὔριοι ξένῳ.
    καί τις τόδ᾽ εἶπε· Δόλιος ἡ ναυκληρία.
1590 πάλιν πλέωμεν· δεξιὰν κέλευε σύ,
σὺ δὲ στρέφ᾽ οἴακ᾽. ἐκ δὲ ταυρείου φόνου
Ἀτρέως σταθεὶς παῖς ἀνεβόησε συμμάχους·
Τί μέλλετ᾽, ὦ γῆς Ἑλλάδος λωτίσματα,
σφάζειν φονεύειν βαρβάρους νεώς τ᾽ ἄπο

stroked its neck and forehead and persuaded it to get on board. Finally, when the ship had received all its cargo, Helen, climbing the ladder with her dainty feet, sat down in the middle of the rowing benches, and next to her sat Menelaus, the supposed dead man. The rest of the Greeks sat down in close formation on the right and left bulkheads, with swords hidden beneath their cloaks. The surge was filled with our shouting as we obeyed the boatswain's orders.

When we were neither too far from the land nor too near, the steersman asked, "Stranger, shall we row further, or is this good enough? You are in charge of the boat." And Menelaus replied, "That's enough." Then taking his sword in his right hand he went up to the prow. Standing there for the bull sacrifice he said nothing about any dead man but as he cut its throat he prayed, "O Poseidon, dweller in the sea, and all you holy daughters of Nereus, bring me and my wife safe and inviolate from this land to Nauplia's shore!" The streams of blood leapt from the animal's neck into the water, a good omen for the foreigner.

Someone said, "This voyage is a trick. Let's row back to land! You, order the ship to starboard, and you, turn the rudder!" But Atreus' son, the bull sacrifice completed, shouted to his friends from where he stood, "Picked fighting men of Greece, no more delaying now! Kill, cut down the barbarians, throw them from the ship into the brine!"

1567–8 del. W. G. Clark

1567 μονάμπυκος Schenkl: -ον L

1576 κελευστοῦ Pierson: κελεύθου L

1583 ἔχει Murray: ἔχων L   1588 οὔριοι Elmsley: -ια L

1590 δεξιὰν Faehse: ἀξίαν L

1595 ῥίπτειν ἐς οἶδμα; ναυβάταις δὲ τοῖσι σοῖς
βοᾷ κελευστὴς τὴν ἐναντίαν ὄπα·
Οὐχ εἶ' ὁ μέν τις λοῖσθον ἀρεῖται δόρυ,
ὁ δὲ ζύγ' ἄξας, ὁ δ' ἀφελὼν σκαλμοῦ πλάτην
καθαιματώσει κρᾶτα πολεμίων ξένων;
1600 ὀρθοὶ δ' ἀνῇξαν πάντες, οἱ μὲν ἐν χεροῖν
κορμοὺς ἔχοντες ναυτικούς, οἱ δὲ ξίφη·
φόνῳ δὲ ναῦς ἐρρεῖτο. παρακέλευσμα δ' ἦν
πρύμνηθεν Ἑλένης· Ποῦ τὸ Τρωικὸν κλέος;
δείξατε πρὸς ἄνδρας βαρβάρους. σπουδῆς δ' ὕπο
1605 ἔπιπτον, οἱ δ' ὠρθοῦντο, τοὺς δὲ κειμένους
νεκροὺς ἂν εἶδες. Μενέλεως δ' ἔχων ὅπλα,
ὅπῃ νοσοῖεν ξύμμαχοι κατασκοπῶν,
ταύτῃ προσῆγε χειρὶ δεξιᾷ ξίφος,
⟨πάντας καθιστὰς ἐς φυγὴν ἐναντίους⟩
ὥστ' ἐκκολυμβᾶν ναός· ἠρήμωσε δὲ
1610 σῶν ναυβατῶν ἐρέτμ'· ἐπ' οἰάκων δὲ βὰς
ἄνακτ' ἐς Ἑλλάδ' εἶπεν εὐθύνειν δόρυ.
οἱ δ' ἱστὸν ᾖραν, οὔριοι δ' ἦκον πνοαί.
βεβᾶσι δ' ἐκ γῆς. διαφυγὼν δ' ἐγὼ φόνον
καθῆκ' ἐμαυτὸν εἰς ἅλ' ἄγκυραν πάρα·
1615 ἤδη δὲ κάμνονθ' ὁρμιατόνων μέ τις
ἀνείλετ' ἐς δὲ γαῖαν ἐξέβησέ σοι
τάδ' ἀγγελοῦντα. σώφρονος δ' ἀπιστίας
οὐκ ἔστιν οὐδὲν χρησιμώτερον βροτοῖς.

ΧΟΡΟΣ
οὐκ ἄν ποτ' ηὔχουν οὔτε σ' οὔθ' ἡμᾶς λαθεῖν

The boatswain shouted the opposite order to your sailors, "Quick! You take a spar as a weapon, you break off one of the thwarts, and you take an oar from its thole! Bloody the heads of these foreign enemies!"

Everyone stood up, one side with oars in their hands, the other with swords. The ship ran with blood. Helen from the stern urged them on: "Where is the glory you won at Troy? Show these barbarians!" In the hard fight men fell down or kept their feet, but those who fell you could see were dead. Menelaus, clothed in armor, watched to see where his friends were weakest and there he plied the sword in his right hand, ⟨putting all his adversaries to flight⟩ so that they leapt into the water from the ship: no oar was left with a rower to man it. Going to the steersman he ordered him to make for Greece. His men raised the mast, and the winds blew favorable.

They have left the country. I myself escaped being killed by throwing myself into the sea near the anchor. I was already worn out when a fisherman picked me up and brought me to land to bring you this news. The best thing for a mortal man is to be sober and skeptical.

Exit MESSENGER *by Eisodos B.*

CHORUS LEADER

I would never have expected, my lord, that Menelaus

1607 ὅπῃ Elmsley: ὅποι L
1608 post h. v. lac. indic. Rassow
1612 ἦραν Diggle: ἦρον L   οὔριοι Hermann: -αι L

189

1620 Μενέλαον, ὦναξ, ὡς ἐλάνθανεν παρών.

ΘΕΟΚΛΥΜΕΝΟΣ

ὦ γυναικείαις τέχναισιν αἱρεθεὶς ἐγὼ τάλας·
ἐκπεφεύγασιν γάμοι με. κεἰ μὲν ἦν ἁλώσιμος
ναῦς διώγμασιν, πονήσας εἷλον ἂν τάχα ξένους·
νῦν δὲ τὴν προδοῦσαν ἡμᾶς τεισόμεσθα σύγγονον,
1625 ἥτις ἐν δόμοις ὁρῶσα Μενέλεων οὐκ εἶπέ μοι.
τοιγὰρ οὔποτ᾽ ἄλλον ἄνδρα ψεύσεται μαντεύμασιν.

ΘΕΡΑΠΩΝ Β

οὗτος, ὤ, ποῖ σὸν πόδ᾽ αἴρεις, δέσποτ᾽, ἐς ποῖον
φόνον;

ΘΕΟΚΛΥΜΕΝΟΣ

οἷπερ ἡ δίκη κελεύει μ᾽· ἀλλ᾽ ἀφίστασ᾽ ἐκποδών.

ΘΕΡΑΠΩΝ Β

οὐκ ἀφήσομαι πέπλων σῶν· μεγάλα γὰρ σπεύδεις
κακά.

ΘΕΟΚΛΥΜΕΝΟΣ

1630 ἀλλὰ δεσποτῶν κρατήσεις δοῦλος ὤν;

ΘΕΡΑΠΩΝ Β

φρονῶ γὰρ εὖ.

ΘΕΟΚΛΥΜΕΝΟΣ

οὐκ ἔμοιγ᾽, εἰ μή μ᾽ ἐάσεις . . .

ΘΕΡΑΠΩΝ Β

οὐ μὲν οὖν σ᾽ ἐάσομεν.

1627n **Θεράπων** Clark: Xo. L

190

could be here without your and our knowing it, but so he was.

THEOCLYMENUS

Woe is me, undone by womanish tricks! My bride has escaped! If pursuit could catch the ship, I would make the effort and capture these foreigners. But as things are, I will punish the sister who has betrayed me. She saw that Menelaus was in the house but did not tell me. Never will she dupe another man with her prophecies!

Theoclymenus starts to go inside. Enter from the skene *a* SECOND SERVANT, *who bars his way.*

SECOND SERVANT

You there, master, where are you going? What murder are you going to commit?

THEOCLYMENUS

I'm going where justice bids me go. Get out of my way!

SECOND SERVANT

(*Taking hold of his cloak*) I will not let go of your garments: you are trying to do a grave wrong.

THEOCLYMENUS

Will you, a slave, control your master?

SECOND SERVANT

Yes, since I have sense.

THEOCLYMENUS

Not in my eyes you don't, unless you allow me . . .

SECOND SERVANT

But I won't allow you.

EURIPIDES

ΘΕΟΚΛΥΜΕΝΟΣ

. . . σύγγονον κτανεῖν κακίστην . . .

ΘΕΡΑΠΩΝ Β

εὐσεβεστάτην μὲν οὖν.

ΘΕΟΚΛΥΜΕΝΟΣ

. . . ἥ με προύδωκεν . . .

ΘΕΡΑΠΩΝ Β

καλήν γε προδοσίαν, δίκαια δρᾶν.

ΘΕΟΚΛΥΜΕΝΟΣ

. . . τἀμὰ λέκτρ᾽ ἄλλῳ διδοῦσα.

ΘΕΡΑΠΩΝ Β

τοῖς γε κυριωτέροις.

ΘΕΟΚΛΥΜΕΝΟΣ

1635   κύριος δὲ τῶν ἐμῶν τίς;

ΘΕΡΑΠΩΝ Β

ὃς ἔλαβεν πατρὸς πάρα.

ΘΕΟΚΛΥΜΕΝΟΣ

ἀλλ᾽ ἔδωκεν ἡ τύχη μοι.

ΘΕΡΑΠΩΝ Β

τὸ δὲ χρεὼν ἀφείλετο.

ΘΕΟΚΛΥΜΕΝΟΣ

οὐ σὲ τἀμὰ χρὴ δικάζειν.

ΘΕΡΑΠΩΝ Β

ἤν γε βελτίω λέγω.

THEOCLYMENUS

. . . to kill my vile sister . . .

SECOND SERVANT

No, your god-fearing sister.

THEOCLYMENUS

. . . who has played traitor to me . . .

SECOND SERVANT

And a noble piece of treachery it was, a righteous act.

THEOCLYMENUS

. . . by giving my bride to another.

SECOND SERVANT

Another with a better claim.

THEOCLYMENUS

Who has a claim to what is mine?

SECOND SERVANT

The man who received her from her father.

THEOCLYMENUS

But chance gave her to me.

SECOND SERVANT

And fate took her away.

THEOCLYMENUS

You should not act as judge in what belongs to me.

SECOND SERVANT

Yes, if I am in the right.

1637 λέγω] φρονῶ F. W. Schmidt

EURIPIDES

ΘΕΟΚΛΥΜΕΝΟΣ

ἀρχόμεσθ᾽ ἄρ᾽, οὐ κρατοῦμεν.

ΘΕΡΑΠΩΝ Β

ὅσια δρᾶν, τὰ δ᾽ ἔκδικ᾽ οὔ.

ΘΕΟΚΛΥΜΕΝΟΣ

κατθανεῖν ἐρᾶν ἔοικας.

ΘΕΡΑΠΩΝ Β

κτεῖνε· σύγγονον δὲ σὴν

1640 οὐ κτενεῖς ἡμῶν ἑκόντων ἀλλ᾽ ἔμ᾽· ὡς πρὸ δεσποτῶν
τοῖσι γενναίοισι δούλοις εὐκλεέστατον θανεῖν.

ΚΑΣΤΩΡ

ἐπίσχες ὀργὰς αἷσιν οὐκ ὀρθῶς φέρῃ,
Θεοκλύμενε, γαίας τῆσδ᾽ ἄναξ· δισσοὶ δέ σε
Διόσκοροι καλοῦμεν, οὓς Λήδα ποτὲ
1645 ἔτικτεν Ἑλένην θ᾽, ἣ πέφευγε σοὺς δόμους.
1646 οὐ γὰρ πεπρωμένοισιν ὀργίζῃ γάμοις·
1650 οὐ μὲν γὰρ αἰεί, τὸν παρόντα δ᾽ ἐς χρόνον
κείνην κατοικεῖν σοῖσιν ἐν δόμοις ἐχρῆν.
ἐπεὶ δὲ Τροίας ἐξανεστάθη βάθρα
καὶ τοῖς θεοῖς παρέσχε τοὔνομ᾽, οὐκέτι
ἐν τοῖσι δ᾽ αὐτοῖς δεῖ νιν ἐζεῦχθαι γάμοις
1655 ἐλθεῖν τ᾽ ἐς οἴκους καὶ συνοικῆσαι πόσει.
1647 οὐδ᾽ ἡ θεᾶς Νηρῇδος ἔκγονος κόρη
ἀδικεῖ σ᾽ ἀδελφὴ Θεονόη, τὰ τῶν θεῶν
1649 τιμῶσα πατρός τ᾽ ἐνδίκους ἐπιστολάς.

1638 τὰ δ᾽ ἔκδικ᾽ οὔ Porson: τάνδ᾽ ἐκδικῶ L

HELEN

THEOCLYMENUS

So I am a subject, not the master.

SECOND SERVANT

You are master—but only to act piously, not wrongfully.

THEOCLYMENUS

You seem to be in love with death.

SECOND SERVANT

Kill me! I will not allow you to kill your sister but only me: it is a glorious thing for a noble slave to die for his mistress.

Enter on the mechane CASTOR *and Polydeuces.*

CASTOR

Theoclymenus, king of this land, halt! Cease from the anger that unjustly controls you! It is the two Dioscuri who call you, sons whom Leda once bore along with Helen, who has fled your house. The marriage you are angry about is one not destined to be. It was not fated that Helen should live for all time in your house but only up to the present: now that Troy's foundations have been destroyed and she has lent her name to the gods, she will live here no longer. She must remain yoked in the same marriage, return home, and live with her husband. And your sister Theonoe, daughter of the Nereid, did you no wrong in honoring the gods' laws and the just behests of her father.

1640 ἔμ’· ὡς Porson: ἐμὲ L
1641 δούλων Dawe
1642n Κάστωρ Bothe: Διόσκοροι L
1650–5 post 1646 trai. Kovacs, del. Willink
1650 οὐ . . . δ’ ἐς H. Cron: εἰ . . . νῦν L
1647 ἔκγονος Matthiae: -γόνη L

1656 ἀλλ' ἴσχε μὲν σῆς συγγόνου μέλαν ξίφος,
νόμιζε δ' αὐτὴν σωφρόνως πράσσειν τάδε.
πάλαι δ' ἀδελφὴν κἂν πρὶν ἐξεσώσαμεν,
ἐπείπερ ἡμᾶς Ζεὺς ἐποίησεν θεούς·
1660 ἀλλ' ἥσσον' ἦμεν τοῦ πεπρωμένου θ' ἅμα
καὶ τῶν θεῶν, οἷς ταῦτ' ἔδοξεν ὧδ' ἔχειν.
σοὶ μὲν τάδ' αὐδῶ, συγγόνῳ δ' ἐμῇ λέγω·
πλεῖ ξὺν πόσει σῷ· πνεῦμα δ' ἕξετ' οὔριον·
σωτῆρε δ' ἡμεῖς σὼ κασιγνήτω διπλὼ
1665 πόντον παριππεύοντε πέμψομεν πάτραν.
ὅταν δὲ κάμψῃς καὶ τελευτήσῃς βίον,
θεὸς κεκλήσῃ [καὶ Διοσκόρων μέτα
σπονδῶν μεθέξεις] ξένιά τ' ἀνθρώπων πάρα
ἕξεις μεθ' ἡμῶν· Ζεὺς γὰρ ὧδε βούλεται.
1670 οὗ δ' ὥρμισέν σε πρῶτα Μαιάδος τόκος
Σπάρτης ἀπάρας τὸν κατ' οὐρανὸν δρόμον,
κλέψας δέμας σὸν μὴ Πάρις γήμειέ σε,
φρουρὸν παρ' Ἀκτὴν τεταμένην νῆσον λέγω,
Ἑλένη τὸ λοιπὸν ἐν βροτοῖς κεκλήσεται,
1675 ἐπεὶ κλοπαίαν σ' ἐκ δόμων ἐδέξατο.
καὶ τῷ πλανήτῃ Μενέλεῳ θεῶν πάρα
μακάρων κατοικεῖν νῆσόν ἐστι μόρσιμον·
τοὺς εὐγενεῖς γὰρ οὐ στυγοῦσι δαίμονες,
τῶν δ' ἀναριθμήτων μᾶλλόν †εἰσιν οἱ πόνοι†.

1659 del. Nauck
1660 ἥσσον' Pierson: -νες L
1667b-8a del. F. W. Schmidt

196

So take your dark sword away from your sister: you must realize that she acted virtuously in this. We might have saved our sister long ago since Zeus made us gods. But we were overruled by fate and the other gods, who decided that these things should be thus.

Those are my words to you. To my sister I say, Sail on with your husband (you will have a favoring breeze), and we, your two brothers, galloping over the sea beside you, will escort you to your own country. When you come to the last lap of your life and die, you will be called a goddess [and in company with the Dioscuri you will receive libations] and like us you will receive gifts from mortals: Zeus wishes it so. The place the son of Maia first brought you on your journey through the sky from Sparta, stealing you away so that Paris might not have you—I mean the island that lies off Akte[30] and guards it—mortals shall henceforth call by the name Helen since it received you stolen from your home. As for the wanderer Menelaus, fate and the gods have ordained for him a life on the Island of the Blest. The gods do not hate the nobly born. But they endure more hardship than do men of no account.

[30] Akte, meaning "promontory" or "headland," was an older name of Attica.

1670 ὥρμισέν Rauchenstein: ὥρισέν L

1671 δρόμον Wilamowitz: δόμων L

1673 φρουρὸν Hermann: -οῦ L   τεταμένην Reiske: τεταγμένη L

1675 κλοπαίαν σ᾽ Herwerden: κλοπὰς L

1679 εἰσιν ἐν πόνοις Madvig: ἀσκοῦσιν πόνοι Dale

ΘΕΟΚΛΥΜΕΝΟΣ

1680 ὦ παῖδε Λήδας καὶ Διός, τὰ μὲν πάρος
νείκη μεθήσω σφῷν κασιγνήτης πέρι·
ἐγώ τ' ἀδελφὴν οὐκέτ' ἂν κτάνοιμ' ἐμήν,
κείνη τ' ἴτω πρὸς οἶκον, εἰ θεοῖς δοκεῖ.
ἴστον δ' ἀρίστης σωφρονεστάτης θ' ἅμα
1685 γεγῶτ' †ἀδελφῆς μονογενοῦς† ἀφ' αἵματος.
καὶ χαίρεθ' Ἑλένης οὕνεκ' εὐγενεστάτης
γνώμης, ὃ πολλαῖς ἐν γυναιξὶν οὐκ ἔνι.

ΧΟΡΟΣ

πολλαὶ μορφαὶ τῶν δαιμονίων,
πολλὰ δ' ἀέλπτως κραίνουσι θεοί·
1690 καὶ τὰ δοκηθέντ' οὐκ ἐτελέσθη,
τῶν δ' ἀδοκήτων πόρον ηὗρε θεός.
τοιόνδ' ἀπέβη τόδε πρᾶγμα.

1682 τ' Willink: δ' L
1683 τ' Lenting: δ' L
1685 fort. ἀδελφὼ (Willink) διογενοῦς

THEOCLYMENUS

O sons of Leda and Zeus, I give up my previous grudge in the matter of your sister! And I will not kill my sister, and Helen may go home if that is the gods' will! Know that you are brothers to a sister who is at once most brave and most virtuous. I wish you joy for the sake of Helen's most noble heart! Not many women have a heart like hers!

Exit CASTOR *and Polydeuces by the* mechane *and* THEOCLYMENUS *and* SECOND SERVANT *into the* skene.

CHORUS LEADER

What heaven sends has many shapes, and many things the gods accomplish against our expectation. What men look for is not brought to pass, but a god finds a way to achieve the unexpected. Such was the outcome of this story.

Exit CHORUS *by Eisodos B.*

PHOENICIAN WOMEN

INTRODUCTION

The story of the siege of Thebes—its attack by Oedipus' son Polynices with his Peloponnesian allies and its defense by his brother Eteocles—was part of the old epic tradition. The story is alluded to by characters in the *Iliad*, and for Hesiod it was, together with the war at Troy, the culminating battle of the heroic age. There were two epic poems, written after Homer but using pre-Homeric materials, that treated Theban legend, the *Oedipodea* and the *Thebaid*, both lost. The sixth-century lyric poet Stesichorus treated the quarrel of the brothers, and a fragment of this poem survives on papyrus. (See the Loeb *Greek Lyric III*, pp. 136–43.) Finally, Aeschylus in his *Seven against Thebes* (467 B.C.) and Sophocles in his *Antigone* (probably late 440s) dramatized this conflict and its aftermath.

Phoenician Women, Euripides' treatment of this story, was probably produced in 410 or 409. It may be the most varied in incident of his plays. It contains, for example, a scene where Antigone in a tower asks her servant to identify the attacking champions, a debate about justice between Eteocles and Polynices cast in the language of the fifth-century sophists, a scene of voluntary self-sacrifice where a divinity demands a young man as a victim and he offers himself, and a scene in which the blind Oedipus appears. Even though the play was already packed with incident when it came from the hand of Euripides, there is evidence that it was expanded in the fourth century and later, and scholarly controversy about the extent of interpolation complicates the task of the interpreter. An overview of the scenes of the play, with remarks on Euripides' mythical innovations, seems the best way to proceed.

Jocasta speaks the prologue. That she is still alive even after the discovery that she married her son and her husband's slayer is a striking innovation vis-à-vis Sophocles, who has her commit suicide. In the Stesichorus fragment, however, she may be the one who gives advice to her sons and tries to avert the dire events prophesied by Teiresias, the role she has in this play. She starts by outlining the history of the Theban royal house, beginning with Cadmus' arrival from Phoenician Tyre to found the city. After describing the fateful birth and exposure of Oedipus, his parricide and incest, his discovery of the truth and self-blinding, and the curse he laid on his sons, she reveals the present situation of the brothers: Eteocles and Polynices, in an attempt to avoid their father's curse, have made a deal that each is to rule Thebes in turn for a year; but Eteocles, his year being over, refused to give up power and banished Polynices, who went to Argos, married the daughter of King Adrastus, and returned with an army to vindicate his claim to the throne. And now Jocasta, in an attempt to avoid war, has arranged a truce so that the two brothers can parley. She prays that Zeus may save Thebes and grant her sons peace and concord. The audience are aware that Thebes will be saved but that the only concord her sons will find is in death. In the next scene Antigone appears with a servant on top of the *skene*. She asks him to identify the leaders of the seven contingents attacking the city, and their excited dialogue, Antigone singing and the servant speaking, makes vivid the danger besetting Thebes. The servant points out gloomily that the attackers have justice on their side and that the gods may take notice.

After their departure the Chorus enters. They are women of Phoenician Tyre who have been sent by their city to serve Apollo in Delphi as temple slaves (presumably for a fixed period) and have stopped at the kindred city of Thebes, where their visit has been unexpectedly prolonged because of the siege. They sing in honorific terms of Delphi, where not only Apollo but also Dionysus is worshiped, and of their blood tie to the city of Thebes. They too note that Polynices' cause is a just one.

Thereafter Polynices enters nervously, sword in hand. He has come to parley but is worried about an ambush. He has a tearful reunion with his mother in which she laments his absence and he the hardships of exile. It is quite characteristic of both Jocasta and Polynices to relate events whose significance they do not understand, though it would be unmistakable to the audience. Polynices' narrative of how he came to Argos and was chosen by Adrastus as his son-in-law shows all the hallmarks of divine guidance of events, and the role of Apollo is explicit in the oracle given to Adrastus that he should marry his daughters to a lion and a boar. But neither mother nor son seems to have any idea that these events are the work of Apollo, who is bringing to pass the second part of his prophecy to Laius, that the whole house would go down in bloody ruin.

Jocasta's attempt at reconciliation thus stands no chance of success, as becomes plain when Eteocles appears. Both brothers are under a curse, but in Eteocles this

205

takes the form of naked ambition. Like some of the sophists in the late fifth century, he says self-aggrandizement, unfettered by justice, is the highest aim of human life and proclaims that since he can take the throne away from Polynices, it would be unmanly to let piety (i.e. his sworn agreement) stand in the way. He is deaf to his mother's appeal to the equality to be found in nature, where daylight and darkness share equally in their yearly round. Polynices, likewise, will not obey his mother's request that he give up besieging his own city. The scene concludes with an exchange of insults and threats conducted in excited trochaic tetrameters.

In their first choral ode, the Chorus had established themselves as pious worshipers of the gods, glorifying Apollo and Delphi. In spite of the grim situation developing in the parley scene, this same stance persists as they tell of the divine origins of Thebes. It was founded, they say, by Apollo's command and is the birthplace of Dionysus. Where Jocasta had seen Thebes as cursed from the beginning (lines 3–5), they tell a different story, one of god-blessed beginnings whose effects continue. They tell the story of the dragon slain by Cadmus, whose teeth he sowed in the soil at Athena's behest. This was the origin of the ruling nobility of Thebes, the Spartoi or "Sown Men," who are its glory, as the Chorus later say. Epaphus, Persephone, Demeter as Mother Earth—all are bidden to come to the defense of this glorious city. All this evokes Thebes' better self, the part that will be saved when the cursed sons of Oedipus are no more.

Then Eteocles comes out accompanied by a messenger he is sending to find Creon: he has, he says, both public and private concerns to discuss with him. (The authorship of this scene opening is disputed: if it was written by Euripides, as the close parallel at *Suppliant Women* 381–98 suggests, the private concern is his sister's marriage to Haemon, which he is afraid he may not live to see.) Creon, for his part, appears at just this moment looking for Eteocles. In the ensuing discussion between the two men two decisions are made: Eteocles decides to choose seven Theban commanders to face the seven Argive champions at the seven gates of Thebes; and he arranges for Teiresias to be consulted, sending Creon's son Menoeceus to fetch him. Since the first decision will cause the fatal meeting of the brothers in battle and the second, as we will see, will secure the salvation of the city, the twofold outcome of the plot is already set in train. The cursed offspring of Oedipus must die, and the other, nobler, side of Thebes' heritage will save the city.

The contrast between the accursed sons of Oedipus and the noble and god-blessed part of Thebes' heritage figures prominently in the following stasimon. In the end of the second stanza the Chorus apparently reflect (the lines are desperately corrupt) on the pollution that attaches to the offspring of Oedipus' incestuous union with his mother. In the third stanza they call the birth of the Sown Men "fairest reproach that Thebes can hear," allude to the miraculous building of Thebes' walls, and hymn the military prowess of the city.

Teiresias arrives next, brought on his way by Menoeceus, Creon's son. In answer to Creon's question, the seer tells him that to save the city he must sacrifice Menoeceus: as a result of the killing of the dragon several generations ago Ares is angry (the dragon was his offspring), and only if a pure-bred Sown Man is sacrificed will Ares (and Earth) be appeased and the city saved. Creon reacts with horror to the idea of sacrificing Menoeceus, and Menoeceus agrees to make a run for it, leaving the country to save his life. Only when Creon has departed does he reveal to the Chorus that he intends to go to the sacred precinct where the dragon was born and slit his own throat, showing thereby the same bravery as a soldier in battle, who is willing to die for his country.

After a choral ode that ends in admiration for his selfless deed the first of two messengers arrive to tell Jocasta of the victory of the Thebans and the rout of the Argives. The city is thus saved. But the messenger has other news of her sons, news he is reluctant to share: they have decided to fight each other in single combat. Jocasta calls Antigone out of the palace, and together they rush to try to stop the duel. After a brief choral ode a second messenger tells an interlocutor (the Chorus in the original version, Creon in the revised text we have) that the brothers have killed one another and that Jocasta in grief has slain herself on top of them. Antigone then arrives with the three corpses and sings a lament, which is followed by a lamentation duet with Oedipus.

Just how Euripides ended his play we cannot tell: the transmitted ending, dubious in grammar and style and contradictory in its dramatic impetus (Antigone wants *both* to follow her father into exile *and* to stay in Thebes and bury Polynices), is unlikely to be from his hand. He need not have written much more: the "salvation of the city" motif has been adequately treated, and the death of the royal brothers has been lamented in sung verse. Perhaps Oedipus with Antigone went off into exile and the

Chorus uttered a final reflection on the inscrutable ways of divinity. We will probably never know.

One motif that runs through much of the play is what could be called the "I know not how" theme, where someone says he doesn't know how a certain ostensibly chance event happened, thereby inviting the audience to speculate on the reason. The reason in this play is always a supernatural one: see 33 (the motive for Oedipus' search for his parents, coinciding with Laius' visit to Delphi), 49 (Oedipus' success with the Sphinx's riddle), 408ff. (how Polynices happened to marry Adrastus' daughter), 1466 (how the Thebans routed the Argives). A related theme is the ironic prayer: 85 (Jocasta prays for concord for her sons), 467–8 (Jocasta prays that "one of the gods" be judge and reconciler, fulfilled when Hades takes this role), 586–7 (the Chorus Leader prays for agreement between the sons). Finally, in the Second Messenger's speech we see how Apollo's prophecy (68) is ironically fulfilled: the brothers "divide" their patrimony when each of them takes a mouthful of dirt.

SELECT BIBLIOGRAPHY

Editions

A. C. Pearson (Cambridge, 1909).
J. U. Powell (London, 1911).
E. Craik (Warminster, 1988).
D. J. Mastronarde (Leipzig, 1988).
———(Cambridge, 1994).

Literary Criticism

M. Arthur, "The Curse of Civilization: the Choral Odes of *Phoenissae*," *HSCP* 81 (1977), 163–85.

D. J. Conacher, "Themes in the Exodus of Euripides' *Phoenissae*," *Phoenix* 21 (1967), 92–101.

H. Erbse, "Beiträge zum Verständnis der euripideischen Phoinissen," *Philologus* 110 (1966), 1–34.

W. H. Friedrich, "Prolegomena zu den Phönissen," *Hermes* 74 (1939), 265–300.

C. Mueller-Goldingen, *Untersuchungen zu den Phönissen des Euripides* (Stuttgart, 1985).

A. Podlecki, "Some Themes in Euripides' *Phoenissae*," *TAPA* 93 (1962), 355–73.

E. Rawson, "Family and Fatherland in Euripides' *Phoenissae*," *GRBS* 11 (1970), 109–27.

J. de Romilly, "The *Phoenican Women* of Euripides: Topicality in Greek Tragedy," *Bucknell Review* 15 (1967), 108–32.

S. Saïd, "Euripide ou l'attente déçue: l'exemple des Phéniciennes," *ASNP* ser. 3, 15 (1985), 501–27.

F. I. Zeitlin, "Thebes: Theater of Self and Society in Athenian Drama," in J. J. Winkler and F. I. Zeitlin, edd., *Nothing To Do with Dionysos? Athenian Drama in Its Social Context* (Princeton, 1990), pp. 130–67.

Dramatis Personae

ΙΟΚΑΣΤΗ	JOCASTA, mother and wife of Oedipus
ΘΕΡΑΠΩΝ	SERVANT
ΑΝΤΙΓΟΝΗ	ANTIGONE, daughter of Oedipus and Jocasta
ΧΟΡΟΣ	CHORUS of Phoenician temple slaves
ΠΟΛΥΝΕΙΚΗΣ	POLYNICES, son of Oedipus living in exile
ΕΤΕΟΚΛΗΣ	ETEOCLES, son of Oedipus living in Thebes
ΚΡΕΩΝ	CREON, brother of Jocasta
ΤΕΙΡΕΣΙΑΣ	TEIRESIAS, a seer of Thebes
ΜΕΝΟΙΚΕΥΣ	MENOECEUS, son of Creon
ΑΓΓΕΛΟΣ Α	MESSENGER
ΑΓΓΕΛΟΣ Β	SECOND MESSENGER
ΟΙΔΙΠΟΥΣ	OEDIPUS

Nonspeaking role: Teiresias' daughter

A Note On Staging

The *skene* represents the royal palace of Thebes. Eisodos A leads to places within Thebes, Eisodos B to the battlefield and foreign parts.

ΦΟΙΝΙΣΣΑΙ

ΙΟΚΑΣΤΗ

[Ὦ τὴν ἐν ἄστροις οὐρανοῦ τέμνων ὁδὸν
καὶ χρυσοκολλήτοισιν ἐμβεβὼς δίφροις]
Ἥλιε, θοαῖς ἵπποισιν εἱλίσσων φλόγα,
ὡς δυστυχῆ Θήβαισι τῇ τόθ᾽ ἡμέρᾳ
5 ἀκτῖν᾽ ἐφῆκας, Κάδμος ἡνίκ᾽ ἦλθε γῆν
τήνδ᾽, ἐκλιπὼν Φοίνισσαν ἐναλίαν χθόνα·
ὃς παῖδα γήμας Κύπριδος Ἁρμονίαν ποτὲ
Πολύδωρον ἐξέφυσε, τοῦ δὲ Λάβδακον
φῦναι λέγουσιν, ἐκ δὲ τοῦδε Λάιον.
10 ἐγὼ δὲ παῖς μὲν κλῄζομαι Μενοικέως,
[Κρέων τ᾽ ἀδελφὸς μητρὸς ἐκ μιᾶς ἔφυ,]
καλοῦσι δ᾽ Ἰοκάστην με· τοῦτο γὰρ πατὴρ
ἔθετο. γαμεῖ δὲ Λάιός μ᾽· ἐπεὶ δ᾽ ἄπαις
ἦν χρόνια λέκτρα τἄμ᾽ ἔχων ἐν δώμασιν,
15 ἐλθὼν ἐρωτᾷ Φοῖβον ἐξαιτεῖ θ᾽ ἅμα
παίδων ἐς οἴκους ἀρσένων κοινωνίαν.
ὁ δ᾽ εἶπεν· Ὦ Θήβαισιν εὐίπποις ἄναξ,
μὴ σπεῖρε τέκνων ἄλοκα δαιμόνων βίᾳ·

1–2 om. papyri, del. Haslam
11 suspectum habuit Geel, del. Paley

PHOENICIAN WOMEN

From the door of the skene JOCASTA *emerges. She is
dressed in dark robes, and her hair is cut as if she were in
mourning.*

JOCASTA

[O you that cut your heavenly path through the stars and
ride in a chariot inlaid with gold,] Sun, who on swift steeds
whirl your blaze in an arc, how unblest for Thebes was the
beam you shed the day when Cadmus came to this country,
leaving his seagirt land in Phoenicia![1] He married Cypris'
daughter Harmonia and begot Polydorus, father, they tell
us, of Labdacus, who sired Laius.

I am called daughter of Menoeceus, [and Creon is my
brother, born of the same mother,] and my name is Jocasta
(for that is what my father named me). Laius was my hus-
band. He had no child, though long married to me, and so
he went and inquired of Phoebus, begging him as he did so
that we two should get male heirs for the house. But Phoe-
bus replied, "King of Thebes, city of fair horses, do not
keep sowing the child-begetting furrow against the gods'

---

[1] I.e. the day Cadmus came to found Thebes was inauspicious.
Tyre, Cadmus' old city, is called "seagirt" because it was an island
until the time of Alexander the Great, who joined it to the main-
land by a mole.

εἰ γὰρ τεκνώσεις παῖδ᾽, ἀποκτενεῖ σ᾽ ὁ φύς,
20 καὶ πᾶς σὸς οἶκος βήσεται δι᾽ αἵματος.
ὁ δ᾽ ἡδονῇ 'νδοὺς ἔς τε βακχείαν πεσὼν
ἔσπειρεν ἡμῖν παῖδα, καὶ σπείρας πατὴρ
γνοὺς τἀμπλάκημα τοῦ θεοῦ τε τὴν φάτιν
λειμῶν᾽ ἐς Ἥρας καὶ Κιθαιρῶνος λέπας
25 δίδωσι βουκόλοισιν ἐκθεῖναι βρέφος,
σφυρῶν σιδηρᾶ κέντρα διαπείρας μέσων·
ὅθεν νιν Ἑλλὰς ὠνόμαζεν Οἰδίπουν.
Πολύβου δέ νιν λαβόντες ἱπποβουκόλοι
φέρουσ᾽ ἐς οἴκους ἔς τε δεσποίνης χέρας
30 ἔθηκαν. ἡ δὲ τὸν ἐμὸν ὠδίνων πόνον
μαστοῖς ὑφεῖτο καὶ πόσιν πείθει τρέφειν.

ἤδη δὲ πυρσαῖς γένυσιν ἐξανδρούμενος
παῖς οὑμὸς ἢ γνοὺς ἤ τινος μαθὼν πάρα
ἔστειχε τοὺς φύσαντας ἐκμαθεῖν θέλων
35 πρὸς δῶμα Φοίβου, Λάιός θ᾽ οὑμὸς πόσις
τὸν ἐκτεθέντα παῖδα μαστεύων μαθεῖν
εἰ μηκέτ᾽ εἴη. καὶ ξυνάπτετον πόδα
ἐς ταὐτὸν ἄμφω Φωκίδος σχιστῆς ὁδοῦ.
καί νιν κελεύει Λαΐου τροχηλάτης·
40 ὦ ξένε, τυράννοις ἐκποδὼν μεθίστασο.
ὁ δ᾽ εἷρπ᾽ ἄναυδος, μέγα φρονῶν. πῶλοι δέ νιν
χηλαῖς τένοντας ἐξεφοίνισσον ποδῶν.

<hr>

21 'νδοὺς Markland: δοὺς C
22 πατὴρ Herwerden: βρέφος C
23 del. Zipperer   26–7 del. Paley (27 iam Valckenaer)
31 τρέφειν Nagel: τεκεῖν C

will: if you sire a son, your own offspring will kill you, and the whole house will be embroiled in bloodshed." But he yielded to pleasure in a drunken moment and sired our child, and having done so, the father, realizing his error and remembering the god's pronouncement, gave the babe to herdsmen to expose in Hera's meadow on rocky Cithaeron, having first passed an iron stake through the middle of his ankles: hence Greece called him Oedipus.[2] The horseherders of Polybus[3] picked him up, brought him to the palace, and placed him in the hands of their mistress. She had him put to the breast, the child my labor pains brought forth, and persuaded her husband to raise him.

When he had come to manhood and his cheeks were tawny with his first beard, my son, discovering something or hearing it from others, went off to the temple of Phoebus to find out who his parents were, and Laius my husband also went there, wishing to learn whether the exposed child was still alive. Their paths coincided at a point on Phocis' Cloven Way.[4] Laius' driver called out to the young man, "Stranger, make way for royalty!" But he just kept walking without a word, being very proud, and the horses' hooves bloodied the tendons of his feet. As a result

---

[2] Oedipus' name (from *oidao*, "swell") alludes to the swelling of his feet that resulted from this operation.   [3] In Sophocles' *Oedipus the King* Polybus is king of Corinth, though other versions of the myth put him in Boeotia, not far from Thebes.

[4] The Cloven Way (σχιστὴ ὁδός) was a portion of the road leading to Delphi from the east: see Pausanias 10.5.3–4. In Euripides' version Oedipus and Laius are traveling in the same direction, the latter more rapidly in a chariot.

ὅθεν (τί τἀκτὸς τῶν κακῶν με δεῖ λέγειν;)
παῖς πατέρα καίνει καὶ λαβὼν ὀχήματα
45 Πολύβῳ τροφεῖ δίδωσιν. ὡς δ᾽ ἐπεζάρει
Σφὶγξ ἁρπαγαῖσι πόλιν ἐμός τ᾽ οὐκ ἦν πόσις,
Κρέων ἀδελφὸς τἀμὰ κηρύσσει λέχη,
ὅστις σοφῆς αἴνιγμα παρθένου μάθοι,
τούτῳ ξυνάψειν λέκτρα. τυγχάνει δέ πως
50 μούσας ἐμὸς παῖς Οἰδίπους Σφιγγὸς μαθὼν
[ὅθεν τύραννος τῆσδε γῆς καθίσταται]
καὶ σκῆπτρ᾽ ἔπαθλα τῆσδε λαμβάνει χθονός,
γαμεῖ δὲ τὴν τεκοῦσαν οὐκ εἰδὼς τάλας
οὐδ᾽ ἡ τεκοῦσα παιδὶ συγκοιμωμένη.
55 τίκτω δὲ παῖδας παιδὶ δύο μὲν ἄρσενας,
Ἐτεοκλέα κλεινήν τε Πολυνείκους βίαν,
κόρας τε δισσάς· τὴν μὲν Ἰσμήνην πατὴρ
ὠνόμασε, τὴν δὲ πρόσθεν Ἀντιγόνην ἐγώ.
μαθὼν δὲ τἀμὰ λέκτρα μητρῴων γάμων
60 ὁ πάντ᾽ ἀνατλὰς Οἰδίπους παθήματα
ἐς ὄμμαθ᾽ αὑτοῦ δεινὸν ἐμβάλλει φόνον,
χρυσηλάτοις πόρπαισιν αἱμάξας κόρας.
ἐπεὶ δὲ τέκνων γένυς ἐμῶν σκιάζεται,
κλήθροις ἔκρυψαν πατέρ᾽, ἵν᾽ ἀμνήμων τύχη
65 γένοιτο πολλῶν δεομένη σοφισμάτων.
ζῶν δ᾽ ἔστ᾽ ἐν οἴκοις. πρὸς δὲ τῆς τύχης νοσῶν

51 del. Valckenaer (51–2 del. Leutsch, 52 om. Π)
60 del. Valckenaer
62 del. Fraenkel

(why should I dwell on irrelevant troubles?) the son killed the father, took his chariot, and gave it to Polybus his foster father. Now when the Sphinx was plundering and vexing the city[5] and my husband was dead, my brother Creon proclaimed that he would give me in marriage to whoever solved the wise maiden's riddle. My son somehow or other managed to learn her song's meaning, [and hence he became king of this land,] took the scepter of this country as his prize, and thus, poor man, unwittingly married his mother, and his mother too was unaware that she was sleeping with her son.

To my own son I bore two sons, Eteocles and glorious Polynices,[6] and two daughters. One daughter her father called Ismene[7] and her elder sister I named Antigone. Now when Oedipus, who endured all manner of sufferings, learned that in marrying me he had married his mother, he committed dreadful slaughter upon his own eyes, bloodying them with brooches of beaten gold. But when my sons' cheeks were darkened with their first beards, they hid their father away behind locked doors so that his fate would be forgotten, though it took much ingenuity to conceal it. He now lives in the palace. Made

[5] The Sphinx, a winged monster with a woman's head and a lion's or dog's body, assailed Thebes, carrying off as prey anyone who could not solve her riddle.　　[6] The epithet "glorious" belongs etymologically to Eteocles, whose name means "man of true glory," and who is normally portrayed as being in the right. Euripides in this play portrays Eteocles as a usurper and Polynices as having juster claim on the throne.

[7] Ismene and the river Ismenus are properly spelled Hismene and Hismenus (see Mastronarde's commentary on line 101), but I have retained the customary English spelling.

217

ἀρὰς ἀρᾶται παισὶν ἀνοσιωτάτας,
θηκτῷ σιδήρῳ δῶμα διαλαχεῖν τόδε.
    τὼ δ' ἐς φόβον πεσόντε, μὴ τελεσφόρους
70 εὐχὰς θεοὶ κραίνωσιν οἰκούντοιν ὁμοῦ,
ξυμβάντ' ἔταξαν τὸν νεώτερον πάρος
φεύγειν ἑκόντα τήνδε Πολυνείκη χθόνα,
Ἐτεοκλέα δὲ σκῆπτρ' ἔχειν μένοντα γῆς,
ἐνιαυτὸν ἀλλάσσοντ'. ἐπεὶ δ' ἐπὶ ζυγοῖς
75 καθέζετ' ἀρχῆς, οὐ μεθίσταται θρόνων,
φυγάδα δ' ἀπωθεῖ τῆσδε Πολυνείκη χθονός.
ὁ δ' Ἄργος ἐλθών, κῆδος Ἀδράστου λαβών,
πολλὴν ἀθροίσας ἀσπίδ' Ἀργείων ἄγει·
ἐπ' αὐτὰ δ' ἐλθὼν ἑπτάπυλα τείχη τάδε
80 πατρῷ' ἀπαιτεῖ σκῆπτρα καὶ μέρη χθονός.
ἐγὼ δ' ἔριν λύουσ' ὑπόσπονδον μολεῖν
ἔπεισα παιδὶ παῖδα πρὶν ψαῦσαι δορός.
ἥξειν δ' ὁ πεμφθείς φησιν αὐτὸν ἄγγελος.
    ἀλλ', ὦ φαεννὰς οὐρανοῦ ναίων πτυχὰς
85 Ζεῦ, σῶσον ἡμᾶς, δὸς δὲ σύμβασιν τέκνοις.
χρὴ δ', εἰ σοφὸς πέφυκας, οὐκ ἐᾶν βροτῶν
τὸν αὐτὸν αἰεὶ δυστυχῆ καθεστάναι.

ΘΕΡΑΠΩΝ
ὦ κλεινὸν οἴκοις Ἀντιγόνη θάλος πατρί,
ἐπεί σε μήτηρ παρθενῶνας ἐκλιπεῖν
90 μεθῆκε μελάθρων ἐς διῆρες ἔσχατον

70 οἰκούντοιν Elmsley: -των C
88n Θεράπων Mastronarde: Παιδαγωγός C

sick by what had befallen him, he pronounced an impious curse on his sons, that they should divide this house with the whetted sword.

The sons, becoming afraid that the gods would bring the curse to fulfillment if they lived together, reached an agreement that Polynices, as younger brother, should be the first to leave the country voluntarily, that Eteocles should stay behind and be king, and that the two should trade places year by year. But once Eteocles was settled on the seat of power, he would not give it up and thrust Polynices from the land as an exile. And he, going to Argos and marrying Adrastus' daughter, gathered together a large force of Argive hoplites and brought them here. Coming to the very walls of this seven-gated city he is demanding his father's scepter and a share in the land. To try to end their strife I persuaded the one son to come to the other under a truce before taking up the spear. The messenger I sent says that he will come.

O Zeus, who inhabit the bright recesses of heaven, save us and grant my sons peace! If you are a wise god, you ought not to allow the same mortal to be always in misery!

Exit JOCASTA into the palace. By means of a ladder behind the skene *a* SERVANT *ascends to its roof. He speaks to Antigone, climbing up behind him.*

SERVANT

Antigone, offspring bringing glory to your father's house, since you begged your mother, she has permitted you to leave your maiden quarters and go to this outermost upper

στράτευμ᾽ ἰδεῖν Ἀργεῖον ἱκεσίαισι σαῖς,
ἐπίσχες, ὡς ἂν προυξερευνήσω στίβον,
μή τις πολιτῶν ἐν τρίβῳ φαντάζεται,
κἀμοὶ μὲν ἔλθῃ φαῦλος ὡς δούλῳ ψόγος,
95 σοὶ δ᾽ ὡς ἀνάσσῃ· πάντα δ᾽ ἐξειδὼς φράσω
ἅ τ᾽ εἶδον εἰσήκουσά τ᾽ Ἀργείων πάρα,
σπονδὰς ὅτ᾽ ἦλθον σῷ κασιγνήτῳ φέρων
ἐνθένδ᾽ ἐκεῖσε δεῦρό τ᾽ αὖ κείνων πάρα.
      ἀλλ᾽ οὔτις ἀστῶν τοῖσδε χρίμπτεται δόμοις·
100 κέδρου παλαιὰν κλίμακ᾽ ἐκπέρα ποδί,
σκόπει δὲ πεδία καὶ παρ᾽ Ἰσμηνοῦ ῥοὰς
Δίρκης τε νᾶμα πολεμίων στράτευμ᾽ ὅσον.

ΑΝΤΙΓΟΝΗ

ὄρεγέ νυν ὄρεγε γεραιὰν νέᾳ
χεῖρ᾽ ἀπὸ κλιμάκων
105 ποδὸς ἴχνος ἐπαντέλλων.

ΘΕΡΑΠΩΝ

ἰδοὺ ξύναψον, παρθέν᾽· ἐς καιρὸν δ᾽ ἔβης·
κινούμενον γὰρ τυγχάνει Πελασγικὸν
στράτευμα, χωρίζουσι δ᾽ ἀλλήλων λόχους.

ΑΝΤΙΓΟΝΗ

ἰὼ πότνια παῖ
110 Λατοῦς Ἑκάτα, κατάχαλκον ἅπαν
πεδίον ἀστράπτει.

---

8 In Athens women of the upper classes lived a secluded life,

room of the house to see the Argive army: halt there so that I can look to see whether any citizens are to be seen in the street. Blame might attach to me as a slave and you as my mistress.[8] Since I am well informed, I shall tell you all that I saw and heard from the Argives when I went from here to there bearing a truce to your brother and also when I brought his truce here.

Well, since none of the citizens is near the house, climb up the ancient cedarwood ladder! Look at the plains and see by the streams of Ismenus and the waters of Dirce the size of the enemy army!

ANTIGONE begins climbing onto the roof.

ANTIGONE
Stretch forth, then, stretch forth your aged
hand to my young one,
raising my foot from the ladder!

SERVANT
(*helping her ascend to the roof*) Here, grasp it, maiden! You have arrived at the right time. The Pelasgian army is now stirring, and they are separating the companies one from another.

ANTIGONE
O lady Hecate,
daughter of Leto,[9] how the whole plain
flashes with bronze!

not usually seen by men who were not relatives. Unmarried girls were closely guarded from the gaze of strangers.

[9] Originally a distinct figure, Hecate is blended in the fifth century with Artemis. Her invocation here suggests the desire to avert disaster.

221

ΘΕΡΑΠΩΝ

οὐ γάρ τι φαύλως ἦλθε Πολυνείκης χθόνα,
πολλοῖς μὲν ἵπποις, μυρίοις δ' ὅπλοις βρέμων.

ΑΝΤΙΓΟΝΗ

ἆρα πυλᾶν κλήθροις χαλκόδετ' ἔμβολ' ⟨ἐν⟩
115 λαϊνέοισιν Ἀμφίονος ὀργάνοις
τείχεος ἥρμοσται;

ΘΕΡΑΠΩΝ

θάρσει· τά γ' ἔνδον ἀσφαλῶς ἔχει πόλις.
[ἀλλ' εἰσόρα τὸν πρῶτον, εἰ βούλῃ μαθεῖν.]

ΑΝΤΙΓΟΝΗ

τίς οὗτος ὁ λευκολόφας,
120 πρόπαρ ὃς ἀγεῖται στρατοῦ
πάγχαλκον ἀσπίδ' ἀμφὶ βραχίονι κουφίζων;

[ΘΕΡΑΠΩΝ

λοχαγός, ὦ δέσποινα.

ΑΝΤΙΓΟΝΗ

τίς, πόθεν γεγώς;
αὔδασον, ὦ γεραιέ, τίς ὀνομάζεται;]

ΘΕΡΑΠΩΝ

125 οὗτος Μυκηναῖος μὲν αὐδᾶται γένος,
Λερναῖα δ' οἰκεῖ νάμαθ', Ἱππομέδων ἄναξ.

114 πυλᾶν Diggle: πύλαι C   χαλκόδετ' ἔμβολ' a: χαλκό-
δετά τ' ἔμ- fere ceteri codd.   ⟨ἐν⟩ Fritzsche
118 del. Diggle
123–4 del. Dindorf

SERVANT

Polynices has come to this land in no mean style: what a din
he makes with his many horsemen and his footsoldiers
beyond count!

ANTIGONE

Have the bronze-bound bars been fitted
‹to› the door barriers
in the stone walls Amphion[10] fashioned?

SERVANT

Have no fear: the inner part of the city is safe. [But look at
the first man, if you are desirous to learn who he is.]

ANTIGONE

Who is he of the white plume
who stands in front of the army to lead it,
bearing lightly upon his arm a shield all of bronze?

[SERVANT

A captain, lady.

ANTIGONE

Who and whence sprung? Tell me, old man, what is his
name?]

SERVANT

He is said to be a Mycenaean by birth, and he dwells by the
waters of Lerna: he is Lord Hippomedon.

---

[10] Legendary builder of Thebes' walls. His lyre-playing is said
to have charmed rocks into forming the walls.

ΑΝΤΙΓΟΝΗ

ἒ ἔ,
ὡς γαῦρος, ὡς φοβερὸς εἰσιδεῖν,
γίγαντι γηγενέτᾳ προσόμοιος,
ἀστερωπὸς ⟨ὥσπερ⟩ ἐν
130 γραφαῖσιν, οὐχὶ πρόσφορος ἀμερίῳ γέννᾳ.

ΘΕΡΑΠΩΝ

τὸν δ᾽ ἐξαμείβοντ᾽ οὐχ ὁρᾷς Δίρκης ὕδωρ;
[λοχαγόν;]

ΑΝΤΙΓΟΝΗ

[ἄλλος ἄλλος ὅδε τευχέων τρόπος.]
τίς δ᾽ οὗτός ἐστι;

ΘΕΡΑΠΩΝ

παῖς μὲν Οἰνέως ἔφυ
Τυδεύς, Ἄρη δ᾽ Αἰτωλὸν ἐν στέρνοις ἔχει.

ΑΝΤΙΓΟΝΗ

135 οὗτος ὁ τᾶς Πολυνείκεος, ὦ γέρον,
αὐτοκασιγνήτᾳ νύμφας
ὁμόγαμος κυρεῖ;
ὡς ἀλλόχρως ὅπλοισι, μειξοβάρβαρος.

ΘΕΡΑΠΩΝ

σακεσφόροι γὰρ πάντες Αἰτωλοί, τέκνον,
140 λόγχαις τ᾽ ἀκοντιστῆρες εὐστοχώτατοι.

[ΑΝΤΙΓΟΝΗ
σὺ δ᾽, ὦ γέρον, πῶς αἰσθάνῃ σαφῶς τάδε;

ANTIGONE

Ah, ah!
How grim, how fearful to look upon,
like a giant born of the earth,
with dazzling visage, ⟨as⟩ in a picture,
not like men of mortal begetting!

SERVANT

Do you not see the man crossing the water of Dirce [, a captain]?

ANTIGONE

[Other, other is the fashion of his arms.] Who is he?

SERVANT

He is Tydeus, son of Oeneus, and Aetolian is the war spirit he bears within his breast.

ANTIGONE

Is this the man
who married the sister
of Polynices' wife?
How strange his weapons are, half-barbarian!

SERVANT

Yes: all the Aetolians, my child, carry light shields and hurl javelins with great accuracy.

[ANTIGONE

But, old sir, how do you come to know so much about these things?

---

129 ⟨ὥσπερ⟩ Nauck
132 suspectum habuit Nauck, del. Leutsch
141–4 del. Stahl

ΘΕΡΑΠΩΝ

σημεῖ᾽ ἰδὼν τότ᾽ ἀσπίδων ἐγνώρισα,
σπονδὰς ὅτ᾽ ἦλθον σῷ κασιγνήτῳ φέρων·
ἃ προσδεδορκὼς οἶδα τοὺς ὡπλισμένους.]

ΑΝΤΙΓΟΝΗ

145   τίς δ᾽ οὗτος ἀμφὶ μνῆμα τὸ Ζήθου περᾷ
κατάβόστρυχος, ὄμμασι γοργὸς
εἰσιδεῖν νεανίας,
λοχαγός, ὡς ὄχλος νιν ὑστέρῳ ποδὶ
πάνοπλος ἀμφέπει;

ΘΕΡΑΠΩΝ

150   ὅδ᾽ ἐστὶ Παρθενοπαῖος, Ἀταλάντης γόνος.

ΑΝΤΙΓΟΝΗ

ἀλλά νιν ἁ κατ᾽ ὄρη μετὰ ματέρος
Ἄρτεμις ἱεμένα τόξοις δαμάσασ᾽ ὀλέσειεν,
ὃς ἐπ᾽ ἐμὰν πόλιν ἔβα πέρσων.

ΘΕΡΑΠΩΝ

εἴη τάδ᾽, ὦ παῖ. σὺν δίκῃ δ᾽ ἥκουσι γῆν·
155   ὃ καὶ δέδοικα μὴ σκοπῶσ᾽ ὀρθῶς θεοί.

ΑΝΤΙΓΟΝΗ

ποῦ δ᾽ ὃς ἐμοὶ μιᾶς ἐγένετ᾽ ἐκ ματρὸς
πολυπόνῳ μοίρᾳ;
ὦ φίλτατ᾽, εἰπέ, ποῦ ᾽στι Πολυνείκης, γέρον;

153 ἐμὰν ‹ἐμὰν› Diggle

SERVANT

I recognized the emblems on their shields, having seen
them before when I went carrying the truce to your
brother. Since I looked at them I know who the armed men
are.]

ANTIGONE

But who is the one who walks near the tomb of Zethus,
a young man with long curls,
grim of face to look upon?
He is a captain, to judge by the armed throng
who follow on his heels.

SERVANT

This is Parthenopaeus, son of Atalanta.

ANTIGONE

May Artemis of the mountains destroy him, and his
mother with him,
shooting and felling them with her arrows!
He has come to my city to sack it!

SERVANT

That is my prayer too, my child! But they are coming to the
land with justice on their side. And I am afraid that the
gods may see this all too clearly.

ANTIGONE

But where is he that was born of one mother with me,
by a fate full of woe?
Dearest old man, tell me, where is Polynices?

EURIPIDES

ΘΕΡΑΠΩΝ

ἐκεῖνος ἑπτὰ παρθένων τάφου πέλας
160 Νιόβης Ἀδράστῳ πλησίον παραστατεῖ.
ὁρᾷς;

ΑΝΤΙΓΟΝΗ

ὁρῶ δῆτ᾽ οὐ σαφῶς, ὁρῶ δέ πως
μορφῆς τύπωμα στέρνα τ᾽ ἐξεικασμένα.
ἀνεμώκεος εἴθε δρόμον νεφέλας
ποσὶν ἐξανύσαιμι δι᾽ αἰθέρος
165 πρὸς ἐμὸν ὁμογενέτορα, περὶ δ᾽ ὠλένας
δέρᾳ φιλτάτᾳ βάλοιμεν χρόνῳ,
φυγάδα μέλεον. ὡς
ὅπλοισι χρυσέοισιν ἐκπρεπής, γέρον,
ἑῴοις ὅμοια φλεγέθων βολαῖς.

ΘΕΡΑΠΩΝ

170 ἥξει δόμους τούσδ᾽, ὥστε σ᾽ ἐμπλῆσαι χαρᾶς,
ἔνσπονδος.

ΑΝΤΙΓΟΝΗ

οὗτος δ᾽, ὦ γεραιέ, τίς κυρεῖ,
ὃς ἅρμα λευκὸν ἡνιοστροφεῖ βεβώς;

ΘΕΡΑΠΩΝ

ὁ μάντις Ἀμφιάραος, ὦ δέσποιν᾽, ὅδε·
σφάγια δ᾽ ἅμ᾽ αὐτῷ, γῇ φιλαιμάτῳ ῥοαί.

ΑΝΤΙΓΟΝΗ

175 ὦ λιπαροζώνου θύγατερ Ἁλίου,
<πότνα> Σελαναία, χρυσόκυκλον φέγγος,

228

SERVANT

He stands over there near the tomb of Niobe's seven
daughters, next to Adrastus. Do you see him?

ANTIGONE

I do not see clearly, but I see somehow,
the outline of his form and the semblance of his chest.
How I wish I could tread, in the sky,
the path of some wind-borne cloud,
go to my own brother, and cast
my arms at long last about his beloved neck,
luckless exile that he is!
How he blazes forth in his golden armor, old man,
gleaming like the rays of the dawn!

SERVANT

He will come to this house under truce to gladden your
heart.

ANTIGONE

But who is this, old man, mounted on a white chariot and
holding the reins?

SERVANT

That is the seer Amphiaraus, my lady. With him are sac-
rificial victims, to provide streams for the earth, which
thirsts for blood.

ANTIGONE

Daughter of gleaming-belted Sun,
⟨Lady⟩ Moon, orb of golden light,

---

¹⁶⁶ βάλοιμεν Diggle: βάλοιμι fere C   ¹⁶⁹ βολαῖς
Wecklein: β- ἡλίου fere C   ¹⁷⁴ γῇ φιλαιμάτῳ Paley: γῆς
φιλαίματοι fere C   ¹⁷⁶ ⟨πότνα⟩ Paley

EURIPIDES

ὡς ἀτρεμαῖα κέντρα πώλοις νέμων
ἰθύνει ⟨δρόμον⟩.
ποῦ δ' ὃς τὰ δεινὰ τῇδ' ἐφυβρίζει πόλει
180 Καπανεύς;

ΘΕΡΑΠΩΝ

ἐκεῖνος προσβάσεις τεκμαίρεται
πύργων, ἄνω τε καὶ κάτω τείχη μετρῶν.

ΑΝΤΙΓΟΝΗ

ἰώ, Νέμεσι καὶ βαρύβρομοι βρονταὶ
Διὸς κεραύνιόν τε φῶς αἰθαλόεν, σύ τοι
μεγαλαγορίαν ὑπεράνορα κοιμίζεις·
185 ὅδ' ἐστίν, αἰχμαλωτίδας ὃς δορὶ Θηβαίας
Μυκηνίσι ⟨γυναιξὶ κομπεῖ κόρας⟩
Λερναίᾳ τε δώσειν τριαίνᾳ,
Ποσειδανίοις Ἀμυμωνίοις
ὕδασι δουλείαν περιβαλών·
190 μήποτε μήποτε τάνδ', ὦ πότνια,
χρυσεοβόστρυχον ὦ Διὸς ἔρνος
Ἄρτεμι, δουλοσύναν τλαίην.

ΘΕΡΑΠΩΝ

ὦ τέκνον, ἔσβα δῶμα καὶ κατὰ στέγας
ἐν παρθενῶσι μίμνε σοῖς, ἐπεὶ πόθου

---

177 κέντρα Paley: κ. καὶ σώφρονα C   νέμων Diggle:
μεταφέρων C   178 ⟨δρόμον⟩ Paley
182–3 βαρύβρομοι βρονταὶ Διὸς Willink: Δ- βα- βρ- C
184 μεγαλαγορίαν Matthiae: μεγαλανορίαν fere C
186 ⟨γυναιξὶ κομπεῖ κόρας⟩ West

230

how firmly he applies the goad to his horses
and guides ⟨his course⟩!
But where is he who uttered the terrible proud words
    against the city,
Capaneus?

SERVANT

He is calculating the approaches to the battlements, mea-
suring the walls from top to bottom.

ANTIGONE

Hear me, Nemesis[11] and the deep-booming thunders
of Zeus and his lightning fire all gleaming!
It is you who lull proud boasting to rest.
This is the man who ⟨boasted⟩ he would give
⟨the maidens⟩ of Thebes as spear captives to ⟨women⟩ of
    Mycenae
and to the Trident of Lerna,
casting upon them servitude
to the waters of Poseidon and Amymone![12]
Never, never, O lady Artemis,
golden-tressed offshoot of Zeus,
may I suffer this slavery!

SERVANT

My child, go into the house and stay in your maiden cham-
ber in the palace, since you have seen what you wished to

[11] The goddess of retribution, who was thought to punish
overconfident boasting.

[12] The spring of Lerna, also called Amymone, was said to have
been created by a blow from Poseidon's trident. Fetching water
from a spring was a task of slave women.

195 ἐς τέρψιν ἦλθες ὧν ἔχρῃζες εἰσιδεῖν.
ὄχλος γάρ, ὡς ταραγμὸς εἰσῆλθεν πόλιν,
χωρεῖ γυναικῶν πρὸς δόμους τυραννικούς,
φιλόψογον δὲ χρῆμα θηλειῶν ἔφυ,
σμικράς τ᾽ ἀφορμὰς ἢν λάβωσι τῶν λόγων
200 πλείους ἐπεσφέρουσιν· ἡδονὴ δέ τις
γυναιξὶ μηδὲν ὑγιὲς ἀλλήλας λέγειν.

ΧΟΡΟΣ

στρ. α

Τύριον οἶδμα λιποῦσ᾽ ἔβαν
ἀκροθίνια Λοξίᾳ
Φοινίσσας ἀπὸ νάσου
205 Φοίβῳ δούλα μελάθρων,
ἵν᾽ ὑπὸ δειράσι νιφοβόλοις
Παρνασσοῦ κατενάσθη,
Ἰόνιον κατὰ πόντον ἐλά-
τᾳ πλεύσασα περιρρύτων
210 ὑπὲρ ἀκαρπίστων πεδίων
Σικελίας Ζεφύρου πνοαῖς
ἱππεύσαντος ἐν οὐρανῷ
κάλλιστον κελάδημα.

ἀντ. α

πόλεος ἐκπροκριθεῖσ᾽ ἐμᾶς
215 καλλιστεύματα Λοξίᾳ

---

13 The Chorus describe themselves as slaves of Loxias
(Apollo), chosen from among their people for their beauty. It is

see. For because the city is in confusion, a crowd of women
has come to the royal palace. Women by nature love to crit-
icize, and once they have found trifling reasons to find
fault, they invent still more, such is the pleasure they take
in speaking ill of one another.

Exit SERVANT *and* ANTIGONE *into the palace. Enter a
group of Phoenician women as* CHORUS *by Eisodos A.* [13]

CHORUS
Leaving the Tyrian sea behind
I have come as choicest offerings for Loxias
from Phoenicia's island city[14]
to serve in Phoebus' temple
where under Parnassus' snow-laden peaks
he has made his home.
By ship through the Ionian sea[15]
I sailed as the West Wind
galloped over Sicily's encircling
barren sea water
and made with its blasts in the sky above
a lovely music.

Chosen from our city
as the fairest gift to Loxias,

likely that we are meant to think of them not as slaves captured in
war but as free women serving Apollo for a fixed period in thanks
to Apollo for some blessing he gave Tyre.

    [14] See note on line 6 above.

    [15] This sea extends west from Greece to Italy and Sicily. The
ship must be imagined as sailing around the Peloponnesus and
into the Corinthian Gulf.

Καδμείαν ἔμολον γᾶν,
κλεινῶν Ἀγηνοριδᾶν
ὁμογενεῖς ἐπὶ Λαΐου
πεμφθεῖσ᾽ ἐνθάδε πύργους.
220 ἴσα δ᾽ ἀγάλμασι χρυσοτεύ-
κτοις Φοίβῳ λάτρις ἐγενόμαν·
ἔτι δὲ Κασταλίας ὕδωρ
περιμένει με κόμας ἐμᾶς
δεῦσαι παρθένιον χλιδὰν
225 Φοιβείαισι λατρείαις.

ἐπῳδ.

ὦ λάμπουσα πέτρα πυρὸς
δικόρυφον σέλας ὑπὲρ ἄκρων
βακχείων Διονύσου,
οἶνά θ᾽ ἃ καθαμέριον
230 στάζεις, τὸν πολύκαρπον
οἰνάνθας ἱεῖσα βότρυν,
ζάθεά τ᾽ ἄντρα δράκοντος οὔ-
ρειαί τε σκοπιαὶ θεᾶν
νιφόβολόν τ᾽ ὄρος ἱερόν, εἱ-
235 λίσσων ἀθανάτους θεοῦ
χορὸς γενοίμαν ἄφοβος
παρὰ μεσόμφαλα γύαλα Φοί-
βου Δίρκαν προλιποῦσα.

233 θεᾶν West: -ῶν C
235 ἀθανάτους Wecklein: -τας vel -του C

234

I have come to the land of Cadmus,
sent to the towers of Laius,
towers that are kin
to the glorious Agenoridae.[16]
Like one of his gold-wrought statues
I entered the service of Phoebus.
The waters of Castalia still await me
to moisten the maidenly
luxuriance of my hair
in the service of Phoebus.

O cliff, shedding a twin-peaked gleam
of fire upon the lofty
sites of Dionysiac transport,[17]
O vine that day by day
drips wine, putting forth
the full-fruited cluster of grape blossom,
O holy cave of the serpent[18]
and mountain lookout of the goddesses,
O sacred mount overspread with snow,
may I dance in honor of the deathless ones
and dance in the god's honor free from fear,
leaving Dirce for Phoebus' vale
at the earth's navel.

[16] Agenoridae (descendants of Agenor) means Tyrians. The kinship is by way of Cadmus, originally a Tyrian.

[17] The two peaks of Parnassus that rise above Delphi were the scene of dances in honor of Dionysus.

[18] The Corycian Cave, abode of the serpent Python, whom Apollo slew. Afterwards it became the haunt of nymphs, alluded to as "goddesses."

στρ. β

νῦν δέ μοι πρὸ τειχέων
240 θούριος μολὼν Ἄρης
αἷμα δάιον φλέγει
τᾷδ', ὃ μὴ τύχοι, πόλει·
κοινὰ γὰρ φίλων ἄχη,
κοινὰ δ', εἴ τι πείσεται
245 ἑπτάπυργος ἅδε γᾶ,
Φοινίσσᾳ χώρᾳ. φεῦ φεῦ.
κοινὸν αἷμα, κοινὰ τέκεα
τᾶς κερασφόρου πέφυκεν Ἰοῦς·
ὧν μέτεστί μοι πόνων.

ἀντ. β

250 ἀμφὶ δὲ πτόλιν νέφος
ἀσπίδων πυκνὸν φλέγει,
σῆμα φοινίου μάχας,
ἃν Ἄρης τάχ' εἴσεται
παισὶν Οἰδίπου φέρων
255 πημονὰν Ἐρινύων.
Ἄργος ὦ Πελασγικόν,
δειμαίνω τὰν σὰν ἀλκὰν
καὶ τὸ θεόθεν· οὐ γὰρ ἄδικον
εἰς ἀγῶνα τόνδ' ἔνοπλος ὁρμᾷ
260 ὃς μετέρχεται δόμους.

259 τάνδ' . . . ὁρμὰν Hermann
260 ὃς Triclinius: παῖς ὃς C: παῖς Battier

But now before the walls
grim Ares has come
and sets war and bloodshed ablaze
for this city: may heaven avert it!
For friends share the woes of friends,
and if this seven-gated city
suffers misfortune,
Phoenicia will share the hurt. Ah ah!
Shared blood, common children
were born from horned Io.[19]
In these troubles I partake.

About the city a thick
cloud of shields flashes,
the sign of murderous battle.
This battle Ares will soon decide
as he brings to Oedipus' sons
the woes of the Erinyes.[20]
O Pelasgian Argos,
I fear your might
and what the gods send. For not unjust
is this contest toward which he presses in armor,
he who comes to recover his house.

[19] Io, daughter of the river god Inachus, was loved by Zeus, who turned her into a heifer to disguise her from his wife Hera. She became the mother of Epaphus, ancestor both of the Tyrians and the Argives. Her connection is not with Thebes in particular but with the Greek race in general.

[20] The agents of divine justice, with particular concern for offenses against kin.

ΠΟΛΥΝΕΙΚΗΣ

τὰ μὲν πυλωρῶν κλῇθρά μ' εἰσεδέξατο
δι' εὐπετείας τειχέων ἔσω μολεῖν.
ὃ καὶ δέδοικα μή με δικτύων ἔσω
λαβόντες οὐκ ἐκφρῶσ' ἀναίμακτον χρόα.

265 ὧν οὕνεκ' ὄμμα πανταχῇ διοιστέον
κἀκεῖσε καὶ τὸ δεῦρο, μὴ δόλος τις ᾖ.
ὡπλισμένος δὲ χεῖρα τῷδε φασγάνῳ
τὰ πίστ' ἐμαυτῷ τοῦ θράσους παρέξομαι.

ὡή, τίς οὗτος; ἢ κτύπον φοβούμεθα;
270 ἅπαντα γὰρ τολμῶσι δεινὰ φαίνεται,
ὅταν δι' ἐχθρᾶς ποὺς ἀμείβηται χθονός.
πέποιθα μέντοι μητρὶ κοὐ πέποιθ' ἅμα,
ἥτις μ' ἔπεισε δεῦρ' ὑπόσπονδον μολεῖν.
ἀλλ' ἐγγὺς ἀλκή (βώμιοι γὰρ ἐσχάραι

275 πέλας πάρεισι) κοὐκ ἔρημα δώματα·
φέρ' ἐς σκοτεινὰς περιβολὰς μεθῶ ξίφος
καὶ τάσδ' ἔρωμαι, τίνες ἐφεστᾶσιν δόμοις.

ξέναι γυναῖκες, εἴπατ', ἐκ ποίας πάτρας
Ἑλληνικοῖσι δώμασιν πελάζετε;

ΧΟΡΟΣ

280 Φοίνισσα μὲν γῆ πατρὶς ἡ θρέψασά με,
Ἀγήνορος δὲ παῖδες ἐκ παίδων δορὸς
Φοίβῳ μ' ἔπεμψαν ἐνθάδ' ἀκροθίνιον.
μέλλων δὲ πέμπειν μ' Οἰδίπου κλεινὸς γόνος
μαντεῖα σεμνὰ Λοξίου τ' ἐπ' ἐσχάρας,

285 ἐν τῷδ' ἐπεστράτευσαν Ἀργεῖοι πόλιν.

238

PHOENICIAN WOMEN

Enter by Eisodos B POLYNICES, *without a retinue, sword in hand, peering in every direction as if afraid of an attack.*

POLYNICES

The gatekeepers' bolts have allowed me to pass easily inside the walls. And so I am afraid that having taken me within their net they will not let me go again without a wound. For this reason I must turn my eyes this way and that for fear of trickery. With this sword in my hand I shall give myself the confidence to venture on.

Ah, who is that? Or am I starting at a mere noise? Everything seems frightful to bold men when their feet tread on enemy territory. Still, I trust my mother—and at the same time mistrust her. She persuaded me to come here under a truce. But help is at hand (for an altar stands nearby) and the house is not without inhabitants: come, let me put up my sword into the dark of its encasement and ask these women standing near the house who they are. (*He sheathes his sword.*)

Foreign ladies, tell me, what country have you left to draw near this Greek house?

CHORUS LEADER

My fathers' land, the land that nurtured me, is Phoenicia; the descendants of Agenor have sent me here to Phoebus in thanks for victory in war. When Oedipus' glorious son was about to send me to Loxias' holy oracle and altars, just then the Argives marched against the city. But you, tell me

---

271 del. Nauck

σὺ δ' ἀντάμειψαί μ', ὅστις ὢν ἐλήλυθας
ἐπτάστομον πύργωμα Θηβαίας χθονός.

ΠΟΛΥΝΕΙΚΗΣ

πατὴρ μὲν ἡμῖν Οἰδίπους ὁ Λαΐου,
ἔτικτε δ' Ἰοκάστη με, παῖς Μενοικέως·
290 καλεῖ δὲ Πολυνείκη με Θηβαῖος λεώς.

ΧΟΡΟΣ

[ὦ συγγένεια τῶν Ἀγήνορος τέκνων,
ἐμῶν τυράννων, ὧν ἀπεστάλην ὕπο.]
γονυπετεῖς ἕδρας προσπίτνω σ', ἄναξ,
τὸν οἴκοθεν σέβουσα νόμον·
295 ἔβας ὦ χρόνῳ γᾶν πατρῴαν.
ἰὼ ἰώ·
πότνια, μόλε πρόδομος, ἀμπέτασον πύλας.
κλύεις, ὦ τεκοῦσα τόνδε μᾶτερ;
τί μέλλεις ὑπώροφα μέλαθρα περᾶν
300 θιγεῖν τ' ὠλέναισιν τέκνου;

ΙΟΚΑΣΤΗ

Φοίνισσαν βοὰν
κλυοῦσ', ὦ νεάνιδες, γηραιοῦ
ποδὸς τρομερὸν ἕλκω ⟨πρὸ δόμων⟩ βάσιν·
ἰὼ τέκνον, χρόνῳ σὸν ὄμ-
305 μα μυρίαις τ' ἐν ἀμέραις
προσεῖδον· ἀμφίβαλλε μα-

291–2 om. Π, del. Haslam
294 σέβουσα νόμον Diggle: ν- σ- C
302–3 γηραιοῦ ποδὸς τρομερὸν ἕλκω ⟨πρὸ δόμων⟩ βάσιν

in your turn who you are that have come to the seven-gated
fortress of Thebes.

POLYNICES

My father is Oedipus, son of Laius, and Menoeceus'
daughter Jocasta is my mother. The people of Thebes call
me Polynices.

[CHORUS LEADER

O kinsman of the sons of Agenor, my royal family, by whom
I was sent!]

CHORUS

(*kneeling before Polynices*) I fall at your knees, my lord,
honoring my native custom!
Ah, you have come at last to your native land!
(*standing up*) Ho there, within!
My queen, come out before the house, open its gates wide!
Do you hear, mother of this man?
Why don't you leave at once your high-roofed house
and take your son in your embrace?

Enter from the skene JOCASTA.

JOCASTA

Your Phoenician cry,
O maidens, I have heard, and my aged
and trembling step I bring slowly ⟨out of doors⟩.
O my son, how long the time,
how many the days since I last saw
your face! Clasp your mother's

---

post Kirchhoff ([ποδὸς] βάσιν) Willink: γηραιῷ ποδὶ τρομερὰν
ἕλκω ποδὸς βάσιν C

στὸν ὠλέναισι ματέρος,
παρηίδων τ᾿ ὄρεγμα δὸς
τριχῶν τε, κυανόχρωτι χαί-
τας πλοκάμῳ δέραν σκιάζων ἁμάν.
310 ἰὼ ἰώ, μόλις φανεὶς
ἄελπτα κἀδόκητα ματρὸς ὠλέναις.
τί φῶ σε; πῶς ἁπάντᾳ
καὶ χερσὶ καὶ λόγοισιν,
πολυέλικτον ἁδονὰν
315 ἐκεῖσε καὶ τὸ δεῦρο περι-
χορεύουσα τέρψιν
παλαιὰν λάβω χαρμονᾶν;
ἰὼ τέκος,
ἔρημον πατρῷον ἔλιπες δόμον
φυγὰς ἀποσταλεὶς ὁμαίμου λώβᾳ,
320 ἦ ποθεινὸς φίλοις,
ἦ ποθεινὸς Θήβαις.
ὅθεν ἐμάν τε λευκόχροα κείρομαι
δακρυόεσσ᾿ ἀνεῖσα πένθει κόμαν,
[ἄπεπλος φαρέων λευκῶν, τέκνον,]
325 δυσόρφναιά τ᾿ ἀμφὶ τρύχη τάδε
σκότι᾿ ἀμείβομαι.
ὁ δ᾿ ἐν δόμοισι πρέσβυς ὀμματοστερὴς
ἀπήνας ὁμοπτέρου τᾶς ἀπο-
ζυγείσας δόμων
330 πόθον ἀμφιδάκρυτον ἀεὶ κατέχων

307–8 δὸς τριχῶν Camper: βοστρύχων C

242

breast to yours,
let me put my hand to your cheeks
and hair, casting the shadow
of your dark curls upon my neck!
(*Embracing him*) Oh, oh, child so late appearing,
unhoped, unlooked for, to your mother's embrace!
(*Circling about him*) What am I to say of you? How can I in
    every way,
by deed of hand and spoken word,
dancing about you
to this side and that
through many turns that give me pleasure,
win the delight of joys long missed?
O my son,
you have left your father's house bereft,
sent into exile by your brother's outrage,
much missed by your friends,
much missed by Thebes!
Hence in grief I have let loose my tresses
and cut this white hair of mine,
[not dressed in white garments, my son,]
and have changed my clothes, putting about my body
these tattered robes, dusky and gloomy.
He in the house, the old man blind,
ever feeling a tearful longing
for the kindred pair
unyoked from the house,

308–9 κυανόχρωτι . . . πλοκάμῳ Geel: -τα . . . πλόκαμον C
309 δέραν σκιάζων Fritzsche: σκ- δ- C
323 δακρυόεσσ᾽ ἀνεῖσα πένθει Hermann: δακρυόεσσαν
ἱεῖσα πενθήρη fere C   324 del. Hartung

ἀνῆξεν μὲν ξίφους
ἐπ' αὐτόχειρά τε σφαγὰν
ὑπὲρ τέραμνά τ' ἀγχόνας,
στενάζων ἀρὰς τέκνοις·
335 σὺν ἀλαλαῖσι δ' αἰὲν αἰαγμάτων
σκότια κρύπτεται.
σὲ δ', ὦ τέκνον, γάμοισι δὴ
κλύω ζυγέντα παιδοποιὸν ἀδονὰν
ξένοισιν ἐν δόμοις ἔχειν,
340 ξένον δὲ κῆδος ἀμφέπειν,
ἄλαστα ματρὶ τᾷδε Λα-
ΐου τε τοῦ πάλαι γένει,
γάμων ἐπακτὸν ἄταν.
ἐγὼ δ' οὔτι σοι πυρὸς ἀνῆψα φῶς
345 νόμιμον [ἐν γάμοις], ὡς πρέπει ματέρι μακαρίᾳ·
ἀνυμέναια δ' Ἰσμηνὸς ἐκηδεύθη
λουτροφόρου χλιδᾶς, ἀνὰ δὲ Θηβαίων
πόλιν ἐσίγαθεν σᾶς ἔσοδοι νύμφας.
350 ὄλοιτο τάδ' εἴτε σίδαρος
εἴτ' Ἔρις εἴτε πατὴρ
ὁ σὸς αἴτιος, εἴτε τὸ δαιμόνιον
κατεκώμασε δώμασιν Οἰδιπόδα·
πρὸς ἐμὲ γὰρ κακῶν ἔμολε τῶνδ' ἄχη.

337 γάμοισι Brunck, Hermann: καὶ γάμοισι fere C
341–2 Λαΐου τε τοῦ πάλαι γένει Hermann: Λαΐῳ τε τῷ
παλαιγενεῖ fere C
345–6 ἐν γάμοις del. Wilamowitz, ὡς πρέπει Nauck
349 ἐσίγαθεν Willink et fort. Π: ἐσιγάθη vel -άθησαν C

rushes now to the sword
of self-slaughter,
now to nooses hung from the rafters,
lamenting the curse on his sons.
With continual cries of woe
he hides himself in the dark.
But you, my son, I hear are yoked
in marriage and have the pleasure of childbegetting
in a foreign house,
with foreigners for kin by marriage,
woe past forgetting to your mother here
and to the race of old Laius,
a marriage curse brought from abroad.
I did not kindle for you the blazing torch
that custom requires [in marriages], as befits a mother
     blessed.[21]
The Ismenus River made this alliance
without the luxurious bath, and in the city
of Thebes none cried aloud at the entrance of your bride.
A curse upon the cause of these things, whether it was the
     sword
or Eris[22] or your father,
or if the power of heaven has run riot
in the house of Oedipus:
for upon me has come the pain of these woes.

[21] In the Greek marriage ceremony, the mother of the groom
held up torches and also (cf. 348) provided a ritual bath for her
son. Thebes' own river is felt to be involved in the latter.

[22] Goddess of strife.

ΧΟΡΟΣ

ΧΟΡΟΣ

355 δεινὸν γυναιξὶν αἱ δι' ὠδίνων γοναί,
καὶ φιλότεκνόν πως πᾶν γυναικεῖον γένος.

ΠΟΛΥΝΕΙΚΗΣ

μῆτερ, φρονῶν εὖ κοὐ φρονῶν ἀφικόμην
ἐχθροὺς ἐς ἄνδρας· ἀλλ' ἀναγκαίως ἔχει
πατρίδος ἐρᾶν ἅπαντας· ὃς δ' ἄλλως λέγει,
360 λόγοισι χαίρει, τὸν δὲ νοῦν ἐκεῖσ' ἔχει.
οὕτω δ' ἐτάρβησ' ἐς φόβον τ' ἀφικόμην
μή τις δόλος με πρὸς κασιγνήτου κτάνῃ,
ὥστε ξιφήρη χεῖρ' ἔχων δι' ἄστεως
κυκλῶν πρόσωπον ἦλθον. ἐν δέ μ' ὠφελεῖ,
365 σπονδαί τε καὶ σὴ πίστις, ἥ μ' ἐσήγαγεν
τείχη πατρῷα· πολύδακρυς δ' ἀφικόμην,
χρόνιος ἰδὼν μέλαθρα καὶ βωμοὺς θεῶν
γυμνάσιά θ' οἷσιν ἐνετράφην Δίρκης θ' ὕδωρ·
ὧν οὐ δικαίως ἀπελαθεὶς ξένην πόλιν
370 ναίω, δι' ὄσσων νᾶμ' ἔχων δακρύρροον.
ἀλλ', ἐκ γὰρ ἄλγους ἄλγος αὖ, σὲ δέρκομαι
κάρα ξυρῆκες καὶ πέπλους μελαγχίμους
ἔχουσαν· οἴμοι τῶν ἐμῶν ἐγὼ κακῶν.
ὡς δεινὸν ἔχθρα, μῆτερ, οἰκείων φίλων.
375 [καὶ δυσλύτους ἔχουσα τὰς διαλλαγάς.
τί γὰρ πατήρ μοι πρέσβυς ἐν δόμοισι δρᾷ,
σκότον δεδορκώς; τί δὲ κασίγνηται δύο;
ἦ που στένουσι τλήμονες φυγὰς ἐμάς;]

CHORUS LEADER

Childbirth and its labor pangs have a surprising effect on women, and all womankind are somehow drawn to their children.

POLYNICES

Mother, it was sensible of me to come to meet my enemy—and also mad. But all men necessarily love their country. Whoever says otherwise takes joy in disputation while his true belief lies elsewhere.

But I am terribly afraid that my brother may kill me by some trick, and so I have come through the city sword in hand and constantly looking around me. Only one thing benefits me, our truce and your trustworthiness. It is this that has brought me into my father's walls. But I arrive in tears: after so long a time I look on the temples and altars of the gods, the gymnasia in which I was trained, and the waters of Dirce. I am unjustly deprived of these things and live in a strange city, my eyes overflowing with tears.

But—here one grief crowns another—I see you with shorn head and garments of black! What misery for me! What a dreadful thing, mother, is hatred between members of one family! [It is hard to settle and reach an understanding. What is my old father doing in the house, blind as he is? What are my two sisters doing? No doubt in their misery lamenting my exile?]

---

361 δ' ἐτάρβησ' a, coni. Hermann: δὲ τάρβους ceteri codd.
369–70 del. West
370 νᾶμ' Musgrave: ὄμμ' fere C
375 suspectum habuit Valckenaer, del. Usener, cl. Σ
376–8 del. Usener

EURIPIDES

ΙΟΚΑΣΤΗ

κακῶς θεῶν τις Οἰδίπου φθείρει γένος·
380 οὕτω γὰρ ἤρξατ᾽, ἄνομα μὲν τεκεῖν ἐμέ,
κακῶς δὲ γῆμαι πατέρα σὸν φῦναί τε σέ.
ἀτὰρ τί ταῦτα; δεῖ φέρειν τὰ τῶν θεῶν.
   ὅπως δ᾽ ἔρωμαι, μή τι σὴν δάκω φρένα,
δέδοιχ᾽, ἃ χρῄζω· διὰ πόθου δ᾽ ἐλήλυθα.

ΠΟΛΥΝΕΙΚΗΣ

385 ἀλλ᾽ ἐξερώτα, μηδὲν ἐνδεὲς λίπῃς·
ἃ γὰρ σὺ βούλῃ, ταῦτ᾽ ἐμοί, μῆτερ, φίλα.

ΙΟΚΑΣΤΗ

[καὶ δή σ᾽ ἐρωτῶ πρῶτον ὧν χρῄζω τυχεῖν·]
τί τὸ στέρεσθαι πατρίδος; ἦ κακὸν μέγα;

ΠΟΛΥΝΕΙΚΗΣ

μέγιστον· ἔργῳ δ᾽ ἐστὶ μεῖζον ἢ λόγῳ.

ΙΟΚΑΣΤΗ

390 τίς ὁ τρόπος αὐτοῦ; τί φυγάσιν τὸ δυσχερές;

ΠΟΛΥΝΕΙΚΗΣ

ἓν μὲν μέγιστον· οὐκ ἔχει παρρησίαν.

ΙΟΚΑΣΤΗ

δούλου τόδ᾽ εἶπας, μὴ λέγειν ἅ τις φρονεῖ.

ΠΟΛΥΝΕΙΚΗΣ

τὰς τῶν κρατούντων ἀμαθίας φέρειν χρεών.

387 om. Π, del. Haslam
393–4 del. Czwalina

248

JOCASTA

Some god is sending the progeny of Oedipus to a terrible ruin. This is how he began: I gave birth unlawfully,[23] your father married me for ill, and thus you were begotten. Yet why should I dwell on this? One must endure what the gods send.

But I am afraid to ask you what I want to know, afraid to grieve your heart. Yet I feel a great longing to ask.

POLYNICES

Ask away, leave nothing out: your desire is mine as well.

JOCASTA

[See, I ask you the first thing I want to know.] What is it like to be deprived of your country? Is it a great calamity?

POLYNICES

The greatest: the reality far surpasses the description.

JOCASTA

What is its nature? What is hard for exiles?

POLYNICES

One thing is most important: no free speech.

JOCASTA

A slave's lot this, not saying what you think.

POLYNICES

You must endure the follies of your ruler.

---

[23] She had a child contrary to Apollo's will.

ΙΟΚΑΣΤΗ

καὶ τοῦτο λυπρόν, συνασοφεῖν τοῖς μὴ σοφοῖς.

ΠΟΛΥΝΕΙΚΗΣ

395 ἀλλ᾽ ἐς τὸ κέρδος παρὰ φύσιν δουλευτέον.

ΙΟΚΑΣΤΗ

αἱ δ᾽ ἐλπίδες βόσκουσι φυγάδας, ὡς λόγος.

ΠΟΛΥΝΕΙΚΗΣ

καλοῖς βλέπουσαί γ᾽ ὄμμασιν, μέλλουσι δέ.

ΙΟΚΑΣΤΗ

399 ἔχουσιν Ἀφροδίτην τιν᾽ ἡδεῖαν κακῶν.

ΠΟΛΥΝΕΙΚΗΣ

398 οὐδ᾽ ὁ χρόνος αὐτὰς διεσάφησ᾽ οὔσας κενάς;

ΙΟΚΑΣΤΗ

400 πόθεν δ᾽ ἐβόσκου, πρὶν γάμοις εὑρεῖν βίον;

ΠΟΛΥΝΕΙΚΗΣ

ποτὲ μὲν ἐπ᾽ ἦμαρ εἶχον, εἶτ᾽ οὐκ εἶχον ἄν.

ΙΟΚΑΣΤΗ

φίλοι δὲ πατρὸς καὶ ξένοι σ᾽ οὐκ ὠφέλουν;

ΠΟΛΥΝΕΙΚΗΣ

εὖ πρᾶσσε· τὰ φίλων δ᾽ οὐδέν, ἤν τις δυστυχῇ.

ΙΟΚΑΣΤΗ

οὐδ᾽ ηὐγένειά σ᾽ ἦρεν εἰς ὕψος μέγαν;

397 βλέπουσαί Hermann, scholiis fretus: βλέπουσί fere C
399 ante 398 trai. anon. Cantabr.   fort. ἔχουσι δ᾽
398 fort. εὖ δ᾽ ὁ χρόνος

JOCASTA

That too is hard, to join fools in their folly.

POLYNICES

Well, to get what he wants a man must suppress his nature
and play the slave.

JOCASTA

Exiles, they say, live on hopes.

POLYNICES

Yes, hopes with loveliness in their glance but delay in their
step.

JOCASTA

They make a man pleasantly in love with his woes.

POLYNICES

But hasn't time shown up their emptiness?

JOCASTA

How did you live before marriage brought you livelihood?

POLYNICES

Sometimes I had enough for the day, sometimes not.

JOCASTA

But did your father's foreign friends not help you?

POLYNICES

You must prosper! Friends vanish if your luck turns sour.

JOCASTA

And did your noble birth not raise you high?

---

401 αὖ Reiske, Valckenaer
404 μέγαν Wecklein: μέγα C

ΠΟΛΥΝΕΙΚΗΣ

405   κακὸν τὸ μὴ 'χειν· τὸ γένος οὐκ ἔβοσκέ με.

ΙΟΚΑΣΤΗ

ἡ πατρίς, ὡς ἔοικε, φίλτατον βροτοῖς.

ΠΟΛΥΝΕΙΚΗΣ

οὐδ' ὀνομάσαι δύναι' ἂν ὡς ἐστὶν φίλον.

ΙΟΚΑΣΤΗ

408   πῶς δ' ἦλθες Ἄργος; τίν' ἐπίνοιαν ἔσχεθες;

ΠΟΛΥΝΕΙΚΗΣ

413   οὐκ οἶδ'· ὁ δαίμων μ' ἐκάλεσεν πρὸς τὴν τύχην.

ΙΟΚΑΣΤΗ

414   σοφὸς γὰρ ὁ θεός· τίνι τρόπῳ δ' ἔσχες λέχος;

ΠΟΛΥΝΕΙΚΗΣ

409   ἔχρησ' Ἀδράστῳ Λοξίας χρησμόν τινα.

ΙΟΚΑΣΤΗ

410   ποῖον; τί τοῦτ' ἔλεξας; οὐκ ἔχω μαθεῖν.

ΠΟΛΥΝΕΙΚΗΣ

κάπρῳ λέοντί θ' ἁρμόσαι παίδων γάμους.

ΙΟΚΑΣΤΗ

412   καὶ σοὶ τί θηρῶν ὀνόματος μετῆν, τέκνον;

ΠΟΛΥΝΕΙΚΗΣ

415   νὺξ ἦν, Ἀδράστου δ' ἦλθον ἐς παραστάδας.

ΙΟΚΑΣΤΗ

κοίτας ματεύων, ἦ φυγὰς πλανώμενος;

POLYNICES
Want is a curse: my lineage did not feed me.

JOCASTA
Dearest to men, it seems, is native soil.

POLYNICES
Your words could not describe how dear it is.

JOCASTA
How did you come to Argos? With what purpose?

POLYNICES
I do not know: heaven called me to my fate.

JOCASTA
The god is wise. But how did you win your bride?

POLYNICES
Loxias gave an oracle to Adrastus.

JOCASTA
What oracle do you mean? I am unclear.

POLYNICES
"To lion and to boar thy daughters marry."

JOCASTA
What share had you, son, in the name of beast?

POLYNICES
It was night: to Adrastus' vestibule I came.

JOCASTA
Seeking a bed, as wandering exile would?

413–4 post 408 trai. Jacobs

ΠΟΛΥΝΕΙΚΗΣ

ἦν ταῦτα· κᾆτά γ' ἦλθεν ἄλλος αὖ φυγάς.

ΙΟΚΑΣΤΗ

τίς οὗτος; ὡς ἄρ' ἄθλιος κἀκεῖνος ἦν.

ΠΟΛΥΝΕΙΚΗΣ

Τυδεύς, ὃν Οἰνέως φασὶν ἐκφῦναι πατρός.

ΙΟΚΑΣΤΗ

420 τί θηρσὶν ὑμᾶς δῆτ' Ἄδραστος ᾔκασεν;

ΠΟΛΥΝΕΙΚΗΣ

στρωμνῆς ἐς ἀλκὴν οὕνεκ' ἤλθομεν πέρι.

ΙΟΚΑΣΤΗ

ἐνταῦθα Ταλαοῦ παῖς συνῆκε θέσφατα;

ΠΟΛΥΝΕΙΚΗΣ

κἄδωκέ γ' ἡμῖν δύο δυοῖν νεάνιδας.

ΙΟΚΑΣΤΗ

ἆρ' εὐτυχεῖς οὖν τοῖς γάμοις ἢ δυστυχεῖς;

ΠΟΛΥΝΕΙΚΗΣ

425 οὐ μεμπτὸς ἡμῖν ὁ γάμος ἐς τόδ' ἡμέρας.

ΙΟΚΑΣΤΗ

πῶς δ' ἐξέπεισας δεῦρό σοι σπέσθαι στρατόν;

ΠΟΛΥΝΕΙΚΗΣ

δισσοῖς Ἄδραστος ὤμοσεν γαμβροῖς τόδε,
[Τυδεῖ τε κἀμοί, σύγγαμος γάρ ἐστ' ἐμός,]

428 del. Jortin

POLYNICES

Just so. And then another exile came.

JOCASTA

Who? He too must have suffered misery!

POLYNICES

Tydeus, who's said to be the son of Oeneus.

JOCASTA

So why did Adrastus liken you to beasts?

POLYNICES

Because we came to blows about a bed.

JOCASTA

Then Talaus' son[24] perceived Apollo's meaning?

POLYNICES

Yes: to us two he married his two daughters.

JOCASTA

Are you happy with your wife, then, or unhappy?

POLYNICES

Up to this hour I make no complaint.

JOCASTA

How did you get an army to come with you?

POLYNICES

Adrastus swore to his two sons-in-law [, Tydeus and me, for he is a sharer with me in marriage,] that he would bring us

[24] I. e. Adrastus.

ἄμφω κατάξειν ἐς πάτραν, πρόσθεν δ' ἐμέ.
430 πολλοὶ δὲ Δαναῶν καὶ Μυκηναίων ἄκροι
πάρεισι, λυπρὰν χάριν, ἀναγκαίαν δέ μοι
διδόντες· ἐπὶ γὰρ τὴν ἐμὴν στρατεύομαι
πόλιν. θεοὺς δ' ἐπώμοσ' ὡς ἀκουσίως
τοῖς φιλτάτοις ἑκοῦσιν ἠράμην δόρυ.
435 ἀλλ' ἐς σὲ τείνει τῶνδε διάλυσις κακῶν,
[μῆτερ, διαλλάξασαν ὁμογενεῖς φίλους]
παῦσαι πόνων σὲ κἀμὲ καὶ πᾶσαν πόλιν.
[πάλαι μὲν οὖν ὑμνηθέν, ἀλλ' ὅμως ἐρῶ·
τὰ χρήματ' ἀνθρώποισι τιμιώτατα
440 δύναμίν τε πλείστην τῶν ἐν ἀνθρώποις ἔχει.
ἀγὼ μεθήκω δεῦρο μυρίαν ἄγων
λόγχην· πένης γὰρ οὐδὲν εὐγενὴς ἀνήρ.]

ΧΟΡΟΣ

καὶ μὴν Ἐτεοκλῆς ἐς διαλλαγὰς ὅδε
χωρεῖ· σὸν ἔργον, μῆτερ Ἰοκάστη, λέγειν
445 τοιούσδε μύθους οἷς διαλλάξεις τέκνα.

ΕΤΕΟΚΛΗΣ

μῆτερ, πάρειμι· τὴν χάριν δέ σοι διδοὺς
ἦλθον. τί χρὴ δρᾶν; ἀρχέτω δέ τις λόγου.
[ὡς ἀμφὶ τείχη καὶ ξυνωρίδας λόχων
τάσσων ἐπέσχον πόλιν, ὅπως κλύοιμί σου
450 κοινὰς βραβείας, αἷς ὑπόσπονδον μολεῖν
τόνδ' εἰσεδέξω τειχέων πείσασά με.]

436 om. Π, del. Nauck
438–42 del. Leidloff

both back from exile, beginning with me. Many nobles of Argos and Mycenae are here, rendering me a favor that I need but that brings me pain: it is my country I am marching against. I swear by the gods that I fight my brother against my will: it is he who wills it. But the ending of these woes depends upon you: [mother, by reconciling those of kindred blood,] rescue yourself and me and the whole city from calamity. [It was said long ago, but I will say it nevertheless: money is held in the highest esteem by mortals, and of all that is in the world of men it has the greatest power. It is to get this that I have come here with ten thousand spearmen. The nobleman who is poor is nothing.]

Enter ETEOCLES *with retinue by Eisodos A.*

CHORUS LEADER

But see, here comes Eteocles to parley. It is your task, mother Jocasta, to say such words as will reconcile your sons.

ETEOCLES

Mother, I am here. I have come as a favor to you. What must be done? Let someone begin the discussion. [For around the walls with their paired divisions I have suspended my marshalling of the citizens so that I may hear from you the judgments you are sharing with us, judgments by which you induced this man, after winning my consent, to come inside the walls under truce.]

He glares fiercely at his brother, who turns away.

448–51 del. Diggle (450–1 suspectos habuit Wecklein)

ΙΟΚΑΣΤΗ

ἐπίσχες· οὔτοι τὸ ταχὺ τὴν δίκην ἔχει,
βραδεῖς δὲ μῦθοι πλεῖστον ἀνύτουσιν σοφόν.
σχάσον δὲ δεινὸν ὄμμα καὶ θυμοῦ πνοάς·
455 οὐ γὰρ τὸ λαιμότμητον εἰσορᾷς κάρα
Γοργόνος, ἀδελφὸν δ' εἰσορᾷς ἥκοντα σόν.
σύ τ' αὖ πρόσωπον πρὸς κασίγνητον στρέφε,
Πολύνεικες· ἐς γὰρ ταὐτὸν ὄμμασιν βλέπων
λέξεις τ' ἄμεινον τοῦδέ τ' ἐνδέξῃ λόγους.
460   παραινέσαι δὲ σφῷν τι βούλομαι σοφόν·
ὅταν φίλος τις ἀνδρὶ θυμωθεὶς φίλῳ
ἐς ἓν συνελθὼν ὄμματ' ὄμμασιν διδῷ,
ἐφ' οἷσιν ἥκει, ταῦτα χρὴ μόνον σκοπεῖν,
κακῶν δὲ τῶν πρὶν μηδενὸς μνείαν ἔχειν.
465   λόγος μὲν οὖν σὸς πρόσθε, Πολύνεικες τέκνον·
σὺ γὰρ στράτευμα Δαναϊδῶν ἥκεις ἄγων,
ἄδικα πεπονθώς, ὡς σὺ φής· κριτὴς δέ τις
θεῶν γένοιτο καὶ διαλλακτὴς κακῶν.

ΠΟΛΥΝΕΙΚΗΣ

ἁπλοῦς ὁ μῦθος τῆς ἀληθείας ἔφυ,
470 κοὐ ποικίλων δεῖ τἄνδιχ' ἑρμηνευμάτων·
ἔχει γὰρ αὐτὰ καιρόν· ὁ δ' ἄδικος λόγος
νοσῶν ἐν αὑτῷ φαρμάκων δεῖται σοφῶν.
ἐγὼ δ' ἀπάρας δωμάτων προυσκεψάμην
τοὐμόν τε καὶ τοῦδ', ἐκφυγεῖν χρῄζων ἀρὰς
475 ἃς Οἰδίπους ἐφθέγξατ' εἰς ἡμᾶς ποτε·
ἐξῆλθον ἔξω τῆσδ' ἑκὼν αὐτὸς χθονός,

JOCASTA

Hold on! Haste does not produce justice. It is deliberate words that most often produce a wise result. Stop your fierce glaring and your angry panting! You are not looking at the severed head of the Gorgon but at your own brother, who has come here. And you, Polynices, turn your face toward your brother. If your glances meet, you will not only speak better but also be better at listening to his words. (*They face one another.*)

Now I want to give the two of you some wise advice. When friend is angry with friend and goes to meet him face to face, he must consider only the business that brought him there and say nothing of any wrongs that happened before.

It is your turn to speak first, Polynices my son. You have come bringing an army of the sons of Danaus, having suffered, as you claim, unjust treatment. May one of the gods be the judge and arbitrator of your troubles!

POLYNICES

Truth's argument is simple, and justice needs no elaborate presentation: all by itself it shows the proper measure. But unjust argument, being diseased in itself, requires clever medicines.

I for my part in leaving home took thought for his interests and mine and tried to escape from the curses Oedipus once uttered against us. I left this land myself of my own

---

453 ἀνύτουσιν Hermann: ἀνύουσιν C
473 δ᾽ ἀπάρας Diggle: δὲ πατρὸς C

δοὺς τῷδ᾽ ἀνάσσειν πατρίδος ἐνιαυτοῦ κύκλον
[ὥστ᾽ αὐτὸς ἄρχειν αὖθις ἀνὰ μέρος λαβὼν
καὶ μὴ δι᾽ ἔχθρας τῷδε καὶ φθόνου μολὼν
480 κακόν τι δρᾶσαι καὶ παθεῖν, ἃ γίγνεται].
ὁ δ᾽ αἰνέσας ταῦθ᾽ ὅρκίους τε δοὺς θεοὺς
ἔδρασεν οὐδὲν ὧν ὑπέσχετ᾽, ἀλλ᾽ ἔχει
τυραννίδ᾽ αὐτὸς καὶ δόμων ἐμὸν μέρος.

καὶ νῦν ἕτοιμός εἰμι τἀμαυτοῦ λαβὼν
485 στρατὸν μὲν ἔξω τῆσδ᾽ ἀποστεῖλαι χθονός,
οἰκεῖν δὲ τὸν ἐμὸν οἶκον ἀνὰ μέρος λαβὼν
καὶ τῷδ᾽ ἀφεῖναι τὸν ἴσον αὖθις ⟨ἐς⟩ χρόνον,
καὶ μήτε πορθεῖν πατρίδα μήτε προσφέρειν
πύργοισι πηκτῶν κλιμάκων προσαμβάσεις·
490 ἃ μὴ κυρήσας τῆς δίκης πειράσομαι
δρᾶν. μάρτυρας δὲ τῶνδε δαίμονας καλῶ,
ὡς πάντα πράσσων σὺν δίκῃ δίκης ἄτερ
ἀποστεροῦμαι πατρίδος ἀνοσιώτατα.

ταῦτ᾽ αὔθ᾽ ἕκαστα, μῆτερ, οὐχὶ περιπλοκὰς
495 λόγων ἀθροίσας εἶπον ἀλλὰ καὶ σοφοῖς
καὶ τοῖσι φαύλοις ἔνδιχ᾽, ὡς ἐμοὶ δοκεῖ.

ΧΟΡΟΣ

ἐμοὶ μέν, εἰ καὶ μὴ καθ᾽ Ἑλλήνων χθόνα
τεθράμμεθ᾽, ἀλλ᾽ οὖν ξυνετά μοι δοκεῖς λέγειν.

ΕΤΕΟΚΛΗΣ

εἰ πᾶσι ταὐτὸ καλὸν ἔφυ σοφόν θ᾽ ἅμα,
500 οὐκ ἦν ἂν ἀμφίλεκτος ἀνθρώποις ἔρις·
νῦν δ᾽ οὔθ᾽ ὅμοιον οὐδὲν οὔτ᾽ ἴσον βροτοῖς

accord, granting this man the right to govern the country for a year. [I was to rule again, taking my turn, and not to come in hatred and ill will toward this man and inflict and suffer harm, which is what is happening.] He agreed to this and swore an oath by the gods but then failed utterly to keep his promises. Instead he holds onto the kingship himself and keeps my share of the house.

Now I am prepared, if I get what is my own, to send the army away from this land, to administer my house, taking my turn, and to relinquish it to this man later ⟨for⟩ the same period, not sacking my country or applying scaling ladders to its towers. But if I do not receive justice, I shall attempt to do these things. I call on the gods to witness that though I am acting justly in all respects, I am being deprived of my country contrary to justice and piety.

I have spoken the precise facts, plain and simple, mother, not marshaling deceitful rhetoric but only saying what is just, it seems to me, in the eyes both of the wise and the simple.

CHORUS LEADER

Though I was not brought up in Greece, to me you seem to be speaking sensibly.

ETEOCLES

If everyone defined justice and wisdom the same way, there would be no quarreling or strife among men. As things stand, the only similarity or equality mortals show is

---

478–80 del. Diggle
487 ⟨ἐς⟩ Jackson

πλὴν ὀνόμασιν· τὸ δ' ἔργον οὐκ ἔστιν τόδε.
ἐγὼ γὰρ οὐδέν, μῆτερ, ἀποκρύψας ἐρῶ·
ἄστρων ἂν ἔλθοιμ' αἰθέρος πρὸς ἀντολὰς
505 καὶ γῆς ἔνερθε, δυνατὸς ὢν δρᾶσαι τάδε,
τὴν θεῶν μεγίστην ὥστ' ἔχειν Τυραννίδα.
τοῦτ' οὖν τὸ χρηστόν, μῆτερ, οὐχὶ βούλομαι
ἄλλῳ παρεῖναι μᾶλλον ἢ σῴζειν ἐμοί·
ἀνανδρία γάρ, τὸ πλέον ὅστις ἀπολέσας
510 τοὔλασσον ἔλαβε. πρὸς δὲ τοῖσδ' αἰσχύνομαι
ἐλθόντα σὺν ὅπλοις τόνδε καὶ πορθοῦντα γῆν
τυχεῖν ἃ χρῄζει· ταῖς γὰρ ἂν Θήβαις τόδε
γένοιτ' ὄνειδος, εἰ Μυκηναίου δορὸς
φόβῳ παρείην σκῆπτρα τἀμὰ τῷδ' ἔχειν.
515 χρῆν δ' αὐτὸν οὐχ ὅπλοισι τὰς διαλλαγάς,
μῆτερ, ποιεῖσθαι· πᾶν γὰρ ἐξαιρεῖ λόγος
ὃ καὶ σίδηρος πολεμίων δράσειεν ἄν.
ἀλλ', εἰ μὲν ἄλλως τήνδε γῆν οἰκεῖν θέλει,
ἔξεστ'· ἐκείνου δ' οὐχ ἑκὼν μεθήσομαι·
520 ἄρχειν παρόν μοι, τῷδε δουλεύσω ποτέ;
   πρὸς ταῦτ' ἴτω μὲν πῦρ, ἴτω δὲ φάσγανα,
ζεύγνυσθε δ' ἵππους, πεδία πίμπλαθ' ἁρμάτων,
ὡς οὐ παρήσω τῷδ' ἐμὴν τυραννίδα.
εἴπερ γὰρ ἀδικεῖν χρή, τυραννίδος πέρι
525 κάλλιστον ἀδικεῖν, τἄλλα δ' εὐσεβεῖν χρεών.

ΧΟΡΟΣ

οὐκ εὖ λέγειν χρὴ μὴ 'πὶ τοῖς ἔργοις καλοῖς·
οὐ γὰρ καλὸν τοῦτ' ἀλλὰ τῇ δίκῃ πικρόν.

in their use of words: the reality to which these refer is not the same.

I shall speak, mother, and hold nothing back. I would go to where heaven's constellations rise, go beneath the earth, if it lay in my power, in order to possess Tyranny,[25] greatest of the gods. Hence, mother, I do not want to yield this good to another: I want to keep it myself. It is unmanly to give up the greater thing and take the lesser. Furthermore I feel shame at the thought that this man, coming with an army and trying to sack the city, should get what he wants. This would be a disgrace for Thebes if from fear of Mycenae's spear[26] I should yield my scepter for him to possess. He ought not to be trying to reach an agreement by force of arms: speech accomplishes everything an enemy's arms might accomplish. Well, if he wants to dwell in this land on other terms, he may do so. But this point I shall never willingly give up: when I can rule, shall I be this man's slave?

Since this is so, let swords advance, yoke your horses, fill the plains with chariots! For I shall never surrender my kingship to him. If one must commit injustice, it is best to do so for the sake of tyranny, being god-fearing in all else.

CHORUS LEADER
Men should not speak fair about ignoble deeds. That is dishonorable and hateful to justice.

[25] I. e. autocratic rule.   [26] Mycenae is used as a virtual synonym for Argos in Greek tragedy.

---

502 ὀνόμασιν Markland, Porson: ὀνομάσαι C
504 αἰθέρος t: ἡλίου C
516 fort. λόγους
520 del. Kirchhoff

ΙΟΚΑΣΤΗ

ὦ τέκνον, οὐχ ἅπαντα τῷ γήρᾳ κακά,
Ἐτεόκλεες, πρόσεστιν· ἀλλ' ἐμπειρία
530 ἔχει τι λέξαι τῶν νέων σοφώτερον.
τί τῆς κακίστης δαιμόνων ἐφίεσαι
Φιλοτιμίας, παῖ; μὴ σύ γ'· ἄδικος ἡ θεός·
πολλοὺς δ' ἐς οἴκους καὶ πόλεις εὐδαίμονας
ἐσῆλθε κἀξῆλθ' ἐπ' ὀλέθρῳ τῶν χρωμένων·
535 ἐφ' ᾗ σὺ μαίνῃ. κεῖνο κάλλιον, τέκνον,
Ἰσότητα τιμᾶν, ἣ φίλους ἀεὶ φίλοις
πόλεις τε πόλεσι συμμάχους τε συμμάχοις
συνδεῖ· τὸ γὰρ ἴσον νόμιμον ἀνθρώποις ἔφυ,
τῷ πλέονι δ' αἰεὶ πολέμιον καθίσταται
540 τοὔλασσον ἐχθρᾶς θ' ἡμέρας κατάρχεται.
καὶ γὰρ μέτρ' ἀνθρώποισι καὶ μέρη σταθμῶν
Ἰσότης ἔταξε κἀριθμὸν διώρισεν,
νυκτός τ' ἀφεγγὲς βλέφαρον ἡλίου τε φῶς
ἴσον βαδίζει τὸν ἐνιαύσιον κύκλον,
545 κοὐδέτερον αὐτοῖν φθόνον ἔχει νικώμενον.
εἶθ' ἥλιος μὲν νύξ τε δουλεύει βροτοῖς
σὺ δ' οὐκ ἀνέξῃ δωμάτων ἔχων ἴσον
καὶ τῷδε νεῖμαι; κᾆτα ποῦ 'στιν ἡ δίκη;
[τί τὴν τυραννίδ', ἀδικίαν εὐδαίμονα,
550 τιμᾷς ὑπέρφευ καὶ μέγ' ἥγησαι τόδε;
περιβλέπεσθαι τίμιον; κενὸν μὲν οὖν.
ἢ πολλὰ μοχθεῖν πόλλ' ἔχων ἐν δώμασιν
βούλῃ; τί δ' ἔστι τὸ πλέον; ὄνομ' ἔχει μόνον·

JOCASTA

My son Eteocles, not all that attends old age is bad: the old
have experience, which can speak more wisely than youth.

Why do you strive for Ambition, the basest of divinities,
my son? Do not do so: she is an unjust goddess! Often she
goes in and out of prosperous cities and houses and ruins
those who have dealings with her! Yet for her you have lost
your senses. Far finer, my son, to honor Equality, which
binds friends to friends, cities to cities, and allies to allies.
For Equality, men find, conduces to lawfulness,[27] whereas
the lesser is always hostile to the greater and making war
against it. In fact, it is Equality that has established mea-
sures and weights for mankind and given them number.
For Night's rayless eyelid walks an equal portion of the
yearly round with the light of Day, and neither of them
feels envy when bested. So then, while daylight and dark-
ness serve mankind's needs, will you, having an equal share
of the house, refuse to accord it to this man? Where then is
justice?

[Why do you so excessively honor tyranny, which is
prosperous injustice? Why regard this as a great thing? Is it
worthwhile to be the object of every gaze? No, it is an
empty thing. Or do you wish to toil mightily because of the
mighty possessions in your house? What is the advantage

---

[27] Or, reading μόνιμον, "stability."

---

538 μόνιμον t   546 βροτοῖς] μέτροις Weil
548 νεῖμαι Salmasius: ἀπονεῖμαι a: -νέμειν b: -νέμων c
v. del. Schoene
549-67 del. Kovacs (552-8 Zipperer, 563-5 Willink, 566-7
Dindorf)

ἐπεὶ τά γ᾽ ἀρκοῦνθ᾽ ἱκανὰ τοῖς γε σώφροσιν.

555 οὔτοι τὰ χρήματ᾽ ἴδια κέκτηνται βροτοί,
τὰ τῶν θεῶν δ᾽ ἔχοντες ἐπιμελούμεθα·
ὅταν δὲ χρῄζωσ᾽ αὔτ᾽ ἀφαιροῦνται πάλιν·
ὁ δ᾽ ὄλβος οὐ βέβαιος ἀλλ᾽ ἐφήμερος.

ἄγ᾽, ἤν σ᾽ ἔρωμαι δύο λόγω προθεῖσ᾽ ἅμα,
560 πότερα τυραννεῖν ἢ πόλιν σῶσαι θέλεις,
ἐρεῖς τυραννεῖν; ἢν δὲ νικήσῃ σ᾽ ὅδε
Ἀργεῖά τ᾽ ἔγχη δόρυ τὸ Καδμείων ἕλῃ,
ὄψῃ δαμασθὲν ἄστυ Θηβαίων τόδε,
ὄψῃ δὲ πολλὰς αἰχμαλωτίδας κόρας
565 βίᾳ πρὸς ἀνδρῶν πολεμίων πορθουμένας.
δαπανηρὸς ἆρ᾽ ὁ πλοῦτος ὃν ζητεῖς ἔχειν
γενήσεται Θήβαισι, φιλότιμος δὲ σύ.]

σοὶ μὲν τάδ᾽ αὐδῶ. σοὶ δέ, Πολύνεικες, λέγω·
ἀμαθεῖς Ἄδραστος χάριτας ἐς σ᾽ ἀνήψατο,
570 ἀσύνετα δ᾽ ἦλθες καὶ σὺ πορθήσων πόλιν.
φέρ᾽, ἢν ἕλῃς γῆν τήνδ᾽, ὃ μὴ τύχοι ποτέ,
πρὸς θεῶν, τρόπαια πῶς ἄρα στήσεις Διί;
πῶς δ᾽ αὖ κατάρξῃ θυμάτων, ἑλὼν πάτραν,
καὶ σκῦλα γράψεις πῶς ἐπ᾽ Ἰνάχου ῥοαῖς;
575 Θήβας πυρώσας τάσδε Πολυνείκης θεοῖς
ἀσπίδας ἔθηκε; μήποτ᾽, ὦ τέκνον, κλέος
τοιόνδε σοι γένοιθ᾽ ὑφ᾽ Ἑλλήνων λαβεῖν.
ἢν δ᾽ αὖ κρατηθῇς καὶ τὰ τοῦδ᾽ ὑπερδράμῃ,
πῶς Ἄργος ἥξεις μυρίους λιπὼν νεκρούς;
580 ἐρεῖ δὲ δή τις· Ὦ κακὰ μνηστεύματα

266

of that? An advantage in name only. A sufficiency is enough for the self-controlled. Mortals do not own wealth as their own property: we merely hold what is the gods' and look after it. When they want it, they take it away again. Wealth is not secure but fleeting.

Come, if I ask you a question, setting two accounts before you at once, whether you would prefer to be king or to save your city, would you say "be king"? But if this man defeats you and the Argive sword conquers the Theban spear, you will see the city of Thebes defeated and see many captive women forcibly carried off as booty by the enemy. And so the wealth you desire to possess will prove costly to Thebes, and you are an ambitious man.]

Those are my words to you. To you, Polynices, I say this. It was a foolish favor Adrastus did you, and your coming here to sack the city was a fool's errand. Come, if you conquer this land—and heaven forbid you should—in the name of the gods how will you set up trophies to Zeus,[28] how will you make burnt offerings, having destroyed your country? What will you inscribe on the spoils by the streams of Inachus?[29] "Having set fire to Thebes Polynices dedicates these shields to the gods"? Never, my son, may you win fame like this from the Greeks! On the other hand, if you are beaten and his forces are superior, how will you return to Argos, having left behind countless dead? Someone will say, "O Adrastus, inflicter on us of ruinous mar-

[28] After a battle the victorious general set up a marker in honor of Zeus Tropaios, "Zeus of the Rout," as thanks for victory.

[29] Chief river of Argos.

572 ἄρα στήσεις Porson: ἀναστήσεις C

Ἄδραστε προσθείς, διὰ μιᾶς νύμφης γάμον
ἀπωλόμεσθα. δύο κακὼ σπεύδεις, τέκνον,
κείνων στέρεσθαι τῶνδέ τ' ἐν μέσῳ πεσεῖν.
μέθετον τὸ λίαν, μέθετον· ἀμαθία δυοῖν,
585 ἐς ταῦθ' ὅταν μόλητον, ἔχθιστον κακόν.

ΧΟΡΟΣ

ὦ θεοί, γένοισθε τῶνδ' ἀπότροποι κακῶν
καὶ ξύμβασίν τιν' Οἰδίπου τέκνοις δότε.

ΕΤΕΟΚΛΗΣ

μῆτερ, οὐ λόγων ἔθ' ἀγών, ἀλλ' ἀναλοῦται χρόνος
οὑν μέσῳ μάτην, περαίνει δ' οὐδὲν ἡ προθυμία·
590 οὐ γὰρ ἂν ξυμβαῖμεν ἄλλως ἢ 'πὶ τοῖς εἰρημένοις,
ὥστ' ἐμὲ σκήπτρων κρατοῦντα τῆσδ' ἄνακτ' εἶναι
χθονός·
τῶν μακρῶν δ' ἀπαλλαγεῖσα νουθετημάτων μ' ἔα.
καὶ σὺ τῶνδ' ἔξω κομίζου τειχέων, ἢ κατθανῇ.

ΠΟΛΥΝΕΙΚΗΣ

πρὸς τίνος; τίς ὧδ' ἄτρωτος ὅστις εἰς ἡμᾶς ξίφος
595 φόνιον ἐμβαλὼν τὸν αὐτὸν οὐκ ἀποίσεται μόρον;

ΕΤΕΟΚΛΗΣ

ἐγγύς, οὐ πρόσω, βέβηκεν· ἐς χέρας λεύσσεις ἐμάς;

ΠΟΛΥΝΕΙΚΗΣ

εἰσορῶ· δειλὸν δ' ὁ πλοῦτος καὶ φιλόψυχον κακόν.

596 ἐς] fort. ἢ

riages, because of the marriage of one bride we have been ruined." It is a double misfortune you are pursuing, my son, losing what you have there and falling short of your goal here.

Let go of this excess, let it go, both of you! When two fools come together, the result is calamity most bitter.

CHORUS LEADER

O gods, avert this calamity and provide some kind of reconciliation for the sons of Oedipus!

ETEOCLES

Mother, it's too late for contests of words: time until the battle is time wasted, and your efforts do no good. We can never reach an agreement except on the terms already named: I hold the scepter and I rule this land. Give up your long admonitions and let me go. (*To Polynices*) And you, take yourself outside the walls—or you're a dead man.

POLYNICES

And who's going to kill me? Who is so invulnerable that he can thrust his murderous sword at me and not receive the death he would inflict?

ETEOCLES

He is standing nearby, not far off. Are you looking at my hands? (*He grasps the hilt of his sword as if to draw it.*)

POLYNICES

I am looking. But Mr. Wealth's a cowardly warrior, afraid to lose his life.

ΕΤΕΟΚΛΗΣ

κᾆτα σὺν πολλοῖσιν ἦλθες πρὸς τὸν οὐδὲν ἐς
μάχην;

ΠΟΛΥΝΕΙΚΗΣ

ἀσφαλὴς γάρ ἐστ' ἀμείνων ἢ θρασὺς στρατηλάτης.

ΕΤΕΟΚΛΗΣ

600 κομπὸς εἶ σπονδαῖς πεποιθώς, αἵ σε σῴζουσιν
θανεῖν.

ΠΟΛΥΝΕΙΚΗΣ

καὶ σέ· δεύτερον δ' ἀπαιτῶ σκῆπτρα καὶ μέρη
χθονός.

ΕΤΕΟΚΛΗΣ

οὐκ ἀπαιτούμεσθ'· ἐγὼ γὰρ τὸν ἐμὸν οἰκήσω δόμον.

ΠΟΛΥΝΕΙΚΗΣ

τοῦ μέρους ἔχων τὰ πλείω;

ΕΤΕΟΚΛΗΣ

        φήμ'· ἀπαλλάσσου δὲ γῆς.

ΠΟΛΥΝΕΙΚΗΣ

ὦ θεῶν βωμοὶ πατρῴων . . .

ΕΤΕΟΚΛΗΣ

        οὓς σὺ πορθήσων πάρει.

ΠΟΛΥΝΕΙΚΗΣ

605 . . . κλύετέ μου . . .

ΕΤΕΟΚΛΗΣ

    τίς δ' ἂν κλύοι σου πατρίδ' ἐπεστρατευμένου;

ETEOCLES

And so you came with many men against such a contempt-ible fighter?

POLYNICES

Yes, for better a safe general than a brash one.

ETEOCLES

You talk big, with the truce to keep you from being killed.

POLYNICES

It keeps you as well. For the second time: I demand the scepter and my share of the land.

ETEOCLES

I don't allow any such demand! I shall manage my own house.

POLYNICES

With more than your share?

ETEOCLES

Yes, that's right. Now leave the country.

POLYNICES

You altars of our fathers' gods . . .

ETEOCLES

Altars you came to ravage!

POLYNICES

. . . hear me!

ETEOCLES

What god would listen to you, on the march against your country?

---

601 δ' Wilamowitz: γ' C

ΠΟΛΥΝΕΙΚΗΣ
καὶ θεῶν τῶν λευκοπώλων δώμαθ᾽ . . .

ΕΤΕΟΚΛΗΣ
οἳ στυγοῦσί σε.

ΠΟΛΥΝΕΙΚΗΣ
. . . ἐξελαυνόμεσθα πατρίδος . . .

ΕΤΕΟΚΛΗΣ
καὶ γὰρ ἦλθες ἐξελῶν.

ΠΟΛΥΝΕΙΚΗΣ
. . . ἀδικίᾳ γ᾽, ὦ θεοί.

ΕΤΕΟΚΛΗΣ
Μυκήναις, μὴ 'νθάδ᾽ ἀνακάλει θεούς.

ΠΟΛΥΝΕΙΚΗΣ
ἀνόσιος πέφυκας . . .

ΕΤΕΟΚΛΗΣ
ἀλλ᾽ οὐ πατρίδος ὡς σὺ πολέμιος.

ΠΟΛΥΝΕΙΚΗΣ
610   . . . ὅς μ᾽ ἄμοιρον ἐξελαύνεις.

ΕΤΕΟΚΛΗΣ
καὶ κατακτενῶ γε πρός.

ΠΟΛΥΝΕΙΚΗΣ
ὦ πάτερ, κλύεις ἃ πάσχω;

ΕΤΕΟΚΛΗΣ
καὶ γὰρ οἷα δρᾷς κλύει.

POLYNICES

And you temples of the white-horsed gods[30] . . .

ETEOCLES

Gods who detest you!

POLYNICES

. . . I am being driven from my country . . .

ETEOCLES

Yes: you came to drive us from it!

POLYNICES

. . . unjustly, O gods!

ETEOCLES

Call on the gods in Mycenae, not here!

POLYNICES

You are godless . . .

ETEOCLES

But not my country's foe, as you are!

POLYNICES

. . . since you expel me without my portion.

ETEOCLES

Yes, and I will kill you into the bargain!

POLYNICES

Father, do you hear what is being done to me?

ETEOCLES

Yes, for he also hears what you are doing!

[30] Amphion and Zethus, sons of Zeus, worshiped as gods.

ΠΟΛΥΝΕΙΚΗΣ

καὶ σύ, μῆτερ;

ΕΤΕΟΚΛΗΣ
    ἀθέμιτόν σοι μητρὸς ὀνομάζειν κάρα.

ΠΟΛΥΝΕΙΚΗΣ

ὦ πόλις.

ΕΤΕΟΚΛΗΣ
    μολὼν ἐς Ἄργος ἀνακάλει Λέρνης ὕδωρ.

ΠΟΛΥΝΕΙΚΗΣ
εἶμι, μὴ πόνει· σὲ δ᾽ αἰνῶ, μῆτερ.

ΕΤΕΟΚΛΗΣ
        ἔξιθι χθονός.

ΠΟΛΥΝΕΙΚΗΣ
615 ἔξιμεν· πατέρα δέ μοι δὸς εἰσιδεῖν.

ΕΤΕΟΚΛΗΣ
        οὐκ ἂν τύχοις.

ΠΟΛΥΝΕΙΚΗΣ
ἀλλὰ παρθένους ἀδελφάς.

ΕΤΕΟΚΛΗΣ
     οὐδὲ τάσδ᾽ ὄψῃ ποτέ.

ΠΟΛΥΝΕΙΚΗΣ
ὦ κασίγνηται.

ΕΤΕΟΚΛΗΣ
    τί ταύτας ἀνακαλεῖς ἔχθιστος ὤν;

POLYNICES

And you, mother?

ETEOCLES

You may not call her mother: the gods' law forbids it!

POLYNICES

O city!

ETEOCLES

Go to Argos and call upon the waters of Lerna!

POLYNICES

I'm going, don't worry! I thank you, mother!

ETEOCLES

Leave the country!

POLYNICES

I'm leaving, but give me permission to see my father.

ETEOCLES

That you shall never get!

POLYNICES

Well, at least my maiden sisters.

ETEOCLES

You will never see them either.

POLYNICES

O sisters!

ETEOCLES

Why do you call on them when you are their enemy?

---

615 ἔξιμεν Musgrave: ἔξειμι C

ΠΟΛΥΝΕΙΚΗΣ

μῆτερ, ἀλλά μοι σὺ χαῖρε.

ΙΟΚΑΣΤΗ

  χαρτὰ γοῦν πάσχω, τέκνον.

ΠΟΛΥΝΕΙΚΗΣ

οὐκέτ᾽ εἰμὶ παῖς σός.

ΙΟΚΑΣΤΗ

  ἐς πόλλ᾽ ἀθλία πέφυκ᾽ ἐγώ.

ΠΟΛΥΝΕΙΚΗΣ

620 ὅδε γὰρ εἰς ἡμᾶς ὑβρίζει.

ΕΤΕΟΚΛΗΣ

  καὶ γὰρ ἀνθυβρίζομαι.

ΠΟΛΥΝΕΙΚΗΣ

ποῦ ποτε στήσῃ πρὸ πύργων;

ΕΤΕΟΚΛΗΣ

  ὡς τί μ᾽ ἱστορεῖς τόδε;

ΠΟΛΥΝΕΙΚΗΣ

ἀντιτάξομαι κτενῶν σε.

ΕΤΕΟΚΛΗΣ

  κἀμὲ τοῦδ᾽ ἔρως ἔχει.

ΙΟΚΑΣΤΗ

ὦ τάλαιν᾽ ἐγώ· τί δράσετ᾽, ὦ τέκν᾽;

ΠΟΛΥΝΕΙΚΗΣ

  αὐτὸ σημανεῖ.

POLYNICES

Mother, you at least I wish joy!

JOCASTA

Yes, much joy have I in what befalls me, my son!

POLYNICES

You have lost your son.

JOCASTA

I am miserable in many ways.

POLYNICES

Yes, since he commits outrage against me.

ETEOCLES

Outrage is being committed against me in turn.

POLYNICES

Where will your station before the battlements be?

ETEOCLES

Why do you ask me that?

POLYNICES

I shall take my stand opposite you to kill you!

ETEOCLES

I too long to do this!

JOCASTA

O unhappy me! What are you going to do, my sons?

ETEOCLES

The event will make it plain.

ΙΟΚΑΣΤΗ

πατρὸς οὐ φεύξεσθ᾽ Ἐρινῦς;

ΠΟΛΥΝΕΙΚΗΣ

ἐρρέτω πρόπας δόμος·

625 ὡς τάχ᾽ οὐκέθ᾽ αἱματηρὸν τοὐμὸν ἀργήσει ξίφος.
τὴν δὲ θρέψασάν με γαῖαν καὶ θεοὺς μαρτύρομαι
ὡς ἄτιμος οἰκτρὰ πάσχων ἐξελαύνομαι χθονός,
δοῦλος ὡς ἀλλ᾽ οὐχὶ ταὐτοῦ πατρὸς Οἰδίπου γεγώς·
κἄν τί σοι, πόλις, γένηται, μὴ ᾽μέ, τόνδε δ᾽ αἰτιῶ·
630 οὐχ ἑκὼν γὰρ ἦλθον, ἄκων δ᾽ †ἐξελαύνομαι χθονός†.
   καὶ σύ, Φοῖβ᾽ ἄναξ Ἀγυιεῦ, καὶ μέλαθρα, χαίρετε,
ἥλικές θ᾽ οὑμοί, θεῶν τε δεξίμηλ᾽ ἀγάλματα.
οὐ γὰρ οἶδ᾽ εἴ μοι προσειπεῖν αὖθις ἔσθ᾽ ὑμᾶς ποτε·
ἐλπίδες δ᾽ οὔπω καθεύδουσ᾽, αἷς πέποιθα σὺν θεοῖς
635 τόνδ᾽ ἀποκτείνας κρατήσειν τῆσδε Θηβαίας χθονός.

ΕΤΕΟΚΛΗΣ

ἔξιθ᾽ ἐκ χώρας· ἀληθῶς δ᾽ ὄνομα Πολυνείκη πατὴρ
ἔθετό σοι θείᾳ προνοίᾳ νεικέων ἐπώνυμον.

ΧΟΡΟΣ

στρ.

Κάδμος ἔμολε τάνδε γᾶν
Τύριος, ᾧ τετρασκελὲς

630 verba ἐξελαύνομαι χθονός ex 627 huc irrepsisse vidit
Schoene, qui ἔριν ἐπαίρομαι χθονί scribit   v. del. Valckenaer
639–40 τετρασκελὲς . . . ἀδάματος Bergk: -ῆς . . . -αστον C: cf.
Ov. Met. 3.16

278

JOCASTA

Will you not flee from your father's Erinyes?

POLYNICES

Let the whole house go to ruin! My sword will have blood:
it will not long be idle. But I call on the land that nourished
me and on the gods, to witness that I am being driven, dis-
honored and in misery, from the country, like a slave, not
the son of Oedipus, who is my father no less than his! If
anything befalls you, O city, blame this man, not me. I
came here not of my own will, and it is under compulsion
that I wage this war.

Farewell to you, Phoebus, Lord of the Ways,[31] farewell,
my house, my agemates, and the statues of the gods, re-
ceivers of sacrifice. I do not know whether I shall ever
again address you. But hope never sleeps, hope which
makes me confident that with the gods' help I will kill this
man and rule Thebes.

Exit POLYNICES by Eisodos B, JOCASTA into the skene.

ETEOCLES

Leave the country! It was all too truly that your father, pro-
phetically inspired, called you Polynices, "man of strife"![32]

Exit ETEOCLES with retinue into the skene.

CHORUS

Cadmus came to this land,
the man of Tyre, for whom a calf, on its four legs,

---

[31] Apollo Aguieus, god of ways, may have been represented on
stage as a statue. Apollo's role in the action is, of course, a sig-
nificant one.   [32] Polynices' name means "much strife."

640 μόσχος ἀδάματος πέσημα
   δίκε τελεσφόρον διδοῦσα
   χρησμόν, οὗ κατοικίσαι
   πεδία νιν τὸ θέσφατον
   πυροφόρα μολόντ᾽ ἔχρη,
645 καλλιπόταμος ὕδατος ἵνα τε
   νοτὶς ἐπέρχεται ῥοαῖς
   Δίρκας χλοηφόρους
   καὶ βαθυσπόρους γύας·
   Βρόμιον ἔνθα τέκετο μά-
650 τηρ Διὸς γάμοισιν,
   κισσὸς ὃν περιστεφὴς
   ἑλικτὸς εὐθὺς ἔτι βρέφος χλοηφόροι-
   σιν ἔρνεσιν κατασκίοι-
   σιν ὀλβίσας ἐνώτισεν,
655 βάκχιον χόρευμα παρθέ-
   νοισι Θηβαΐαισι
   καὶ γυναιξὶν εὐίοις.

ἀντ.

   ἔνθα φόνιος ἦν δράκων
   Ἄρεος, ὠμόφρων φύλαξ,
   νάματ᾽ ἔνυδρα καὶ ῥέεθρα
660 χλοερὰ δεργμάτων κόραισι
   πολυπλάνοις ἐπισκοπῶν·

643 νιν Dindorf: μὲν C   644 μολόντ᾽ Wilamowitz: δόμων
C   ἔχρη Bergk: ἔχρησε C
646 ῥοαῖς Willink: γυίαις C: γάνος Mastronarde

unbent to the yoke,
threw itself down, fulfilling
prophecy in the place
where the oracle ordained he should come
to live in the wheat-bearing fields,[33]
the place where by Dirce's stream
the dew of lovely rivers
visits the grassy
and luxuriant plains.
There it was that Bromius' mother[34] gave birth to him
when she had lain with Zeus,
and about him, though still a babe,
forthwith the curling ivy
with its shoots of shady green
covered him in blessedness,
the Bacchic god worshiped in dancing
by maids and matrons
of Thebes in their ecstasy.

In that place was the deadly serpent
of Ares, fierce-tempered guardian:
over the watery eddies
and fresh streams he kept watch
with gazing eye that ever moved.

[33] Cadmus, ordered by his father Agenor to find his sister Europa, who had been abducted by Zeus, went to Delphi. Apollo told him to follow a calf and to found a city where the animal lay down.

[34] Semele, impregnated by Zeus, gave birth to Dionysus, also called Bromius.

ὃν ἐπὶ χέρνιβας μολὼν
Κάδμος ὄλεσε μαρμάρῳ,
κρᾶτα φόνιον ὀλεσίθηρος
665 ὠλένας κιχὼν βολαῖς,
δίας ‹δ᾽› ἀμάτορος
Παλλάδος ‹δίκεν› φραδαῖς
669 ἐς βαθυσπόρους γύας
668 γαπετεῖς ὀδόντας.
670 ἔνθεν ἐξανῆκε γᾶ
πάνοπλον ὄψιν ὑπὲρ ἄκρων ὅρων χθονός·
σιδαρόφρων δέ νιν φόνος
φίλᾳ ξυνῆψε γᾷ πάλιν.
αἵματος δ᾽ ἔδευσε γαῖαν,
ἅ νιν εὐαλίοισι
675 δεῖξεν αἰθέρος πνοαῖς.
ἐπῳδ.

καὶ σέ, τὸν προμάτορος
Ἰοῦς ποτ᾽ ἔκγονον
Ἔπαφον, ὦ Διὸς γένεθλον,
ἐκάλεσ᾽ ἐκάλεσ᾽,
‹ἰώ,› βαρβάρῳ βοᾷ,
680 ἰώ, βαρβάροις λιταῖς·

665 κιχὼν Kock: δικὼν C   666 ‹δ᾽› Brunck
667 ‹δίκεν› post Wilamowitz Mastronarde
669 ante 668 trai. Mastronarde
668 ὀδόντας Conradt: δικὼν ὀδόντας C
673 φίλᾳ ξυνῆψε γᾷ πάλιν Kovacs: π- ξ- φ- γ- fere C
677 Ἰοῦς] πόρτιός Willink   679 ‹ἰώ› Willink

Going in quest of lustral water
Cadmus slew him with a stone,
smiting and bloodying his head with the cast
of his beast-slaying arm.
⟨And⟩ at the word of the bright one,
her of no mother, Pallas, ⟨he threw⟩
onto the luxuriant plains
the teeth that fell to earth.
Then earth put forth
on its topmost bourne a vision of men full-armored.
But cruel slaughter
joined them once more to dear earth's embrace.
It moistened with blood the earth
that had brought them forth
to the lovely sun and the air of heaven.[35]

You also, offspring
of our foremother Io,
Epaphus, son of Zeus,[36]
you I invoke, invoke,
⟨halloo,⟩ with barbarian shout,
halloo, with barbarian prayer:

[35] This myth tells the origin of the Theban aristocracy, the Spartoi or Sown Men. The warlike men who sprang from the dragon's teeth were mostly killed in battle with each other, but some survived to beget the best fighters of Thebes. Thebes' warriors therefore can be called Sown Men, for instance in lines 795 and 1245 below.

[36] See note on line 248 above.

βᾶθι βᾶθι τάνδε γᾶν·
σοί νιν ἔκγονοι κτίσαν,
καὶ διώνυμοι θεαί,
Περσέφασσα καὶ φίλα
685 Δαμάτηρ θεά,
πάντων ἄνασσα,
πάντων δὲ Γᾶ τροφός,
κτήσαντο· πέμπε πυρφόρους
θεάς, ἄμυνε τᾷδε γᾷ·
πάντα δ' εὐπετῆ θεοῖς.

ΕΤΕΟΚΛΗΣ

690 χώρει σὺ καὶ κόμιζε τὸν Μενοικέως
Κρέοντ', ἀδελφὸν μητρὸς Ἰοκάστης ἐμῆς,
λέγων τάδ', ὡς οἰκεῖα καὶ κοινὰ χθονὸς
θέλω πρὸς αὐτὸν συμβαλεῖν βουλεύματα
πρὶν ἐς μάχην τε καὶ δορὸς τάξιν μολεῖν.
695 καίτοι ποδῶν σῶν μόχθον ἐκλύει παρών·
ὁρῶ γὰρ αὐτὸν πρὸς δόμους στείχοντ' ἐμούς.

ΚΡΕΩΝ

ἦ πόλλ' †ἐπῆλθον† εἰσιδεῖν χρῄζων σ', ἄναξ
Ἐτεόκλεες, πέριξ δὲ Καδμείων πύλας
φυλακάς τ' ἐπῆλθον σὸν δέμας θηρώμενος.

683 καὶ Major: ᾇ C
690–6 del. Willink
697 ἐμόχθησ' Geel

come, O come to the land,
for your offspring founded it,
and the goddesses called the Twain,
Persephassa and the dear
goddess Demeter,
mistress of all,
all-nurturing earth,[37]
have won it for their own.[38] Escort the torch-bearing
goddesses and protect this land:
all things are easy for gods.

Enter from the skene ETEOCLES, *speaking to one of his
retinue.*

ETEOCLES

Go and fetch Creon, son of Menoeceus, the brother of my
mother Jocasta, and tell him that I wish to confer with him
on private matters and state affairs before we begin battle.

But he has saved you trouble by appearing: I see him
coming to my house.

Enter CREON *by Eisodos B.*

CREON

It has been hard work to find you, my lord Eteocles: I
walked all around the Theban walls and guard posts look-
ing for you.

---

[37] Demeter is here identified with Ge (Earth), as if her name
were Gemeter (Earth-mother).

[38] Demeter Thesmophoros had a shrine on the citadel of
Thebes.

ΕΤΕΟΚΛΗΣ

700 καὶ μὴν ἐγὼ σ' ἔχρῃζον εἰσιδεῖν, Κρέον·
πολλῶν γὰρ ηὗρον ἐνδεεῖς διαλλαγάς,
ὡς ἐς λόγους συνῆψα Πολυνείκει μολών.

ΚΡΕΩΝ

ἤκουσα μεῖζον αὐτὸν ἐς Θήβας φρονεῖν,
κήδει τ' Ἀδράστου καὶ στρατῷ πεποιθότα.
705 ἀλλ' ἐς θεοὺς χρὴ ταῦτ' ἀναρτήσαντ' ἔχειν·
ἃ δ' ἐμποδὼν μάλιστα, ταῦθ' ἥκω φράσων.

ΕΤΕΟΚΛΗΣ

τὰ ποῖα ταῦτα; τὸν λόγον γὰρ ἀγνοῶ.

ΚΡΕΩΝ

ἥκει τις αἰχμάλωτος Ἀργείων πάρα.

ΕΤΕΟΚΛΗΣ

λέγει δὲ δὴ τί τῶν ἐκεῖ νεώτερον;

ΚΡΕΩΝ

710 μέλλειν πέριξ πυκνοῖσι Καδμείων πόλιν
ὅπλοις ἑλίξειν αὐτίκ' Ἀργείων στρατόν.

ΕΤΕΟΚΛΗΣ

ἐξοιστέον τἄρ' ὅπλα Καδμείων πόλει.

ΚΡΕΩΝ

ποῖ; μῶν νεάζων οὐχ ὁρᾷς ἃ χρή σ' ὁρᾶν;

ΕΤΕΟΚΛΗΣ

ἐκτὸς τάφρων τῶνδ', ὡς μαχουμένους τάχα.

703 ἐς Wecklein: ἢ C

286

ETEOCLES

Well, I wanted to see you as well, Creon. I found the truce to be very unsatisfactory when I went to parley with Polynices.

CREON

I have heard that he has become haughty toward Thebes: his marriage tie with Adrastus and his army give him confidence.

But we must commit all that to the gods. I have come to tell you what is most immediate.

ETEOCLES

What's that? I do not know what you're reporting.

CREON

We have a prisoner from the Argive side.

ETEOCLES

What does he say that's new of matters there?

CREON

They mean to encircle Thebes with close-ranked arms.

ETEOCLES

Thebes then must take its arms outside the walls.

CREON

Where? Are you too young to see what you should see?

ETEOCLES

Outside the moat, to fight our foes at once.

---

708 fort. αὐτομόλος ἐναντίων πάρα
710 πυκνοῖσι Reiske: πύργοισι C

EURIPIDES

ΚΡΕΩΝ

715 σμικρὸν τὸ πλῆθος τῆσδε γῆς, οἱ δ' ἄφθονοι.

ΕΤΕΟΚΛΗΣ

ἐγᾦδα κείνους τοῖς λόγοις ὄντας θρασεῖς.

ΚΡΕΩΝ

ἔχει τιν' ὄγκον τἄργος Ἑλλήνων πάρα.

ΕΤΕΟΚΛΗΣ

θάρσει· τάχ' αὐτῶν πεδίον ἐμπλήσω φόνου.

ΚΡΕΩΝ

θέλοιμ' ἄν· ἀλλὰ τοῦθ' ὁρῶ πολλοῦ πόνου.

ΕΤΕΟΚΛΗΣ

720 ὡς οὐ καθέξω τειχέων ἔσω στρατόν.

ΚΡΕΩΝ

καὶ μὴν τὸ νικᾶν <γ'> ἐστι πᾶν εὐβουλίας.

ΕΤΕΟΚΛΗΣ

βούλῃ τράπωμαι δῆθ' ὁδοὺς ἄλλας τινάς;

ΚΡΕΩΝ

πάσας γε, πρὶν κίνδυνον εἰσάπαξ μολεῖν.

ΕΤΕΟΚΛΗΣ

724 εἰ νυκτὸς αὐτοῖς προσβάλοιμεν ἐκ λόχου;

ΚΡΕΩΝ

727 ἐνδυστυχῆσαι δεινὸν εὐφρόνης κνέφας.

ΕΤΕΟΚΛΗΣ

726 ἴσον φέρει νύξ, τοῖς δὲ τολμῶσιν πλέον.

288

CREON

Thebes' force is slight, the enemy army large.

ETEOCLES

Yes, but their bravery is all in words.

CREON

Argos' prestige among the Greeks is great.

ETEOCLES

No fear! I'll fill the plain soon with their blood!

CREON

I hope you may: but this requires much work.

ETEOCLES

Know this: I shall not coop my men within.

CREON

But victory lies entirely with good counsel.

ETEOCLES

You wish me then to ponder other routes?

CREON

Yes, all of them before you risk your all.

ETEOCLES

How if by night we attack them from an ambush?

CREON

It's easy in the dark to come to grief.

ETEOCLES

Night levels and to bold men gives advantage.

---

^{721} ⟨γ'⟩ Lenting   εὐβουλίας Schoene et fort. Σ: -ία vel -ίᾳ
C $^{724-32}$ hoc ordine Wecklein

ΚΡΕΩΝ

725 εἴπερ σφαλείς γε δεῦρο σωθήσῃ πάλιν.

ΕΤΕΟΚΛΗΣ

730 βαθύς γέ τοι Διρκαῖος ἀναχωρεῖν πόρος.

ΚΡΕΩΝ

731 ἅπαν κάκιον τοῦ φυλάσσεσθαι καλῶς.

ΕΤΕΟΚΛΗΣ

728 ἀλλ' ἀμφὶ δεῖπνον οὖσι προσβάλω δόρυ;

ΚΡΕΩΝ

729 ἔκπληξις ἂν γένοιτο· νικῆσαι δὲ δεῖ.

ΕΤΕΟΚΛΗΣ

732 τί δ' εἰ καθιππεύσαιμεν Ἀργείων στρατόν;

ΚΡΕΩΝ

κἀκεῖ πέφαρκται λαὸς ἅρμασιν πέριξ.

ΕΤΕΟΚΛΗΣ

τί δῆτα δράσω; πολεμίοισι δῶ πόλιν;

ΚΡΕΩΝ

735 μὴ δῆτα· βουλεύου δ', ἐπείπερ εἶ σοφός.

ΕΤΕΟΚΛΗΣ

τίς οὖν πρόνοια γίγνεται σοφωτέρα;

ΚΡΕΩΝ

ἕπτ' ἄνδρας αὐτοῖς φασιν, ὡς ἤκουσ' ἐγώ . . .

ΕΤΕΟΚΛΗΣ

τί προστετάχθαι δρᾶν; τὸ γὰρ σθένος βραχύ.

CREON

Yes, if you get home safely from disaster.

ETEOCLES

Well, Dirce's ford *is* deep for a retreat.

CREON

Best counsel is to be well on one's guard.

ETEOCLES

Shall I attack them, then, while they're at dinner?

CREON

That would cause fright, but victory's what we need.

ETEOCLES

Why not tread down the Argives with our cavalry?

CREON

There too they're guarded well, ringed round by chariots.

ETEOCLES

What shall I do? Put Thebes in enemy hands?

CREON

No, no! If you are wise, deliberate!

ETEOCLES

What wiser plan is there than what I've said?

CREON

I've heard report that seven of their men . . .

ETEOCLES

Are ordered to do what? This force is slight.

ΚΡΕΩΝ

. . . λόχων ἄνακτας ἑπτὰ προσκεῖσθαι πύλαις.

ΕΤΕΟΚΛΗΣ

740 τί δῆτα δρῶμεν; ἀπορίαν γὰρ οὐ μενῶ.

ΚΡΕΩΝ

ἕπτ᾽ ἄνδρας αὐτοῖς καὶ σὺ πρὸς πύλαις ἑλοῦ.

ΕΤΕΟΚΛΗΣ

λόχων ἀνάσσειν ἢ μονοστόλου δορός;

ΚΡΕΩΝ

λόχων, προκρίνας οἵπερ ἀλκιμώτατοι.

ΕΤΕΟΚΛΗΣ

ξυνῆκ᾽· ἀμύνειν τειχέων προσαμβάσεις.

ΚΡΕΩΝ

745 καὶ ξυστρατήγους ⟨γ᾽⟩· εἷς δ᾽ ἀνὴρ οὐ πάνθ᾽ ὁρᾷ.

ΕΤΕΟΚΛΗΣ

θάρσει προκρίνας ἢ φρενῶν εὐβουλίᾳ;

ΚΡΕΩΝ

ἀμφότερ᾽· ἐν ἀπολειφθὲν γὰρ οὐδὲν θατέρου.

ΕΤΕΟΚΛΗΣ

ἔσται τάδ᾽· ἐλθὼν ἑπτάπυργον ἐς κύκλον
τάξω λοχαγοὺς πρὸς πύλαισιν, ὡς λέγεις,
750 ἴσους ἴσοισι πολεμίοισιν ἀντιθείς.
ὄνομα δ᾽ ἑκάστου διατριβὴ πολλὴ λέγειν,
ἐχθρῶν ὑπ᾽ αὐτοῖς τείχεσιν καθημένων.

739 ἄνακτας Matthiae: ἀνάσσειν C

292

CREON
. . . are placed before the seven gates as captains.

ETEOCLES
What shall we do? I can't stand helplessness.

CREON
Choose seven yourself to meet them at the gates.

ETEOCLES
To captain companies or to fight alone?

CREON
To captain: choose the bravest of your men.

ETEOCLES
I see: to keep the enemy from the walls.

CREON
And share command: one man cannot see all.

ETEOCLES
For bravery shall I choose them or for prudence?

CREON
Both: neither's any good without the other.

ETEOCLES
It shall be so. I shall go to the city's seven-towered circuit
and station the captains at the gates, as you recommend,
setting an equal number of defenders to face the enemy.
To tell you the name of each man would consume too
much time with the enemy encamped at our very gates.

742–3 del. Czwalina   745 ⟨γ’⟩ Lenting   δ’ del. Polle
747 ἀμφότερ’· ἐν . . . θατέρου Wecklein: ἀμφότερον . . .
θάτερον C
748 κύκλον Musgrave: πόλιν C

[ἀλλ᾽ εἶμ᾽, ὅπως ἂν μὴ καταργῶμεν χέρα.
καί μοι γένοιτ᾽ ἀδελφὸν ἀντήρη λαβεῖν
755 καὶ ξυσταθέντα διὰ μάχης ἑλεῖν δορὶ
κτανεῖν θ᾽, ὃς ἦλθε πατρίδα πορθήσων ἐμήν.]
    γάμους δ᾽ ἀδελφῆς Ἀντιγόνης παιδός τε σοῦ
Αἵμονος, ἐάν τι τῆς τύχης ἐγὼ σφαλῶ,
σοὶ χρὴ μέλεσθαι· τὴν δόσιν δ᾽ ἐχέγγυον
760 τὴν πρόσθε ποιῶ νῦν ἐπ᾽ ἐξόδοις ἐμαῖς.
[μητρὸς δ᾽ ἀδελφὸς εἶ· τί δεῖ μακρηγορεῖν;
τρέφ᾽ ἀξίως νιν σοῦ τε τήν τ᾽ ἐμὴν χάριν.
πατὴρ δ᾽ ἐς αὐτὸν ἀμαθίαν ὀφλισκάνει,
ὄψιν τυφλώσας· οὐκ ἄγαν σφ᾽ ἐπήνεσα·
765 ἡμᾶς δ᾽ ἀραῖσιν, ἢν τύχῃ, κατακτενεῖ.]
    ἓν δ᾽ ἐστὶν ἡμῖν ἀργόν, εἴ τι θέσφατον
οἰωνόμαντις Τειρεσίας ἔχει φράσαι,
τοῦδ᾽ ἐκπυθέσθαι ταῦτ᾽· ἐγὼ δὲ παῖδα σὸν
Μενοικέα, σοῦ πατρὸς αὐτεπώνυμον,
770 ἄξοντα πέμψω δεῦρο Τειρεσίαν, Κρέον·
σοὶ μὲν γὰρ ἡδὺς ἐς λόγους ἀφίξεται,
ἐγὼ δὲ τέχνην μαντικὴν ἐμεμψάμην
ἤδη πρὸς αὐτόν, ὥστε μοι μομφὰς ἔχειν.
[πόλει δὲ καὶ σοὶ ταῦτ᾽ ἐπισκήπτω, Κρέον·
775 ἤνπερ κρατήσῃ τἀμά, Πολυνείκους νέκυν
μήποτε ταφῆναι τῇδε Θηβαίᾳ χθονί,
θνῄσκειν δὲ τὸν θάψαντα, κἂν φίλων τις ᾖ.
σοὶ μὲν τάδ᾽ εἶπον· προσπόλοις δ᾽ ἐμοῖς λέγω·]
    ἐκφέρετε τεύχη πάνοπλά τ᾽ ἀμφιβλήματα
780 ὡς εἰς ἀγῶνα τὸν προκείμενον δορὸς

[Well, I shall go so that my hand may not be idle. May it be my lot to find my brother facing me, close with him, conquer him in battle, and kill him, since he came to sack my city!]

As for the marriage of my sister Antigone and your son Haemon, you must see to it if I have one of Fortune's falls. My previous betrothal of her I now confirm as I go forth. [You are the brother of my mother. Need I say more? Maintain her in appropriate style for your sake and mine. My father wins the name of fool with regard to himself since he put out his own eyes. I do not praise him overmuch. But it may be that he will kill us with his curses.]

One thing I have left undone, asking the prophet Teiresias to tell us any prophecies he has. But I will send your son Menoeceus, your father's namesake, to bring him here, Creon. He will gladly come to talk to you. I, however, have already criticized his mantic art to his face, and so he bears me a grudge. [But upon you and the city I lay this charge, Creon: If I am successful, let Polynices' body never be buried in this land of Thebes, and let anyone who buries him be put to death, though it be one of his kin. To you I say this. To my servants I say:]

(*to servants*) Bring forth my weapons and my armor for the spear fight that lies before me [so that I may now set

---

753–6 del. Paley

761–5 del. West (763–5 Paley, Fraenkel, 753–65 dos Santos Alves)

770 ἄξοντα Markland: λαβόντα C

774–7 del. Walter

778 om. II, del. Kirchhoff

[ὁρμώμεθ᾽ ἤδη ξὺν δίκῃ νικηφόρῳ].
τῇ δ᾽ Εὐλαβείᾳ, χρησιμωτάτῃ θεῶν,
προσευχόμεσθα τήνδε διασῶσαι πόλιν.

ΧΟΡΟΣ

στρ.

ὦ πολύμοχθος Ἄρης, τί ποθ᾽ αἵματι
785 καὶ θανάτῳ κατέχῃ Βρομίου παράμουσος ἑορταῖς;
οὐκ ἐπὶ καλλιχόροις στεφάνοισι νεάνιδος ὥρας
βόστρυχον ἀμπετάσας λωτοῦ κατὰ πνεύματα μέλπῃ
μοῦσαν ἐν ᾇ χάριτες χοροποιοί,
ἀλλὰ σὺν ὁπλοφόροις, στρατὸν Ἀργείων
ἐπιπνεύσας
790 αἵματι Θήβας,
κῶμον ἀναυλότατον προχορεύεις,
οὐ ποδὶ θυρσομανεῖ νεβρίδων μέτα,
δίνας ⟨δ᾽⟩ ἅρμασι καὶ ψαλίων
τετραβάμοσι μωνυχοπώλων
ἱππείαις ἐπὶ χεύμασι βαίνων
Ἰσμηνοῖο θοάζεις·
Ἀργείοις ⟨δ᾽⟩ ἐπέπνευσας

781 om. Π, del. Haslam   785 κατέχεις . . . ἑορτάς Jack-
son   789 ὁπλοφόφῳ Schenkl (tum 790 ἅλματι Schenkl;
οἵματι Willink, ᾄσματι Badham)
790a ἅλμασι Leutsch   791 οὐ ποδὶ Zakas: οὐδ᾽ ὑπὸ C
792 δίνας ⟨δ᾽⟩ Willink: δινεύεις C   μωνυχοπώλων Weid-
gen: μώνυχα πῶλον fere C   793–4 ἱππείαις . . . Ἰσμηνοῖο
Murray (Ἰσμ- Mastronarde): Ἰσμηνοῦ τ᾽ . . . ἱππείαισι C
794 ⟨δ᾽⟩ ἐπέπνευσας Willink: ἐπιπνεύσας C

out with the aid of justice that brings victory]! I pray to
Lady Caution, most beneficial of the gods, to bring this city
through to safety!

Servants bring armor out of the skene. *Exit* ETEOCLES
with retinue by Eisodos B.

CHORUS

O Ares, god of toils, why are you possessed
by bloodshed and death, why jar discordantly with
    Bromius' feasts?[39]
Not for you, amid the fair garlands that lovely youth wear
    to the dance,
to spread your loosened locks and sing, to the breathed
    melody of pipes,
the songs in which resides the grace of dancing;
no, you breathe the Argive army
upon Thebes' race,
and with armed men you lead the chorus in revelry unfit
    for the pipe,
not on ecstatic feet, dressed in fawnskin.
⟨Rather⟩ with chariots and the four-foot
riding of bridled horses
you make eddies whirl
as you tread Ismenus' streams.
⟨And⟩ against the Argives your breath hurls forth to meet
    them

---

[39] Dionysus is here mentioned as patron of music and dance,
his role at the City Dionysia, at which tragedy was performed.

795 Σπαρτῶν γένναν,
ἀσπιδοφέρμονα κῶμον ἀρήιον
ἀντίπαλον, κατὰ λάινα τείχεα
χαλκῷ κοσμήσας.
ἦ δεινά τις Ἔρις θεός, ἃ τάδε
μήσατο πήματα γᾶς βασιλεῦσιν,
800 Λαβδακίδαις πολυμόχθοις.

ἀντ.

ὦ ζαθέων πετάλων πολυθηρότα-
τον νάπος, Ἀρτέμιδος χιονοτρόφον ὄμμα Κιθαιρών,
μήποτε τὸν θανάτῳ προτεθέντα, λόχευμ᾽ Ἰοκάστας,
ὤφελες Οἰδιπόδαν θρέψαι, βρέφος ἔκβολον οἴκων,
805 χρυσοδέτοις περόναις ἐπίσαμον·
μηδὲ τὸ παρθένιον πτερόν, οὔρειον τέρας, ἐλθεῖν
πένθεα γαίας
Σφίγγ᾽ ἀπομουσοτάταισι σὺν ᾠδαῖς,
ἅ ποτε Καδμογενῆ τετραβάμοσι
χαλαῖς τείχεσι χριμπτομένα
φέρεν αἰθέρος εἰς ἄβατον φῶς
810 γένναν· τάνδ᾽ ὁ κατὰ χθονὸς Ἅιδας
Καδμείοις ἐπιπέμπει·
δυσδαίμων δ᾽ ἔρις ἄλλα
θάλλει παίδων
Οἰδιπόδα κατὰ δώματα καὶ πόλιν.

796 κῶμον ἀρήιον West: θίασον ἔνοπλον C
800 om. Π, del. Nauck
807b Σφίγγ᾽ ἀπομουσοτάταισι Nauck: Σφιγγὸς ἀμουσ- C

the race of the Sown Men,[40]
shield-bearing revelers of war,
whom you have decked
in bronze along the battlements of stone.
Dread is the goddess Strife, she
who wrought these woes for this land's royal house,
the Labdacids of many sorrows.

O glade of sacred foliage, glade of many beasts,
Artemis' delight, snow-nurturing Cithaeron,
would that you had never reared Jocasta's offspring
    Oedipus,
the child exposed for death and cast from the house,
child with the mark of the golden brooch upon him!
Would that the winged maid, portent brought forth by the
    mountain, had not come
to vex the land,
the Sphinx with her song unblessed by the Muse,[41]
who with her four taloned feet,
hovering over the walls,
carried off to the pathless realms of sky
the youth of Cadmus' city. Hades who dwells below
sent her against the Cadmeans.
But it is another strife,
the strife of sons, that blooms in misery
in the house and city of Oedipus.

[40] See note on line 675 above.
[41] See note on line 46 above.

---

810 τάνδ' Willink: ἂν fere C

οὐ γὰρ ὃ μὴ καλὸν οὔποτ' ἔφυ καλόν,
815 †οὐδ' οἱ μὴ νόμιμοι
παῖδες ματρὶ λόχευμα μίασμα πατρός·
ἡ δὲ συναίμονος εἰς λέχος ἦλθεν†
⟨. . . . .⟩.

ἐπῳδ.

ἔτεκες, ὦ Γαῖ, ἔτεκές ποτε,
βάρβαρον ὡς ἀκοὰν ἐδάην ἐδάην ποτ' ἐν οἴκοις,
820 τὰν ἀπὸ θηροτρόφου φοινικολόφοιο δράκοντος
γένναν ὀδοντοφυᾶ, Θήβαις κάλλιστον ὄνειδος·
Ἁρμονίας δέ ποτ' εἰς ὑμεναίους
ἤλυθον οὐρανίδαι, φόρμιγγί τε τείχεα Θήβας
τᾶς Ἀμφιονίας τε λύρας ὕπο πύργος ἀνέστα
825 διδύμων ποταμῶν πόρον ἀμφὶ μέσον,
Δίρκα χλοεροτρόφον ᾇ πεδίον
πρόπαρ Ἰσμηνοῦ καταδεύει,
Ἰώ θ' ἁ κερόεσσα προμάτωρ
Καδμείων βασιλῆας ἐγείνατο·
830 μυριάδας δ' ἀγαθῶν ἑτέροις ἑτέ-
ρας μεταμειβομένα πόλις ἅδ' ἐπ' ἄκροις
στεφάνοις ἕστακεν Ἀρείοις.

815–7 desperati: fort. ἶνες δ' οὐκ ὀρθοὶ / [παῖδες] ⟨πικρὸν⟩
ματρὶ λόχευμα, μίασμά ⟨τε⟩ / πατρί, σύναιμον ὃς ἐς λέχος
ἦλθεν ⟨πατροφόνος πολυπενθής⟩ ([παῖδες] Kirchhoff,
σύναιμον ὃς Paley, ⟨πατροφόνος πολυπενθής⟩ Mastronarde)
817 post h. v. lac. indic. edd.   818 ὦ ἔτεκές ⟨ποτε⟩ Γαῖ,
ἔτεκές ποτε Willink   826 Δίρκα Burges: -ας C
832 στεφάνοις ἕστακεν Ἀρείοις Diggle, Willink: ἕστακ'
Ἀρηίοις στεφάνοισιν fere C

What is not fine is never fine,[42]
and sons so unlawfully begotten
are ⟨an unwelcome⟩ embrace to their mother ⟨and⟩ a stain
to their father, who shared her incestuous bed
⟨as a luckless parricide⟩.

You bore, O Earth, you bore long ago
(so runs the barbarian tale I heard at home)
the race sprung from the beast-brood serpent with crimson crest,
race which grew from its teeth, fairest reproach that Thebes can hear.[43]
There came to the marriage of Harmonia once
the gods, sons of Heaven, and with the lyre
and the charm of Amphion's strings the fortress arose[44]
on the narrow land between the two rivers,
where Dirce alongside Ismenus
waters the fruitful plain.
Io, my horned ancestress
begat the kings of the Cadmeans.
Getting countless blessings on top of countless others,
this city stands high
in the crowns Ares bestows.

[42] The next three lines of this stanza are desperately corrupt, and a line is probably missing at the end. I translate my illustrative conjecture without any confidence that it is even approximately right.

[43] Birth from the teeth of a serpent can be treated as a reproach of bestial origins, but to Thebes it is a source of pride.

[44] See note on line 115 above.

ΤΕΙΡΕΣΙΑΣ

ἡγοῦ πάροιθε, θύγατερ· ὡς τυφλῷ ποδὶ
835   ὀφθαλμὸς εἶ σύ, ναυβάταισιν ἄστρον ὥς·
δεῦρ᾽ ἐς τὸ λευρὸν πέδον ἴχνος τιθεῖσ᾽ ἐμὸν
πρόβαινε, μὴ σφαλῶμεν· ἀσθενὴς πατήρ·
κλήρους τέ μοι φύλασσε παρθένῳ χερί,
οὓς ἔλαβον οἰωνίσματ᾽ ὀρνίθων μαθὼν
840   θάκοισιν ἐν ἱεροῖσιν οὗ μαντεύομαι.
τέκνον Μενοικεῦ, παῖ Κρέοντος, εἰπέ μοι
πόση τις ἡ ᾽πίλοιπος ἄστεως ὁδὸς
πρὸς πατέρα τὸν σόν· ὡς ἐμὸν κάμνει γόνυ,
πυκνὴν δὲ βαίνων ἤλυσιν μόλις περῶ.

ΚΡΕΩΝ

845   θάρσει· πέλας γάρ, Τειρεσία, φίλοισι σοῖς
ἔσθ᾽ ὁρμίσαι σὸν πόδα· λαβοῦ δ᾽ αὐτοῦ, τέκνον·
ὡς παῖς ἔτ᾽ ἀπτὴν πούς τε πρεσβύτου φιλεῖ
χειρὸς θυραίας ἀναμένειν κουφίσματα.

ΤΕΙΡΕΣΙΑΣ

εἶέν, πάρεσμεν· τί με καλεῖς σπουδῇ, Κρέον;

ΚΡΕΩΝ

850   οὔπω λελήσμεθ᾽· ἀλλὰ σύλλεξαι σθένος

---

846 ἔσθ᾽ ὁρμίσαι Kvíčala: ἐξορμίσαι fere C
847 παῖς ἔτ᾽ ἀπτὴν Hermann: πᾶς ἀπήνη C

---

45 We do not know how these "lot tablets" were used in divination.

Enter by Eisodos A TEIRESIAS, *a staff in his hand and a wreath of gold on his head. His other hand rests on the shoulder of his daughter, who goes before him and carries the lot tablets her father uses in divination.* MENOECEUS *accompanies them.*

TEIRESIAS

Lead on, my daughter! You are the eyes that guide my blind steps, as a star guides sailors. Now as you set my feet here on this level ground, go before me to keep me from stumbling (your father is weak) and guard with your maiden hand my lot tablets of divination, the ones I took when I heard what the bird omens were in the holy seat where I prophesy.[45]

My lad, Menoeceus, son of Creon, tell me how long a city road still remains until we reach your father. My knees are growing weary, and as I must take so many steps, my progress is slow.

CREON

Courage, Teiresias! You can now moor your footsteps near your friends. Take his arm, my son. For like a child still unfledged, the step of an old man usually awaits the help of another's hand.

Menoeceus helps Teiresias move forward to face Creon, then releases him.

TEIRESIAS

Well then, here I am. Why did you summon me so urgently, Creon?

CREON

I have not yet forgotten the reason. But collect your

303

καὶ πνεῦμ' ἄθροισον, αἶπος ἐκβαλὼν ὁδοῦ.

ΤΕΙΡΕΣΙΑΣ

κόπῳ παρεῖμαι γοῦν Ἐρεχθειδῶν ἄπο
δεῦρ' ἐκκομισθεὶς τῆς πάροιθεν ἡμέρας·
κἀκεῖ γὰρ ἦν τις πόλεμος Εὐμόλπου δορός,
855 οὗ καλλινίκους Κεκροπίδας ἔθηκ' ἐγώ·
καὶ τόνδε χρυσοῦν στέφανον, ὡς ὁρᾷς, ἔχω
λαβὼν ἀπαρχὰς πολεμίων σκυλευμάτων.

ΚΡΕΩΝ

οἰωνὸν ἐθέμην καλλίνικα σὰ στέφη·
ἐν γὰρ κλύδωνι κείμεθ', ὥσπερ οἶσθα σύ,
860 δορὸς Δαναϊδῶν, καὶ μέγας Θήβαις ἀγών.
βασιλεὺς μὲν οὖν βέβηκε κοσμηθεὶς ὅπλοις
ἤδη πρὸς ἀλκὴν Ἐτεοκλῆς Μυκηνίδα·
ἐμοὶ δ' ἐπέσταλκ' ἐκμαθεῖν σέθεν πάρα
τί δρῶντες ἂν μάλιστα σώσαιμεν πόλιν.

ΤΕΙΡΕΣΙΑΣ

865 Ἐτεοκλέους μὲν οὕνεκ' ἂν κλῄσας στόμα
χρησμοὺς ἐπέσχον· σοὶ δ', ἐπεὶ χρῄζεις μαθεῖν,
λέξω. νοσεῖ γὰρ ἥδε γῆ πάλαι, Κρέον,
ἐξ οὗ 'τεκνώθη Λάιος βίᾳ θεῶν
πόσιν τ' ἔφυσε μητρὶ μέλεον Οἰδίπουν·

861–3 del. Willink propter 865–7a
869–80 del. Fraenkel, 868–80 Reeve

46 "Land of the Erechthidae" is a poetic periphrasis for Athens, and "sons of Cecrops" for the Athenians. Erechtheus was

strength and recover your breath, putting your steep journey behind you.

TEIRESIAS

It is true that I am weary: I traveled here from the land of the Erechthidae[46] yesterday. There too there was war, led by Eumolpus,[47] and I caused the sons of Cecrops to win a glorious victory over him. I wear this golden chaplet, as you see, which I received as first fruits of the enemy spoils.

CREON

I regard your victory chaplet as a good omen. War with the sons of Danaus surges about us, as you know, and for Thebes the stakes are high. Our king Eteocles has already gone off, decked with armor, to fight the Myceneans. He has bidden me ask you what we must do to save the city.

TEIRESIAS

Were it for Eteocles' sake, I would have held my tongue and refused to prophesy. But to you, since you ask me, I will speak. The land has been diseased for a long time, Creon, ever since Laius had a child against the gods' wishes and begot unlucky Oedipus as husband to his

one of the most important of the legendary kings of Athens. His temple, the Erechtheum, stood next to the temple of Athena Parthenos (the Parthenon) on the Athenian acropolis. Cecrops was another early king.

[47] Eumolpus, king of Thrace, attacked Athens during the reign of Erechtheus. The attack was averted when, on the advice of seers, Erechtheus' daughter gave herself as a voluntary sacrificial victim, much as Menoeceus does at the end of this scene. Euripides had dramatized this story in his *Erechtheus*, put on probably in 422.

870 αἵ θ᾽ αἱματωποὶ δεργμάτων διαφθοραὶ
θεῶν σόφισμα κἀπίδειξις Ἑλλάδι.
ἃ συγκαλύψαι παῖδες Οἰδίπου χρόνῳ
χρῄζοντες, ὡς δὴ θεοὺς ὑπεκδραμούμενοι,
ἥμαρτον ἀμαθῶς· οὔτε γὰρ γέρα πατρὶ
875 οὔτ᾽ ἔξοδον διδόντες ἄνδρα δυστυχῆ
ἐξηγρίωσαν· ἐκ δ᾽ ἔπνευσ᾽ αὐτοῖς ἀρὰς
δεινάς, νοσῶν τε καὶ πρὸς ἠτιμασμένος.
ἀγὼ τί οὐ δρῶν, ποῖα δ᾽ οὐ λέγων ἔπη
ἐς ἔχθος ἦλθον παισὶ τοῖσιν Οἰδίπου;
880 ἐγγὺς δὲ θάνατος αὐτόχειρ αὐτοῖς, Κρέον.
πολλοὶ δὲ νεκροὶ περὶ νεκροῖς πεπτωκότες
Ἀργεῖα καὶ Καδμεῖα μείξαντες μέλη
πικροὺς γόους δώσουσι Θηβαίᾳ χθονί.
σύ τ᾽ ὦ τάλαινα συγκατασκάπτῃ πόλι,
885 εἰ μὴ λόγοις τις τοῖς ἐμοῖσι πείσεται.
[ἐκεῖνο μὲν γὰρ πρῶτον ἦν, τῶν Οἰδίπου
μηδένα πολίτην μηδ᾽ ἄνακτ᾽ εἶναι χθονός,
ὡς δαιμονῶντας κἀνατρέψοντας πόλιν.
ἐπεὶ δὲ κρεῖσσον τὸ κακόν ἐστι τἀγαθοῦ,
890 μί᾽ ἔστιν ἄλλη μηχανὴ σωτηρίας.]
    ἀλλ᾽ οὐ γὰρ εἰπεῖν οὔτ᾽ ἐμοὶ τόδ᾽ ἀσφαλὲς
πικρόν τε τοῖσι τὴν τύχην κεκτημένοις
πόλει παρασχεῖν φάρμακον σωτηρίας,
ἄπειμι. χαίρεθ᾽· εἷς γὰρ ὢν πολλῶν μέτα
895 τὸ μέλλον, εἰ χρή, πείσομαι· τί γὰρ πάθω;

871 σωφρόνισμα Herwerden

306

mother. The bloody destruction of his eyes is the gods' subtle contrivance for giving a lesson to Greece. The sons of Oedipus, wishing to cover this up, thinking that they could outstrip the gods, erred grievously. Since they did not grant their father his privileges or allow him to go out, they made the unhappy man violently angry. He breathed out terrible curses on them, being sick and also treated insultingly. I did and said everything I could but came to be hated by the sons of Oedipus. Death by their own hand is near them, Creon. Corpse falling upon corpse in great numbers, Argive and Theban limbs mingled together, will cause the land of Thebes bitter keening. And you, poor city, will be destroyed together with your soldiery unless someone pays heed to my words. [The best thing would be that no son of Oedipus should be either citizen or ruler of the land since they are under a divine curse and will overturn the city. But since the evil part is stronger than the good, there is one other way to secure safety.]

But it is unsafe for me to speak these words, and it will be galling to those who are touched by this fate that I should give the city its life-saving medicine: I'm going away. Farewell! If I must I will suffer, as one man among many, what is to come. What can I do?

He turns to go, but Creon restrains him.

---

878 κἀγὼ King
882 μέλη Markland: βέλη C
885 λόγοις τις τοῖς ἐμοῖσι Porson: λόγοισι τοῖς ἐμοῖς τις C
886–90 del. Fraenkel

ΚΡΕΩΝ

ἐπίσχες αὐτοῦ, πρέσβυ.

ΤΕΙΡΕΣΙΑΣ
μὴ 'πιλαμβάνου.

ΚΡΕΩΝ

μεῖνον, τί φεύγεις μ';

ΤΕΙΡΕΣΙΑΣ
ἡ τύχη σ', ἀλλ' οὐκ ἐγώ.

ΚΡΕΩΝ

φράσον πολίταις καὶ πόλει σωτηρίαν.

ΤΕΙΡΕΣΙΑΣ
βούλῃ σὺ μέντοι κοὐχὶ βουλήσῃ τάχα.

ΚΡΕΩΝ

900 καὶ πῶς πατρῴαν γαῖαν οὐ σῶσαι θέλω;

ΤΕΙΡΕΣΙΑΣ
θέλεις ἀκοῦσαι δῆτα καὶ σπουδὴν ἔχεις;

ΚΡΕΩΝ

ἐς γὰρ τί μᾶλλον δεῖ προθυμίαν ἔχειν;

ΤΕΙΡΕΣΙΑΣ
[κλύοις ἂν ἤδη τῶν ἐμῶν θεσπισμάτων.]
πρῶτον δ' ἐκεῖνο βούλομαι σαφῶς μαθεῖν,
905 ποῦ 'στιν Μενοικεύς, ὅς με δεῦρ' ἐπήγαγεν;

ΚΡΕΩΝ

ὅδ' οὐ μακρὰν ἄπεστι, πλησίον δὲ σοῦ.

CREON

Stop where you are, old sir!

TEIRESIAS

Unhand me!

CREON

Stay, why do you run from me?

TEIRESIAS

It is not I who do so but your fate.

CREON

Tell the city and its citizens how they may survive.

TEIRESIAS

You wish it now, but soon you will not.

CREON

How can I not wish to save my country?

TEIRESIAS

You want to hear it? You are eager?

CREON

What should I be more eager for?

TEIRESIAS

[You will soon hear my prophecies.] But first I want to know this: where is Menoeceus, who brought me here?

CREON

He stands near you, not far off.

---

903 del. Diggle (903–4 iam Zipperer)

ΤΕΙΡΕΣΙΑΣ

ἀπελθέτω νυν θεσφάτων ἐμῶν ἑκάς.

ΚΡΕΩΝ

ἐμὸς πεφυκὼς παῖς ἃ δεῖ σιγήσεται.

ΤΕΙΡΕΣΙΑΣ

βούλῃ παρόντος δῆτά σοι τούτου φράσω;

ΚΡΕΩΝ

910 κλύων γὰρ ἂν τέρποιτο τῆς σωτηρίας.

ΤΕΙΡΕΣΙΑΣ

ἄκουε δή νυν θεσφάτων ἐμῶν ὁδόν
[ἃ δρῶντες ἂν σώσαιτε Καδμείων πόλιν]·
σφάξαι Μενοικέα τόνδε δεῖ σ' ὑπὲρ πάτρας,
σὸν παῖδ', ἐπειδὴ τὴν τύχην αὐτὸς καλεῖς.

ΚΡΕΩΝ

915 τί φῄς; τίν' εἶπας τόνδε μῦθον, ὦ γέρον;

ΤΕΙΡΕΣΙΑΣ

ἅπερ πέφηνε· ταῦτα κἀνάγκη σε δρᾶν.

ΚΡΕΩΝ

ὦ πολλὰ λέξας ἐν βραχεῖ λόγῳ κακά.

ΤΕΙΡΕΣΙΑΣ

σοί γ', ἀλλὰ πατρίδι μεγάλα καὶ σωτήρια.

ΚΡΕΩΝ

οὐκ ἔκλυον, οὐκ ἤκουσα· χαιρέτω πόλις.

912 om. codex unus, del. Kirchhoff cl. 864
916 πέφηνε Camper: πέφυκε C

TEIRESIAS
Let him then withdraw, far from my prophecies.

CREON
He is my son and will keep any secrets he must.

TEIRESIAS
Then you want me to speak in his presence?

CREON
Yes: he will be glad to hear what will keep us safe.

TEIRESIAS
Hear then the course of my prophecies [by performing which you will save the city]: you must slaughter your son Menoeceus here, for the country's sake: you yourself asked for your fate.

CREON
What are you saying? What tale is this, old sir?

TEIRESIAS
The one that has been revealed: this is what you must do.

CREON
Such woe in so few words!

TEIRESIAS
Woe for you, but for your country the great secret of its survival.

CREON
I have not heard it, not listened! Country be damned!

---

⁹¹⁷ λόγῳ Nauck: χρόνῳ C

ΤΕΙΡΕΣΙΑΣ

920 ἀνὴρ ὅδ᾽ οὐκέθ᾽ αὑτός· ἐκνεύει πάλιν.

ΚΡΕΩΝ

χαίρων ἴθ᾽· οὐ γὰρ σῶν με δεῖ μαντευμάτων.

ΤΕΙΡΕΣΙΑΣ

ἀπόλωλεν ἀλήθει᾽, ἐπεὶ σὺ δυστυχεῖς;

ΚΡΕΩΝ

ὦ πρός σε γονάτων καὶ γερασμίου τριχὸς . . .

ΤΕΙΡΕΣΙΑΣ

τί προσπίτνεις με; δυσφύλακτ᾽ αἴνει κακά.

ΚΡΕΩΝ

925 . . . σίγα, πόλει δὲ τούσδε μὴ λέξῃς λόγους.

ΤΕΙΡΕΣΙΑΣ

ἀδικεῖν κελεύεις μ᾽· οὐ σιωπήσαιμεν ἄν.

ΚΡΕΩΝ

τί δή με δράσεις; παῖδά μου κατακτενεῖς;

ΤΕΙΡΕΣΙΑΣ

ἄλλοις μελήσει ταῦτ᾽, ἐμοὶ δ᾽ εἰρήσεται.

ΚΡΕΩΝ

ἐκ τοῦ δ᾽ ἐμοὶ τόδ᾽ ἦλθε καὶ τέκνῳ κακόν;

ΤΕΙΡΕΣΙΑΣ

930 [ὀρθῶς μ᾽ ἐρωτᾷς κἀς ἀγῶν᾽ ἔρχῃ λόγων.]
δεῖ τόνδε θαλάμαις, οὗ δράκων ὁ γηγενὴς

924 αἴνει anon. Cantabr.: αἰτῇ fere C
930 del. Herwerden

TEIRESIAS

This man is much changed: he shies back!

CREON

Farewell and be gone! I have no need of prophecies from *you*!

TEIRESIAS

Has truth been destroyed because you are suffering?

CREON

(*kneeling before him as a suppliant*) By your knees I beg you and by your white hair . . .

TEIRESIAS

Why do you supplicate me? Your woes cannot be avoided: accept them!

CREON

. . . say nothing: do not tell the city these prophecies!

TEIRESIAS

What you ask is wrong: I shall not be silent.

CREON

What will you do to me? Kill my son?

TEIRESIAS

Others will see to that: I shall speak.

CREON

Why has this woe come upon me and my son?

TEIRESIAS

[You are right to ask me and to enter a contest of words.] This boy must be slaughtered in the chamber where the

ἐγένετο Δίρκης ναμάτων ἐπίσκοπος,
σφαγέντα φόνιον αἷμα γῇ δοῦναι χοάς,
Κάδμῳ παλαιῶν Ἄρεος ἐκ μηνιμάτων,
935 ὃς γηγενεῖ δράκοντι τιμωρεῖ φόνον·
καὶ ταῦτα δρῶντες σύμμαχον κτήσεσθ᾽ Ἄρη.
χθὼν δ᾽ ἀντὶ καρποῦ καρπὸν ἀντί θ᾽ αἵματος
αἷμ᾽ ἢν λάβῃ βρότειον, ἕξετ᾽ εὐμενῆ
Γῆν, ἥ ποθ᾽ ἡμῖν χρυσοπήληκα στάχυν
940 Σπαρτῶν ἀνῆκεν· ἐκ γένους δὲ δεῖ θανεῖν
τοῦδ᾽ ὃς δράκοντος γέννος ἐκπέφυκε παῖς.
σὺ δ᾽ ἐνθάδ᾽ ἡμῖν λοιπὸς εἶ Σπαρτῶν γένους
ἀκέραιος ἔκ τε μητρὸς ἀρσένων τ᾽ ἄπο
[οἱ σοί τε παῖδες. Αἵμονος μὲν οὖν γάμοι
945 σφαγὰς ἀπείργουσ᾽. οὐ γάρ ἐστιν ἤθεος.
κεἰ μὴ γὰρ εὐνῆς ἥψατ᾽, ἀλλ᾽ ἔχει λέχος].
οὗτος δὲ πῶλος τῇδ᾽ ἀνειμένος πόλει
θανὼν πατρῴαν γαῖαν ἐκσώσειεν ἄν.
πικρὸν δ᾽ Ἀδράστῳ νόστον Ἀργείοισί τε
950 θήσει, μέλαιναν κῆρ᾽ ἐπ᾽ ὄμμασιν βαλών,
κλεινάς τε Θήβας. τοῖνδ᾽ ἑλοῦ δυοῖν πότμοιν
τὸν ἕτερον· ἢ γὰρ παῖδα σῶσον ἢ πόλιν.

τὰ μὲν παρ᾽ ἡμῶν πάντ᾽ ἔχεις· ἡγοῦ, τέκνον,
πρὸς οἶκον. ὅστις δ᾽ ἐμπύρῳ χρῆται τέχνῃ
955 μάταιος· ἢν μὲν πικρὰ σημήνας τύχῃ,
ἐχθρὸς καθέστηχ᾽ οἷς ἂν οἰωνοσκοπῇ·
ψευδῆ δ᾽ ὑπ᾽ οἴκτου τοῖσι χρωμένοις λέγων
ἀδικεῖ τὰ τῶν θεῶν. Φοῖβον ἀνθρώποις μόνον
χρῆν θεσπιῳδεῖν, ὃς δέδοικεν οὐδένα.

earthborn snake, guardian of Dirce's waters, came to birth:
he must give the earth a libation of blood because of the
ancient grudge of Ares against Cadmus: Ares is now aveng-
ing the death of the earthborn snake. If you do this, you
will have Ares as your ally. And if the ground receives off-
spring in place of offspring and mortal blood for blood,
Earth will be propitious to you, Earth who once sent forth
the gold-helmeted harvest of the Sown Men. One of this
race must die, one begotten from the jaw of the snake. You
are one of the last remaining members of the Sown Men
here, of pure lineage on your mother's and father's side.
[And so are your children. Haemon's coming marriage pre-
vents him from being slaughtered, for he is not a man un-
wed. Even if he has not yet experienced the bed of love,
still he has a wife.] This colt, sacrificial animal for the city,
will rescue his fatherland by his death. Sorry is the home-
coming he will give Adrastus and the Argives, casting black
death upon their eyes, and glorious will he make Thebes.
Of these two fates choose one: save your son or your city.

You have heard all I have to say. Lead me home, daugh-
ter! Anyone who practices divination is a fool. If he hap-
pens to give unwelcome prophecies, the recipients regard
him as an enemy. But if he pities those who consult him
and tells them lies, he wrongs the gods. Only Phoebus
should prophesy to men: he fears no man.

---

934 Κάδμῳ Valckenaer: -ου C
944–6 del. Willink (946 iam Valckenaer)
955 πικρὰ Valckenaer: ἐχθρὰ fere C

ΧΟΡΟΣ

960 Κρέον, τί σιγᾷς γῆρυν ἄφθογγον σχάσας;
κἀμοὶ γὰρ οὐδὲν ἧσσον ἔκπληξις πάρα.

ΚΡΕΩΝ

τί δ' ἄν τις εἴποι; δῆλον οἵ γ' ἐμοὶ λόγοι.
ἐγὼ γὰρ οὔποτ' ἐς τόδ' εἶμι συμφορᾶς
ὥστε σφαγέντα παῖδα προσθεῖναι πόλει.

965 πᾶσιν γὰρ ἀνθρώποισι φιλότεκνος βίος,
οὐδ' ἂν τὸν αὑτοῦ παῖδά τις δοίη κτανεῖν.
μή μ' εὐλογείτω τἀμά τις κτείνων τέκνα·
αὐτὸς δ', ἐν ὡραίῳ γὰρ ἕσταμεν βίου,
θνῄσκειν ἕτοιμος πατρίδος ἐκλυτήριον.

970 ἀλλ' εἶα, τέκνον, πρὶν μαθεῖν πᾶσαν πόλιν,
ἀκόλαστ' ἐάσας μάντεων θεσπίσματα,
φεῦγ' ὡς τάχιστα τῆσδ' ἀπαλλαχθεὶς χθονός.
[λέξει γὰρ ἀρχαῖς καὶ στρατηλάταις τάδε,
πύλας ἐφ' ἑπτὰ καὶ λοχαγέτας μολών.]

975 κἂν μὲν φθάσωμεν, ἔστι σοι σωτηρία·
ἢν δ' ὑστερήσῃς, οἰχόμεσθα, κατθανῇ.

ΜΕΝΟΙΚΕΥΣ

ποῖ δῆτα φεύγω; τίνα πόλιν; τίνα ξένων;

ΚΡΕΩΝ

ὅπου χθονὸς τῆσδ' ἐκποδὼν μάλιστ' ἔσῃ.

ΜΕΝΟΙΚΕΥΣ

οὔκουν σὲ φράζειν εἰκός, ἐκπονεῖν δ' ἐμέ;

Exit TEIRESIAS *and his daughter by Eisodos A.*

CHORUS LEADER

Creon, why are you silent, uttering no sound? I am no less startled than you.

CREON

What can one say? Yet what I must say is clear. Never shall I go so far in wretchedness as to offer my child to the city for slaughter! All men alive love their children, and no one would give his own child to be killed. I do not want the praise of someone who kills my children! I myself am ready to die to rescue my country: I am a fitting age to do so.

But quick, my son! Before the whole city learns of this, abandon these wanton oracles of seers and leave the country as fast as you can! [For he will report these things to the authorities and the generals, going to the seven gates and their captains.] If we are quick, your life may be saved. But if you are too late, we are done for, you will be killed!

MENOECEUS

Where shall I flee? To what city or what host?

CREON

Where you will be furthest from this land.

MENOECEUS

Should you not give the orders and I carry them out?

973–4 del. Willink (974 suspectum habuit Valckenaer cl. Σ, del. Wecklein)

ΚΡΕΩΝ

980 Δελφοὺς περάσας . . .

ΜΕΝΟΙΚΕΥΣ
ποῖ με χρή, πάτερ, μολεῖν;

ΚΡΕΩΝ
. . . Αἰτωλίδ᾽ ἐς γῆν.

ΜΕΝΟΙΚΕΥΣ
ἐκ δὲ τῆσδε ποῖ περῶ;

ΚΡΕΩΝ
Θεσπρωτὸν οὖδας.

ΜΕΝΟΙΚΕΥΣ
σεμνὰ Δωδώνης βάθρα;

ΚΡΕΩΝ
ἔγνως.

ΜΕΝΟΙΚΕΥΣ
τί δὴ τόδ᾽ ἔρυμά μοι γενήσεται;

ΚΡΕΩΝ
πόμπιμος ὁ δαίμων.

ΜΕΝΟΙΚΕΥΣ
χρημάτων δὲ τίς πόρος;

ΚΡΕΩΝ
985 ἐγὼ πορεύσω χρυσόν.

ΜΕΝΟΙΚΕΥΣ
εὖ λέγεις, πάτερ.
χώρει νυν· ὡς σὴν πρὸς κασιγνήτην μολών,

318

CREON

Pass through Delphi . . .

MENOECEUS

And then where must I go, father?

CREON

. . . and go to Aetolia.

MENOECEUS

Where shall I go from there?

CREON

To the land of Thesprotia.

MENOECEUS

The holy sanctuary of Dodona?

CREON

That's it.

MENOECEUS

How will this protect me?

CREON

The god will convey you.

MENOECEUS

What money shall I have?

CREON

I will send money.

MENOECEUS

Your plan is good, father. Go on your way. I shall go to your

---

983 δὴ τόδ' Musgrave: δῆτ' C

ἧς πρῶτα μαστὸν εἵλκυσ᾽, Ἰοκάστην λέγω,
μητρὸς στερηθεὶς ὀρφανός τ᾽ ἀποζυγείς,
προσηγορήσας εἶμι καὶ σώσω βίον.

ΚΡΕΩΝ

990 ἀλλ᾽ εἶα, χώρει· μὴ τὸ σὸν κωλυέτω.

ΜΕΝΟΙΚΕΥΣ

γυναῖκες, ὡς εὖ πατρὸς ἐξεῖλον φόβον,
κλέψας λόγοισιν, ὥσθ᾽ ἃ βούλομαι τυχεῖν·
ὅς μ᾽ ἐκκομίζει, πόλιν ἀποστερῶν τύχης,
καὶ δειλίᾳ δίδωσι. καὶ συγγνωστὰ μὲν
995 γέροντι, τοὐμὸν δ᾽ οὐχὶ συγγνώμην ἔχει,
προδότην γενέσθαι πατρίδος ἤ μ᾽ ἐγείνατο.
ὡς οὖν ἂν εἰδῆτ᾽, εἶμι καὶ σώσω πόλιν
ψυχήν τε δώσω τῆσδ᾽ ὑπερθανὼν χθονός.
αἰσχρὸν γάρ· οἱ μὲν θεσφάτων ἐλεύθεροι
1000 κοὐκ εἰς ἀνάγκην δαιμόνων ἀφιγμένοι
στάντες παρ᾽ ἀσπίδ᾽ οὐκ ὀκνήσουσιν θανεῖν,
πύργων πάροιθε μαχόμενοι πάτρας ὕπερ,
ἐγὼ δέ, πατέρα καὶ κασίγνητον προδοὺς
πόλιν τ᾽ ἐμαυτοῦ, δειλὸς ὡς ἔξω χθονὸς
1005 ἄπειμ᾽, ὅπου δ᾽ ἂν ζῶ, κακὸς φανήσομαι;
μὰ τὸν μετ᾽ ἄστρων Ζῆν᾽ Ἄρη τε φοίνιον,
ὃς τοὺς ὑπερτείλαντας ἐκ γαίας ποτὲ
Σπαρτοὺς ἄνακτας τῆσδε γῆς ἱδρύσατο.
ἀλλ᾽ εἶμι καὶ στὰς ἐξ ἐπάλξεων ἄκρων
1010 σφάξας ἐμαυτὸν σηκὸν ἐς μελαμβαθῆ
δράκοντος, ἔνθ᾽ ὁ μάντις ἐξηγήσατο,

sister Jocasta, whose breast I first sucked when I was left orphaned from my mother. I shall say goodbye to her and then go and save my life.

CREON

Then go quickly: let her not prevent your departure!

Exit CREON by Eisodos A. Menoeceus is silent until he is out of earshot.

MENOECEUS

Women, how effectively I took my father's fear away, stealing it from him by talk so that I could get my heart's desire! He is trying to send me away, depriving the city of its fate and making me out to be a coward. To be sure, in an old man this is pardonable, but there would be no pardon for me if I betrayed the country that begot me. Know this: I shall go and save the city, giving my life for the country and dying for it. The contrast would otherwise be disgraceful. On the one hand, men under no compulsion from oracles or the gods stand by their shields and do not shrink from death. And on the other, shall I betray father, brother, and my own city, leave the country like a coward, and be shown up as base wherever I live? No, by Zeus enthroned among the stars and by Ares, god of slaughter, who established the Sown Men, rising out of the earth, as rulers of this land! I shall go now, take my stand upon the high battlements, slit my own throat above the deep black precinct of the serpent, the place the seer named, and set the city free. You

---

989 προσηγορήσας Hartung et Σ: -ήσων C et Σ alter
995 fort. τεκόντι   998 ὑπερθανὼν Barnes: -εῖν C
999 αἰσχρῶς Heimsoeth

ἐλευθερώσω γαῖαν· εἴρηται λόγος.
[στείχω δέ, θανάτου δῶρον οὐκ αἰσχρὸν πόλει
δώσων, νόσου δὲ τήνδ' ἀπαλλάξω χθόνα.
1015 εἰ γὰρ λαβὼν ἕκαστος ὅ τι δύναιτό τις
χρηστὸν διέλθοι τοῦτο κἀς κοινὸν φέροι
πατρίδι, κακῶν ἂν αἱ πόλεις ἐλασσόνων
πειρώμεναι τὸ λοιπὸν εὐτυχοῖεν ἄν.]

ΧΟΡΟΣ

στρ.

ἔβας ἔβας,
ὦ πτεροῦσσα, Γᾶς λόχευμα
1020 νερτέρου τ' Ἐχίδνας,
Καδμείων ἁρπαγά,
πολύφθορος πολύστονος
μειξοπάρθενον δάιον τέρας,
φοιτάσι πτεροῖς
1025 χαλαῖσί τ' ὠμοσίτοις·
Διρκαίων ἅ ποτ' ἐκ τόπων νέους
πεδαίρουσ' ἄλυρον ἀμφὶ μοῦσαν,
ὀλομέναν γ' Ἐρινύν,
1030 ἔφερες ἔφερες ἄχεα πατρίδι
φόνια· φόνιος ἐκ θεῶν
ὃς τάδ' ἦν ὁ πράξας.
ἰάλεμοι δὲ ματέρων,
ἰάλεμοι δὲ παρθένων

1013–8 del. Scheurleer   1016 fort. φέρων
1023 μειξοπάρθενον a (coni. Valckenaer): -ος ceteri codd.

have heard all I have to say. [I go in order to give the city the not ignoble gift of my death, and I shall free this land from plague. If each man were to take whatever useful thing he might do, examine it thoroughly, and contribute it to the common good, cities would have less trouble and prosper henceforth and forever.]

Exit MENOECEUS *by Eisodos A.*

CHORUS

You came, you came,
O winged one, offspring of Earth
and of the Snake of the Underworld,
plunderer of the Cadmeans,
killer of many, source of many tears,
half-maiden portent of ruin!
On roving wings you came
and with talons for eating raw flesh!
From the region of Dirce you took
young men away by plying your lyreless Muse,
a cursed Erinys,[48]
and brought upon the country
woes murderous: murderous was the god's hand
who wrought all this.
Keening of mothers,
keening of maids

---

[48] The Sphinx's "Muse" was her riddle (in verse), and she killed those who could not solve it. It is called an Erinys because an Erinys too is sent by the gods for destruction.

1029 γ' Diggle: τ' C: del. Hartung

1035 ἐστέναζον οἴκοις·
ἰηιήιον βοάν,
ἰηιήιον μέλος
ἄλλος ἄλλοτ᾽ ἐποτότυζε
διαδοχαῖς ἀνὰ πτόλιν.
βροντᾷ δὲ στεναγμὸς
1040 ἀχά τ᾽ ἦν ὅμοιος,
ὁπότε πόλεος ἀφανίσειεν
ἁ πτεροῦσσα παρθένος τιν᾽ ἀνδρῶν.

ἀντ.

χρόνῳ δ᾽ ἔβα
Πυθίαις ἀποστολαῖσιν
Οἰδίπους ὁ τλάμων
1045 Θηβαίαν τάνδε γᾶν
τότ᾽ ἀσμένοις, πάλιν δ᾽ ἄχη·
ματρὶ γὰρ γάμους δυσγάμους τάλας
καλλίνικος ὢν
αἰνιγμάτων συνάπτει,
1050 μιαίνει δὲ πτόλιν, δι᾽ αἱμάτων δ᾽
ἀμείβει μυσαρὸν εἰς ἀγῶνα
καταβαλὼν ἀραῖσι
τέκεα μέλεος. ἀγάμεθ᾽ ἀγάμεθ᾽,
1055 ὃς ἐπὶ θάνατον οἴχεται
γᾶς ὑπὲρ πατρῴας,
Κρέοντι μὲν λιπὼν γόους,

1038a ἄλλοτ᾽ Diggle: ἄλλον C
1040 ἀχά Musgrave (ἀχαί Π): ἰα- C

324

broke forth in their houses.
The cry "Ah me!"
the song "Ah me!"
by different voices at different times
was uttered in succession in the city.
The groans and lamentations
were like the sound of thunder
whenever the winged maid
took from the city one of its men.

In time there came
by the sending of Pytho[49]
Oedipus the doomed
to this land of Thebes,
at first bringing joy, then later grief.
For with his mother he made a marriage that was no
    marriage, poor man,
glorious in victory
over the riddle,
and brought pollution upon the city, and now in deeds of
    blood
his sons he brings into a blood-stained contest,
hurling them into it with his curse,
luckless man. I marvel, marvel,
at him who goes to his death
to save his country,
leaving lamentation to Creon

[49] Apollo "sent" Oedipus to Thebes in that he wanted Laius to
be killed by his son.

τὰ δ᾽ ἑπτάπυργα κλῇθρα γᾶς
καλλίνικα θήσων.
1060 γενοίμεθ᾽ ὧδε ματέρες
γενοίμεθ᾽ εὔτεκνοι, φίλα
Παλλάς, ἃ δράκοντος αἷμα
λιθόβολον κατηργάσω,
Καδμείαν μέριμναν
ὁρμάσασ᾽ ἐπ᾽ ἔργον,
1065 ὅθεν ἐπέσυτο τάνδε γαῖαν
ἁρπαγαῖσι δαιμόνων τις ἄτα.

ΑΓΓΕΛΟΣ

ὠή, τίς ἐν πύλαισι δωμάτων κυρεῖ;
ἀνοίγετ᾽· ἐκπορεύετ᾽ Ἰοκάστην δόμων.
ὠὴ μάλ᾽ αὖθις· διὰ μακροῦ μέν, ἀλλ᾽ ὅμως.
1070 [ἔξελθ᾽, ἄκουσον, Οἰδίπου κλεινὴ δάμαρ,
λήξασ᾽ ὀδυρμῶν πενθίμων τε δακρύων.]

ΙΟΚΑΣΤΗ

ὦ φίλτατ᾽, οὔ που ξυμφορὰν ἥκεις φέρων
Ἐτεοκλέους θανόντος, οὗ παρ᾽ ἀσπίδα
βέβηκας αἰεὶ πολεμίων εἴργων βέλη;
1075 [τί μοί ποθ᾽ ἥκεις καινὸν ἀγγελῶν ἔπος;]
τέθνηκεν ἢ ζῇ παῖς ἐμός; σήμαινέ μοι.

ΑΓΓΕΛΟΣ

ζῇ, μὴ τρέσῃς, τοῦδ᾽ ὥς σ᾽ ἀπαλλάξω φόβου.

1069 in fine dist. Jackson   1070–1 post Bruhn et Harber-
ton del. Reeve   1072 οὔ που Kirchhoff: ἦ που fere C
1075 del. Hartung cl. Σ

but making the land's seven-towered fortress
glorious in victory.
May we be mothers, may we,
of fair children like these,
dear Pallas! It was you who inspired
the serpent's bloody death by stoning
and set the tensed effort of Cadmus
on the path to completion.[50]
From this deed there rushed against the land
the snatching ruinous hand of heaven.

Enter by Eisodos B a soldier of Eteocles as MESSENGER.

MESSENGER

(*knocking on the door*) Ho there! Who is manning the
palace gate? Open up: bring Jocasta out! (*silence*) Ho there
once more, though far off you be! [Illustrious wife of Oedi-
pus, come out and hear! Cease your lamentations and your
tears of grief!]

Enter JOCASTA *from the* skene.

JOCASTA

Dear man, you have not come, I trust, to bring the bad
news of Eteocles' death? You always stood by his shield
hand and protected him from enemy weapons. [What un-
toward event have you come to report?] Is my son dead or
alive? Tell me.

MESSENGER

Alive, no fear: of that care I will free you.

---

[50] See above, lines 657–68.

ΙΟΚΑΣΤΗ

τί δ'; ἑπτάπυργοι πῶς ἔχουσι περιβολαί;

ΑΓΓΕΛΟΣ

ἑστᾶσ' ἄθραυστοι κοὐκ ἀνήρπασται πόλις.

ΙΟΚΑΣΤΗ

1080 ἦλθον δὲ πρὸς κίνδυνον Ἀργείου δορός;

ΑΓΓΕΛΟΣ

ἀκμήν γ' ἐπ' αὐτήν· ἀλλ' ὁ Καδμείων Ἄρης
κρείσσων κατέστη τοῦ Μυκηναίου δορός.

ΙΟΚΑΣΤΗ

ἓν εἰπὲ πρὸς θεῶν, εἴ τι Πολυνείκους πέρι
οἶσθ'· ὡς μέλει μοι καὶ τόδ', εἰ λεύσσει φάος.

ΑΓΓΕΛΟΣ

1085 ζῇ σοι ξυνωρὶς ἐς τόδ' ἡμέρας τέκνων.

ΙΟΚΑΣΤΗ

εὐδαιμονοίης. πῶς γὰρ Ἀργεῖον δόρυ
πυλῶν ἀπεστήσασθε πυργηρούμενοι;
λέξον, γέροντα τυφλὸν ὡς κατὰ στέγας
ἐλθοῦσα τέρψω, τῆσδε γῆς σεσωμένης.

ΑΓΓΕΛΟΣ

1090 ἐπεὶ Κρέοντος παῖς ὁ γῆς ὑπερθανὼν
πύργων ἐπ' ἄκρων στὰς μελάνδετον ξίφος
λαιμῶν διῆκε, τῇδε γῇ σωτηρίαν,
λόχους ἔνειμεν ἑπτὰ καὶ λοχαγέτας
πύλας ἐφ' ἑπτά, φύλακας Ἀργείου δορός,
1095 σὸς παῖς, ἐφέδρους ⟨θ'⟩ ἱππότας μὲν ἱππόταις

JOCASTA
And how are the seven-gated battlements?

MESSENGER
Unbreached: the city has not been taken.

JOCASTA
Did they come into danger from the Argive spear?

MESSENGER
Yes, to the utmost pitch: but Cadmean war spirit vanquished the Mycenean spear.

JOCASTA
One thing more, by the gods: do you know anything about Polynices? It matters greatly to me that he is living.

MESSENGER
Your two sons are alive until this hour.

JOCASTA
Blessings on you! But how, when you were besieged, did you force the Argive army from the gates? Tell me so that I may go and gladden the blind old man in the house with the news that this land has been rescued.

MESSENGER
When Creon's son, who died on the land's behalf, had stood on the top of the battlements and plunged the dark sword into his throat, achieving survival for this land, your son allotted seven companies and seven captains to the seven gates to ward off the Argive spear. ⟨And⟩ he stationed reserves for both cavalry and hoplite forces so

---

1092 σωτηρίαν Diggle: σωτήριον C
1095 ⟨θ'⟩ Valckenaer

ἔταξ', ὁπλίτας δ' ἀσπιδηφόροις ἔπι,
ὡς τῷ νοσοῦντι τειχέων εἴη δορὸς
ἀλκὴ δι' ὀλίγου. περγάμων δ' ἀπ' ὀρθίων
λεύκασπιν εἰσορῶμεν Ἀργείων στρατὸν
1100 Τευμησσὸν ἐκλιπόντα, καὶ τάφρου πέλας
†δρόμῳ ξυνῆψαν† ἄστυ Καδμείας χθονός.
παιὰν δὲ καὶ σάλπιγγες ἐκελάδουν ὁμοῦ
ἐκεῖθεν ἔκ τε τειχέων ἡμῶν πάρα.
[καὶ πρῶτα μὲν προσῆγε Νηίσταις πύλαις
1105 λόχον πυκναῖσιν ἀσπίσιν πεφρικότα
ὁ τῆς κυναγοῦ Παρθενοπαῖος ἔκγονος,
ἐπίσημ' ἔχων οἰκεῖον ἐν μέσῳ σάκει,
ἑκηβόλοις τόξοισιν Ἀταλάντην κάπρον
χειρουμένην Αἰτωλόν. ἐς δὲ Προιτίδας
1110 πύλας ἐχώρει σφάγι' ἔχων ἐφ' ἅρματι
ὁ μάντις Ἀμφιάραος, οὐ σημεῖ' ἔχων
ὑβρισμέν' ἀλλὰ σωφρόνως ἄσημ' ὅπλα.
Ὠγύγια δ' ἐς πυλώμαθ' Ἱππομέδων ἄναξ
ἔστειχ' ἔχων σημεῖον ἐν μέσῳ σάκει
1115 στικτοῖς Πανόπτην ὄμμασιν δεδορκότα,
τὰ μὲν σὺν ἄστρων ἐπιτολαῖσιν ὄμματα
βλέποντα, τὰ δὲ κρύπτοντα δυνόντων μέτα,
ὡς ὕστερον θανόντος εἰσορᾶν παρῆν.
Ὁμολωίσιν δὲ τάξιν εἶχε πρὸς πύλαις
1120 Τυδεύς, λέοντος δέρος ἔχων ἐπ' ἀσπίδι
χαίτῃ πεφρικός· δεξιᾷ δὲ λαμπάδα
Τιτὰν Προμηθεὺς ἔφερεν ὡς πρήσων πόλιν.
ὁ σὸς δὲ Κρηναίαισι Πολυνείκης πύλαις

that any part of the wall that was in trouble should have relief close at hand. Then from the lofty battlements we espied the Argive army with its white shields coming from Teumessus: at the circle of our trench they broke into a run and ringed the Cadmean citadel about. The paean of war and the trumpet resounded from the enemy side and from ours within the fortifications.

[And first the huntswoman's son Parthenopaeus brought his company, bristling with close-ranked shields, to the Neïstan Gate. He had a fitting symbol in the middle of his shield, Atalanta overcoming the Aetolian boar with her far-darting arrows. To the Proetid Gate came the seer Amphiaraus with sacrificial victims on his chariot. He had no arrogant device but a shield modestly unmarked.

Hippomedon marched to the Ogygian Gate. In the center of his shield was the all-seeing Argus, with eyes dappling his body, some opening in concert with rising stars and some closing with setting ones, as we later could see after his death.

Tydeus was stationed near the Homoloïd Gate, wearing on his shield the pelt of a lion with bristling mane. In his right hand he carried a torch, a Titan Prometheus, in order to burn the city.

Your son Polynices brought his soldiery against the

1101 fort. βρόχου συνῆψαν ἄστυ Καδμεῖον δίκην   v. del. Kirchhoff
1104–40 del. Morus

Ἄρη προσῆγε· Ποτνιάδες δ᾽ ἐπ᾽ ἀσπίδι
1125 ἐπίσημα πῶλοι δρομάδες ἐσκίρτων φόβῳ,
εὖ πως στρόφιγξιν ἔνδοθεν κυκλούμεναι
πόρπαχ᾽ ὑπ᾽ αὐτόν, ὥστε μαίνεσθαι δοκεῖν.
ὁ δ᾽ οὐκ ἔλασσον Ἄρεος ἐς μάχην φρονῶν
Καπανεὺς προσῆγε λόχον ἐπ᾽ Ἠλέκτραις πύλαις·
1130 σιδηρονώτοις δ᾽ ἀσπίδος κύκλοις ἐπῆν
γίγας ἐπ᾽ ὤμοις γηγενὴς ὅλην πόλιν
φέρων μοχλοῖσιν ἐξανασπάσας βάθρων,
ὑπόνοιαν ἡμῖν οἷα πείσεται πόλις.
ταῖς δ᾽ ἑβδόμαις Ἄδραστος ἐν πύλαισιν ἦν,
1135 ἑκατὸν ἐχίδναις ἀσπίδ᾽ ἐκπληρῶν γραφῇ,
ὕδρας ἔχων λαιοῖσιν ἐν βραχίοσιν
Ἀργεῖον αὔχημ᾽· ἐκ δὲ τειχέων μέσων
δράκοντες ἔφερον τέκνα Καδμείων γνάθοις.
παρῆν δ᾽ ἑκάστου τῶνδέ μοι θεάματα
1140 ξύνθημα παραφέροντι ποιμέσιν λόχων.]
καὶ πρῶτα μὲν τόξοισι καὶ μεσαγκύλοις
ἐμαρνάμεσθα σφενδόναις θ᾽ ἑκηβόλοις
πέτρων τ᾽ ἀραγμοῖς· ὡς δ᾽ ἐνικῶμεν μάχῃ,
ἔκλαγξε Τυδεὺς καὶ σὸς ἐξαίφνης γόνος·
1145 Ὦ τέκνα Δαναῶν, πρὶν κατεξάνθαι βολαῖς,
τί μέλλετ᾽ ἄρδην πάντες ἐμπίπτειν πύλαις,
γυμνῆτες ἱππῆς ἁρμάτων τ᾽ ἐπιστάται;
ἠχῆς δ᾽ ὅπως ἤκουσαν, οὔτις ἀργὸς ἦν·
πολλοὶ δ᾽ ἔπιπτον κρᾶτας αἱματούμενοι,
1150 ἡμῶν τ᾽ ἐς οὖδας εἶδες ἂν πρὸ τειχέων
πυκνοὺς κυβιστητῆρας ἐκπεπνευκότας·

Crenaean Gate. Upon his shield pranced in panic the wild mares of Potniae,[51] skillfully twisting upon pivots from inside the shield, below the shield strap itself, so that they seem to be insane.

Capaneus, whose pride in war is like that of Ares himself, brought his company against the Electran gates. Upon the iron-backed circle of his shield was an earthborn Giant, who had pried up the whole city from its foundations with a crowbar and was carrying it on his back, an indication of what our city would suffer.

At the seventh gate was Adrastus, who had pictured on his shield a hundred snakes, hydras he bore on his left arm, an Argive boast. And from the middle of the battlements the snakes were bearing off with their teeth the Thebans' children. I got to see each of these sights when I took round the watchword to the captains of the companies.]

At first we fought with bows, javelins, and slings, distance weapons, and with showers of stones. When we were prevailing in the fight, at once Tydeus and your son shouted out, "Sons of the Danaans, before we are torn to pieces by missiles, quick, charge the gates all in a body, light-armed troops, cavalry, chariot drivers, and all!" When they heard this cry, no one was idle: many fell to the ground with bloodied heads, and you could have seen on our earth large numbers of divers, their life's breath gone,

---

[51] The flesh-eating horses of Glaucus of Potniae, which Heracles had to overcome.

1151 ἐκπεπτωκότας Madvig, ἐκνενευκότας Markland

ξηρὰν δ' ἔδευον γαῖαν αἵματος ῥοαῖς.

ὁ δ' Ἀρκάς, οὐκ Ἀργεῖος, Ἀταλάντης γόνος
τυφῶς πύλαισιν ὥς τις ἐμπεσὼν βοᾷ
1155 πῦρ καὶ δικέλλας, ὡς κατασκάψων πόλιν·
ἀλλ' ἔσχε μαργῶντ' αὐτὸν ἐναλίου θεοῦ
Περικλύμενος παῖς λᾶαν ἐμβαλὼν κάρᾳ
ἁμαξοπληθῆ, γεῖσ' ἐπάλξεων ἄπο·
ξανθὸν δὲ κρᾶτα διεπάλυνε καὶ ῥαφὰς
1160 ἔρρηξεν ὀστέων, ἄρτι δ' οἰνωπὸν γένυν
καθημάτωσεν· οὐδ' ἀποίσεται βίον
τῇ καλλιτόξῳ μητρὶ Μαινάλου κόρῃ.

ἐπεὶ δὲ τάσδ' ἐσεῖδεν εὐτυχεῖς πύλας,
ἄλλας ἐπῄει παῖς σός, εἱπόμην δ' ἐγώ.
1165 ὁρῶ δὲ Τυδέα καὶ παρασπιστὰς πυκνοὺς
Αἰτωλίσιν λόγχαισιν εἰς ἄκρον στόμα
πύργων ἀκοντίζοντας, ὥστ' ἐπάλξεων
λιπεῖν ἐρίπνας φύλακας· ἀλλά νιν πάλιν
κυναγὸς ὡσεὶ παῖς σὸς ἐξαθροίζεται,
1170 πύργοις δ' ἐπέστησ' αὖθις. ἐς δ' ἄλλας πύλας
ἠπειγόμεσθα, τοῦτο παύσαντες νοσοῦν.

Καπανεὺς δὲ πῶς εἴποιμ' ἂν ὡς ἐμαίνετο;
μακραύχενος γὰρ κλίμακος προσαμβάσεις
ἔχων ἐχώρει, καὶ τοσόνδ' ἐκόμπασεν,
1175 μηδ' ἂν τὸ σεμνὸν πῦρ νιν εἰργαθεῖν Διὸς
τὸ μὴ οὐ κατ' ἄκρων περγάμων ἑλεῖν πόλιν.
καὶ ταῦθ' ἅμ' ἠγόρευε καὶ πετρούμενος
ἀνεῖρφ' ὑπ' αὐτὴν ἀσπίδ' εἱλίξας δέμας,
κλίμακος ἀμείβων ξέστ' ἐνηλάτων βάθρα.

before the walls. They dampened the thirsty earth with streams of their blood.

The son of Atalanta, an Arcadian, not an Argive, hurled himself against the gates like a whirlwind and shouted for fire and pickaxes to raze the city to the ground. But in his fury he was checked by Periclymenus, son of the seagod, who hurled at his head a rock that would fill a wagon, a coping stone from the battlements. It shattered his blond head, broke the sutures of the skull, and bloodied his cheeks, with the new bloom of youth upon them. He will not return alive to his mother of the lovely bow, the girl of Maenalus.

When he saw that these gates were doing well, your son went to others, and I with him. I saw Tydeus and his massed companions hurling their Aetolian lances at the topmost edge of the gate so that the guards left the high battlements. But your son like a master of hounds brought them back together and set them upon the tower again. When we had cured this malady, we rush off to other gates.

How can I describe the way Capaneus raged? With a long-necked ladder in his hands he came on and uttered this boast, that not even the holy fire of Zeus would stop him from razing the city's topmost towers to the ground. With these words on his lips up he climbed, pelted with stones and coiling his body under his shield, passing from

---

1168 φύλακας nescioquis ap. Valckenaer: φυγάδας C

1180 ἤδη δ' ὑπερβαίνοντα γεῖσα τειχέων
βάλλει κεραυνῷ Ζεύς νιν· ἐκτύπησε δὲ
χθών, ὥστε δεῖσαι πάντας· ἐκ δὲ κλιμάκων
[ἐσφενδονᾶτο χωρὶς ἀλλήλων μέλη,
κόμαι μὲν εἰς Ὄλυμπον, αἷμα δ' ἐς χθόνα,
1185 χεῖρες δὲ καὶ κῶλ' ὡς κύκλωμ' Ἰξίονος]
εἱλίσσετ'· ἐς γῆν δ' ἔμπυρος πίπτει νεκρός.
   ὡς δ' εἶδ' Ἄδραστος Ζῆνα πολέμιον στρατῷ,
ἔξω τάφρου καθεῖσεν Ἀργείων στρατόν.
οἱ δ' αὖ παρ' ἡμῶν δεξιὸν Διὸς τέρας
1190 ἰδόντες ἐξήλαυνον, ἁρμάτων ὄχοι
ἱππῆς ὁπλῖται, κὰς μέσ' Ἀργείων ὅπλα
συνῆψαν ἔγχη· πάντα δ' ἦν ὁμοῦ κακά·
ἔθρωσκον ἐξέπιπτον ἀντύγων ἄπο,
τροχοί τ' ἐπήδων ἄξονές τ' ἐπ' ἄξοσιν
1195 νεκροί τε νεκροῖς ἐξεσωρεύονθ' ὁμοῦ.
   πύργων μὲν οὖν γῆς ἔσχομεν κατασκαφὰς
ἐς τὴν παροῦσαν ἡμέραν· εἰ δ' εὐτυχὴς
ἔσται τὸ λοιπὸν ἥδε γῆ, θεοῖς μέλει.
[καὶ νῦν γὰρ αὐτὴν δαιμόνων ἔσωσέ τις.]

[ΧΟΡΟΣ
1200 καλὸν τὸ νικᾶν· εἰ δ' ἀμείνον' οἱ θεοὶ
γνώμην ἔχουσιν, εὐτυχὴς εἴην ἐγώ.]

ΙΟΚΑΣΤΗ
καλῶς τὰ τῶν θεῶν καὶ τὰ τῆς τύχης ἔχει·

1183–5 del. Nauck   1188 στρατόν] fort. λεών
1190 ὄχοι Musgrave: ὄχους fere C

336

one smooth rung to the next. Now, as he mounted the top of the battlements, Zeus struck him with his lightning bolt. The earth resounded and everyone grew afraid. From the ladder[52] he rolled, and his corpse fell in flames to the ground.

When Adrastus saw that Zeus was his army's enemy, he withdrew the Argive forces beyond the ditch. Our side, seeing Zeus's favorable omen, moved out after them, chariots, cavalry, and hoplites, and rushing into the midst of the Argive army they charged their spears. In one place could be seen all manner of ruin: men leapt or were thrown from their chariots, wheels hurtled through the air, and axles were piled upon axles, corpses upon corpses.

We have checked the destruction of this land's towers for today. Whether the country will be fortunate henceforth lies with the gods. [For even now some god has saved it.]

[CHORUS LEADER
Victory is a fine thing. If the gods have a better disposition than before, may I be happy!]

JOCASTA
What the gods and fortune have done is good: my sons are

---

[52] After this phrase the manuscripts give (bracketed words deleted by Nauck) "[his limbs were hurled in opposite directions, his hair to Olympus, his blood to the ground, while like Ixion on his wheel his arms and legs] rolled, and his corpse fell in flames to the ground."

1193 ἔθρῳσκον Earle: ἔθνησκον C   1195 τε Fritzsche:
δὲ C   1199 om. plerique codd.
1200–1 suspectos habuit Paley, del. Harberton

παῖδές τε γάρ μοι ζῶσι κἀκπέφευγε γῆ.
Κρέων δ' ἔοικε τῶν ἐμῶν νυμφευμάτων
1205 τῶν τ' Οἰδίπου δύστηνος ἀπολαῦσαι κακῶν,
παιδὸς στερηθείς, τῇ πόλει μὲν εὐτυχῶς,
ἰδίᾳ δὲ λυπρῶς. ἀλλ' ἄνελθέ μοι πάλιν,
τί τἀπὶ τούτοις παῖδ' ἐμὼ δρασείετον.

ΑΓΓΕΛΟΣ
ἔα τὰ λοιπά· δεῦρ' ἀεὶ γὰρ εὐτυχεῖς.

ΙΟΚΑΣΤΗ
1210 τοῦτ' εἰς ὕποπτον εἶπας· οὐκ ἐατέον.

ΑΓΓΕΛΟΣ
μεῖζον τί χρῄζεις παῖδας ἢ σεσωμένους;

ΙΟΚΑΣΤΗ
καὶ τἀπίλοιπά γ' εἰ καλῶς πράσσω κλυεῖν.

ΑΓΓΕΛΟΣ
μέθες μ'· ἔρημος παῖς ὑπασπιστοῦ σέθεν.

ΙΟΚΑΣΤΗ
κακόν τι κεύθεις καὶ στέγεις ὑπὸ σκότῳ.

ΑΓΓΕΛΟΣ
1215 οὐκ ἄν γε λέξαιμ' ἐπ' ἀγαθοῖσί σοι κακά.

ΙΟΚΑΣΤΗ
ἢν μή γε φεύγων ἐκφύγῃς πρὸς αἰθέρα.

ΑΓΓΕΛΟΣ
αἰαῖ· τί μ' οὐκ εἴασας ἐξ εὐαγγέλου
φήμης ἀπελθεῖν, ἀλλὰ μηνῦσαι κακά;

alive and the land has escaped harm. Poor Creon, it seems, has reaped misfortune from my marriage to Oedipus since he has lost his son: it was good fortune for the city but pain for him personally. But go back to your story: what are my two sons planning to do after this?

MESSENGER

Do not ask the sequel! Up to this point your fortune is good.

JOCASTA

Your words raise fears: I must not let them go.

MESSENGER

Do you crave more than that your sons should live?

JOCASTA

I want to hear if the rest of my fortune is good.

MESSENGER

Let me go: your son needs his subordinate.

JOCASTA

You keep some trouble hidden in the dark.

MESSENGER

I will not tell you woe on top of blessing.

JOCASTA

(restraining him) You will unless you fly to the upper air.

MESSENGER

Ah, ah! Why not let me go away after bringing good news, why compel me to reveal misfortune? Your two sons, with

---

¹²¹⁵ σοι Reiske: σοῖς fere C

EURIPIDES

τὼ παῖδε τὼ σὼ μέλλετον, τολμήματα
1220 αἴσχιστα, χωρὶς μονομαχεῖν παντὸς στρατοῦ.
[λέξαντες Ἀργείοισι Καδμείοισί τε
ἐς κοινὸν οἷον μήποτ' ὤφελον λόγον.
Ἐτεοκλέης δ' ὑπῆρξ' ἀπ' ὀρθίου σταθεὶς
πύργου, κελεύσας σῖγα κηρῦξαι στρατῷ·
1225 ἔλεξε δ'· Ὦ γῆς Ἑλλάδος στρατηλάται,
Δαναῶν ἀριστῆς, οἵπερ ἤλθετ' ἐνθάδε,
Κάδμου τε λαός, μήτε Πολυνείκους χάριν
ψυχὰς ἀπεμπολᾶτε μήθ' ἡμῶν ὕπερ.
ἐγὼ γὰρ αὐτὸς τόνδε κίνδυνον μεθεὶς
1230 μόνος συνάψω συγγόνῳ τὠμῷ μάχην·
κἂν μὲν κτάνω τόνδ', οἶκον οἰκήσω μόνος,
ἡσσώμενος δὲ τῷδε παραδώσω μόνῳ·
ὑμεῖς δ' ἀγῶν' ἀφέντες, Ἀργεῖοι, χθόνα
νίσεσθε, βίοτον μὴ λιπόντες ἐνθάδε·
1235 Σπαρτῶν τε λαὸς ἅλις ὃς κεῖται νεκρός.
τοσαῦτ' ἔλεξε· σὸς δὲ Πολυνείκης γόνος
ἐκ τάξεων ὤρουσε κἀπῄνει λόγους.
πάντες δ' ἐπερρόθησαν Ἀργεῖοι τάδε
Κάδμου τε λαὸς ὡς δίκαι' ἡγούμενοι.
1240 ἐπὶ τοῖσδε δ' ἐσπείσαντο κἀν μεταιχμίοις
ὅρκους συνῆψαν ἐμμενεῖν στρατηλάται.
ἤδη δ' ἔκρυπτον σῶμα παγχάλκοις ὅπλοις
δισσοὶ γέροντος Οἰδίπου νεανίαι·
φίλοι δ' ἐκόσμουν, τῆσδε μὲν πρόμον χθονὸς
1245 Σπαρτῶν ἀριστῆς, τὸν δὲ Δαναϊδῶν ἄκροι.
ἔσταν δὲ λαμπρὼ χρῶμά τ' οὐκ ἠλλαξάτην

340

shameful brashness, mean to separate from their armies and fight in single combat. [To the Argive and the Cadmeans together they spoke words I wish they had never spoken. Eteocles began it: standing on the high battlements he ordered the herald to call for silence, saying "You generals of the land of Greece, princes of the Danaans who have come here, and you people of Cadmus, you need not sell your lives for Polynices or for me. I myself, averting this danger, shall join in single combat with my brother. And if I kill him, I shall manage our house by myself, but if I am defeated I shall give it into his sole possession. You Argives, abandoning the struggle, will go back to your land and not leave your lives behind here. Enough too of the Sown Men are lying dead."

Those were his words. Your son Polynices rushed from the ranks and praised this speech. And all the Argives and all the people of Cadmus roared their approval, thinking the terms just. On these terms the generals poured libations, and in the space between the lines they gave oaths that they would abide by them.

And now they proceeded to cover their bodies in their bronze panoplies, these two young sons of old Oedipus. They were adorned in armor by their friends, Thebes' champion by the Sown Men's champions, his brother by the chiefs of the sons of Danaus. They stood there gleaming and did not blanch as they yearned eagerly to hurl their

---

1221–58 del. Paley
1232 ἡσσημένος Diggle
1235 ὅς] ὅσος aliquot recentiores

μαργῶντ᾽ ἐπ᾽ ἀλλήλοισιν ἱέναι δόρυ.
παρεξιόντες δ᾽ ἄλλος ἄλλοθεν φίλων
λόγοις ἐθάρσυνόν τε κἀξηύδων τάδε·

1250 Πολύνεικες, ἐν σοὶ Ζηνὸς ὀρθῶσαι βρέτας
τρόπαιον Ἄργει τ᾽ εὐκλεᾶ δοῦναι λόγον·
Ἐτεοκλέα δ᾽ αὖ· Νῦν πόλεως ὑπερμαχεῖς,
νῦν καλλίνικος γενόμενος σκήπτρων κρατεῖς.
τάδ᾽ ἠγόρευον παρακαλοῦντες ἐς μάχην.

1255 μάντεις δὲ μῆλ᾽ ἔσφαζον, ἐμπύρου τ᾽ ἀκμῆς
ῥήξεις ἐνώμων, ὑγρότητ᾽ ἐναντίαν,
ἄκραν τε λαμπάδ᾽, ἣ δυοῖν ὅρους ἔχει,
νίκης τε σῆμα καὶ τὸ τῶν ἡσσωμένων.]
ἀλλ᾽, εἴ τιν᾽ ἀλκὴν ἢ σοφοὺς ἔχεις λόγους

1260 ἢ φίλτρ᾽ ἐπῳδῶν, στεῖχ᾽, ἐρήτυσον τέκνα
δεινῆς ἁμίλλης· ὡς ὁ κίνδυνος μέγας
[καὶ τἆθλα δεινά· δάκρυά σοι γενήσεται
δισσοῖν στερείσῃ τῇδ᾽ ἐν ἡμέρᾳ τέκνοιν].

ὦ τέκνον ἔξελθ᾽ Ἀντιγόνη δόμων πάρος.

1265 [οὐκ ἐν χορείαις οὐδὲ παρθενεύμασιν
νῦν σοι προχωρεῖ δαιμόνων κατάστασις,
ἀλλ᾽ ἄνδρ᾽ ἀρίστω καὶ κασιγνήτω σέθεν
ἐς θάνατον ἐκνεύοντε κωλῦσαί σε δεῖ
ξὺν μητρὶ τῇ σῇ μὴ πρὸς ἀλλήλοιν θανεῖν.]

1270 τίν᾽, ὦ τεκοῦσα μῆτερ, ἔκπληξιν νέαν
φίλοις αὐτεῖς τῶνδε δωμάτων πάρος;

spears at one another. From one quarter and another came one and another of their friends and spoke these encouraging words: "Polynices, it lies in your power to raise aloft the trophy of Zeus and to bring glory to Argos"; and to Eteocles: "Now you are the city's champion; now when you have won a glorious victory you will hold the scepter."

That is what they said, exhorting them to battle. The seers proceeded to sacrifice victims and observed the fissures at the tips of sacrificial flame, denoting an unfavorable moistness, and the peak of the fire, which portends two things, either victory or defeat.]

So if you have any strength to save them or clever words or incantatory charms, go, rescue your sons from the dread contest: the danger is great [and the prize is a terrible one: tears will be your portion if you lose your two sons today]!

JOCASTA

Daughter Antigone, come out before the palace! [It is not in choral dances or girlish pursuits that the fortune sent by the gods proceeds for you: the two heroes, your brothers, are veering toward death, and you and your mother must prevent their being killed each at the other's hand.]

Enter ANTIGONE *from the* skene.

ANTIGONE

Mother who bore me, what startling news are you announcing to your near and dear before the house?

1255 ἐμπύρου τ’ ἀκμῆς Geel: -ους τ’ -ὰς C
1256 ῥήξεις Geel: ῥ- τ’ C   1262–3 del. Valckenaer
1263 στερείσῃ Reiske: -ήσῃ fere C
1265–9 del. Fraenkel

ΙΟΚΑΣΤΗ

ὦ θύγατερ, ἔρρει σῶν κασιγνήτων βίος.

ΑΝΤΙΓΟΝΗ

πῶς εἶπας;

ΙΟΚΑΣΤΗ

αἰχμὴν ἐς μίαν καθέστατον.

ΑΝΤΙΓΟΝΗ

οἲ 'γώ, τί λέξεις, μῆτερ;

ΙΟΚΑΣΤΗ

οὐ φίλ', ἀλλ' ἔπου.

ΑΝΤΙΓΟΝΗ

1275 ποῖ, παρθενῶνας ἐκλιποῦσ';

ΙΟΚΑΣΤΗ

ἀνὰ στρατόν.

ΑΝΤΙΓΟΝΗ

αἰδούμεθ' ὄχλον.

ΙΟΚΑΣΤΗ

οὐκ ἐν αἰσχύνῃ τὰ σά.

ΑΝΤΙΓΟΝΗ

δράσω δὲ δὴ τί;

ΙΟΚΑΣΤΗ

συγγόνων λύσεις ἔριν.

ΑΝΤΙΓΟΝΗ

τί δρῶσα, μῆτερ;

JOCASTA

My daughter, your brothers' lives rush to ruin.

ANTIGONE

What do you mean?

JOCASTA

They are set to fight one another.

ANTIGONE

What can you mean, mother? Ah me!

JOCASTA

No welcome meaning. But come with me.

ANTIGONE

Where shall I go, leaving my maiden chamber?

JOCASTA

To the battlefield.

ANTIGONE

I feel shame before the crowd.

JOCASTA

Your circumstances do not allow shame.

ANTIGONE

But what shall I do?

JOCASTA

End your brothers' quarrel.

ANTIGONE

How, mother?

ΙΟΚΑΣΤΗ

προσπίτνουσ' ἐμοῦ μέτα.

ἡγοῦ σὺ πρὸς μεταίχμι'· οὐ μελλητέον.

1280 ἔπειγ' ἔπειγε, θύγατερ· ὡς, ἢν μὲν φθάσω
παῖδας πρὸ λόγχης, οὑμὸς ἐν φάει βίος·
[ἢν δ' ὑστερήσῃς, οἰχόμεσθα, κατθανῇ·]
θανοῦσι δ' αὐτοῖς συνθανοῦσα κείσομαι.

ΧΟΡΟΣ

στρ.

αἰαῖ αἰαῖ, τρομερὰν φρίκᾳ

1285 τρομερὰν φρέν' ἔχω· διὰ σάρκα δ' ἐμὰν
ἔλεος ἔλεος ἔμολε μα-
τέρος δειλαίας.
δίδυμα τέκεα πότερος ἄρα
πότερον αἱμάξει—

1290 ἰώ μοι πόνων, ἰὼ Ζεῦ καὶ γᾶ—
ὁμογενῆ δέραν, ὁμογενῆ ψυχὰν
δι' ἀσπίδων, δι' αἱμάτων;
τάλαιν' ἐγὼ τάλαινα,

1295 πότερον ἄρα νέκυν ὀλόμενον ἀχήσω;

ἀντ.

φεῦ δᾶ φεῦ δᾶ, δίδυμοι θῆρες,
φόνιαι ψυχαὶ δορὶ παλλομένῳ
πέσεα πέσεα δάι' αὐ-
τίχ' αἱμάξετον·

1300 τάλανες, ὅτι ποτὲ μονομάχον

1282 (=976) om. aliquot codd., del. Grotius

JOCASTA

Join me in supplicating them. (*to the Messenger*) You, lead us to the battlefield: we must not delay. Hurry, hurry, daughter: if I reach my sons before their battle, I will still live in the sun's light. [But if you are too late, you will be killed—woe is me.] But if they are dead, I shall lie next to them in death.

Exit by Eisodos B JOCASTA, ANTIGONE, *and* MESSENGER.

CHORUS

Ah, ah, ah, ah, trembling with fear,
trembling is my heart in my breast, and through my flesh
runs pity, pity for
the woeful mother.
The two sons—which of them
will draw blood from the other
(alas for my woes, alas Zeus and Earth),
draw blood from his brother's neck, his brother's life
by weapons, by deed of slaughter?
Ah, luckless me,
for whose death, whose corpse, shall I lament?

O woe, O woe, twin beasts,
murderous hearts, with the brandished spear
they will at once
accomplish their fell slaying slaying:
luckless men, whatever brought them

1290 καὶ Diggle et Willink: ἰὼ C   1293 τάλαινα] τάλαιν᾽·
⟨αἰαῖ⟩ Willink   1294–5 ἀχήσω Elmsley: ἰαχ- C
1297 παλλομένῳ Diggle: -όμεναι C

ἐπὶ φρέν᾽ ἠλθέτην.
βοᾷ βαρβάρῳ στενακτὰν ἀχὰν
μελομέναν νεκροῖς δάκρυσι θρηνήσω.
σχεδὸν τύχα, πέλας φόνος·
1305 κρινεῖ ξίφος τὸ μέλλον.
πότμος ἄποτμος ὁ φόνος ἕνεκ᾽ Ἐρινύων.

[—ἀλλὰ γὰρ Κρέοντα λεύσσω τόνδε δεῦρο συννεφῆ
πρὸς δόμους στείχοντα, παύσω τοὺς παρεστῶτας
γόους.

ΚΡΕΩΝ

1310 οἴμοι, τί δράσω; πότερ᾽ ἐμαυτὸν ἢ πόλιν
στένω δακρύσας, ἣν πέριξ ἔχει νέφος
τοιοῦτον ὥστε δι᾽ Ἀχέροντος ἰέναι;
ἐμός τε γὰρ παῖς γῆς ὄλωλ᾽ ὑπερθανών,
τοὔνομα λαβὼν γενναῖον, ἀνιαρὸν δ᾽ ἐμοί·
1315 ὃν ἄρτι κρημνῶν ἐκ δρακοντείων ἑλὼν
αὐτοσφαγῆ δύστηνος ἐκόμισ᾽ ἐν χεροῖν.
βοᾷ δὲ δῶμα πᾶν· ἐγὼ δ᾽ ἥκω μετὰ
γέρων ἀδελφὴν γραῖαν Ἰοκάστην, ὅπως
λούσῃ προθῆταί τ᾽ οὐκέτ᾽ ὄντα παῖδ᾽ ἐμόν.
1320 τοῖς γὰρ θανοῦσι χρὴ τὸν οὐ τεθνηκότα
τιμὰς διδόντα χθόνιον εὐσεβεῖν θεόν.

1302 ἀχὰν Wecklein: ἰαχὰν C   1305 ξίφος Hermann:
φάος C   1306 πότμος Dindorf: ἄποτμος C: τὸ μέλλον ᾆ /
πότμος Willink (vide ad 1293)
1308–53 Creontis personam hic interpolatam esse vidit Di

348

to the thought of single combat!
With barbarian clamor I shall utter in tears
a groaning cry fit for the dead.
Their fate is nigh, the slaughter near:
the sword shall give verdict for the future.
How grim a fate is this slaughter the Erinyes have made!

[Enter by Eisodos A CREON.[53]

CHORUS LEADER
But I see Creon coming to the palace with clouded brow: I
shall cease from my present lamentations.

CREON
Ah, ah, what shall I do? Shall I weep and groan for myself
or my city, so set about by a cloud of woe as to send it down
to Acheron? My son is dead, perished for his country,
having won a name that is noble but painful for me. I have
just now taken him, self-slain, from the dragon cliffs and
brought him back in my arms. My whole house is wailing.
And now I, old man that I am, have come in search of old
Jocasta so that she may wash my dead son's body and lay it
out for burial. For the living must honor the dead and
reverence the god of the underworld.

---

[53] The scene preceding the entrance of the second messenger
seems to have been reworked to accommodate another appear-
ance of Creon. New lines have been added and original lines cut. I
have marked the whole of 1308–53 as spurious while realizing that
the new scene may contain some lines salvaged from the old.

Benedetto (praeeunte Leidloff), quo auctore 1308–34 et fere
1338–53 del. Fraenkel, 1335–7 Kovacs

EURIPIDES

ΧΟΡΟΣ

βέβηκ' ἀδελφὴ σὴ δόμων ἔξω, Κρέον,
κόρη τε μητρὸς Ἀντιγόνη κοινῷ ποδί.

ΚΡΕΩΝ

ποῖ κἀπὶ ποίαν συμφοράν; σήμαινέ μοι.

ΧΟΡΟΣ

1325 ἤκουσε τέκνα μονομάχῳ μέλλειν δορὶ
ἐς ἀσπίδ' ἥξειν βασιλικῶν δόμων ὕπερ.

ΚΡΕΩΝ

πῶς φής; νέκυν τοι παιδὸς ἀγαπάζων ἐμοῦ
οὐκ ἐς τόδ' ἦλθον ὥστε καὶ τάδ' εἰδέναι.

ΧΟΡΟΣ

ἀλλ' οἴχεται μὲν σὴ κασιγνήτη πάλαι·
1330 δοκῶ δ' ἀγῶνα τὸν περὶ ψυχῆς, Κρέον,
ἤδη πεπρᾶχθαι παισὶ τοῖσιν Οἰδίπου.

ΚΡΕΩΝ

οἴμοι, τὸ μὲν σημεῖον εἰσορῶ τόδε,
σκυθρωπὸν ὄμμα καὶ πρόσωπον ἀγγέλου
στείχοντος, ὃς πᾶν ἀγγελεῖ τὸ δρώμενον.

ΑΓΓΕΛΟΣ Β

1335 ὦ τάλας ἐγώ, τίν' εἴπω μῦθον ἢ τίνας γόους;

ΚΡΕΩΝ

οἰχόμεσθ'· οὐκ εὐπροσώποις φροιμίοις ἄρχῃ λόγου.

ΑΓΓΕΛΟΣ Β

ὦ τάλας, δισσῶς αὐτῶ· μεγάλα γὰρ φέρω κακά.

PHOENICIAN WOMEN

CHORUS LEADER

Your sister has left the house, Creon, and with her
Antigone, her daughter.

CREON

Left for where and with what event in view? Tell me.

CHORUS LEADER

She heard that her sons were about to fight a duel for the
royal palace.

CREON

What? I was tending the body of my son and did not know
of this.

CHORUS LEADER

Well, your sister went off some time ago, Creon. I think
that the sons of Oedipus have already accomplished their
deadly struggle.

Enter by Eisodos B a follower of Eteocles as SECOND MES-
SENGER.

CREON

Ah, ah, I see a sign here, the gloomy eye and expression of
the arriving messenger, who will tell everything that has
happened.

SECOND MESSENGER

O misery, what word shall I utter, what lament?

CREON

We are undone: it is with joyless prelude that you begin
your tale.

SECOND MESSENGER

O misery! I say it twice, for terrible is the news I bear.

ΚΡΕΩΝ

πρὸς πεπραγμένοισιν ἄλλοις πήμασιν. λέγεις δὲ τί;

ΑΓΓΕΛΟΣ Β

οὐκέτ᾽ εἰσὶ σῆς ἀδελφῆς παῖδες ἐν φάει, Κρέον.

ΚΡΕΩΝ

1340 αἰαῖ·
μεγάλα μοι θροεῖς πάθεα καὶ πόλει.
ὦ δώματ᾽ εἰσηκούσατ᾽ Οἰδίπου τάδε,
παίδων ὁμοίαις συμφοραῖς ὀλωλότων;

ΧΟΡΟΣ

ὥστ᾽ ἂν δακρῦσαί γ᾽, εἰ φρονοῦντ᾽ ἐτύγχανεν.

ΚΡΕΩΝ

1345 οἴμοι ξυμφορᾶς βαρυποτμωτάτας,
οἴμοι κακῶν δύστηνος, ὦ τάλας ἐγώ.

ΑΓΓΕΛΟΣ Β

εἰ καὶ τὰ πρὸς τούτοισί γ᾽ εἰδείης κακά.

ΚΡΕΩΝ

καὶ πῶς γένοιτ᾽ ἂν τῶνδε δυσποτμώτερα;

ΑΓΓΕΛΟΣ Β

τέθνηκ᾽ ἀδελφὴ σὴ δυοῖν παίδοιν μέτα.

ΧΟΡΟΣ

1350 ἀνάγετ᾽ ἄγετε κωκυτόν, ἐπὶ κάρᾳ
⟨τίθε⟩τε λευκοπήχεις κτύπους χεροῖν.

1344 ὥστ᾽ ἂν δακρῦσαί Hartung: ὥστε δ- vel ὥστ᾽ ἐκδ- C
1350 ἄγετε Mastronarde: ἀνάγετε C

CREON

In addition to other past woes. What is your news?

SECOND MESSENGER

Your sister's sons look no more on the light, Creon.

CREON

Ah, ah!
Great are the sufferings you utter, for me and for my city.
O house of Oedipus, do you hear these words,
that the sons are dead by like misfortune?

CHORUS LEADER

Yes, it hears and would weep if it were conscious.

CREON

Alas for calamity most grievous,
alas for disaster, what misery!

SECOND MESSENGER

And how if you were to learn of further misfortunes?

CREON

What misfortune beyond this can there be?

SECOND MESSENGER

Your sister is dead along with her two sons.

CHORUS

Raise, raise the lament, strike
the head with your pale hands!

1351 ⟨τίθε⟩τε Diggle

EURIPIDES

ΚΡΕΩΝ

ὦ τλῆμον, οἷον τέρμον᾽, Ἰοκάστη, βίου
γάμων τε τῶν σῶν Σφιγγὸς αἰνιγμοῖς ἔτλης.]

⟨ΧΟΡΟΣ⟩

πῶς καὶ πέπρακται διπτύχων παίδων φόνος
1355 ἀρᾶς τ᾽ ἀγώνισμ᾽ Οἰδίπου; σήμαινέ μοι.

ΑΓΓΕΛΟΣ Β

τὰ μὲν πρὸ πύργων εὐτυχήματα χθονὸς
οἶσθ᾽· οὐ μακρὰν γὰρ τειχέων περιπτυχαί
[ὥστ᾽ οὐχ ἅπαντά σ᾽ εἰδέναι τὰ δρώμενα].
    ἐπεὶ δὲ χαλκέοις σῶμ᾽ ἐκοσμήσανθ᾽ ὅπλοις
1360 οἱ τοῦ γέροντος Οἰδίπου νεανίαι,
ἔστησαν ἐλθόντ᾽ ἐς μέσον μεταίχμιον
[δισσὼ στρατηγὼ καὶ διπλὼ στρατηλάτα]
ὡς εἰς ἀγῶνα μονομάχου τ᾽ ἀλκὴν δορός.
βλέψας δ᾽ ἐπ᾽ Ἄργος ἧκε Πολυνείκης ἀράς·
1365 Ὦ πότνι᾽ Ἥρα, σὸς γάρ εἰμ᾽, ἐπεὶ γάμοις
ἔζευξ᾽ Ἀδράστου παῖδα καὶ ναίω χθόνα,
δός μοι κτανεῖν ἀδελφόν, ἀντήρη δ᾽ ἐμὴν
καθαιματῶσαι δεξιὰν νικηφόρον.
[αἴσχιστον αἰτῶν στέφανον, ὁμογενῆ κτανεῖν.
1370 πολλοῖς δ᾽ ἐπήει δάκρυα τῆς εὐχῆς ὅση,
κἄβλεψαν ἀλλήλοισι διαδόντες κόρας.]
    Ἐτεοκλέης δὲ Παλλάδος χρυσάσπιδος
βλέψας πρὸς οἶκον ηὔξατ᾽· Ὦ Διὸς κόρη,
δὸς ἔγχος ἡμῖν καλλίνικον †ἐκ χερὸς†
1375 ἐς στέρν᾽ ἀδελφοῦ τῆσδ᾽ ἀπ᾽ ὠλένης βαλεῖν

354

CREON

Poor Jocasta, what a death, what an ending to your marriage you endured because of the Sphinx's riddles.]

‹CHORUS LEADER›

How was the slaughter of the two sons accomplished, their struggle with the curse of Oedipus? Tell me.

SECOND MESSENGER

You know the country's successes before the towers: the encircling wall is not far off [so that you know all that has happened].

When old Oedipus' young sons had decked themselves in bronze armor, they went to the space between the armies [, the two generals and two leaders,] and took their stand to fight in single combat. Looking toward Argos Polynices spoke this prayer: "Lady Hera, I am yours since I have married Adrastus' daughter and dwell in the land. Grant that I may kill my brother and bloody my right hand, his enemy, in victory!" [He asked for a disgraceful crown, killing a brother. Many wept at the enormity of the prayer, exchanging glances with one another.]

Eteocles, looking toward the temple of Pallas of the Golden Shield, prayed, "Daughter of Zeus, grant that I may hurl my victorious spear from my hand into my

---

1353 αἰνιγμοῖς Geel: -οὺς C
1354n ‹Xo.› Di Benedetto, Fraenkel
1358 del. Wecklein
1362 del. Valckenaer
1369–71 del. Valckenaer
1370 εὐχῆς Hermann: τύχης C
1374 εὐστόχως Wecklein

355

[κτανεῖν θ᾽ ὃς ἦλθε πατρίδα πορθήσων ἐμήν].
ἐπεὶ δ᾽ ἀνήφθη πυρσὸς ὡς Τυρσηνικῆς
σάλπιγγος ἠχή, σῆμα φοινίου μάχης,
ᾖξαν δράμημα δεινὸν ἀλλήλοις ἔπι.
1380 κάπροι δ᾽ ὅπως θήγοντες ἀγρίαν γένυν
ξυνῆψαν, ἀφρῷ διάβροχοι γενειάδας.
ᾖσσον δὲ λόγχαις· ἀλλ᾽ ὑφίζανον κύκλοις,
ὅπως σίδηρος ἐξολισθάνοι μάτην.
εἰ δ᾽ ὄμμ᾽ ὑπερσχὸν ἴτυος ἅτερος μάθοι,
1385 λόγχην ἐνώμα, στόματι προφθῆναι θέλων.
ἀλλ᾽ εὖ προσῆγον ἀσπίδων κεγχρώμασιν
ὀφθαλμόν, ἀργὸν ὥστε γίγνεσθαι δόρυ.
[πλείων δὲ τοῖς ὁρῶσιν ἐστάλασσ᾽ ἱδρὼς
ἢ τοῖσι δρῶσι διὰ φίλων ὀρρωδίαν.]
1390   Ἐτεοκλέης δὲ ποδὶ μεταψαίρων πέτρον
ἴχνους ὑπόδρομον, κῶλον ἐκτὸς ἀσπίδος
τίθησι· Πολυνείκης δ᾽ ἀπήντησεν δορί,
πληγὴν σιδήρῳ παραδοθεῖσαν εἰσιδών,
κνήμην τε διεπέρασεν Ἀργεῖον δόρυ·
1395 στρατὸς δ᾽ ἀνηλάλαξε Δαναϊδῶν ἅπας.
κἀν τῷδε μόχθῳ γυμνὸν ὦμον εἰσιδὼν
ὁ πρόσθε τρωθεὶς †στέρνα Πολυνείκους βίᾳ†
διῆκε λόγχην, κἀπέδωκεν ἡδονὰς
Κάδμου πολίταις, ἀπὸ δ᾽ ἔθραυσ᾽ ἄκρον δόρυ.
1400 ἐς δ᾽ ἄπορον ἥκων δορὸς ἐπὶ σκέλος πάλιν
χωρεῖ, λαβὼν δ᾽ ἀφῆκε μάρμαρον πέτρον
μέσον δ᾽ ἄκοντ᾽ ἔθραυσεν· ἐξ ἴσου δ᾽ Ἄρης
ἦν, κάμακος ἀμφοῖν χεὶρ᾽ ἀπεστερημένοιν.

brother's chest [and kill the man who came to sack my country]!"

When the voice of the Etruscan trumpet, sign of murderous battle, was set ablaze like a torch, they hurtled upon each other in a dread rush. Like wild boars that sharpen their savage tusks they clashed, with foam dripping down their beards. They lunged at each other with lances but each hid behind the circle of his shield so that the iron would slip off harmlessly. If one saw the other's face above the rim, he aimed his spear, wishing to hit him first with his spearpoint. But each effectively covered his eyes with the embossed shield rim so that the spear did no harm. [More sweat dripped from the spectators than from the combatants, so fearful were they for their friends.]

Eteocles, brushing aside with his foot a stone that was slipping beneath his tread, stuck his leg outside his shield. Polynices, seeing that his iron point had a chance to strike, went at him with his spear, and his Argive weapon pierced the shinguard. The whole army of the sons of Danaus raised a shout. While this was going on, the one already wounded, seeing an exposed shoulder, thrust his spear at Polynices and gave pleasure to the citizens of Cadmus, but his spear point broke off. Since he now had no spear, he retreated step by step, then taking up a gleaming stone he hurled it and broke Polynices' spear in the middle. The battle was now equal since both their hands had been deprived of spears.

ἐνθένδε κώπας ἁρπάσαντε φασγάνων
1405 ἐς ταὐτὸν ἧκον, συμβαλόντε δ' ἀσπίδας
πολὺν ταραγμὸν ἀμφιβάντ' εἶχον μάχης.
καί πως νοήσας Ἐτεοκλῆς τὸ Θεσσαλὸν
ἐσήγαγεν σόφισμ' ὁμιλίᾳ χθονός·
ἐξαλλαγεὶς γὰρ τοῦ παρεστῶτος πόνου,
1410 λαιὸν μὲν ἐς τοὔπισθεν ἀναφέρει πόδα,
πρόσω τὰ κοῖλα γαστρὸς εὐλαβούμενος,
προβὰς δὲ κῶλον δεξιὸν δι' ὀμφαλοῦ
καθῆκεν ἔγχος σφονδύλοις τ' ἐνήρμοσεν.
ὁμοῦ δὲ κάμψας πλευρὰ καὶ νηδὺν τάλας
1415 σὺν αἱματηραῖς σταγόσι Πολυνείκης πίτνει.
ὁ δ', ὡς κρατῶν δὴ καὶ νενικηκὼς μάχῃ,
ξίφος δικὼν ἐς γαῖαν ἐσκύλευέ νιν,
τὸν νοῦν πρὸς αὑτὸν οὐκ ἔχων, ἐκεῖσε δέ.
ὃ καί νιν ἔσφηλ'· ἔτι γὰρ ἐμπνέων βραχύ,
1420 σῴζων σίδηρον ἐν λυγρῷ πεσήματι,
μόλις μέν, ἐξέτεινε δ' εἰς ἧπαρ ξίφος
Ἐτεοκλέους ὁ πρόσθε Πολυνείκης πεσών.
γαῖαν δ' ὀδὰξ ἑλόντες ἀλλήλοιν πέλας
πίπτουσιν ἄμφω καὶ διώρισαν κράτος.

ΧΟΡΟΣ

1425 φεῦ φεῦ, κακῶν σῶν σ', Οἰδίπους, ὅσον στένω·
τὰς σὰς δ' ἀρὰς ἔοικεν ἐκπλῆσαι θεός.

ΑΓΓΕΛΟΣ Β

ἄκουε δή νυν καὶ τὰ πρὸς τούτοις κακά.
ἐπεὶ τέκνω πεσόντ' ἐλειπέτην βίον,

Now they grasped their sword hilts and closed on each other, and the dashing together of their shields as they stood against each other caused a great battle din. And somehow Eteocles thought of the Thessalian stratagem (he had visited that country) and applied it: he let up on pressing his enemy, drew his left foot back while carefully guarding his abdomen in front, advanced his right leg, and thrust his sword through the navel to the backbone. With flanks and belly doubled over the luckless Polynices falls, gushing blood. His brother, thinking he was now master, victorious in the fight, threw his sword on the ground and proceeded to strip off Polynices' armor, paying attention to the task and not to himself. This was his undoing. Polynices still had a little breath in him and in his death fall had kept his sword. And thus Polynices, who had fallen first, managed with great effort to run his sword through Eteocles' liver. They lie fallen near each other, mouthfuls of earth between their teeth: thus they divided the sovereignty.

CHORUS LEADER

Ah, Oedipus, how I grieve for your misfortunes: it seems that some god has fulfilled your curse.

SECOND MESSENGER

Hear then the woes that followed on these. At the point when the two sons had fallen and were dying, their luckless

---

1422 suspectum habuit Paley, del. Paulson
1424 καὶ t, coni. Denniston: κοὺ C: cf. 68
1425 σῶν σ’, Οἰδίπους, ὅσον Blaydes: σῶν, Οἰδίπου, σ’ ὅσον C

ἐν τῷδε μήτηρ ἡ τάλαινα †προσπίτνει†
1430 [σὺν παρθένῳ τε καὶ προθυμίᾳ ποδός].
τετρωμένους δ' ἰδοῦσα καιρίους σφαγὰς
ᾤμωξεν· Ὦ τέκν', ὑστέρα βοηδρόμος
πάρειμι. προσπίτνουσα δ' ἐν μέρει τέκνα
ἔκλαι' ἐθρήνει, τὸν πολὺν μαστῶν πόνον
1435 στένουσ', ἀδελφή θ' ἡ παρασπίζουσ' ὁμοῦ·
Ὦ γηροβοσκὼ μητρός—Ὦ γάμους ἐμοὺς
προδόντ' ἀδελφὼ φιλτάτω. στέρνων δ' ἄπο
φύσημ' ἀνεὶς †δύστλητον† Ἐτεοκλῆς ἄναξ
ἤκουσε μητρός, κἀπιθεὶς ὑγρὰν χέρα
1440 φωνὴν μὲν οὐκ ἀφῆκεν, ὀμμάτων δ' ἄπο
προσεῖπε δακρύοις, ὥστε σημῆναι φίλα.
ὁ δ' ἦν ἔτ' ἔμπνους, πρὸς κασιγνήτην δ' ἰδὼν
γραῖάν τε μητέρ' εἶπε Πολυνείκης τάδε·
Ἀπωλόμεσθα, μῆτερ· οἰκτίρω δέ σε
1445 καὶ τήνδ' ἀδελφὴν καὶ κασίγνητον νεκρόν.
φίλος γὰρ ἐχθρὸς ἐγένετ', ἀλλ' ὅμως φίλος.
θάψον δέ μ', ὦ τεκοῦσα, καὶ σύ, σύγγονε,
ἐν γῇ πατρῴᾳ, καὶ πόλιν θυμουμένην
παρηγορεῖτον, ὡς τοσόνδε γοῦν τύχω
1450 χθονὸς πατρῴας, κεἰ δόμους ἀπώλεσα.
ξυνάρμοσον δὲ βλέφαρά μου τῇ σῇ χερί,
μῆτερ—τίθησι δ' αὐτὸς ὀμμάτων ἔπι—
καὶ χαίρετ'· ἤδη γάρ με περιβάλλει σκότος.
ἄμφω δ' ἅμ' ἐξέπνευσαν ἄθλιον βίον.
1455 μήτηρ δ', ὅπως ἐσεῖδε τήνδε συμφοράν,
ὑπερπαθήσασ' ἥρπασ' ἐκ νεκρῶν ξίφος

mother came suddenly on the scene [with maiden daughter and eagerness of foot]. When she saw that they were mortally wounded, she cried out in pain, "O children, my help has come too late!" Falling on her sons in turn she wept and lamented, sighing for the lost effort of suckling them, and so did their sister, who accompanied her: "Sons, support of your mother's old age!" and "Dear brothers, who have not seen to my marriage." Lord Eteocles, his breath coming labored from his chest, heard his mother. He laid a damp hand upon her, and though he said no word, yet with the tears in his eyes he spoke, uttering his love. His brother Polynices still had breath, and looking at his sister and aged mother he said, "My life is over, mother. But it is you I pity and my sister here and my dead brother. My brother became my foe, but he was brother still. Bury me, my mother and sister, in my native soil, assuaging the city's anger, so that I may get at least this much of my native land even if I have lost my house. Close my eyes with your hand, mother"—here he laid her hand himself upon his eyes—"and farewell! Already darkness is covering me."

Both thus together breathed out the last of their unblessed lives. And seeing this the mother, in a fit of passion, snatched up a sword from the corpses and did a dreadful

---

1429 ἐπέρχεται Wecklein
1430 del. Markland
1434 μαστῶν] μάτην Nauck

κἄπραξε δεινά· διὰ μέσου γὰρ αὐχένος
ὠθεῖ σίδηρον, ἐν δὲ τοῖσι φιλτάτοις
θανοῦσα κεῖται περιβαλοῦσ᾽ ἀμφοῖν χέρας.
1460   ἀνῇξε δ᾽ ὀρθὸς λαὸς εἰς ἔριν λόγων,
ἡμεῖς μὲν ὡς νικῶντα δεσπότην ἐμόν,
οἱ δ᾽ ὡς ἐκεῖνον· ἦν δ᾽ ἔρις στρατηλάταις.
[οἱ μὲν πατάξαι πρόσθε Πολυνείκη δορί,
οἱ δ᾽ ὡς θανόντων οὐδαμοῦ νίκη πέλοι.
1465   κἂν τῷδ᾽ ὑπεξῆλθ᾽ Ἀντιγόνη στρατοῦ δίχα.]
οἱ δ᾽ εἰς ὅπλ᾽ ᾖσσον· εὖ δέ πως προμηθίᾳ
καθῆστο Κάδμου λαὸς ἀσπίδων ἔπι,
κἄφθημεν οὔπω τεύχεσι πεφαργμένον
Ἀργεῖον ἐσπεσόντες ἐξαίφνης στρατόν.
1470   κοὐδεὶς ὑπέστη, πεδία δ᾽ ἐξεπίμπλασαν
φεύγοντες, ἔρρει δ᾽ αἷμα μυρίον νεκρῶν
λόγχαις πιτνόντων. ὡς δ᾽ ἐνικῶμεν μάχῃ,
οἱ μὲν Διὸς τροπαῖον ἵστασαν βρέτας,
οἱ δ᾽ ἀσπίδας συλῶντες Ἀργείων νεκρῶν
1475   σκυλεύματ᾽ εἴσω τειχέων ἐπέμπομεν.
ἄλλοι δὲ τοὺς θανόντας Ἀντιγόνης μέτα
νεκροὺς φέρουσιν ἐνθάδ᾽ οἰκτίσαι φίλοις.
    πόλει δ᾽ ἀγῶνες οἱ μὲν εὐτυχέστατοι
τῇδ᾽ ἐξέβησαν, οἱ δὲ δυστυχέστατοι.

ΧΟΡΟΣ

1480   οὐκ εἰς ἀκοὰς ἔτι δυστυχία
δώματος ἥκει· πάρα γὰρ λεύσσειν

1463–4 del. Harberton

362

deed. She thrust the iron blade through the middle of her throat and now lies dead among her beloved sons, embracing them both in her arms.

The soldiery rose to their feet and began to quarrel, with our side claiming victory for my master, and the other side for Polynices: the leaders were wrangling. [Some said that Polynices struck first with his spear, but others that dead men are in no wise victorious. At this point Antigone withdrew quietly from the army.] The men rushed for their weapons. By some happy providence the Cadmean host had been sitting next to their shields, and we fell on the Argive army quickly when they were still unprotected. None of them stood his ground: they covered the plain in their flight, and blood flowed copiously from those slain with the spear. When we were victorious, some of us proceeded to raise the trophy image of Zeus, while others stripped off the shields from the Argive dead and took them inside the walls as prizes of war. Others together with Antigone are carrying the dead here for their kin to mourn.

For this city some of its struggles have ended in good fortune, others in bad.

Exit SECOND MESSENGER *by Eisodos A. Enter by Eisodos B* ANTIGONE *with a retinue of soldiers bearing the corpses of Eteocles, Polynices, and Jocasta.*

CHORUS LEADER
Now no longer do we hear of the house's misfortune: our

1465 del. Valckenaer
1478–9 τῇ μὲν . . . / οἵδ᾽ . . . τῇ δὲ Kock cl. Σ

πτώματα νεκρῶν τρισσῶν ἤδη
τάδε πρὸς μελάθροις κοινῷ θανάτῳ
σκοτίαν αἰῶνα λαχόντων.

ΑΝΤΙΓΟΝΗ

1485   οὐ προκαλυπτομένα
βοτρυχώδεος ἁβρὰ παρῆδος
οὐδ᾽ ὑπὸ παρθενίας τὸν ὑπὸ βλεφάροις
φοίνικ᾽, ἐρύθημα προσώπου,
αἰδομένα φέρομαι βάκχα νεκύων,
1490   κράδεμνα δικοῦσα κόμας ἀπ᾽ ἐμᾶς,
στολίδος κροκόεσσαν ἀνεῖσα τρυφάν,
ἀγεμόνευμα νεκροῖσι πολύστονον. αἰαῖ, ἰώ μοι.
ὦ Πολύνεικες, ἔφυς ἄρ᾽ ἐπώνυμος· ὤμοι, Θῆβαι·
1495   σὰ δ᾽ ἔρις—οὐκ ἔρις, ἀλλὰ φόνῳ φόνος—
Οἰδιπόδα δόμον
ὤλεσε κρανθεῖσ᾽ αἵματι δεινῷ,
αἵματι λυγρῷ.
†τίνα προσῳδὸν†
ἢ τίνα μουσοπόλον στοναχὰν ἐπὶ
1500   δάκρυσι δάκρυσιν, ὦ δόμος, ὦ δόμος,
ἀγκαλέσωμαι,
τρισσὰ φέρουσα τάδ᾽ αἵματα σύγγονα,
ματέρα καὶ τέκνα, χάρματ᾽ Ἐρινύος;
ἃ δόμον Οἰδιπόδα πρόπαρ ὤλεσε,
1505   τᾶς ἀγρίας ὅτε

1491 στολίδος . . . τρυφάν Porson: -ίδα . . . -ᾶς C
1494 Θήβαις Hermann

364

eyes can see here near the house three bodies of the slain,
who have lost in shared death the light of life.

ANTIGONE

Not covering up
the delicate skin of my cheek adorned with curls
nor concealing from maiden modesty
the crimson below my eyes, my face's blush,
I rush forth a bacchant of the dead,
hurling my mantilla from my tresses
and loosening my luxuriant saffron-colored robe,
a mournful escorter of the dead: alas, ah me!
O Polynices, how true your name has proved:[54] ah ah,
   Thebes!
Your strife—no strife but bloodshed upon bloodshed—
destroyed the house of Oedipus,
being brought to fulfillment in murder dread,
in murder grim.
What tuneful,
what muse-inspired groan amidst
weeping weeping, O house, O house,
shall I summon to my aid
as I bear these three slain bodies of kinsmen,
mother and sons, to gladden the Erinys?
She destroyed Oedipus' house long before
when he solved the intelligible song

[54] See above, note on line 637.

1498 τίνα πρῶτ᾽ ᾠδὰν Willink

δυσξυνέτου ξυνετὸν μέλος ἔγνω
Σφιγγὸς ἀοιδοῦ σῶμα φονεύσας.
ἰώ μοί μοι·
τίς Ἑλλὰς ἢ βάρβαρος ἢ
1510   τῶν προπάροιθ' εὐγενετᾶν
ἕτερος ἔτλα κακῶν τοσῶνδ'
αἵματος ἀμερίου
τοιάδ' ἄχεα φανερά;
τάλαιν', ὡς ἐλελίζῃ·
1515   τίς ἄρ' ὄρνις δρυὸς ἢ
ἐλάτας ἀκροκόμοις ἃμ πετάλοις
μονομάτορσιν ὀδυρμοῖ-
σιν ἐμοῖς <εἷσ'> ἄχεσιν συνῳδός;
αἴλινον αἰάγμασιν ἃ τούσδε προκλαίω,
1520   μονάδ' αἰῶνα διάξουσα τὸν αἰεὶ
χρόνον ἐν λειβομένοισιν δακρύοις·
αἰαῖ·
†τίν' ἐπὶ πρῶτον ἀπὸ† χαίτας
1525   σπαραγμοῖσιν ἀπαρχὰς
βάλω, ματρὸς ἐμᾶς ἢ διδύμοις
ἀγαλάκτοις παρὰ μαστοῖς
ἢ πρὸς ἀδελφῶν
οὐλόμεν' αἰκίσματα νεκρῶν;

1516 ἃμ πετάλοις Willink: εμ πεταλοις Π: ἀμφὶ κλάδοις
fere C
    1517 μονομάτορσιν Wilamowitz: -μάτερος C
    1518 <εἷσ'> post Paley (<εἷσιν> ἐμοῖς) Willink
    1524 αἰαῖ Willink: ε Π: om. C   τίνα πρῶτ' ἔπι Willink

of the fierce and baffling creature
and slew the singer Sphinx's body.
Ah me, ah me,
what woman Greek or foreign or
what other scion of ancient nobility
has endured of mortal bloodshed's
woes so many,
such manifest pains?
Poor woman, what keening you raise!
What bird then on oak's or
fir tree's lofty mane of leaves
will <come> to sing with lonely mother's plaint
in concert with my woes?
These my dead I mourn here with woeful cries of "Sing
    sorrow,"
I who am doomed to live a life bereft
with streaming tears for all time to come.

She tears out some of her hair.

Ah me!
On whom first shall I cast
first fruits of the tearing of my hair,
on my mother's two
milkless breasts
or on my brothers'
poor ravaged bodies?

1526 ἢ King: ἐν C
1527 ἀγαλάκτοις Headlam: γάλακτος C

1530 ὀτοτοτοῖ
λεῖπε σοὺς δόμους, ὄμμ' ἀλαὸν φέρων,
πάτερ γεραιέ, δεῖξον, ⟨ὦ⟩
Οἰδιπόδα, σὸν αἰῶνα μέλεον, ὃς ἔτι
δώμασιν ἀέριον ὄμμασι σκότον
1535 σοῖσι βαλὼν ἕλκεις μακρόπονον ζόαν.
κλύεις, ὦ κατ' αὐλὰν
ἀλαίνων γεραιὸν
πόδ' ἢ δεμνίοις δύ-
στανος ἰαύων;

OIΔIΠΟΥΣ

τί μ', ὦ παρθένε, βακτρεύμασι τυφλοῦ
1540 ποδὸς ἐξάγαγες ἐς φῶς
λεχήρη σκοτίων ἐκ θαλάμων οἰκ-
τροτάτοισιν δακρύοισιν,
πολιὸν αἰθερῶδες εἴδωλον ἢ
νέκυν ἔνερθεν ἢ
1545 πτανὸν ὄνειρον;

ANTIΓONH

δυστυχὲς ἀγγελίας ἔπος εἴσῃ,
πάτερ, οὐκέτι σοι τέκνα λεύσσει
φάος οὐδ' ἄλοχος, παραβάκτροις

1531 ὄμμ' ἀλαὸν Willink: ἀ. ὄμμα C
1532 ⟨ὦ⟩ Willink
1534 ὄμμασι σκότον Willink: σ- ὄ- C
1535 μακρόπονον Nauck: μακρόπνουν fere C

368

She throws it on the corpses

Alas!
Leave your house behind, blind though your eyes be,
⟨O⟩ aged father Oedipus, and show
your miserable fate, you that still
within the house, having cast upon your eyes
a murky darkness, drag out your life of long toil!
Do you hear, you that in the courtyard
wander with aged step
or in your wretchedness
lie abed?

Enter OEDIPUS *from the* skene, *supported by a staff.*

OEDIPUS

Why, daughter, have your brought me out
into the light, my blind footsteps guided by a stick,
bedridden though I am, from my dark chamber
by your pitiable cries,
a gray and insubstantial phantom,
a dead man from the nether world,
or a winged dream?

ANTIGONE

Luckless is the message you will hear,
father: your sons no longer look on the light,
nor your wife, who toiled in caring for you

1537 πόδ' ἢ Schoene: πόδα C
1543 αἰθερῶδες Willink: αἰθέρος ἀφανὲς C
1545 ὄνειρον ⟨ὥς⟩ Willink   1546 εἴσῃ Battier: οἴσῃ C

ἃ πόδα σὸν τυφλόπουν θεραπεύμασιν αἰὲν ἐμόχθει,
1550 ⟨ὦ⟩ πάτερ, ὤμοι.

ΟΙΔΙΠΟΥΣ

ὤμοι ἐγὼ παθέων· πάρα γὰρ στοναχαῖς τάδ' ἀυτεῖν.
τρισσαὶ ψυχαὶ ποίᾳ μοίρᾳ,
πῶς ἔλιπον φάος; ὦ τέκνον, αὔδα.

ΑΝΤΙΓΟΝΗ

1555 οὐκ ἐπ' ὀνείδεσιν οὐδ' ἐπιχάρμασιν,
ἀλλ' ὀδύναισι λέγω· σὸς ἀλάστωρ
ξίφεσιν βρίθων
καὶ πυρὶ καὶ σχετλίαισι μάχαις ἐπὶ παῖδας ἔβα
σούς,
ὦ πάτερ, ὤμοι.

ΟΙΔΙΠΟΥΣ

1560 αἰαῖ.

ΑΝΤΙΓΟΝΗ

τί τόδε καταστένεις;

ΟΙΔΙΠΟΥΣ

τέκνα.

ΑΝΤΙΓΟΝΗ

δι' ὀδύνας ἔβας·
εἰ δὲ τέθριππά γ' ἔθ' ἅρματα λεύσσων
ἀελίου τάδε σώματα νεκρῶν
ὄμματος αὐγαῖς σαῖς ἐπενώμας;

1550 ⟨ὦ⟩ Hermann, Seidler
1551 στοναχαῖς Geel: στενάχειν C

370

and like a staff tended your blind footsteps,
alas, dear father!

OEDIPUS

O misery! That is what I must groan and shout aloud.
What fate made three souls
leave the light? Tell me, my child!

ANTIGONE

Not to reproach you nor to rejoice at your misfortune
but in grief I tell you: the avenging spirit you sent forth,
with its cargo of swords
and fire and cruel battle, went against your sons,
alas, dear father!

OEDIPUS

Ah me!

ANTIGONE

What is this sigh you make?

OEDIPUS

My sons!

ANTIGONE

You are in pain!
But how if still seeing the sun's chariot
you had cast your eyes' gaze
on these corpses?

1561 τέκν᾽· Αν. ⟨οἶδα·⟩ δι᾽ Jackson
1562 δὲ Wilamowitz: τὰ C   ἔθ᾽ Seidler, Hermann: ἐς C

ΟΙΔΙΠΟΥΣ

1565 τῶν μὲν ἐμῶν τεκέων φανερὸν κακόν·
ἁ δὲ τάλαιν᾿ ἄλοχος τίνι μοι, τέκνον, ὤλετο μοίρᾳ;

ΑΝΤΙΓΟΝΗ

δάκρυα γοερὰ
φανερὰ πᾶσι τιθεμένα,
τέκεσι μαστὸν ἔφερεν ἔφερεν
ἱκέτις ἱκέτιν ὁρομένα.

1570 ηὗρε δ᾿ ἐν Ἠλέκτραισι πύλαις τέκνα
λωτοτρόφον κατὰ λείμακα λόγχαις
κοινὸν ἐνυάλιον †μάτηρ† ὥστε λέοντας ἐναύλους
μαρναμένους, ἐπὶ τραύμασι δ᾿ αἵματος

1575 ἤδη ψυχρὰν λοιβὰν φονίαν,
ἃν ἔλαχ᾿ Ἅιδας, ὤπασε δ᾿ Ἄρης·
χαλκόκροτον δὲ λαβοῦσα νεκρῶν πάρα φάσγανον
εἴσω
σαρκὸς ἔβαψεν, ἄχει δὲ τέκνων ἔπεσ᾿ ἀμφὶ
νεκροῖσιν·
πάντα δ᾿ ἐν ἄματι τῷδε συνάγαγεν,

1580 ὦ πάτερ, ἁμετέροισιν ἄχη μελάθροις
θεὸς τάδ᾿ ὃς τελευτᾷ.

[ΧΟΡΟΣ

πολλῶν κακῶν κατῆρξεν Οἰδίπου δόμοις
τόδ᾿ ἦμαρ· εἴη δ᾿ εὐτυχέστερος βίος.

1570-6 del. Diggle, def. Cropp, *CQ* 47 (1997), 570–4
1573 ἐνυαλίου *μέρος* Willink
1574 τραύμασι δ᾿ Musgrave: τραύμασι τ᾿ a: τραύμασιν rell.

PHOENICIAN WOMEN

OEDIPUS

My sons' woe is clear.
But my poor wife—child, what fate destroyed her?

ANTIGONE

Making her clamorous tears
manifest to all,
she brought, she brought in a rush to her sons
as suppliant her suppliant breast.
She found them at the Electran gate
in a clovery meadow with lances
in common battle fighting like lions in a den,
found upon their wounds the cold
gore's libation already poured out,
libation of Ares given to Hades.
Taking the bronze-beaten sword from the dead
she plunged it into her body and in grief sank down over
    her sons' corpses.
All these woes were gathered in one day
upon our house, father,
by the god who has fulfilled these things.[55]

[CHORUS LEADER

This day has been the beginning of many woes for the
house of Oedipus. May our life be more fortunate!

[55] It is likely that from here to the end the play has been re-
worked for some later production, new material displacing old. I
have bracketed the passage, though some of the lines in the new
scene might have been salvaged from the old.

1581 τάδ' ὃς Diggle: ὃς τάδε fere C
1582–1766 ab Euripide abiudicat Leidloff (1737–66 om. Π)

ΚΡΕΩΝ

οἴκτων μὲν ἤδη λήγεθ᾽, ὡς ὥρα τάφου
1585 μνήμην τίθεσθαι· τῶνδε δ᾽, Οἰδίπου, λόγων
ἄκουσον· ἀρχὰς τῆσδε γῆς ἔδωκέ μοι
Ἐτεοκλέης παῖς σός, γάμων φερνὰς διδοὺς
Αἵμονι κόρης τε λέκτρον Ἀντιγόνης σέθεν.
οὔκουν σ᾽ ἐάσω τήνδε γῆν οἰκεῖν ἔτι·
1590 σαφῶς γὰρ εἶπε Τειρεσίας οὐ μή ποτε
σοῦ τήνδε γῆν οἰκοῦντος εὖ πράξειν πόλιν.
ἀλλ᾽ ἐκκομίζου. καὶ τάδ᾽ οὐχ ὕβρει λέγω
οὐδ᾽ ἐχθρὸς ὤν σοι, διὰ δὲ τοὺς ἀλάστορας
τοὺς σοὺς δεδοικὼς μή τι γῆ πάθῃ κακόν.

ΟΙΔΙΠΟΥΣ

1595 ὦ μοῖρ᾽, ἀπ᾽ ἀρχῆς ὥς μ᾽ ἔφυσας ἄθλιον
καὶ τλήμον᾽, εἴ τις ἄλλος ἀνθρώπων ἔφυ·
ὃν καὶ πρὶν ἐς φῶς μητρὸς ἐκ γονῆς μολεῖν
ἄγονον Ἀπόλλων Λαΐῳ μ᾽ ἐθέσπισεν
φονέα γενέσθαι πατρός· ὦ τάλας ἐγώ.
1600 ἐπεὶ δ᾽ ἐγενόμην, αὖθις ὁ σπείρας πατὴρ
κτείνει με νομίσας πολέμιον πεφυκέναι·
χρῆν γὰρ θανεῖν νιν ἐξ ἐμοῦ· πέμπει δέ με
μαστὸν ποθοῦντα θηρσὶν ἄθλιον βοράν·
οὗ σῳζόμεσθα· Ταρτάρου γὰρ ὤφελεν
1605 ἐλθεῖν Κιθαιρὼν εἰς ἄβυσσα χάσματα,
ὅς μ᾽ οὐ διώλεσ᾽, ἀλλὰ δουλεῦσαι †τέ μοι†
δαίμων ἔδωκε Πόλυβον ἀμφὶ δεσπότην.

1600 αὖθις] αὐτὸς Nauck, αὐτίχ᾽ Geel, εὐθὺς Seyffert

374

CREON[56]

Stop lamenting now! It's time to speak of burial. Hear these words, Oedipus: your son Eteocles has given me the right to rule this land when he gave Haemon the marriage dowry and union with your daughter Antigone. Accordingly I will no longer permit you to dwell in this land: Teiresias said plainly that the city would never prosper while you dwelt here. So take yourself away. I do not say this from highhandedness or as your enemy but to prevent harm to the land from the avenging spirits besetting you.

OEDIPUS

O fate, how miserable you have made me from the start, how wretched if any man ever was! Even before I came forth into the light from my mother's womb and was still unborn Apollo prophesied to Laius that I would be my father's murderer: O the misery! And when I was born, the father who begot me tried to kill me, regarding me as his enemy (for he was fated to be killed at my hands), and he sent me, still reaching out for the breast, to be in my misery food for wild beasts! There I was rescued. O how I wish Cithaeron had gone down into the deep chasms of Tartarus! It failed to end my life, and instead fate made me a slave in the train of my master Polybus.[57] Luckless man

---

[56] Creon, in the revised production, is still on stage, having entered at line 1307.

[57] The text here is uncertain.

1606–7 δουλεύσας γ' ἐμοὶ / αἰῶν' Stahl   post ἀλλὰ lac. indic. Murray (oportebat post δουλεῦσαι)

κτανὼν δ᾽ ἐμαυτοῦ πατέρ᾽ ὁ δυσδαίμων ἐγὼ
ἐς μητρὸς ἦλθον τῆς ταλαιπώρου λέχος
1610 παῖδάς τ᾽ ἀδελφοὺς ἔτεκον, οὓς ἀπώλεσα,
ἀρὰς παραλαβὼν Λαΐου καὶ παισὶ δούς.
οὐ γὰρ τοσοῦτον ἀσύνετος πέφυκ᾽ ἐγὼ
ὥστ᾽ εἰς ἔμ᾽ ὄμματ᾽ ἔς τ᾽ ἐμῶν παίδων βίον
ἄνευ θεῶν του ταῦτ᾽ ἐμηχανησάμην.
1615 εἶέν· τί δράσω δῆθ᾽ ὁ δυσδαίμων ἐγώ;
τίς ἡγεμών μοι ποδὸς ὁμαρτήσει τυφλοῦ;
ἥδ᾽ ἡ θανοῦσα; ζῶσά γ᾽ ἂν σάφ᾽ οἶδ᾽ ὅτι.
ἀλλ᾽ εὔτεκνος ξυνωρίς; ἀλλ᾽ οὐκ ἔστι μοι.
ἀλλ᾽ ἔτι νεάζων αὐτὸς εὕροιμ᾽ ἂν βίον;
1620 πόθεν; τί μ᾽ ἄρδην ὧδ᾽ ἀποκτείνεις, Κρέον;
ἀποκτενεῖς γάρ, εἴ με γῆς ἔξω βαλεῖς.
οὐ μὴν ἑλίξας γ᾽ ἀμφὶ σὸν χεῖρας γόνυ
κακὸς φανοῦμαι· τὸ γὰρ ἐμόν ποτ᾽ εὐγενὲς
οὐκ ἂν προδοίην, οὐδέ περ πράσσων κακῶς.

ΚΡΕΩΝ

1625 σοί τ᾽ εὖ λέλεκται γόνατα μὴ χρῴζειν ἐμά,
ἐγὼ δὲ ναίειν σ᾽ οὐκ ἐάσαιμ᾽ ἂν χθόνα.
νεκρῶν δὲ τῶνδε τὸν μὲν ἐς δόμους χρεὼν
ἤδη κομίζειν, τόνδε δ᾽, ὃς πέρσων πόλιν
πατρίδα σὺν ἄλλοις ἦλθε, Πολυνείκους νέκυν
1630 ἐκβάλετ᾽ ἄθαπτον τῆσδ᾽ ὅρων ἔξω χθονός.
κηρύξεται δὲ πᾶσι Καδμείοις τάδε·
ὃς ἂν νεκρὸν τόνδ᾽ ἢ καταστέφων ἁλῷ
ἢ γῇ καλύπτων θάνατον ἀνταλλάξεται·

that I am, having killed my own father I came to my poor mother's bed and begot sons who were brothers. These I have now destroyed, putting on my children the curses I received from my father. For of course I am not so lacking in sense that I brought this ruin on my own eyes and the lives of my sons without the prompting of some god.

Well, then, what am I to do, wretch that I am? Who will come and guide my blind footsteps? The dead woman here? I am sure she would have were she alive. My two lovely sons then? They are mine no longer. Am I still vigorous enough to find my own livelihood? Where? Why are you destroying me so utterly, Creon? It will be my death if you banish me from the country. Yet I will not entwine my arms about your knees and show myself to be base. I shall never betray the noble blood that once was mine, even though I fare so ill.

CREON

Your not grasping my knees—that was well said. I shall never permit you to live in this land.

As for these dead men, we must take one of them into the palace, but this one, the corpse of Polynices, who came with allies to sack his native city—cast him unburied beyond the country's boundaries. This proclamation will be made to all the citizens of Cadmus: whoever is caught garlanding this corpse or covering it with earth will receive

ἐᾶν δ' ἄκλαυτον, ἄταφον, οἰωνοῖς βοράν.

1635 σὺ δ' ἐκλιποῦσα τριπτύχους θρήνους νεκρῶν
κόμιζε σαυτήν, Ἀντιγόνη, δόμων ἔσω
καὶ παρθενεύου τὴν ἰοῦσαν ἡμέραν
μένουσ', ἐν ᾗ σε λέκτρον Αἵμονος μένει.

ΑΝΤΙΓΟΝΗ

ὦ πάτερ, ἐν οἵοις κείμεθ' ἄθλιοι κακοῖς.

1640 ὡς σὲ στενάζω τῶν τεθνηκότων πλέον·
οὐ γὰρ τὸ μέν σοι βαρὺ κακῶν, τὸ δ' οὐ βαρύ,
ἀλλ' εἰς ἅπαντα δυστυχὴς ἔφυς, πάτερ.
ἀτὰρ σ' ἐρωτῶ τὸν νεωστὶ κοίρανον·
τί τόνδ' ὑβρίζεις πατέρ' ἀποστέλλων χθονός;

1645 τί θεσμοποιεῖς ἐπὶ ταλαιπώρῳ νεκρῷ;

ΚΡΕΩΝ

Ἐτεοκλέους βουλεύματ', οὐχ ἡμῶν, τάδε.

ΑΝΤΙΓΟΝΗ

ἄφρονά γε, καὶ σὺ μῶρος ὃς ἐπίθου τάδε.

ΚΡΕΩΝ

πῶς; τἀντεταλμέν' οὐ δίκαιον ἐκπονεῖν;

ΑΝΤΙΓΟΝΗ

οὔκ, ἢν πονηρά γ' ᾖ κακῶς τ' εἰρημένα.

ΚΡΕΩΝ

1650 τί δ'; οὐ δικαίως ὅδε κυσὶν δοθήσεται;

ΑΝΤΙΓΟΝΗ

οὐκ ἔννομον γὰρ τὴν δίκην πράσσεσθέ νιν.

death as his reward: leave him unwept, unburied, as food for birds.

You, Antigone, leave off lamenting these three corpses and take yourself into the palace. Live as an unmarried girl, waiting for the day that is coming, the day of your marriage to Haemon.

ANTIGONE

Father, in what miseries we are sunk! I grieve more for you than for the dead! For it is not that one of your misfortunes is heavy while another is not: no, you are miserable in everything, father.

But I ask you, the new ruler: why do you commit outrage against my father in banishing him from the land? Why legislate for a miserable corpse?

CREON

This was Eteocles' decision, not my own.

ANTIGONE

And a foolish decision it was, and you are a fool for following it.

CREON

What? Is it not right to carry out orders?

ANTIGONE

Not if they are bad and badly given.

CREON

Is it not justice to give this man to the dogs?

ANTIGONE

No: the penalty you exact from him is not lawful.

ΚΡΕΩΝ

εἴπερ γε πόλεως ἐχθρὸς ἦν οὐκ ἐχθρὸς ὤν.

ΑΝΤΙΓΟΝΗ

οὔκουν ἔδωκε †τῇ τύχῃ τὸν δαίμονα†;

ΚΡΕΩΝ

καὶ τῷ τάφῳ νυν τὴν δίκην παρασχέτω.

ΑΝΤΙΓΟΝΗ

1655 τί πλημμελήσας, τὸ μέρος εἰ μετῆλθε γῆς;

ΚΡΕΩΝ

ἄταφος ὅδ᾽ ἀνήρ, ὡς μάθῃς, γενήσεται.

ΑΝΤΙΓΟΝΗ

ἐγώ σφε θάψω, κἂν ἀπεννέπῃ πόλις.

ΚΡΕΩΝ

σαυτὴν ἄρ᾽ ἐγγὺς τῷδε συνθάψεις νεκρῷ.

ΑΝΤΙΓΟΝΗ

ἀλλ᾽ εὐκλεές τοι δύο φίλω κεῖσθαι πέλας.

ΚΡΕΩΝ

1660 λάζυσθε τήνδε κὰς δόμους κομίζετε.

ΑΝΤΙΓΟΝΗ

οὐ δῆτ᾽, ἐπεὶ τοῦδ᾽ οὐ μεθήσομαι νεκροῦ.

ΚΡΕΩΝ

ἔκριν᾽ ὁ δαίμων, παρθέν᾽, οὐχ ἃ σοὶ δοκεῖ.

1653 τὴν δίκην τῷ δαίμονι Purgold

380

CREON

Yes it is: though no enemy, he became his city's enemy.

ANTIGONE

Has he not paid the penalty to the god?[58]

CREON

So let him pay the penalty in the manner of his burial as well.

ANTIGONE

What was his fault if he came to get his share of the land?

CREON

To tell you plainly, this man shall not be buried!

ANTIGONE

I shall bury him, though the city forbid it.

CREON

You will dig your own grave, then, next to his.

ANTIGONE

Well, it is a glorious thing for two relatives to lie close together.

CREON

(to his retinue) Seize her and bring her into the house!

ANTIGONE

(falling to her knees and holding Polynices) No: I shall not let go of this corpse.

CREON

Fate has decided this matter, maiden, differently from you.

---

[58] I translate Purgold's conjecture without any confidence that it is right.

ΑΝΤΙΓΟΝΗ

κἀκεῖνο κέκριται, μὴ 'φυβρίζεσθαι νεκρούς.

ΚΡΕΩΝ

ὡς οὔτις ἀμφὶ τῷδ' ὑγρὰν θήσει κόνιν.

ΑΝΤΙΓΟΝΗ

1665 ναί, πρός σε τῆσδε μητρὸς Ἰοκάστης, Κρέον.

ΚΡΕΩΝ

μάταια μοχθεῖς· οὐ γὰρ ἂν τύχοις τάδε.

ΑΝΤΙΓΟΝΗ

σὺ δ' ἀλλὰ νεκρῷ λουτρὰ περιβαλεῖν μ' ἔα.

ΚΡΕΩΝ

ἐν τοῦτ' ἂν εἴη τῶν ἀπορρήτων πόλει.

ΑΝΤΙΓΟΝΗ

ἀλλ' ἀμφὶ τραύματ' ἄγρια τελαμῶνας βαλεῖν.

ΚΡΕΩΝ

1670 οὐκ ἔσθ' ὅπως σὺ τόνδε τιμήσεις νέκυν.

ΑΝΤΙΓΟΝΗ

ὦ φίλτατ', ἀλλὰ στόμα γε σὸν προσπτύξομαι.

ΚΡΕΩΝ

οὐ μὴ ἐς γάμους σοὺς συμφορὰν κτήσῃ γόοις;

ΑΝΤΙΓΟΝΗ

ἦ γὰρ γαμοῦμαι ζῶσα παιδὶ σῷ ποτε;

1672 οὐ μὴ Kirchhoff: οὐκ C

ANTIGONE

This too has been decided: no outrage for the dead.

CREON

No one shall put moist earth about this man.

ANTIGONE

By my mother Jocasta here, yes they will, Creon.

CREON

You toil to no purpose: you will never win consent for this.

ANTIGONE

Well, at least let me wash the body.

CREON

That would be one of the things the citizens may not do.

ANTIGONE

Well, at least let me bandage these cruel wounds.

CREON

Never shall you honor this corpse!

ANTIGONE

Dear brother, I will at least embrace and kiss you. (*She kisses him.*)

CREON

No: you court disaster for your marriage by your lamentation.

ANTIGONE

What? Shall I live to marry your son?

ΚΡΕΩΝ

πολλή σ' ἀνάγκη· ποῖ γὰρ ἐκφεύξῃ λέχος;

ΑΝΤΙΓΟΝΗ

1675 νὺξ ἆρ' ἐκείνη Δαναΐδων μ' ἕξει μίαν.

ΚΡΕΩΝ

εἶδες τὸ τόλμημ' οἷον ἐξωνείδισεν;

ΑΝΤΙΓΟΝΗ

ἴστω σίδηρος ὅρκιόν τέ μοι ξίφος.

ΚΡΕΩΝ

τί δ' ἐκπροθυμῇ τῶνδ' ἀπηλλάχθαι γάμων;

ΑΝΤΙΓΟΝΗ

συμφεύξομαι τῷδ' ἀθλιωτάτῳ πατρί.

ΚΡΕΩΝ

1680 γενναιότης σοι, μωρία δ' ἔνεστί τις.

ΑΝΤΙΓΟΝΗ

καὶ ξυνθανοῦμαί γ', ὡς μάθῃς περαιτέρω.

ΚΡΕΩΝ

ἴθ', οὐ φονεύσεις παῖδ' ἐμόν, λίπε χθόνα.

ΟΙΔΙΠΟΥΣ

ὦ θύγατερ, αἰνῶ μέν σε τῆς προθυμίας.

ΑΝΤΙΓΟΝΗ

ἀλλ' εἰ γαμοίμην, σὺ δὲ μόνος φεύγοις, πάτερ;

---

59 The daughters of Danaus on their wedding night murdered their cousins, the sons of Aegyptus, whom they were forced to marry.

CREON

You must: where will you go to escape marriage?

ANTIGONE

My marriage night will make me one of the Danaids.[59]

CREON

Do you see the effrontery of her insults?

ANTIGONE

Iron be my witness and the sword of oath!

CREON

Why do you take care to be quit of this marriage?

ANTIGONE

I will join this poor father of mine in exile.

CREON

That is noble of you but a bit foolish.

ANTIGONE

Yes, and what's more I will die with him.

CREON

Go, you will not kill my son: leave the land.

(?) *Exit* CREON *with retinue into the* skene. *Antigone rises to her feet.*

OEDIPUS

Daughter, my thanks, to be sure, for your good will.

ANTIGONE

Well, what would happen if I married and you went into exile alone?

ΟΙΔΙΠΟΥΣ

1685 μέν' εὐτυχοῦσα· τἄμ' ἐγὼ στέρξω κακά.

ΑΝΤΙΓΟΝΗ

καὶ τίς σε τυφλὸν ὄντα θεραπεύσει, πάτερ;

ΟΙΔΙΠΟΥΣ

πεσὼν ὅπου μοι μοῖρα κείσομαι πέδῳ.

ΑΝΤΙΓΟΝΗ

ὁ δ' Οἰδίπους ποῦ καὶ τὰ κλείν' αἰνίγματα;

ΟΙΔΙΠΟΥΣ

ὄλωλ'· ἐν ἦμάρ μ' ὤλβισ', ἐν δ' ἀπώλεσεν.

ΑΝΤΙΓΟΝΗ

1690 οὔκουν μετασχεῖν κἀμὲ δεῖ τῶν σῶν κακῶν;

ΟΙΔΙΠΟΥΣ

αἰσχρὰ φυγὴ θυγατρὶ σὺν τυφλῷ πατρί.

ΑΝΤΙΓΟΝΗ

οὔ, σωφρονούσῃ γ', ἀλλὰ γενναία, πάτερ.

ΟΙΔΙΠΟΥΣ

προσάγαγέ νύν με, μητρὸς ὡς ψαύσω σέθεν.

ΑΝΤΙΓΟΝΗ

ἰδού, γεραιᾶς φιλτάτης ψαῦσον χερί.

ΟΙΔΙΠΟΥΣ

1695 ὦ μῆτερ, ὦ ξυνάορ' ἀθλιωτάτη.

ΑΝΤΙΓΟΝΗ

οἰκτρὰ πρόκειται, πάντ' ἔχουσ' ὁμοῦ κακά.

OEDIPUS

Stay and be happy: I will endure my own misfortunes.

ANTIGONE

But who will tend you in your blindness, father?

OEDIPUS

I shall lie on the ground there where I am fated to fall.

ANTIGONE

Where then is Oedipus and his famous riddles?

OEDIPUS

Perished: one day made me blessed, another destroyed me.

ANTIGONE

Shall I not share then in your troubles?

OEDIPUS

For a daughter to be exiled with her blind father is disgraceful.

ANTIGONE

Not disgraceful but noble—provided she is sensible.

OEDIPUS

Take me to your mother, then, so that I may touch her.

ANTIGONE

(leading Oedipus to her) There! Put your hand to the dear old woman.

OEDIPUS

O mother, O wife most wretched!

ANTIGONE

She lies there pitiably, enduring all woes at once.

EURIPIDES

ΟΙΔΙΠΟΥΣ
Ἐτεοκλέους δὲ πτῶμα Πολυνείκους τε ποῦ;

ΑΝΤΙΓΟΝΗ
τώδ᾽ ἐκτάδην σοι κεῖσθον ἀλλήλοιν πέλας.

ΟΙΔΙΠΟΥΣ
πρόσθες τυφλὴν χεῖρ᾽ ἐπὶ πρόσωπα δυστυχῆ.

ΑΝΤΙΓΟΝΗ
1700 ἰδού, θανόντων σῶν τέκνων ἅπτου χερί.

ΟΙΔΙΠΟΥΣ
ὦ φίλα πεσήματ᾽ ἄθλι᾽ ἀθλίου πατρός.

ΑΝΤΙΓΟΝΗ
ὦ φίλτατον δῆτ᾽ ὄνομα Πολυνείκους ἐμοί.

ΟΙΔΙΠΟΥΣ
νῦν χρησμός, ὦ παῖ, Λοξίου περαίνεται.

ΑΝΤΙΓΟΝΗ
ὁ ποῖος; ἀλλ᾽ ἦ πρὸς κακοῖς ἐρεῖς κακά;

ΟΙΔΙΠΟΥΣ
1705 ἐν ταῖς Ἀθήναις κατθανεῖν μ᾽ ἀλώμενον.

ΑΝΤΙΓΟΝΗ
ποῦ; τίς σε πύργος Ἀτθίδος προσδέξεται;

ΟΙΔΙΠΟΥΣ
ἱερὸς Κολωνός, δώμαθ᾽ ἱππίου θεοῦ.
ἀλλ᾽ εἶα, τυφλῷ τῷδ᾽ ὑπηρέτει πατρί,
ἐπεὶ προθυμῇ τῆσδε κοινοῦσθαι φυγῆς.

OEDIPUS

And where are the bodies of Eteocles and Polynices?

ANTIGONE

(*leading him to them*) They lie here stretched out near each other.

OEDIPUS

Put my blind hands upon their unfortunate faces.

ANTIGONE

(*doing so*) There! With your hands touch your sons who have perished.

OEDIPUS

Dear fallen ones, wretched sons of a wretched father!

ANTIGONE

O Polynices, name I love best!

OEDIPUS

Now, my daughter, the prophecy of Loxias is being fulfilled.

ANTIGONE

What prophecy? Will you speak of misery on top of misery?

OEDIPUS

That I must wander and die in Athens.

ANTIGONE

Where? What fort in Attica will receive you?

OEDIPUS

Colonus the holy, the house of the god of horses. But come, serve me, your blind father, since you are eager to share in my exile.

ΑΝΤΙΓΟΝΗ

1710 ἴθ᾽ ἐς φυγὰν τάλαιναν· ὄρεγε χέρα φίλαν,
πάτερ γεραιέ, πομπίμαν
ἔχων ἔμ᾽ ὥστε ναυσίπομπον αὔραν.

ΟΙΔΙΠΟΥΣ

ἰδού·
πορεύομαι, τέκνον· σύ μοι
1715 ποδαγὸς ἀθλία γενοῦ.

ΑΝΤΙΓΟΝΗ

γενόμεθα γενόμεθ᾽, ἄθλιοί
γε δῆτα Θηβαιᾶν μάλιστα παρθένων.

ΟΙΔΙΠΟΥΣ

πόθι γεραιὸν ἴχνος τίθημι;
βάκτρα πόθι φέρω, τέκνον.

ΑΝΤΙΓΟΝΗ

1720 τᾷδε τᾷδε βᾶθί μοι,
τᾷδε τᾷδε πόδα τίθει,
ὥστ᾽ ὄνειρον ἰσχύν.

ΟΙΔΙΠΟΥΣ

ἰὼ ἰώ, δυστυχεστάτας φυγὰς
ἀλαίνειν τὸν γέροντά μ᾽ ἐκ πάτρας.
1725 ἰὼ ἰώ, δεινὰ δείν᾽ ἐγὼ τλάς.

ΑΝΤΙΓΟΝΗ

τί τλάς; τί τλάς; οὐχ ὁρᾷ Δίκα κακούς,

1716 ἄθλιοί Porson: -αί C
1722 ἰσχύν Π et Σ, coni. Hermann: ἰσχὺν ἔχων C

ANTIGONE

Go into miserable exile! Stretch out your beloved hand,
dear father, and take me
as escort, like a ship-escorting breeze.

OEDIPUS

There!
I am going, daughter: be for me
my luckless guide.

ANTIGONE

That I have been, have been, luckless
beyond the lot of Theban maidens!

OEDIPUS

Where shall I put my aged foot?
Where shall I take my staff, child?

ANTIGONE

This way, this way walk,
this way, this way plant your steps,
strengthless as a dream.

OEDIPUS

Ah me, ah me, for me, an old man,
to wander in miserable exile from my land!
Ah, ah, what terrible terrible things I have suffered!

ANTIGONE

Why, why say "suffered"? Justice does not behold the
wicked

1724 ἀλαίνειν Musgrave: ἐλαύνων C

οὐδ' ἀμείβεται βροτῶν ἀσυνεσίας.

ΟΙΔΙΠΟΥΣ

ὅδ' εἰμὶ μοῦσαν ὃς ἐπὶ καλ-
λίνικον οὐράνιον ἔβαν
1730 <μειξο>παρθένου κόρας
αἴνιγμ' ἀσύνετον εὑρών.

ΑΝΤΙΓΟΝΗ

Σφιγγὸς ἀναφέρεις ὄνειδος;
ἄπαγε τὰ πάρος εὐτυχήματ' αὐδῶν.
τάδε σ' ἐπέμενε μέλεα πάθεα
1735 φυγάδα πατρίδος ἄπο γενόμενον,
ὦ πάτερ, θανεῖν που.

ποθεινὰ δάκρυα παρὰ φίλαισι παρθένοις
λιποῦσ' ἄπειμι πατρίδος ἀποπρὸ γαίας
ἀπαρθένευτ' ἀλωμένα.

ΟΙΔΙΠΟΥΣ

1740 φεῦ τὸ χρήσιμον φρενῶν

ΑΝΤΙΓΟΝΗ

ἐς πατρός γε συμφορὰς
εὐκλεᾶ με θήσει.
τάλαιν' ἐγὼ <σῶν> συγγόνου θ' ὑβρισμάτων,
ὃς ἐκ δόμων νέκυς ἄθαπτος οἴχεται
1745 μέλεος, ὄν, εἴ με καὶ θανεῖν, πάτερ, χρεών,
σκότια γᾷ καλύψω.

1730 <μειξο>παρθένου Wilamowitz

and does not requite mortal folly.[60]

OEDIPUS

I am the man who mounted heaven-high in victory
over the song
of the ⟨part-⟩maiden creature
and solved her baffling riddle.

ANTIGONE

Do you renew your reproach of the Sphinx?
Speak of your former good fortunes as you depart.
These are the miseries that await you,
to go from your land as an exile
and die somewhere, my father.

Leaving to my maiden friends tears of longing
I go far from my country
to wander in no maiden fashion.

OEDIPUS

Oh what nobility of heart!

ANTIGONE

Yes, where my father's woes are concerned
it will give me glory.
Alas for the violence done against ⟨you⟩ and against my
    brother,
who has perished from the house as an unburied corpse
poor man, whom I, though I must die for it,
shall secretly hide in earth.

---

[60] These two lines are obscure.

1743 ⟨σῶν⟩ Matthiae

ΟΙΔΙΠΟΥΣ

1749 σὺ δ᾽ ἀμφιβωμίοις λιταῖς
1747 πρὸς ἥλικας φάνηθι σάς.

ΑΝΤΙΓΟΝΗ

1748 ἅλις ὀδυρμάτων ἐμῶν·
1750 κόρον ἔχουσ᾽ ἐμῶν κακῶν.

ΟΙΔΙΠΟΥΣ

ἴθ᾽ ἀλλὰ Βρόμιος ἵνα τε ση-
κὸς ἄβατος ὄρεσι μαινάδων.

ΑΝΤΙΓΟΝΗ

Καδμείαν ᾧ νεβρίδα
1755 στολιδωσαμένα ποτ᾽ ἐγὼ Σεμέλας
θίασον ἱερὸν ὄρεσιν ἀνεχόρευσα,
χάριν ἀχάριτον ἐς θεοὺς διδοῦσα.

ΟΙΔΙΠΟΥΣ

ὦ πάτρας κλεινῆς πολῖται, λεύσσετ᾽· Οἰδίπους ὅδε,
ὃς τὰ κλείν᾽ αἰνίγματ᾽ ἔγνων καὶ μέγιστος ἦν ἀνήρ,
1760 ὃς μόνος Σφιγγὸς κατέσχον τῆς μιαιφόνου κράτη,
νῦν ἄτιμος αὐτὸς οἰκτρὸς ἐξελαύνομαι χθονός.
ἀλλὰ γὰρ τί ταῦτα θρηνῶ καὶ μάτην ὀδύρομαι;
τὰς γὰρ ἐκ θεῶν ἀνάγκας θνητὸν ὄντα δεῖ φέρειν.

1747–9 hoc ordine Diggle
1749 ἀμφιβωμίοις λιταῖς Wecklein: ἀμφὶ βωμίους λιτάς C
1761 αὐτὸς οἰκτρὸς] οἰκτρὸς οἰκτρῶς Hermann

OEDIPUS

With entreaties near the altar
appear to your agemates.

ANTIGONE

Enough of lamentations:
they have had their fill of my troubles.

OEDIPUS

Well, then, come to the place on the maenads' mountains
where Dionysus' untrodden grove is.

ANTIGONE

I once girt myself in his honor
with Cadmean fawnskin
and led upon the mountains Semele's holy company:
my service won me no thanks.

OEDIPUS

Citizens of a glorious country, see! I, Oedipus, who solved
the famous riddle and was a man of great stature, who
alone checked the power of the murderous Sphinx, am
now being driven from the land all unhonored and in pite-
ous state. But why should I lament this and weep to no
purpose? Being mortal, I must bear the necessities sent by
the gods.

Exit by Eisodos B OEDIPUS *and* ANTIGONE (*exit* CREON
into the skene *unless he has exited at 1682*).

ΧΟΡΟΣ

ὦ μέγα σεμνὴ Νίκη, τὸν ἐμὸν
1765   βίοτον κατέχοις
καὶ μὴ λήγοις στεφανοῦσα.]

CHORUS LEADER
Victory, may you have my life in your charge and never
cease garlanding my head!]

Exit CHORUS *by Eisodos A.*

ORESTES

INTRODUCTION

Orestes, produced in 408, just before the poet left Athens for the court of Archelaus of Macedon, has a plot that seems to be the poet's free invention. The familiar tale of Clytaemestra's murder of her husband Agamemnon and her death in turn at the hands of their son Orestes is the background. The action picks up at the point where the poet's earlier *Electra* had left off, but minus the *deus ex machina*: in our play six days have gone by since Clytaemestra's funeral, and no divine help has appeared. Thereafter an entirely novel plot is set in motion.

The situation is set out in the prologue, spoken by Electra as her brother lies asleep in a bed set before the palace. Orestes, unlike his namesake in Aeschylus, has not gone to Delphi for purification but is still in Argos, tormented by visions of the Erinyes and by horror at what he has done. The people of Argos, stirred up by Agamemnon's enemies, are outraged at his deed, and he and his sister Electra are about to be put on trial and, if found guilty, executed by stoning. They are even being prevented from leaving the country: all the ways are guarded. Their only hope is their father's brother Menelaus, who has just returned to Greece with his wife Helen after long wanderings. Electra knows that he has arrived at the port of Nauplia and is watching for his return. Helen is already indoors, sent ahead under cover of darkness for fear that the Argives will throw stones at her.

Instead of the expected Menelaus the first person to appear is Helen, emerging from the *skene*. Utterly selfish, she asks Electra, already preoccupied with her brother, to go to Clytaemestra's grave and make an offering on her behalf. Electra declines politely and suggests sending Helen's own daughter Hermione, who is summoned from indoors and goes off. After Helen goes back into the *skene*, Electra comments on the worthlessness of her character. The universal detestation in which Helen is held in the play will have a role in making the later attempt on her life seem excusable or even laudable.

After a Chorus of Argive women enter—amusingly, since Electra keeps hushing them so that they won't waken Orestes, and they keep loudly protesting that they are making no noise—a scene ensues in which we see the loving care of the two siblings for each other. First we see Electra's solicitude for Orestes, who has gone for six days without eating or bathing. Then Orestes suffers from a brief attack of the Erinyes, whom he puts to flight by threatening to shoot them with a bow and arrows. When the attack is over he in his turn is worried about Electra, and he sends her indoors to take some rest. This is of practical importance since the following scene features Menelaus and Tyndareus in addition to Orestes, and an Athenian dramatist had only three actors at his disposal.

After a choral ode on the Erinyes, the long-awaited Menelaus arrives. His attitude is one of almost clinical detachment as he asks for details of Orestes' situation, a hopeless one without his help. Just then Tyndareus, father of Helen and Clytaemestra, arrives. Tyndareus vituperates

Orestes, condemning him roundly for the murder of his mother. (His reasons are somewhat complex: see below.) Orestes makes a speech of self-excuse to him, and Tyndareus is so enraged that he promises to take an active hand in securing Orestes' condemnation and stomps off toward the center of the city, where the trial is to take place, threatening Menelaus with expulsion from Sparta (where both live) if he helps Orestes against the Argives. After his departure Orestes appeals once more to Menelaus, but the latter all but says outright that he will not help him. Almost certainly he exits not in the direction of the city center but toward Nauplia. Orestes shouts charges of cowardice at his retreating back.

With no break we see Orestes' friend and accomplice Pylades coming down the eisodos from the city center, through which he has come on his journey from his native Phocis. Pylades has the loyalty that Menelaus so conspicuously lacks. Though he is under a sentence of banishment (his father banished him for his part in the murder of Clytaemestra), he resolves to help Orestes with his troubles. The two decide that Orestes' only hope is to try to persuade the Argives that he deserves pity. They exit, Pylades supporting Orestes in his weakness.

We learn the result of the trial from a messenger speech. Though the hero Diomedes speaks in favor of allowing him to go into exile and an anonymous Argive even goes so far as to say that Orestes should be rewarded for killing a woman whose conduct threatened the whole community, his enemies carry the day, and he and his sister are condemned to death, the only concession being that they are allowed to take their own lives.

When Orestes and Pylades return from the assembly, the siblings plan to stab themselves and ask Pylades to bury them. But Pylades indicates that he means to perish with them. Additionally he suggests that before they die they take revenge on the cowardly and faithless Menelaus by killing Helen. This not only would pay him back for abandoning them but would also mean killing a woman who richly deserves to die, whose wantonness has caused so many deaths. Orestes approves. Then Electra makes a new suggestion: once they have killed Helen they should seize Menelaus' daughter Hermione as a hostage to force Menelaus to help them by persuading the people to let them live. The two men go in, and Electra and the Chorus of Argive women keep a watch for Hermione, who is expected to return soon from making offerings at Clytaemestra's grave.

Helen's voice is heard within, calling for help as she is being attacked. Hermione arrives and is duly sent in. Then out comes a most remarkable messenger, one of the Phrygian slaves Helen has brought back with her from Troy. He has escaped while the murder plot was in progress and tells what happened. His "report" is sung, an aria not only of enormous length but also written in a style that reads almost like a parody of late-Euripidean monody. What he has to report is that Orestes and Pylades, on the point of killing Helen, were interrupted by the escape of the slaves from their imprisonment elsewhere in the palace and by the arrival of Hermione, whom the men promptly seized. And when they resumed their attempt on Helen's life, she mysteriously vanished, stolen away, he thinks, by the gods or magic. Orestes comes out after the slave, thinks of sending him back indoors, but finally decides to let him go so that he can bring the news to Menelaus of his daughter's danger.

In the next scene Menelaus comes, convinced, despite what the Phrygian has told him, that his wife has been killed but bent on at least rescuing his daughter. He is about to attack the doors when Orestes appears on the roof holding a sword at Hermione's throat, accompanied by Pylades and Electra, who hold torches and are ready to burn the palace down. (This was what Pylades suggested doing if their attempt on Helen was not successful.) Menelaus blusters but is cowed by the threat to his daughter.

Orestes has just given the order to fire the palace, perhaps in order to force Menelaus to a decision, and Menelaus has called on the Argives to come to his aid when Apollo appears on the *mechane* along with Helen. His speech, compounded of revelations and dispositions for the future, starts out by confirming the miraculous rescue of Helen from death: she is Zeus's daughter and was used by him to foment the Trojan War and thereby reduce the population of the earth, and now she will go to live in heaven with her deified brothers. Orestes must go into exile for a year, stand trial at Athens, and be acquitted. He is to marry Hermione, at whose throat he is now holding a sword, and return to rule in Argos. Pylades is to marry Electra. Menelaus must return to Sparta, leaving Orestes to rule in Argos: Apollo will arrange a reconciliation between Orestes and the citizens since it was he who compelled Orestes to murder his mother. Orestes confesses that Apollo's oracles have proved true, drops his sword, and promises to marry Hermione as soon as her father agrees to the marriage. Menelaus likewise consents to

Apollo's disposition and offers his daughter's hand. "Go and hold Peace, fairest of the gods, in honor," the god tells them and departs with Helen for her new abode in the stars.

There have been various ways of making sense of this most baffling play. (For a summary of the history of interpretation see Porter 1994, pp. 1–44.) Early nineteenth-century critics (most influentially A. W. Schlegel) found fault with Euripides as a decadent dramatist who abandoned classical decorum and dignity and pandered to the tastes of his audience by producing a sensational but incoherent set of melodramatic scenes. This view was essentially revived in the late twentieth century, though without the querulous tone: West and Willink in their introductions, as well as other scholars, have emphasized the novelty and excitement of the play and have seen Euripides as having principally these qualities in view rather than issues of a more serious nature.

This stance is a reaction to the concerns of earlier twentieth-century scholars, who saw in the play one or another serious purpose or *arrière pensée*. Thus in the view of Verrall 1905, Euripides is attacking the unrealistic treatment of the myth by his predecessors, showing what kind of man it would take, in the world as it actually is, to kill his mother, not a hero but a violent and anti-social criminal. Reinhardt 1960 and others see the deliberate creation of an absurd and nonsensical world, the analogue of the world of war and intellectual anguish that, it is argued, set the mood of the late fifth century.

A general interpretation of this puzzling play, which raises so many difficult questions, is beyond the scope of this introduction. Instead, I end with a list of queries, some of which have received little or no attention in the scholarly literature. Why does Orestes remain in Argos after the murder of his mother instead of going, as the custom was for murderers, to foreign soil (Delphi in other versions) for cleansing? Is this merely a means to allow Euripides to develop his highly original plot, or are we to see Orestes' neglect of the forms of religion as significant? Would the audience have been shocked or surprised that Orestes attends the funeral of the woman he murdered? Why do Electra and Orestes speak often (though not invariably) as if the Erinyes were purely a subjective phenomenon? In particular, why does Orestes tell Menelaus (396) that he suffers from σύνεσις, understanding, the consciousness of what he has done, rather than from goddesses of retribution, and why does Electra tell her brother (258–9) that his Erinyes are a hallucination? Does Orestes have a bow (268–70) given to him by Apollo (such a gift appeared in a version by the lyric poet Stesichorus), or is this a figment of his imagination? Are the Erinyes in the "mad scene" real though invisible entities, or are they projections of Orestes' psyche? If they are real, is their dispersal caused by the bow (supposing it to exist), or is their disappearance after being threatened a dramatically useful coincidence? What kind of attitude or attitudes is the audience being invited to take toward the two principals: sympathy with their plight? revulsion at the violent means they adopt? sympathy followed by revulsion in the course of the play? or some mixture of basic sympathy with a feeling that they are acting throughout on misguided presuppositions?

It is most unusual for the threat in a Greek tragedy to come from the populace as a whole, as it does here. Are the people of Argos portrayed as they are because Euripides is expressing his disgust with the excesses and irrationality of the Athenian democracy? Or are we not meant to think about the populace as such but rather about men such as Talthybius, Aegisthus' friends, and Tyndareus, who lead them to pass an unmerciful verdict on the siblings? Or are we meant to think that stoning was after all a reasonable response to Orestes' failure to observe religious custom in the matter of purification?

Aristotle complained that the character of Menelaus was baser than the plot required (*Poetics* 1454a28–9 and 1461b19–21). Many have found this judgment unintelligible: after all, Menelaus' desertion of Orestes and Electra is a prime motivation for the plot against Helen and Hermione, and so one supposes that had he not been cowardly in defense of his nephew and niece, the plot would have been impossible. Did Aristotle perhaps have a different understanding of Menelaus' role? Orestes says after the event (1058–9) that Menelaus deliberately did not intervene because he had his eye on the kingship (cf. also 1108, 1146–7, and 1596). Could Aristotle have thought that Menelaus was not only a coward but also deviously plotting to rule Argos as well as Sparta, counting on the throne's being vacant if Orestes died, and might this attempted usurpation have been the baseness unnecessary to the plot of which he complains? Is it possible to sustain this view of the action without excesses of Verrallian ingenuity?

Tyndareus' role also raises questions. The Spartan's motive in opposing help to Orestes could have been, as Pylades guesses it to be (751), anger at the death of his daughter. This would have been perfectly intelligible. Instead, he vituperates Clytaemestra as strongly as anyone in the play and says she has merely gotten her just deserts. He objects only to the fact that it was Orestes who killed her. He propounds some quite principled-sounding reasons for his view, claiming that killing people who have killed others leads to an endless cycle, and that in the good old days people were exiled, never executed. Curiously, execution is just what he threatens Orestes with (and ends up proposing, by proxy, in the assembly) and just what he says his daughter deserved, but perhaps Euripides did not wish us to concentrate on this contradiction. Is Tyndareus drawn the way he is to represent a principled man, the embodiment of traditional Spartan respect for law, and are we then to read in his reaction the moral revulsion decent people must take toward Orestes' deed? Or is he an irascible old man, and one who is instantly unsympathetic to the Athenian audience because of what he is, one of the hated Spartans? Or are we meant to find his explicit motivation so contradictory and confused that we look for some hidden purpose, perhaps some deep plot concocted with Menelaus to annex Argos to Sparta?

Other questions could be asked as well, but the foregoing may suffice to show that the play is a difficult one to interpret, perhaps the most difficult of all Euripidean plays that have come down to us. Not the least part of the difficulty is that the play was immensely popular in antiquity: it was repeatedly revived and hence was more exposed to interpolation than most plays we have, which complicates the interpreter's work as well as the editor's.

SELECT BIBLIOGRAPHY

Editions

N. Wedd (Cambridge, 1895).
V. Di Benedetto (Florence, 1965).
C. W. Willink (Oxford, 1986).
M. L. West (Warminster, 1987).

Literary Criticism

A. P. Burnett, *Catastrophe Survived: Euripides' Plays of Mixed Reversal* (Oxford, 1971), pp. 183–222.

C. F. Fuqua, "The World of Myth in Euripides' *Orestes*," *Traditio* 34 (1978), 1–28.

N. Greenberg, "Euripides' *Orestes*, an Interpretation," *HSCP* 66 (1962), 157–92.

D. Kovacs, "Rationalism, Naive and Malign, in Euripides' *Orestes*," in J. F. Miller, C. Damon, and K. S. Myers, edd., *Vertis in usum. Studies in Honor of Edward Courtney* (Leipzig, 2002), pp. 277–86.

F. J. Nisetich, "The Silencing of Pylades (*Orestes* 1591–92)," *AJP* 107 (1986), 46–54.

M. J. O'Brien, "Tantalus in Euripides' *Orestes*," *RhM* 131 (1988), 30–45.

G. Perrotta, "Studi euripidei II. L'*Oreste*," *SIFC* 6 (1928), 89–138.

J. R. Porter, *Studies in Euripides'* Orestes (Leiden, 1994).

K. Reinhardt, "Die Sinneskrise bei Euripides," in *Tradition und Geist* (Göttingen, 1960), 227–56 (=*Euripides*, ed. E.-R. Schwinge [Darmstadt, 1968], pp. 507–42).

J. de Romilly, "L'assemblée du peuple dans l'*Oreste* d'Euripide," in *Studi classici in onore di Q. Cataudella* (Catania, 1972), vol. 1, pp. 237–51.

W. Steidle, *Studien zum antiken Drama* (Munich, 1968), pp. 96–117.

A. W. Verrall, *Essays on Four Plays of Euripides* (Cambridge, 1905), pp. 199–264.

R. P. Winnington-Ingram, "Euripides: *poietes sophos*," *Arethusa* 2 (1969), 127–42.

Dramatis Personae

ΗΛΕΚΤΡΑ	ELECTRA, sister of Orestes
ΕΛΕΝΗ	HELEN, wife of Menelaus
ΧΟΡΟΣ	CHORUS of Argive women
ΟΡΕΣΤΗΣ	ORESTES, son of Agamemnon and Clytaemestra
ΜΕΝΕΛΑΟΣ	MENELAUS, brother of Agamemnon
ΤΥΝΔΑΡΕΩΣ	TYNDAREUS, father of Helen and Clytaemestra
ΠΥΛΑΔΗΣ	PYLADES, kinsman and friend of Orestes
ΑΓΓΕΛΟΣ	MESSENGER
ΕΡΜΙΟΝΗ	HERMIONE, daughter of Menelaus and Helen
ΦΡΥΞ	PHRYGIAN, one of Helen's slaves
ΑΠΟΛΛΩΝ	APOLLO

Nonspeaking roles: Hermione in the opening scene, and Helen, Hermione, Pylades, and Electra in the final scene.

A Note On Staging

The *skene* represents the royal palace of Argos. Eisodos A leads to Clytaemestra's tomb and the port of Nauplia, Eisodos B to Agamemnon's tomb and the Argive agora.

411

ΟΡΕΣΤΗΣ

Οὐκ ἔστιν οὐδὲν δεινόν, ὧδ' εἰπεῖν ἔπος,
οὐδὲ πάθος οὐδὲ ξυμφορὰ θεήλατος,
ἧς οὐκ ἂν ἄραιτ' ἄχθος ἀνθρώπου φύσις.
ὁ γὰρ μακάριος (κοὐκ ὀνειδίζω τύχας)
5 Διὸς πεφυκώς, ὡς λέγουσι, Τάνταλος
κορυφῆς ὑπερτέλλοντα δειμαίνων πέτρον
ἀέρι ποτᾶται· καὶ τίνει ταύτην δίκην,
ὡς μὲν λέγουσιν, ὅτι θεοῖς ἄνθρωπος ὢν
κοινῆς τραπέζης ἀξίωμ' ἔχων ἴσον,
10 ἀκόλαστον ἔσχε γλῶσσαν, αἰσχίστην νόσον.
οὗτος φυτεύει Πέλοπα, τοῦ δ' Ἀτρεὺς ἔφυ,

---

¹ ὡς Blaydes   ¹⁰ εἶχε Wecklein

---

¹ Or, removing the commas in line 1, "There is no word so
shocking to utter, no suffering, no god-sent affliction."

² Tantalus, king of Sipylus in Asia Minor, appears in *Odyssey*
11.582–92 as one of the great sinners in the Underworld, where he
is "tantalized," his hunger and thirst tormented by fruit and water
he cannot reach. Punishment by overhanging stone is mentioned
in Archilochus fr. 91.14 W. His suspension in air seems to be a
Euripidean invention: see below, note to line 984.

412

ORESTES

At the beginning of the play ORESTES *lies asleep on a bed or*
pallet outside the skene, *which represents the royal palace*
of Argos. Next to him sits ELECTRA.

ELECTRA

There is virtually nothing horrific, no suffering, no god-
sent affliction,[1] whose burden man, being what he is, might
not shoulder. Tantalus was a prosperous man (and I do not
reproach him with his good fortune), the son of Zeus, they
say: now he is suspended in the clouds, in constant fear of a
rock hanging above his head.[2] He pays this penalty, so men
say, because though enjoying, as a mortal, equal rank with
the gods at their shared table, he had an unbridled tongue,
a most disgraceful malady.[3] This man begot Pelops, who
was the father of Atreus. For Atreus the Goddess,[4] card-

---

[3] Perhaps alluding to the story that when Zeus granted him a
wish he asked for all the pleasures that the gods have (Zeus kept
his promise but nullified the pleasures by suspending a rock over
him); or to the story that he divulged the gods' secrets to men.
Other sources say that he stole the gods' nectar and ambrosia and
gave them to mortals; or that he tested the gods' omniscience by
killing and cooking his son Pelops and serving him to them.

[4] Fate is meant. An alternative reading makes the goddess
Strife the subject.

ᾧ στέμματα ξήνασ᾽ ἐπέκλωσεν θεὰ
ἔριν, Θυέστῃ πόλεμον ὄντι συγγόνῳ
θέσθαι· τί τἄρρητ᾽ ἀναμετρήσασθαί με δεῖ;
[ἔδαισε δ᾽ οὖν νιν τέκν᾽ ἀποκτείνας Ἀτρεύς.]
   Ἀτρέως δέ (τὰς γὰρ ἐν μέσῳ σιγῶ τύχας)
ὁ κλεινός, εἰ δὴ κλεινός, Ἀγαμέμνων ἔφυ
Μενέλεώς τε Κρήσσης μητρὸς Ἀερόπης ἄπο.
γαμεῖ δ᾽ ὁ μὲν δὴ τὴν θεοῖς στυγουμένην
Μενέλαος Ἑλένην, ὁ δὲ Κλυταιμήστρας λέχος
ἐπίσημον εἰς Ἕλληνας Ἀγαμέμνων ἄναξ·
ᾧ παρθένοι μὲν τρεῖς ἔφυμεν ἐκ μιᾶς,
Χρυσόθεμις Ἰφιγένειά τ᾽ Ἠλέκτρα τ᾽ ἐγώ,
ἄρσην τ᾽ Ὀρέστης, μητρὸς ἀνοσιωτάτης,
ἣ πόσιν ἀπείρῳ περιβαλοῦσ᾽ ὑφάσματι
ἔκτεινεν· ὧν δ᾽ ἕκατι, παρθένῳ λέγειν
οὐ καλόν· ἐῶ τοῦτ᾽ ἀσαφὲς ἐν κοινῷ σκοπεῖν.
   Φοίβου δ᾽ ἀδικίαν μὲν τί δεῖ κατηγορεῖν;
πείθει δ᾽ Ὀρέστην μητέρ᾽ ἥ σφ᾽ ἐγείνατο
κτεῖναι, πρὸς οὐχ ἅπαντας εὔκλειαν φέρον.
ὅμως δ᾽ ἀπέκτειν᾽ οὐκ ἀπειθήσας θεῷ,
κἀγὼ μετέσχον, οἷα δὴ γυνή, φόνου
[Πυλάδης θ᾽, ὃς ἡμῖν συγκατείργασται τάδε].
ἐντεῦθεν ἀγρίᾳ συντακεὶς νόσῳ δέμας
τλήμων Ὀρέστης ὅδε πεσὼν ἐν δεμνίοις
κεῖται, τὸ μητρὸς δ᾽ αἷμά νιν τροχηλατεῖ
μανίαισιν· ὀνομάζειν γὰρ αἰδοῦμαι θεὰς

13 ἔριν a: Ἔρις b

414

ing out her tufts of wool, spun a destiny of strife, that he should make war on his brother Thyestes. But why should I go over the shocking tale? [At any rate, Atreus killed Thyestes' children and made a feast for him.]

To Atreus (I pass over intervening events) were born Agamemnon the glorious, if indeed glorious he is, and Menelaus: their mother was the Cretan Aërope. Menelaus married the god-detested Helen, and king Agamemnon married Clytaemestra, a notable match in Greek eyes. To him were born three daughters, Chrysothemis, Iphigenia, and myself, Electra, and a son, Orestes, all from a single godless mother: she entangled her husband in an endless woven garment and killed him. Why she did so it does not befit a maiden to say: for discussion in public I leave this unclear.

Why should I charge Apollo with injustice? Yet he did persuade Orestes to kill the mother who gave him birth, an act not everyone found glorious. In spite of that he killed her, in obedience to the god, and I too had such part as a woman may have in this murder [as did Pylades who accomplished these things with us]. Ever since then poor Orestes here, his body wasting away with a cruel disease, has taken to his bed, whirled in madness by the blood of his mother. I shrink from naming the goddesses, the

---

15 del. Markland
33 del. Herwerden
34 δέμας Hermann: νοσεῖ C

†Εὐμενίδας† αἳ τόνδ᾿ ἐξαμιλλῶνται φόβον.
ἕκτον δὲ δὴ τόδ᾿ ἦμαρ ἐξ ὅτου σφαγαῖς
40 θανοῦσα μήτηρ πυρὶ καθήγνισται δέμας,
ὧν οὔτε σῖτα διὰ δέρης ἐδέξατο,
οὐ λούτρ᾿ ἔδωκε χρωτί· χλανιδίων δ᾿ ἔσω
κρυφθείς, ὅταν μὲν σῶμα κουφισθῇ νόσου
ἔμφρων δακρύει, ποτὲ δὲ δεμνίων ἄπο
45 πηδᾷ δρομαῖος, πῶλος ὡς ὑπὸ ζυγοῦ.
ἔδοξε δ᾿ Ἄργει τῷδε μήθ᾿ ἡμᾶς στέγαις,
μὴ πυρὶ δέχεσθαι, μήτε προσφωνεῖν τινα
μητροκτονοῦντας· κυρία δ᾿ ἥδ᾿ ἡμέρα
ἐν ᾗ διοίσει ψῆφον Ἀργείων πόλις
50 εἰ χρὴ θανεῖν νὼ λευσίμῳ πετρώματι
[ἢ φάσγανον θήξαντ᾿ ἐπ᾿ αὐχένος βαλεῖν].
ἐλπίδα δὲ δή τιν᾿ ἔχομεν ὥστε μὴ θανεῖν·
ἥκει γὰρ ἐς γῆν Μενέλεως Τροίας ἄπο,
λιμένα δὲ Ναυπλίειον ἐκπληρῶν πλάτῃ
55 ἀκταῖσιν ὁρμεῖ, δαρὸν ἐκ Τροίας χρόνον
ἄλαισι πλαγχθείς· τὴν δὲ δὴ πολύστονον
Ἑλένην, φυλάξας νύκτα, μή τις εἰσιδὼν
μεθ᾿ ἡμέραν στείχουσαν ὧν ὑπ᾿ Ἰλίῳ
παῖδες τεθνᾶσιν, ἐς πέτρων ἔλθῃ βολάς,
60 προὔπεμψεν ἐς δῶμ᾿ ἡμέτερον· ἔστιν δ᾿ ἔσω
κλαίουσ᾿ ἀδελφὴν συμφοράς τε δωμάτων.
ἔχει δὲ δή τιν᾿ ἀλγέων παραψυχήν·

38 Εὐμενίδας] ποτνιάδας Stadtmüller   v. del. Nauck, tum
fort. νιν pro γὰρ 37

Eumenides,[5] who work to create this fear. This is now the sixth day since our slaughtered mother's body has been purified by the pyre. During this time he has neither swallowed food nor bathed. He lies covered in a blanket, and when his body finds relief from his malady, he is sane and weeps, while at other times he leaps from the bedding and runs about like an unyoked colt.

Argos has decreed that no one is to receive us under his roof or at his fireside or even speak to us since we are matricides. And this is the appointed day on which the city will vote whether we two must die by stoning [or someone must whet a sword and thrust it upon our necks].

But we do have *some* hope of escaping death: Menelaus has returned home from Troy. Filling the harbor at Nauplia with his fleet he lies at anchor near the headlands. He has wandered for a long time after leaving Troy. As for Helen, cause of so much woe, he waited for nightfall and sent her on ahead to our house so that those whose sons died at Troy might not see her walking by day and throw stones at her. She is now inside, weeping for her sister and for the house's misfortunes. But she does have some comfort in her grief. She left an unmarried daughter, Her-

---

[5] Electra appears to contradict herself by saying that she shrinks from naming the goddesses and then calling them the Eumenides. Possibly Euripides wrote something like "the goddess of madness," and "Eumenides" was a marginal note accidentally incorporated into the text.

---

[51] del. Herwerden
[56] πολυκτόνον Musgrave

ἦν γὰρ κατ' οἴκους ἔλιφ', ὅτ' ἐς Τροίαν ἔπλει,
παρθένον ἐμῇ τε μητρὶ παρέδωκεν τρέφειν
65 Μενέλαος, ἀγαγὼν Ἑρμιόνην Σπάρτης ἄπο,
ταύτῃ γέγηθε κἀπιλήθεται κακῶν.
    βλέπω †δὲ πᾶσαν εἴσοδον† πότ' ὄψομαι
Μενέλαον ἥκονθ'· ὡς τά γ' ἄλλ' ἐπ' ἀσθενοῦς
ῥώμης ὀχούμεθ', ἤν τι μὴ κείνου πάρα
70 σωθῶμεν. ἄπορον χρῆμα δυστυχῶν δόμος.

ΕΛΕΝΗ

ὦ παῖ Κλυταιμήστρας τε κἀγαμέμνονος,
παρθένε μακρὸν δὴ μῆκος Ἠλέκτρα χρόνου,
πῶς, ὦ τάλαινα, σύ τε κασίγνητός τε σὸς
τλήμων Ὀρέστης, μητρὸς ὃς φονεὺς ἔφυ;
75 προσφθέγμασιν γὰρ οὐ μιαίνομαι σέθεν,
ἐς Φοῖβον ἀναφέρουσα τὴν ἁμαρτίαν.
καίτοι στένω γε τὸν Κλυταιμήστρας μόρον,
ἐμῆς ἀδελφῆς, ἥν, ἐπεὶ πρὸς Ἴλιον
ἔπλευσ' ὅπως ἔπλευσα θεομανεῖ πότμῳ,
80 οὐκ εἶδον, ἀπολειφθεῖσα δ' αἰάζω τύχας.

ΗΛΕΚΤΡΑ

Ἑλένη, τί σοι λέγοιμ' ἂν ἅ γε παροῦσ' ὁρᾷς
[ἐν συμφοραῖσι τὸν Ἀγαμέμνονος γόνον];
ἐγὼ μὲν ἄυπνος πάρεδρος ἀθλίῳ νεκρῷ
(νεκρὸς γὰρ οὗτος οὕνεκα σμικρᾶς πνοῆς)

67 fort. δ' ἐπ' ἀκτάς, εἰς ὁδὸν cl. 55 et 1311–2
74 ὃς Porson: ὅδε vel ὧδε C
82 del. Kirchhoff

mione, at home when she sailed for Troy, and Menelaus entrusted her to my mother to raise, bringing her from Sparta. In her she takes her joy and forgets her troubles.

Now I look down every road,[6] wondering when I shall see Menelaus' arrival. In all else we have little strength to keep us afloat unless he lends some aid to save us. A house in misfortune is a helpless thing.

Enter from the skene HELEN. *She carries in her hands a lock of her hair and a vessel containing funeral libations.*

HELEN

Daughter of Clytaemestra and Agamemnon, Electra, unmarried now for so long, how are you faring, poor woman, you and your brother, unhappy Orestes who murdered his mother? Speaking to you does not bring pollution upon me: I attribute any guilt to Phoebus. Yet I do lament the death of my sister Clytaemestra. After my unfortunate voyage to Ilium—a voyage caused by god-sent madness—I never saw her again, and in my bereavement I lament her sad fate.

ELECTRA

Helen, why should I describe to you what you can see right before you [that Agamemnon's son is in trouble]? I sit here without sleep beside this luckless corpse (and a corpse is what he is except that he breathes a little). As for *his* trou-

---

[6] There are several reasons (among them, that only one of the eisodoi leads to the harbor) for thinking that this line is corrupt.

85 θάσσω· τὰ τούτου δ᾽ οὐκ ὀνειδίζω κακά.
σὺ δ᾽ ἡ μακαρία μακάριός θ᾽ ὁ σὸς πόσις
ἥκετον ἐφ᾽ ἡμᾶς ἀθλίως πεπραγότας.

ΕΛΕΝΗ

πόσον χρόνον δὲ δεμνίοις πέπτωχ᾽ ὅδε;

ΗΛΕΚΤΡΑ

ἐξ οὗπερ αἷμα γενέθλιον κατήνυσεν.

ΕΛΕΝΗ

90 ὦ μέλεος, ἡ τεκοῦσά θ᾽ ὡς διώλετο.

ΗΛΕΚΤΡΑ

οὕτως ἔχει τάδ᾽ ὥστ᾽ ἀπείρηκεν κακοῖς.

ΕΛΕΝΗ

πρὸς θεῶν, πίθοι᾽ ἂν δῆτά μοί τι, παρθένε;

ΗΛΕΚΤΡΑ

ὅσ᾽ ἄσχολός γε συγγόνου προσεδρίᾳ.

ΕΛΕΝΗ

βούλῃ τάφον μοι πρὸς κασιγνήτης μολεῖν;

ΗΛΕΚΤΡΑ

95 μητρὸς κελεύεις τῆς ἐμῆς; τίνος χάριν;

ΕΛΕΝΗ

κόμης ἀπαρχὰς καὶ χοὰς φέρουσ᾽ ἐμάς.

ΗΛΕΚΤΡΑ

σοὶ δ᾽ οὐχὶ θεμιτὸν πρὸς φίλων στείχειν τάφον;

93 ὅσ᾽ Herwerden: ὡς C

420

bles I say nothing by way of reproach about them. You and your husband, both fortunate, have arrived to find us faring badly.

HELEN
How long has he been lying in bed?

ELECTRA
Ever since he shed his mother's blood.

HELEN
Poor man, and poor woman too, for the way she died!

ELECTRA
That is how our woes stand: hence his collapse.

HELEN
Maiden, I beg you: would you do me a favor?

ELECTRA
Yes, to the extent I can: I am occupied with sitting by my brother.

HELEN
Are you willing to go to my sister's tomb?

ELECTRA
You mean my mother's tomb? Why?

HELEN
To bring her a hair offering and libations.

ELECTRA
But are you not allowed to visit your sister's tomb?

ΕΛΕΝΗ

δεῖξαι γὰρ Ἀργείοισι σῶμ' αἰσχύνομαι.

ΗΛΕΚΤΡΑ

ὀψέ γε φρονεῖς εὖ, τότε λιποῦσ' αἰσχρῶς δόμους.

ΕΛΕΝΗ

100 ὀρθῶς ἔλεξας· οὐ φίλως δέ μοι λέγεις.

ΗΛΕΚΤΡΑ

αἰδὼς δὲ δὴ τίς σ' ἐς Μυκηναίους ἔχει;

ΕΛΕΝΗ

δέδοικα πατέρας τῶν ὑπ' Ἰλίῳ νεκρῶν.

ΗΛΕΚΤΡΑ

δεινὸν γὰρ Ἄργει γ' ἀναβοᾷ διὰ στόμα.

ΕΛΕΝΗ

σύ νυν χάριν μοι τὸν φόβον λύσασα δός.

ΗΛΕΚΤΡΑ

105 οὐκ ἂν δυναίμην μητρὸς ἐσβλέψαι τάφον.

ΕΛΕΝΗ

αἰσχρόν γε μέντοι προσπόλους φέρειν τάδε.

ΗΛΕΚΤΡΑ

τί δ' οὐχὶ θυγατρὸς Ἑρμιόνης πέμπεις δέμας;

ΕΛΕΝΗ

ἐς ὄχλον ἕρπειν παρθένοισιν οὐ καλόν.

103 γ' Matthiae: τ' C

HELEN

No: shame prevents me from showing myself to the Argives.

ELECTRA

Your good sense comes late: previously you left your home disgracefully.

HELEN

Your words are true but unkindly spoken.

ELECTRA

But what inhibition do you feel toward the Myceneans?[7]

HELEN

I am afraid of the fathers of those who died at Troy.

ELECTRA

Yes: in Argos your name is fearsomely shouted out.

HELEN

So do me a favor and relieve me of this fear.

ELECTRA

I could not look on my mother's tomb.

HELEN

But it wouldn't be proper for servants to bring these offerings.

ELECTRA

Well, why don't you send your daughter Hermione?

HELEN

It's not good for unmarried girls to appear in public.

---

[7] Tragedy uses "Mycenae" and "Mycenean" as synonyms for "Argos" and "Argive."

ΗΛΕΚΤΡΑ

καὶ μὴν τίνοι γ᾽ ἂν τῇ τεθνηκυίᾳ τροφάς.

ΕΛΕΝΗ

110 [ὀρθῶς ἔλεξας, πείθομαί τέ σοι, κόρη.]
ναί, πέμψομέν γε θυγατέρ᾽· εὖ γάρ τοι λέγεις.
ὦ τέκνον, ἔξελθ᾽, Ἑρμιόνη, δόμων πάρος
καὶ λαβὲ χοὰς τάσδ᾽ ἐν χεροῖν κόμας τ᾽ ἐμάς,
ἐλθοῦσα δ᾽ ἀμφὶ τὸν Κλυταιμήστρας τάφον
115 μελίκρατ᾽ ἄφες γάλακτος οἰνωπόν τ᾽ ἄχνην,
καὶ στᾶσ᾽ ἐπ᾽ ἄκρου χώματος λέξον τάδε·
Ἑλένη σ᾽ ἀδελφὴ ταῖσδε δωρεῖται χοαῖς,
φόβῳ προσελθεῖν μνῆμα σόν, ταρβοῦσά γε
Ἀργεῖον ὄχλον. πρευμενῆ δ᾽ ἄνωγέ νιν
120 ἐμοί τε καὶ σοὶ καὶ πόσει γνώμην ἔχειν
τοῖν τ᾽ ἀθλίοιν τοῖνδ᾽, οὓς ἀπώλεσεν θεός.
ἃ δ᾽ εἰς ἀδελφὴν καιρὸς ἐκπονεῖν ἐμέ,
ἅπανθ᾽ ὑπισχνοῦ νερτέρων δωρήματα.
ἴθ᾽, ὦ τέκνον μοι, σπεῦδε καὶ χοὰς τάφῳ
125 δοῦσ᾽ ὡς τάχιστα τῆς πάλιν μέμνησ᾽ ὁδοῦ.

ΗΛΕΚΤΡΑ

ὦ φύσις, ἐν ἀνθρώποισιν ὡς μέγ᾽ εἶ κακόν
[σωτήριον δὲ τοῖς καλῶς κεκτημένοις].
ἴδετε γὰρ ἄκρας ὡς ἀπέθρισεν τρίχας,
σῴζουσα κάλλος· ἔστι δ᾽ ἡ πάλαι γυνή.
130 θεοί σε μισήσειαν, ὥς μ᾽ ἀπώλεσας
καὶ τόνδε πᾶσάν θ᾽ Ἑλλάδ᾽.

ELECTRA

But she would be repaying her dead aunt for raising her.

HELEN

[Your suggestion is good and I will take it, maiden.] Yes, I will send my daughter: your advice is good.

Hermione, daughter, come out in front of the house! (*Enter Hermione from the* skene.) Take these libations and my hair offering in your hands. Go to the tomb of Clytaemestra and around it pour out the milk and honey mixture and the foaming wine. Then stand on top of the grave mound and say, "These libations are a gift to you from your sister Helen. She was afraid to approach your tomb for fear of the Argive multitude." Then ask her to show a kindly spirit to me, to you, and to my husband, and also to these two luckless ones the god has ruined. Promise her all the funeral offerings it is appropriate to make for a sister. (*She hands her the offerings.*) Go quickly, my daughter, and when you have given the libations to the tomb, remember to come back with all speed.

Exit Hermione by Eisodos A, HELEN *into the* skene.

ELECTRA

O inborn nature, what a curse you are to mankind [but a salvation to those who have a good one]! See how she cut off just the ends of her hair, trying to keep her beauty unchanged! She is the old Helen still. May the gods' hatred fall upon you for ruining me and him and all of Greece!

---

110 del. Sansone   111 ναί Paley: καὶ C   127 om.
unus cod., del. Klinkenberg   δὲ Wecklein: τε fere C
128 γὰρ Duport: παρ' C

ὦ τάλαιν᾽ ἐγώ·

αἵδ᾽ αὖ πάρεισι τοῖς ἐμοῖς θρηνήμασιν
φίλαι ξυνῳδοί· τάχα μεταστήσουσ᾽ ὕπνου
τόνδ᾽ ἡσυχάζοντ᾽, ὄμμα δ᾽ ἐκτήξουσ᾽ ἐμὸν
135 δακρύοις, ἀδελφὸν ὅταν ὁρῶ μεμηνότα.
ὦ φίλταται γυναῖκες, ἡσύχῳ ποδὶ
χωρεῖτε, μὴ ψοφεῖτε, μηδ᾽ ἔστω κτύπος.
φιλία γὰρ ἡ σὴ πρευμενὴς μὲν ἀλλ᾽ ὅμως
[τόνδ᾽ ἐξεγεῖραι συμφορὰ γενήσεται].

140 σῖγα σῖγα, λεπτὸν ἴχνος ἀρβύλας
τίθετε, μὴ κτυπεῖτ᾽·
ἀποπρὸ βᾶτ᾽ ἐκεῖσ᾽ ἀποπρό μοι κοίτας.

στρ. α

ΧΟΡΟΣ

ἰδού, πείθομαι.

ΗΛΕΚΤΡΑ

145 ἆ ἆ σύριγγος ὅπως πνοὰ
λεπτοῦ δόνακος, ὦ φίλα, φώνει μοι.

ΧΟΡΟΣ

ἴδ᾽ ἀτρεμαῖον ὡς ὑπόροφον φέρω
βοάν.

ΗΛΕΚΤΡΑ

ναί, οὕτως·

138 ὅμως Π (u.v.) et duo codd.: ἐμοὶ plerique C
139 del. Diggle praeeunte Willink

Enter by Eisodos B Argive women as CHORUS.

Oh misery! Here they are again, my friends who sing in harmony with my laments! They will awaken my brother at once from his peaceful sleep, making my eyes melt with tears when I see his insanity!

Dear friends, walk with quiet step, make no noise, let there be no clattering! To be sure, your friendship is kindly meant, yet still! [It would be a great misfortune to wake this man up.]

Softly, softly, your footsteps lightly
place, take care to make no sound!
Go back from the bed, please, go back!

CHORUS

There: I am doing as you say.

ELECTRA

Ah, ah! Please speak no louder than the breath
of a panpipe's slender reed, my friends!

CHORUS

See how gentle is the voice
I bring indoors![8]

ELECTRA

Yes, that's the way:

---

[8] Or, with Musgrave's conjecture, "See how gently I utter my soporific tones!"

140n Electrae continuant tt: Xo. fere C
141 τίθετε Hermann: τιθεῖτε fere C   κτυπεῖτ᾽ Π u. v., t:
κτυπεῖτε μηδ᾽ ἔστω κτύπος C   147 ὑπνοφόρον Musgrave

κάταγε κάταγε, πρόσιθ᾽ ἀτρέμας, ἀτρέμας ἴθι·
150 λόγον ἀπόδος ἐφ᾽ ὅ τι χρέος ἐμόλετέ ποτε.
χρόνια γὰρ πεσὼν ὅδ᾽ εὐνάζεται.

μεσῳδ.

ΧΟΡΟΣ
πῶς ἔχει; λόγου μετάδος, ὦ φίλα·
τίνα τύχαν εἴπω; τίνα δὲ συμφοράν;

ΗΛΕΚΤΡΑ
155 ἔτι μὲν ἐμπνέει, βραχὺ δ᾽ ἀνασθμαίνει.

ἀντ. α

ΧΟΡΟΣ
τί φῄς; ὦ τάλας.

ΗΛΕΚΤΡΑ
ὀλεῖς, εἰ βλέφαρα κινήσεις
ὕπνου γλυκυτάταν φερομένῳ χάριν.

ΧΟΡΟΣ
160 μέλεος ἐχθίστων θεόθεν ἐργμάτων,
τάλας.

ΗΛΕΚΤΡΑ
φεῦ μόχθων.
ἄδικος ἄδικα τότ᾽ ἄρ᾽ ἔλακεν ἔλακεν, ἀπό-
φονον ὅτ᾽ ἐπὶ τρίποδι Θέμιδος ἄρ᾽ ἐδίκασε
165 φόνον ὁ Λοξίας ἐμᾶς ματέρος.

155 ἀνασθμαίνει Musgrave: ἀναστένει C

come near, come near, approach gently, gently tread,
and tell me for what purpose you have come.
For at long last he has fallen asleep.

CHORUS

How do things stand with him? Share with us what you can
 tell, dear friend.
What shall I say is his condition, his plight?

ELECTRA

He breathes, to be sure, but draws his breath in short
 gasps.

CHORUS

What's this? O poor man!

ELECTRA

It will be the death of him if you disturb his closed eyes
while he enjoys the sweet gift of sleep.

CHORUS

Poor man, ruined by hateful deeds
sent by the gods.

ELECTRA

Ah, what troubles he has!
Unjust the god, and unjust the commands Loxias[9] uttered,
 uttered
when on the tripod of Themis he pronounced the doom
of unnatural murder upon my mother.

[9] Another name for Apollo.

στρ. β

ΧΟΡΟΣ

ὁρᾷς; ἐν πέπλοισι κινεῖ δέμας.

ΗΛΕΚΤΡΑ

σὺ γάρ νιν, τάλαινα,
θοώξασ᾽ ἔλασας ἐξ ὕπνου.

ΧΟΡΟΣ

εὕδειν μὲν οὖν ἔδοξα.

ΗΛΕΚΤΡΑ

170 οὐκ ἀφ᾽ ἡμῶν, οὐκ ἀπ᾽ οἴκων
πάλιν ἀνὰ πόδα σὸν εἱλίξεις
μεθεμένα κτύπου;

ΧΟΡΟΣ

ὑπνώσσει.

ΗΛΕΚΤΡΑ

λέγεις εὖ.
πότνια, πότνια Νύξ,
175 ὑπνοδότειρα τῶν πολυπόνων βροτῶν,
Ἐρεβόθεν ἴθι, μόλε μόλε κατάπτερος
τὸν Ἀγαμεμνόνιον ἐπὶ δόμον.
180 ὑπὸ γὰρ ἀλγέων ὑπό τε συμφορᾶς
διοιχόμεθ᾽, οἰχόμεθ᾽· ἆ
κτύπον ἀγάγετ᾽· οὐχὶ σῖγα
σῖγα φυλασσομένα
185 στόμα τὸ σὸν ἀκέλαδον ἀποπρὸ λέχεος ἥ-
συχον ὕπνου χάριν παρέξεις, φίλα;

ORESTES

CHORUS

Look! He stirs in his blankets!

ELECTRA

Yes, because you, unfeeling one,
have driven him from sleep by your shouting.

CHORUS

But no, I think he sleeps.

ELECTRA

Will you not leave us, leave our house,
ply your steps backwards
and stop this clattering?

CHORUS

He slumbers.

ELECTRA

That is good.
O mistress, mistress Night,
giver of sleep to trouble-laden mortals,
come from Erebos, come winging
to the house of Agamemnon.
Because of our woes, our calamity,
we are lost, lost. Ah,
you made a clatter! Won't you guard
your tongues in silence, silence, my friends,
making no noise, far from his bed,
and grant him the boon of quiet sleep?

---

167 τάλαινα Willink: ὦ τ- C

168 ἔλασας Willink: ἐλάσασα a: ἔβαλες b

182 οἰχόμεθ᾽. ἆ Willink (praeeunte Biehl): οἰχόμεθα fere C

185 στόμα τὸ σὸν ἀκέλαδον Willink: στόματος ἀνὰ κέλαδον
fere C   ἀποπρὸ Musgrave: ἀπὸ C

ἀντ. β

ΧΟΡΟΣ

θρόει τίς κακῶν τελευτὰ μένει.

ΗΛΕΚΤΡΑ

θανεῖν ⟨νιν⟩, τί δ᾽ ἄλλο;
οὐδὲ γὰρ πόθον ἔχει βορᾶς.

ΧΟΡΟΣ

190 πρόδηλος ἄρ᾽ ὁ πότμος.

ΗΛΕΚΤΡΑ

ἐξέθυσ᾽ ὁ Φοῖβος ἡμᾶς
μέλεον ἀπόφονον αἷμα δοὺς
πατροφόνου ματρός.

ΧΟΡΟΣ

δίκᾳ μέν.

ΗΛΕΚΤΡΑ

καλῶς δ᾽ οὔ.
195 ἔκανες ἔθανες, ὦ
τεκομένα με μᾶτερ, ἀπὸ δ᾽ ὤλεσας
πατέρα τέκνα τε τάδε σέθεν ἀφ᾽ αἵματος·
200 ὀλόμεθ᾽ ἰσονέκυες ὀλόμεθα.
ὅδε γὰρ ἐν νεκροῖς τό τ᾽ ἐμὸν οἴχεται
βίου τὸ πλέον μέρος· ἐν
στοναχαῖσι δὲ καὶ γόοισι
205 δάκρυσί τ᾽ ἐννυχίοις
ἄγαμος ἄτεκνος ἔτι ⟨βίον ἀ⟩βίοτον ἁ
μέλεος ἐς τὸν αἰὲν ἕλκω χρόνον.

CHORUS

Tell us how his calamity will end.

ELECTRA

With ⟨his⟩ death, how else?
He has no desire even for food.

CHORUS

So his fate is all too plain.

ELECTRA

Phoebus has slaughtered us for sacrifice,
giving us the unnatural murder
of the mother who slew our father.

CHORUS

It was justice.

ELECTRA

But digraceful.
You slew, you were slain,
mother who bore me, but you have destroyed
my father and the children born from your blood.
We are dead, dead, mere corpses!
This man is among the dead, and as for me,
the better part of my life has vanished:
in sighs and in lamentation
and nightly tears
unwed and childless I, the luckless one, still drag out
my life ⟨that is no life⟩ all my days.

---

188 ⟨νιν⟩ Willink   201 ὅδε Weil: σύ τε fere C
204 δὲ Willink: τε C
206 ἄγαμος Hermann: ἄ- ἐπὶ δ᾽ C   ἔτι ⟨βίον ἀ⟩βίοτον
Willink: ἅτε βίοτον C

ΧΟΡΟΣ

ὅρα παροῦσα, παρθέν᾽ Ἠλέκτρα, πέλας,
μὴ κατθανών σε σύγγονος λέληθ᾽ ὅδε·
210   οὐ γάρ μ᾽ ἀρέσκει τῷ λίαν παρειμένῳ.

ΟΡΕΣΤΗΣ

ὦ φίλον ὕπνου θέλγητρον, ἐπίκουρον νόσου,
ὡς ἡδύ μοι προσῆλθες ἐν δέοντί τε.
ὦ πότνια Λήθη τῶν κακῶν, ὡς εἶ σοφὴ
καὶ τοῖσι δυστυχοῦσιν εὐκταία θεός.
215   πόθεν ποτ᾽ ἦλθον δεῦρο; πῶς δ᾽ ἀφικόμην;
ἀμνημονῶ γάρ, τῶν πρὶν ἀπολειφθεὶς φρενῶν.

ΗΛΕΚΤΡΑ

ὦ φίλταθ᾽, ὥς μ᾽ ηὔφρανας εἰς ὕπνον πεσών.
βούλῃ θίγω σου κἀνακουφίσω δέμας;

ΟΡΕΣΤΗΣ

λαβοῦ λαβοῦ δῆτ᾽, ἐκ δ᾽ ὄμορξον ἀθλίου
220   στόματος ἀφρώδη πελανὸν ὀμμάτων τ᾽ ἐμῶν.

ΗΛΕΚΤΡΑ

ἰδού· τὸ δούλευμ᾽ ἡδύ, κοὐκ ἀναίνομαι
ἀδέλφ᾽ ἀδελφῇ χειρὶ θεραπεύειν μέλη.

ΟΡΕΣΤΗΣ

ὑπόβαλε πλευροῖς πλευρὰ καὐχμώδη κόμην
ἄφελε προσώπου· λεπτὰ γὰρ λεύσσω κόραις.

216 φρενῶν] ακων Π (unde ⟨κ⟩ακῶν Willink)

434

CHORUS

Maiden Electra, you stand nearby: make sure that your
brother has not died without your knowing it. His body is
so slack: I don't like it.

ORESTES

(*awakening*) O sleep's enchantment, friend and helper
against sickness, how sweet was your visitation, how
timely! O lady Oblivion-of-woes, what a wise goddess you
are, and how often those in misfortune invoke you!

What place did I leave to get here? How did I arrive? I
cannot remember: my former state of mind has left me.

ELECTRA

Dearest brother, how you cheered me when you fell
asleep! Shall my hands soothe your distress?

ORESTES

Yes, take hold, take hold of me, wipe the residue of foam
from my luckless mouth and eyes.

She wipes his face.

ELECTRA

There! Such a menial task is a pleasure, and I do not refuse
to tend my brother's body with sisterly touch.

ORESTES

Support my side with yours and brush back the unkempt
hair from my face: I cannot see clearly.

ΗΛΕΚΤΡΑ

225 ὦ βοστρύχων πινῶδες ἀθλίων κάρα,
ὡς ἠγρίωσαι διὰ μακρᾶς ἀλουσίας.

ΟΡΕΣΤΗΣ

κλῖνόν μ' ἐς εὐνὴν αὖθις· ὅταν ἀνῇ νόσος
μανιάς, ἄναρθρός εἰμι κἀσθενῶ μέλη.

ΗΛΕΚΤΡΑ

ἰδού. φίλον τοι τῷ νοσοῦντι δέμνια,
230 ἀνιαρὸν ὄντα κτῆμ', ἀναγκαῖον δ' ὅμως.

ΟΡΕΣΤΗΣ

αὖθίς μ' ἐς ὀρθὸν στῆσον, ἀνακύκλει δέμας·
δυσάρεστον οἱ νοσοῦντες ἀπορίας ὕπο.

ΗΛΕΚΤΡΑ

ἦ κἀπὶ γαίας ἁρμόσαι πόδας θέλεις,
χρόνιον ἴχνος θείς; μεταβολὴ πάντων γλυκύ.

ΟΡΕΣΤΗΣ

235 μάλιστα· δόξαν γὰρ τόδ' ὑγιείας ἔχει·
κρεῖσσον δὲ τὸ δοκεῖν, κἂν ἀληθείας ἀπῇ.

ΗΛΕΚΤΡΑ

ἄκουε δή νυν, ὦ κασίγνητον κάρα,
ἕως ἐῶσί σ' εὖ φρονεῖν Ἐρινύες.

ΟΡΕΣΤΗΣ

λέξεις τι καινόν· κεἰ μὲν εὖ, χάριν φέρεις·
240 εἰ δ' ἐς βλάβην τιν', ἅλις ἔχω τοῦ δυστυχεῖν.

225 ἀθλίων Diggle: ἄθλιον C

ELECTRA

O filthy head of ill-starred hair, how savage you have become by being so long unwashed!

ORESTES

Lay me back down again on my bed: when my mad affliction lets up, my limbs are slack and weak.

ELECTRA

There! When a man's sick, he loves his bed: nuisance though it may be, it's what he must have.

ORESTES

Set me up straight again, turn me about: the sick are hard to please, being so helpless.

ELECTRA

Do you want me to put your feet on the ground? It is some time since you walked: change is always pleasant.

ORESTES

Yes: that has the look of health to it, and better to seem so even if it falls short of reality.

ELECTRA

Listen to me then, brother, while the Erinyes allow you your sanity.

ORESTES

You're about to tell me some news. If it's good, you will have gratitude: if it's about some trouble, I already have enough misfortune.

ΗΛΕΚΤΡΑ

Μενέλαος ἥκει, σοῦ κασίγνητος πατρός,
ἐν Ναυπλίᾳ δὲ σέλμαθ᾽ ὥρμισται νεῶν.

ΟΡΕΣΤΗΣ

πῶς εἶπας; ἥκει φῶς ἐμοῖς καὶ σοῖς κακοῖς
ἀνὴρ ὁμογενὴς καὶ χάριτας ἔχων πατρός;

ΗΛΕΚΤΡΑ

245 ἥκει (τὸ πιστὸν τόδε λόγων ἐμῶν δέχου)
Ἑλένην ἀγόμενος Τρωικῶν ἐκ τειχέων.

ΟΡΕΣΤΗΣ

εἰ μόνος ἐσώθη, μᾶλλον ἂν ζηλωτὸς ἦν·
εἰ δ᾽ ἄλοχον ἄγεται, κακὸν ἔχων ἥκει μέγα.

ΗΛΕΚΤΡΑ

ἐπίσημον ἔτεκε Τυνδάρεως †εἰς τὸν ψόγον†
250 γένος θυγατέρων δυσκλεές τ᾽ ἀν᾽ Ἑλλάδα.

ΟΡΕΣΤΗΣ

σύ νυν διάφερε τῶν κακῶν, ἔξεστι γάρ,
καὶ μὴ μόνον λέγ᾽ ἀλλὰ καὶ φρόνει τάδε.

ΗΛΕΚΤΡΑ

οἴμοι, κασίγνητ᾽, ὄμμα σὸν ταράσσεται,
ταχὺς δὲ μετέθου λύσσαν, ἄρτι σωφρονῶν.

249 ἀστῶν ψόγῳ Willink

438

ELECTRA

Your uncle Menelaus has arrived: his galleys are moored at
Nauplia.

ORESTES

What's this you say? Has he come as a beacon of rescue to
you and me in our troubles, a kinsman and one who owes
my father a debt of gratitude?

ELECTRA

He has come—take this as the pledge of my words'
truth[10]—and he brings Helen from the walls of Troy.

ORESTES

Had he survived alone, his fate would have been more
enviable: if he brings his wife, he has come home bringing
a great bane.

ELECTRA

Marked for censure were the daughters Tyndareus bore,
ill-famed throughout Greece.

ORESTES

Take care then to be different from the wicked, since you
can: do not merely mouth these sentiments but have them
in your heart.

He begins to show signs of distress.

ELECTRA

Ah, ah, your eyes are becoming disturbed, brother! How
quickly you have fallen into madness, though you were just
now sane!

[10] Perhaps raising her hand in attestation.

ΟΡΕΣΤΗΣ

255 ὦ μῆτερ, ἱκετεύω σε, μὴ 'πίσειέ μοι
τὰς αἱματωποὺς καὶ δρακοντώδεις κόρας.
αὗται γὰρ αὗται πλησίον θρῴσκουσ' ἐμοῦ.

ΗΛΕΚΤΡΑ

μέν', ὦ ταλαίπωρ', ἀτρέμα σοῖς ἐν δεμνίοις·
ὁρᾷς γὰρ οὐδὲν ὧν δοκεῖς σάφ' εἰδέναι.

ΟΡΕΣΤΗΣ

260 ὦ Φοῖβ', ἀποκτενοῦσί μ' αἱ κυνώπιδες
γοργῶπες, ἐνέρων ἱέρεαι, δειναὶ θεαί.

ΗΛΕΚΤΡΑ

οὗτοι μεθήσω· χεῖρα δ' ἐμπλέξασ' ἐμὴν
σχήσω σε πηδᾶν δυστυχῆ πηδήματα.

ΟΡΕΣΤΗΣ

μέθες· μί' οὖσα τῶν ἐμῶν Ἐρινύων
265 μέσον μ' ὀχμάζεις, ὡς βάλῃς ἐς Τάρταρον.

ΗΛΕΚΤΡΑ

οἲ 'γὼ τάλαινα, τίν' ἐπικουρίαν λάβω,
ἐπεὶ τὸ θεῖον δυσμενὲς κεκτήμεθα;

ΟΡΕΣΤΗΣ

δὸς τόξα μοι κερουλκά, δῶρα Λοξίου,
οἷς μ' εἶπ' Ἀπόλλων ἐξαμύνασθαι θεάς,
270 εἴ μ' ἐκφοβοῖεν μανιάσιν λυσσήμασιν.

257 post 270 trai. Burges
268–70 del. Cropp

ORESTES

Mother, I beg you, don't sic on me those bloody-faced, snaky maidens! Here they come leaping toward me!

ELECTRA

Poor man, keep still in your bed! You don't actually see anything you think you see!

ORESTES

Phoebus, these bitch-faced fierce-eyed ones mean to kill me, these priestesses of the dead, dread goddesses!

ELECTRA

I will not let you go.[11] I shall twine my arms about you and restrain you from your miserable leaping. (*She tries to restrain her brother.*)

ORESTES

Let me go! You are one of my Erinyes and have grasped me about the waist to hurl me into Tartarus! (*He breaks loose.*)

ELECTRA

O woe is me, what help can I find with heaven for my enemy? (*She covers her head with her garments.*)

ORESTES

(*speaking to an imaginary attendant*) Give me my bow of horn, gift of Loxias! Apollo told me to keep off the goddesses with it if they should frighten me with raving

---

[11] Electra's words, *outoi metheso*, are pretty clearly an allusion to the words of Apollo, *outoi prodoso*, "I will not abandon you," in Aeschylus' *Eumenides* 64 (cf. *Libation Bearers* 269).

441

EURIPIDES

βεβλήσεταί τις θεῶν βροτησίᾳ χερί,
εἰ μὴ 'ξαμείψει χωρὶς ὀμμάτων ἐμῶν.
οὐκ εἰσακούετ'; οὐχ ὁρᾶθ' ἑκηβόλων
τόξων πτερωτὰς γλυφίδας ἐξορμωμένας;
275 ἆ ἆ·
τί δῆτα μέλλετ'; ἐξακρίζετ' αἰθέρα
πτεροῖς· τὰ Φοίβου δ' αἰτιᾶσθε θέσφατα.
      ἔα·
τί χρῆμ'; ἀλύω, πνεῦμ' ἀνεὶς ἐκ πλευμόνων.
ποῖ ποῖ ποθ' ἡλάμεσθα δεμνίων ἄπο;
ἐκ κυμάτων γὰρ αὖθις αὖ γαλήν' ὁρῶ.
280 σύγγονε, τί κλαίεις κρᾶτα θεῖσ' ἔσω πέπλων;
αἰσχύνομαί σοι μεταδιδοὺς πόνων ἐμῶν
ὄχλον τε παρέχων παρθένῳ νόσοις ἐμαῖς.
μὴ τῶν ἐμῶν ἕκατι συντήκου κακῶν·
σὺ μὲν γὰρ ἐπένευσας τάδ', εἴργασται δ' ἐμοὶ
285 μητρῷον αἷμα· Λοξίᾳ δὲ μέμφομαι,
ὅστις μ' ἐπάρας ἔργον ἀνοσιώτατον,
τοῖς μὲν λόγοις ηὔφρανε, τοῖς δ' ἔργοισιν οὔ.
οἶμαι δὲ πατέρα τὸν ἐμόν, εἰ κατ' ὄμματα
ἐξιστόρουν νιν μητέρ' εἰ κτεῖναί με χρή,
290 πολλὰς γενείου τοῦδ' ἂν ἐκτεῖναι λιτὰς
μήποτε τεκούσης ἐς σφαγὰς ὦσαι ξίφος,
εἰ μήτ' ἐκεῖνος ἀναλαβεῖν ἔμελλε φῶς
ἐγώ θ' ὁ τλήμων τοιάδ' ἐκπλήσειν κακά.
      καὶ νῦν ἀνακάλυπτ', ὦ κασιγνήτη, κάρα,

286 ἔργον ἀνόσιον τελεῖν Diggle

442

madness.[12] (*threatening with an imaginary bow*) Some goddess is going to be struck by a mortal hand if she doesn't move out of my sight! Aren't you listening? Don't you see the feathered arrows darting from my far-shooting bow? No, no! No more delaying! Mount up to the upper air with your wings: it's Phoebus' oracles you should blame!

(*returning to sanity*) But what is this? I'm raving and out of breath. Where ever have I leapt to from my bed? After the storm waves I once more see calm.

Sister, why are you weeping and covering your head with your garments? I feel ashamed that I am giving you a share in my woes and causing trouble to a girl by my disease. Do not melt in tears on account of my misfortunes. Although you gave your consent, it was I who shed my mother's blood. Yet it is Loxias that I blame, seeing that he spurred me on to commit a most unholy deed, then gave me the comfort of words but not deeds. I think that if I had asked my father face to face whether I should kill my mother, he would have put out his hand repeatedly to my chin, begging me never to thrust a sword into my mother's throat since he was not going to come back to life and I in my wretchedness would have to endure ills like these.

And now, sister, uncover your head and cease your

---

[12] A scholiast tells us that in later productions of the play the actors mimed the actions of an archer with an imaginary bow. He also says that what Orestes ought properly to do (i. e. did in the original staging) was to use a real bow, presumably handed to him by Electra. Though this creates some staging difficulties, it is conceivable that he is right on both counts.

---

295 ἐκ δακρύων τ᾽ ἄπελθε, κεἰ μάλ᾽ ἀθλίως
ἔχομεν. ὅταν δὲ τἄμ᾽ ἀθυμήσαντ᾽ ἴδῃς,
σύ μου τὸ δεινὸν καὶ διαφθαρὲν φρενῶν
ἴσχναινε παραμυθοῦ θ᾽· ὅταν δὲ σὺ στένῃς,
ἡμᾶς παρόντας χρή σε νουθετεῖν φίλα·
300 ἐπικουρίαι γὰρ αἵδε τοῖς φίλοις καλαί.
    ἀλλ᾽, ὦ τάλαινα, βᾶσα δωμάτων ἔσω
ὕπνῳ τ᾽ ἄυπνον βλέφαρον ἐκταθεῖσα δὸς
σίτων τ᾽ ὄρεξαι λουτρά τ᾽ ἐπιβαλοῦ χροΐ.
εἰ γὰρ προλείψεις ἢ προσεδρίᾳ νόσον
305 κτήσῃ τιν᾽, οἰχόμεσθα· σὲ γὰρ ἔχω μόνην
ἐπίκουρον, ἄλλων, ὡς ὁρᾷς, ἔρημος ὤν.

ΗΛΕΚΤΡΑ

οὐκ ἔστι· σὺν σοὶ καὶ θανεῖν αἱρήσομαι
καὶ ζῆν· ἔχει γὰρ ταὐτόν· ἢν σὺ κατθάνῃς,
γυνὴ τί δράσω; πῶς μόνη σωθήσομαι,
310 ἀνάδελφος ἀπάτωρ ἄφιλος; εἰ δὲ σοὶ δοκεῖ,
δρᾶν χρὴ τάδ᾽. ἀλλὰ κλῖνον εἰς εὐνὴν δέμας,
καὶ μὴ τὸ ταρβοῦν κἀκφοβοῦν σ᾽ ἐκ δεμνίων
ἄγαν ἀποδέχου, μένε δ᾽ ἐπὶ στρωτοῦ λέχους.
κἂν μὴ νοσῇ γάρ, ἀλλὰ δοξάζῃ νοσεῖν,
315 κάματος βροτοῖσιν ἀπορία τε γίγνεται.

ΧΟΡΟΣ

στρ.

αἰαῖ·
δρομάδες ὦ πτεροφόροι
ποτνιάδες θεαί,

weeping, even if our situation is bad. Whenever you see me despondent, you must cure the grim derangement of my mind and encourage me. And when *you* are groaning, I must stand by you and offer friendly admonition. Aid like this is proper for kin to offer.

So, poor woman, go into the house, give your sleepless eyelids over to rest, take some nourishment, and bathe yourself. For if you collapse or by sitting over me catch some illness, my life is over. You are the only helper I have: I have no others, as you see.

ELECTRA

(*uncovering her head*) I cannot do it: I shall choose both death and life in your company. For it comes to the same thing: if you die, what am I as a woman to do? How can I survive all alone, being without brother, father, or friend? Still, if you think it best, I must do as you say. But lie down on the bed and try not to be too receptive to the panic that makes you run from your couch, but stay within its covers. For even if mortals are not ill but only think they are, the result is weariness and despair.

Exit ELECTRA into the skene. *Orestes returns to his bed.*

CHORUS

Ah, ah!
Swift-running winged ones,
goddesses of madness,

---

³⁰⁴ προλείψεις Paley cl. *Hec.* 438: π- μ' C

ἀβάκχευτον αἶ θίασον ἐλάχετ᾽ ἐν
320 δάκρυσι καὶ γόοις,
μελάγχρωτες Εὐμενίδες, αἵτε τὸν
ταναὸν αἰθέρ᾽ ἀμπάλλεσθ᾽, αἵματος
τινύμεναι δίκαν, τινύμεναι φόνου,
καθικετεύομαι καθικετεύομαι,
325 τὸν Ἀγαμέμνονος γόνον ἐάσατ᾽ ἐκ-
λαθέσθαι λύσσας μανιάδος φοιτα-
λέου. φεῦ μόχθων οἵων, ὦ τάλας,
ὀρεχθεὶς ἔρρεις,
τρίποδος ἄπο φάτιν ἃν ὁ Φοῖ-
330 βος ἔλακεν ἔλακε δεξάμενος ἀνὰ δάπεδον,
ἵνα μεσόμφαλοι λέγονται μυχοί.

ἀντ.

ὦ Ζεῦ·
τίς ἔλεος τίς ὅδ᾽ ἀγὼν
φόνιος ἔρχεται,
335 θοάζων σε τὸν μέλεον; ᾧ δάκρυα
δάκρυσι συμβάλλει
χορεύων τις ἐς δόμον ἀλαστόρων,
ματέρος αἷμα σᾶς ὅς σ᾽ ἀναβακχεύει.
κατολοφύρομαι κατολοφύρομαι.
340 ὁ μέγας ὄλβος οὐ μόνιμος ἐν βροτοῖς·
ἀνὰ δὲ λαῖφος ὥς τις ἀκάτου θοᾶς
τινάξας δαίμων κατέκλυσεν δεινῶν

who have as your portion a worshipful band, unblest by
    Bacchus,
amidst tears and groans,
dark-hued Eumenides, you that gallop over
the far-spreading upper air,
exacting, exacting the penalty for bloodshed,
I entreat you, entreat you,
let the son of Agamemnon
put from his mind his raving madness,
the wandering of his wits: poor man, what work
you put your hand to, what ruin you suffered,
when from the holy tripod you received
the word that Phoebus uttered, uttered in the sacred
    precinct
where, 'tis said, are the inner recesses of Earth's navel![13]

O Zeus!
What pity, what struggle
comes in blood
as it spurs you on, poor man? To you tears
upon tears he brings,
that nameless avenging spirit dancing into the house
who drives you to madness for your mother's murder.
I weep, I weep for you.
Great good fortune among mortals is not lasting:
some god, shaking it like the sail of a swift ship,
overwhelms it in waves of fearful trouble,

[13] Delphi was thought to be the navel (i.e. central point) of
Earth, and the story was told that eagles released simultaneously
at the eastern- and westernmost edge of the world met over
Delphi.

πόνων ὡς πόντου λάβροις ὀλεθρίοι-
σιν ἐν κύμασιν.
345 τίνα †γὰρ ἔτι† πάρος οἶκον ἄλ-
λον ἕτερον ἢ τὸν ἀπὸ θεογόνων γάμων,
τὸν ἀπὸ Ταντάλου, σέβεσθαί με χρή;

—καὶ μὴν βασιλεὺς ὅδε δὴ στείχει
Μενέλαος ἄναξ, πολὺς ἁβροσύνη,
350 δῆλος ὁρᾶσθαι τοῦ Τανταλιδῶν
ἐξ αἵματος ὤν. ὦ χιλιόναυν
στρατὸν ὁρμήσας ἐς γῆν Ἀσίαν,
χαῖρ', εὐτυχίᾳ δ' αὐτὸς ὁμιλεῖς,
355 θεόθεν πράξας ἅπερ ηὔχου.

ΜΕΝΕΛΑΟΣ
ὦ δῶμα, τῇ μέν σ' ἡδέως προσδέρκομαι
Τροίαθεν ἐλθών, τῇ δ' ἰδὼν καταστένω·
κύκλῳ γὰρ εἱλιχθεῖσαν ἀθλίοις κακοῖς
οὐπώποτ' ἄλλην μᾶλλον εἶδον ἑστίαν.
360 Ἀγαμέμνονος μὲν γὰρ τύχας ἠπιστάμην
[καὶ θάνατον, οἵῳ πρὸς δάμαρτος ὤλετο],
Μαλέᾳ προσίσχων πρῷραν· ἐκ δὲ κυμάτων
ὁ ναυτίλοισι μάντις ἐξήγγειλέ μοι
Νηρέως προφήτης Γλαῦκος, ἀψευδὴς θεός,
365 ὅς μοι τόδ' εἶπεν ἐμφανῶς κατασταθείς·
Μενέλαε, κεῖται σὸς κασίγνητος θανών,
λουτροῖσιν ἀλόχου περιπεσὼν πανυστάτοις.
δακρύων δ' ἔπλησεν ἐμέ τε καὶ ναύτας ἐμοὺς

deadly and boisterous
like those of the main.
But what other house
shall I rather honor than this, the house of Tantalus,
descended from marriage with the gods?

Enter MENELAUS *with retinue by Eisodos A.*

CHORUS LEADER

But look, here comes king Menelaus, resplendent in luxury: his looks mark him plainly as from the blood of the sons of Tantalus. Leader of the thousand-ship fleet to Asia, hail! All on your own you consort with Prosperity and have from the gods all the success you prayed for!

MENELAUS

O house, I look on you in one way with pleasure, being just returned from Troy, but in another way I groan as I look at you: never have I seen another hearth more surrounded by miserable woes. I learned of the death of Agamemnon [and his murder at the hands of his wife] as I was putting into Malea: from the waves the sailors' seer announced it to me, Glaucus, prophet of Nereus, unerring god. He appeared before my eyes and said, "Menelaus, your brother lies dead, having received his last bath from his wife." Thus he filled my sailors' eyes and mine with tears. But when

---

345 δὲ τίνα Willink
349 πολὺς Willink: πολὺ δ' vel πολλῇ C: ποδὸς Kirchhoff
361 del. Dindorf

πολλῶν. ἐπεὶ δὲ Ναυπλίας ψαύω χθονός,
370 ἤδη δάμαρτος ἐνθάδ' ἐξορμωμένης,
δοκῶν Ὀρέστην παῖδα τὸν Ἀγαμέμνονος
φίλαισι χερσὶ περιβαλεῖν καὶ μητέρα,
ὡς εὐτυχοῦντας, ἔκλυον ἀλιτύπων τινὸς
τῆς Τυνδαρείας παιδὸς ἀνόσιον φόνον.
375 καὶ νῦν ὅπου 'στὶν εἴπατ', ὦ νεάνιδες,
Ἀγαμέμνονος παῖς, ὃς τὰ δείν' ἔτλη κακά.
βρέφος γὰρ ἦν τότ' ἐν Κλυταιμήστρας χεροῖν
ὅτ' ἐξέλειπον μέλαθρον ἐς Τροίαν ἰών,
ὥστ' οὐκ ἂν αὐτὸν γνωρίσαιμ' ἂν εἰσιδών.

ΟΡΕΣΤΗΣ

380 ὅδ' εἴμ' Ὀρέστης, Μενέλεως, ὃν ἱστορεῖς.
ἑκὼν ἐγώ σοι τἀμὰ μηνύσω κακά.
τῶν σῶν δὲ γονάτων πρωτόλεια θιγγάνω
ἱκέτης, ἀφύλλους στόματος ἐξάπτων λιτάς·
σῶσόν μ' (ἀφῖξαι δ' αὐτὸν ἐς καιρὸν) κακῶν.

ΜΕΝΕΛΑΟΣ

385 ὦ θεοί, τί λεύσσω; τίνα δέδορκα νερτέρων;

ΟΡΕΣΤΗΣ

εὖ γ' εἶπας· οὐ γὰρ ζῶ κακοῖς, φάος δ' ὁρῶ.

ΜΕΝΕΛΑΟΣ

ὡς ἠγρίωσαι πλόκαμον αὐχμηρόν, τάλας.

384 αὐτὸν Schaefer: αὐτὸς C

450

we touched land at Nauplia and my wife had already set out for here, though I thought I would embrace his son Orestes and his mother with loving arms, and supposed they would be prospering, I heard from a sailor about the unholy murder of Tyndareus' daughter.

Tell me now, young women, where the son of Agamemnon is, he who brought himself to do this grievous wrong. He was a babe in Clytaemestra's arms when I left the palace on my way to Troy, so I would not know him by sight.

Orestes leaves his couch and kneels before Menelaus.

ORESTES
Here, Menelaus: I am the Orestes you are looking for. I will reveal my misfortunes to you of my own accord. But as a first offering I grasp your knees as a suppliant and add the prayer of my mouth, unadorned by boughs.[14] Save me from disaster: you have come in the very nick of time!

MENELAUS
Gods! What do I see, what corpse am I looking at?

ORESTES
You are right: I am dead from my troubles, though I still see the light of day.

MENELAUS
Poor man, how wild you look with your filthy hair!

---

[14] It is normal for a suppliant to carry a leafy bough adorned with tufts of wool. Orestes apparently keeps this suppliant posture until line 544.

EURIPIDES

ΟΡΕΣΤΗΣ

οὐχ ἡ πρόσοψίς μ᾽ ἀλλὰ τἄργ᾽ ἀκίζεται.

ΜΕΝΕΛΑΟΣ

δεινὸν δὲ λεύσσεις ὀμμάτων ξηραῖς κόραις.

ΟΡΕΣΤΗΣ

390   τὸ σῶμα φροῦδον· τὸ δ᾽ ὄνομ᾽ οὐ λέλοιπέ με.

ΜΕΝΕΛΑΟΣ

ὦ παρὰ λόγον μοι σὴ φανεῖσ᾽ ἀμορφία.

ΟΡΕΣΤΗΣ

ὅδ᾽ εἰμί, μητρὸς τῆς ταλαιπώρου φονεύς.

ΜΕΝΕΛΑΟΣ

ἤκουσα· φείδου δ᾽, ὀλιγάκις λέγων κακά.

ΟΡΕΣΤΗΣ

φειδόμεθ᾽· ὁ δαίμων δ᾽ ἐς ἐμὲ πλούσιος κακῶν.

ΜΕΝΕΛΑΟΣ

395   τί χρῆμα πάσχεις; τίς σ᾽ ἀπόλλυσιν νόσος;

ΟΡΕΣΤΗΣ

ἡ σύνεσις, ὅτι σύνοιδα δείν᾽ εἰργασμένος.

ΜΕΝΕΛΑΟΣ

πῶς φής; σοφόν τοι τὸ σαφές, οὐ τὸ μὴ σαφές.

ΟΡΕΣΤΗΣ

λύπη μάλιστά γ᾽ ἡ διαφθείρουσά με . . .

---

388 h. v. et 390 inter se trai. Willink
393 λέγων Kvíčala: -ειν C

452

ORESTES
It is not my looks but my deeds that mar me.

MENELAUS
How terrible is the glance you shoot from parched eyes!

ORESTES
My body is dead and gone, but my name has not left me.

MENELAUS
How unexpected it is to find you so disfigured!

ORESTES
It is I, the killer of my poor mother.

MENELAUS
So I have heard: but be sparing and do not dwell on your troubles.

ORESTES
Sparing is what I am: but the god is lavish in troubles for me.

MENELAUS
What is wrong with you? What malady is destroying you?

ORESTES
Understanding: the awareness that I have done dreadful things.

MENELAUS
What do you mean? Clarity is the wise thing, not unclarity.

ORESTES
What destroys me most of all is grief . . .

ΜΕΝΕΛΑΟΣ

δεινὴ γὰρ ἡ θεός, ἀλλ᾽ ὅμως ἰάσιμος.

ΟΡΕΣΤΗΣ

400 . . . μανίαι τε, μητρὸς αἵματος τιμωρίαν.

ΜΕΝΕΛΑΟΣ

ἤρξω δὲ λύσσης πότε; τίς ἡμέρα τότ᾽ ἦν;

ΟΡΕΣΤΗΣ

ἐν ᾗ τάλαιναν μητέρ᾽ ἐξώγκουν τάφῳ.

ΜΕΝΕΛΑΟΣ

πότερα κατ᾽ οἴκους ἢ προσεδρεύων πυρᾷ;

ΟΡΕΣΤΗΣ

ἐκτός, φυλάσσων ὀστέων ἀναίρεσιν.

ΜΕΝΕΛΑΟΣ

405 παρῆν τις ἄλλος, ὃς σὸν ὤρθενεν δέμας;

ΟΡΕΣΤΗΣ

Πυλάδης γ᾽, ὁ συνδρῶν αἷμα καὶ μητρὸς φόνον.

ΜΕΝΕΛΑΟΣ

φαντασμάτων δὲ τάδε νοσεῖς ποίων ὕπο;

ΟΡΕΣΤΗΣ

ἔδοξ᾽ ἰδεῖν τρεῖς Νυκτὶ προσφερεῖς κόρας.

ΜΕΝΕΛΑΟΣ

οἶδ᾽ ἃς ἔλεξας, ὀνομάσαι δ᾽ οὐ βούλομαι.

---

400 τιμωρίαν Diggle: -ίαι C: τιμάοροι Renehan
404 ἐκτός Wecklein: νυκτός C

MENELAUS
A dread goddess but nonetheless one that can be healed.

ORESTES
... and fits of madness, in requital for my mother's blood.

MENELAUS
When did your frenzy begin? On what day?

ORESTES
The day I was heaping up a tomb for my poor mother.

MENELAUS
Were you in the house or sitting near her pyre?

ORESTES
Outdoors: I was waiting for the gathering of the bones.

MENELAUS
Was anyone else there to hold your body up?

ORESTES
Yes, Pylades, my accomplice in my mother's blood.

MENELAUS
What sort of visions cause you this malady?

ORESTES
In my imagination I saw three maidens who looked like Night.

MENELAUS
I know the maidens you mean, but I do not wish to name them.

ΟΡΕΣΤΗΣ

410 σεμναὶ γάρ· εὐπαίδευτα δ᾽ ἀπετρέπου λέγειν.

ΜΕΝΕΛΑΟΣ

αὗταί σε βακχεύουσι συγγενῆ φόνον.

ΟΡΕΣΤΗΣ

οἴμοι διωγμῶν οἷς ἐλαύνομαι τάλας.

ΜΕΝΕΛΑΟΣ

οὐ δεινὰ πάσχειν δεινὰ τοὺς εἰργασμένους.

ΟΡΕΣΤΗΣ

ἀλλ᾽ ἔστιν ἡμῖν ἀναφορὰ τῆς συμφορᾶς ...

ΜΕΝΕΛΑΟΣ

415 μὴ θάνατον εἴπῃς· τοῦτο μὲν γὰρ οὐ σοφόν.

ΟΡΕΣΤΗΣ

... Φοῖβος, κελεύσας μητρὸς ἐκπρᾶξαι φόνον.

ΜΕΝΕΛΑΟΣ

ἀμαθέστερός γ᾽ ὢν τοῦ καλοῦ καὶ τῆς δίκης.

ΟΡΕΣΤΗΣ

δουλεύομεν θεοῖς, ὅ τι ποτ᾽ εἰσὶν οἱ θεοί.

ΜΕΝΕΛΑΟΣ

κᾆτ᾽ οὐκ ἀμύνει Λοξίας τοῖς σοῖς κακοῖς;

ΟΡΕΣΤΗΣ

420 μέλλει· τὸ θεῖον δ᾽ ἐστὶ τοιοῦτον φύσει.

ΜΕΝΕΛΑΟΣ

πόσον χρόνον δὲ μητρὸς οἴχονται πνοαί;

---

410 ἀπετρέπου Hermann: ἀποτρέπου C: ἀπετράπου Diggle

ORESTES

Yes, they are dread goddesses: your refusal to name them shows good breeding.

MENELAUS

These are the ones who madden you because of kindred bloodshed.

ORESTES

Ah, how they hound and pursue me in my misery!

MENELAUS

It is not monstrous that those who have done monstrous things should suffer them.

ORESTES

Well, my recourse in disaster . . .

MENELAUS

Don't say "is death": *that* isn't wise.

ORESTES

. . . is Phoebus, who ordered me to murder my mother.

MENELAUS

Yes, and little knowledge he showed of what is decent and right.

ORESTES

We are slaves of the gods, whatever "the gods" are.

MENELAUS

Then does Loxias give you no help in your troubles?

ORESTES

He bides his time: that's the way gods are.

MENELAUS

How long since your mother breathed her last?

ΟΡΕΣΤΗΣ

ἕκτον τόδ᾽ ἦμαρ· ἔτι πυρὰ θερμὴ τάφου.

ΜΕΝΕΛΑΟΣ

ὡς ταχὺ μετῆλθόν σ᾽ αἷμα μητέρος θεαί.

‹ΟΡΕΣΤΗΣ

ταχὺν πιθέσθαι γ᾽· ὁ δὲ θεὸς σῶσαι βραδύς.

ΜΕΝΕΛΑΟΣ

σοφὸς δὲ μείνας ἐκτὸς αἰτίας θεός.›

ΟΡΕΣΤΗΣ

οὐ σοφὸς ἀληθῶς ἐς φίλους ὁ φὺς κακός.

ΜΕΝΕΛΑΟΣ

425   πατρὸς δὲ δή τί σ᾽ ὠφελεῖ τιμωρία;

ΟΡΕΣΤΗΣ

οὔπω· τὸ μέλλον δ᾽ ἴσον ἀπραξίᾳ λέγω.

ΜΕΝΕΛΑΟΣ

τὰ πρὸς πόλιν δὲ πῶς ἔχεις δράσας τάδε;

ΟΡΕΣΤΗΣ

μισούμεθ᾽ οὕτως ὥστε μὴ προσεννέπειν.

ΜΕΝΕΛΑΟΣ

οὐδ᾽ ἥγνισαι σὸν αἷμα κατὰ νόμον χεροῖν;

ΟΡΕΣΤΗΣ

430   ἐκκλῇομαι γὰρ δωμάτων ὅποι μόλω.

423 post h. v. lac. indic. Kirchhoff
424 ἀληθῶς Bothe (-ῶς) et Willink (del. δ'): ἀληθὴς δ' C
ὁ φὺς Willink: ἔφυς C

ORESTES

This is the sixth day: her pyre is still warm.

MENELAUS

How swiftly the goddesses have pursued you for your mother's blood.

‹ORESTES

Yes: I was swift to obey, but the god is slow to save.

MENELAUS

The god is wise in keeping clear of blame.›

ORESTES

No one who is unfaithful to his friends is truly wise.

MENELAUS

But really, has your avenging of your father helped you at all?

ORESTES

Not yet: in my eyes delay is the same as inaction.

MENELAUS

But the city, how do you stand with it since committing this deed?

ORESTES

I am so detested that no one speaks to me.

MENELAUS

But have you not been cleansed of the blood on your hands in the customary way?

ORESTES

No: wherever I go they shut me from their homes.

EURIPIDES

ΜΕΝΕΛΑΟΣ
τίνες πολιτῶν δ᾽ ἐξαμιλλῶνταί †σε γῆς†;

ΟΡΕΣΤΗΣ
Οἴαξ, τὸ Τροίας μῖσος ἀναφέρων πατρί.

ΜΕΝΕΛΑΟΣ
συνῆκα· Παλαμήδους σε τιμωρεῖ φόνου.

ΟΡΕΣΤΗΣ
οὗ γ᾽ οὐ μετῆν μοι· διὰ τριῶν δ᾽ ἀπόλλυμαι.

ΜΕΝΕΛΑΟΣ
435   τίς δ᾽ ἄλλος; ἦ πού τινες ἀπ᾽ Αἰγίσθου φίλων;

ΟΡΕΣΤΗΣ
οὗτοί μ᾽ ὑβρίζουσ᾽· ὧν πόλις τὰ νῦν κλύει.

ΜΕΝΕΛΑΟΣ
Ἀγαμέμνονος δὲ σκῆπτρ᾽ ἐᾷ σ᾽ ἔχειν πόλις;

ΟΡΕΣΤΗΣ
πῶς, οἵτινες ζῆν οὐκ ἐῶσ᾽ ἡμᾶς ἔτι;

ΜΕΝΕΛΑΟΣ
τί δρῶντες; ἦ τι σαφὲς ἔχεις εἰπεῖν ἐμοί;

431 λέγε vel τάδε Willink
435 τινες Heimsoeth: τῶν C
439 ἦ τι Hermann cl. Σ: ὅ τι καὶ C

---

15 Palamedes, Oeax's brother, was framed on a charge of trea-
son by his rival Odysseus and stoned to death.

MENELAUS

But which of the citizens are behind this?

ORESTES

It's Oeax: he blames my father for the hateful occurrence at Troy.[15]

MENELAUS

I catch your drift: he is punishing you for the murder of Palamedes.

ORESTES

Which I had nothing to do with. Three things are causing my death.[16]

MENELAUS

Who else attacks you? Perhaps some of Aegisthus' party?

ORESTES

Yes, they treat me outrageously. And the city now does their bidding.

MENELAUS

Does the city allow you to hold Agamemnon's scepter?

ORESTES

Scepter? They will not allow me even to live!

MENELAUS

But what are they doing? Can you tell me anything definite?

---

[16] The three are Clytaemestra's murder, Palamedes' death, and (still to be mentioned) Aegisthus' friends. Alternatively we may translate "I am ruined by it at two removes" (West), with Oeax venting his anger against Odysseus first on his commander Agamemnon and then on Agamemnon's son.

ΟΡΕΣΤΗΣ

440 ψῆφος καθ᾽ ἡμῶν οἴσεται τῇδ᾽ ἡμέρᾳ.

[ΜΕΝΕΛΑΟΣ

φεύγειν πόλιν τήνδ᾽; ἢ θανεῖν ἢ μὴ θανεῖν;

ΟΡΕΣΤΗΣ

θανεῖν ὑπ᾽ ἀστῶν λευσίμῳ πετρώματι.]

ΜΕΝΕΛΑΟΣ

κᾆτ᾽ οὐχὶ φεύγεις γῆς ὑπερβάλλων ὅρους;

ΟΡΕΣΤΗΣ

κύκλῳ γὰρ εἱλισσόμεθα παγχάλκοις ὅπλοις.

ΜΕΝΕΛΑΟΣ

445 ἰδίᾳ πρὸς ἐχθρῶν ἢ πρὸς Ἀργείας χερός;

ΟΡΕΣΤΗΣ

πάντων πρὸς ἀστῶν, ὡς θάνω· βραχὺς λόγος.

ΜΕΝΕΛΑΟΣ

ὦ μέλεος, ἥκεις συμφορᾶς ἐς τοὔσχατον.

ΟΡΕΣΤΗΣ

ἐς σ᾽ ἐλπὶς ἡμὴ καταφυγὰς ἔχει κακῶν.
ἀλλ᾽ ἀθλίως πράσσουσιν εὐτυχὴς μολὼν
450 μετάδος φίλοισι σοῖσι σῆς εὐπραξίας,
καὶ μὴ μόνος τὸ χρηστὸν ἀπολαβὼν ἔχε,
ἀλλ᾽ ἀντιλάζου καὶ πόνων ἐν τῷ μέρει,
χάριτας πατρῴας ἐκτίνων ἐς οὕς σε δεῖ.
ὄνομα γάρ, ἔργον δ᾽ οὐκ ἔχουσιν οἱ φίλοι
455 οἱ μὴ ᾽πὶ ταῖσι συμφοραῖς ὄντες φίλοι.

462

ORESTES
A vote will be taken against me today.

[MENELAUS
Banishment from the city? To be put to death or spared?

ORESTES
To be put to death by stoning at the hands of the citizens.]

MENELAUS
Then why aren't you fleeing across the border?

ORESTES
I am surrounded by panoplies of bronze.

MENELAUS
By the private forces of your enemies or an army of Argos?

ORESTES
In a word: by all the citizens, to bring about my death.

MENELAUS
Poor man, you have reached the limit of misfortune.

ORESTES
You are my hoped-for refuge from trouble!

So, since I am in misery and you arrive in prosperity, give a share of your good fortune to your kinsman! Don't take all the good and keep it to yourself but accept some trouble too in your turn by repaying to those you should the debt of gratitude you owe my father. Those who are not friends in misfortune have only the name of friendship, not its reality.

441–2 del. Weil

ΧΟΡΟΣ

καὶ μὴν γέροντι δεῦρ' ἁμιλλᾶται ποδὶ
ὁ Σπαρτιάτης Τυνδάρεως, μελάμπεπλος
κουρᾷ τε θυγατρὸς πενθίμῳ κεκαρμένος.

ΟΡΕΣΤΗΣ

Μενέλα', ἀπωλόμεσθα· Τυνδάρεως ὅδε
460   στείχει πρὸς ἡμᾶς, οὗ μάλιστ' αἰδώς μ' ἔχει
ἐς ὄμματ' ἐλθεῖν τοῖσιν ἐξειργασμένοις.
καὶ γάρ μ' ἔθρεψε σμικρὸν ὄντα, πολλὰ δὲ
φιλήματ' ἐξέπλησε, τὸν Ἀγαμέμνονος
παῖδ' ἀγκάλαισι περιφέρων, Λήδα θ' ἅμα,
465   τιμῶντέ μ' οὐδὲν ἧσσον ἢ Διοσκόρω·
οἷς, ὦ τάλαινα καρδία ψυχή τ' ἐμή,
ἀπέδωκ' ἀμοιβὰς οὐ καλάς. τίνα σκότον
λάβω προσώπῳ; ποῖον ἐπίπροσθεν νέφος
θῶμαι, γέροντος ὀμμάτων φεύγων κόρας;

ΤΥΝΔΑΡΕΩΣ

470   ποῦ ποῦ θυγατρὸς τῆς ἐμῆς ἴδω πόσιν,
Μενέλαον; ἐπὶ γὰρ τῷ Κλυταιμήστρας τάφῳ
χοὰς χεόμενος ἔκλυον ὡς ἐς Ναυπλίαν
ἥκοι σὺν ἀλόχῳ πολυετὴς σεσωμένος.
ἄγετέ με· πρὸς γὰρ δεξιὰν αὐτοῦ θέλω
475   στὰς ἀσπάσασθαι, χρόνιος εἰσιδὼν φίλον.

ΜΕΝΕΛΑΟΣ

ὦ πρέσβυ, χαῖρε, Ζηνὸς ὁμόλεκτρον κάρα.

Enter TYNDAREUS with attendants by Eisodos A.

CHORUS LEADER
But look, here comes the Spartan Tyndareus, hurrying with aged step. He is dressed in black and his hair is shorn in grief for his daughter.

ORESTES
Menelaus, I'm done for! Tyndareus is coming toward us: I feel the greatest hesitation to appear before him after what I have done. He took care of me when I was a child, showing me much affection and carrying "Agamemnon's boy" around in his arms. So did Leda, and the two of them honored me equally with the Dioscuri.[17] O unhappy heart, unhappy soul, I have given them no good return for their kindness. What darkness can I find to enshroud my face? What cloud can I put in front of it as I try to escape the old man's glance?

TYNDAREUS
Where can I find my daughter's husband Menelaus? As I was pouring libations at the tomb of Clytaemestra I heard that he has arrived in Nauplia, safe and sound after many years away. Bring me forward! I want to approach Menelaus' right hand and clasp it in greeting: I have not seen my kinsman for a long time.

MENELAUS
Old Tyndareus, who once shared your wife with Zeus, I wish you joy!

---

[17] The sons of Zeus, Castor and Polydeuces, Leda's twin sons.

---

459 Μενέλα᾽, ἀπωλόμεσθα Elmsley: ἀπωλόμην, Μενέλαε C: vide *Euripidea Altera* 102–3

ΤΥΝΔΑΡΕΩΣ

ὦ χαῖρε καὶ σύ, Μενέλεως, κήδευμ᾽ ἐμόν.
ἔα· [τὸ μέλλον ὡς κακὸν τὸ μὴ εἰδέναι.]
ὁ μητροφόντης ὅδε πρὸ δωμάτων δράκων

480 στίλβει νοσώδεις ἀστραπάς, στύγημ᾽ ἐμόν.
Μενέλαε, προσφθέγγῃ νιν, ἀνόσιον κάρα;

ΜΕΝΕΛΑΟΣ

τί γάρ; φίλου μοι πατρός ἐστιν ἔκγονος.

ΤΥΝΔΑΡΕΩΣ

κείνου γὰρ ὅδε πέφυκε, τοιοῦτος γεγώς;

ΜΕΝΕΛΑΟΣ

πέφυκεν· εἰ δὲ δυστυχεῖ, τιμητέος.

ΤΥΝΔΑΡΕΩΣ

485 βεβαρβάρωσαι, χρόνιος ὢν ἐν βαρβάροις.

ΜΕΝΕΛΑΟΣ

Ἑλληνικόν τοι τὸν ὁμόθεν τιμᾶν ἀεί.

ΤΥΝΔΑΡΕΩΣ

καὶ τῶν νόμων γε μὴ πρότερον εἶναι θέλειν.

ΜΕΝΕΛΑΟΣ

πᾶν τοὐξ ἀνάγκης δοῦλόν ἐστ᾽ ἐν τοῖς σοφοῖς.

ΤΥΝΔΑΡΕΩΣ

κέκτησό νυν σὺ τοῦτ᾽, ἐγὼ δ᾽ οὐ κτήσομαι.

478 τὸ . . . εἰδέναι del. Wecklein

TYNDAREUS

Joy to you too, son-in-law Menelaus!
  (*catching sight of Orestes*) But what is this? [How terrible not to know the future.] Here is a mother-killing snake before the palace, with sickness in his darting glance: how I loathe him! Menelaus, are you talking to him, the godless wretch?

MENELAUS

Of course: he is the son of a man dear to me.

TYNDAREUS

Can a man like this really be *his* son?

MENELAUS

Yes, and if he is in misfortune, I must honor this relation.

TYNDAREUS

You have turned barbarian from being so long among barbarians.

MENELAUS

Well, it's a Greek custom always to honor blood relatives.

TYNDAREUS

Yes, and not to try to be above the law.

MENELAUS

The intelligent regard all actions done from compulsion as slavish.

TYNDAREUS

You hold to that opinion: I won't.

ΜΕΝΕΛΑΟΣ

490 ὀργὴ γὰρ ἅμα σου καὶ τὸ γῆρας οὐ σοφόν.

ΤΥΝΔΑΡΕΩΣ

πρὸς τόνδ᾽ ἀγών τις ἀσοφίας ἥκει πέρι·
εἰ τὰ καλὰ πᾶσι φανερὰ καὶ τὰ μὴ καλά,
τούτου τίς ἀνδρῶν ἐγένετ᾽ ἀσυνετώτερος,
ὅστις τὸ μὲν δίκαιον οὐκ ἐσκέψατο
495 οὐδ᾽ ἦλθεν ἐπὶ τὸν κοινὸν Ἑλλήνων νόμον;
ἐπεὶ γὰρ ἐξέπνευσεν Ἀγαμέμνων βίον
κάρα θυγατρὸς τῆς ἐμῆς πληγεὶς ὕπο
498 (αἴσχιστον ἔργον· οὐ γὰρ αἰνέσω ποτέ),
500 χρῆν αὐτὸν ἐπιθεῖναι μὲν αἵματος δίκην
ὁσίαν διώκοντ᾽, ἐκβαλεῖν τε δωμάτων
μητέρα· τὸ σῶφρόν τ᾽ ἔλαβ᾽ ἂν ἀντὶ συμφορᾶς
καὶ τοῦ νόμου τ᾽ ἂν εἴχετ᾽ εὐσεβής τ᾽ ἂν ἦν.
νῦν δ᾽ ἐς τὸν αὐτὸν δαίμον᾽ ἦλθε μητέρι·
505 κακὴν γὰρ αὐτὴν ἐνδίκως ἡγούμενος,
αὐτὸς κακίων μητέρ᾽ ἐγένετο κτανών.
ἐρήσομαι δέ, Μενέλεως, τοσόνδε σε·
εἰ τόνδ᾽ ἀποκτείνειεν ὁμόλεκτρος γυνή,
χὠ τοῦδε παῖς αὖ μητέρ᾽ ἀνταποκτενεῖ,
510 κἄπειθ᾽ ὁ κείνου γενόμενος φόνῳ φόνον
λύσει, πέρας δὴ ποῖ κακῶν προβήσεται;
καλῶς ἔθεντο ταῦτα πατέρες οἱ πάλαι·
ἐς ὀμμάτων μὲν ὄψιν οὐκ εἴων περᾶν
οὐδ᾽ εἰς ἀπάντημ᾽ ὅστις αἷμ᾽ ἔχων κυροῖ,
515 φυγαῖσι δ᾽ ὁσιοῦν, ἀνταποκτείνειν δὲ μή.

ORESTES

ORESTES

MENELAUS

No, there's folly in your age and irascibility.

TYNDAREUS

It's this man who's on trial for folly: if good and bad are
manifest to all, what man has ever shown himself more
foolish than he has, seeing that he did not consider justice
or have recourse to the common law of the Greeks? When
Agamemnon breathed his last, struck on the head by my
daughter (a most disgraceful deed, which I shall never
condone), then he ought as prosecutor to have imposed
a murder penalty consistent with piety and expelled his
mother from the house. Instead of disaster he would have
won praise for moderation, and he would have stuck close
to the law and been god-fearing. But as it is, his lot proved
to be the same as his mother's. He rightly considered her to
be wicked, yet he showed himself more wicked than she
was by committing matricide.

Menelaus, let me ask you just this: if Orestes were to be
killed by his wedded wife, and his son in his turn kills his
mother, and then *his* son requites that murder with mur-
der, where's the limit to calamity? Our ancestors of old or-
dered this matter well: though they forbade anyone with
blood on his hands to come into their sight or meet them, it
was by exile, not retaliatory killing, that they said purity

---

491 ἀσοφίας Bothe: σοφίας C: possis μωρίας vel ἀμαθίας
497 κάρα . . . πληγεὶς ὕπο Brunck: πληγεὶς . . . ὑπὲρ κάρα C
499 nil omissum: hic et 719 quod numeri cum summa versuum
non quadrant, id incuria veterum editorum factum est
502 ἔλαβ' ἂν Bergk: ἔλαβεν C
506 μητέρ' ἐγένετο Porson: ἐγένετο μητέρα C

ἀεὶ γὰρ εἷς ἔμελλ᾽ ἐνέξεσθαι φόνῳ,
τὸ λοίσθιον μίασμα λαμβάνων χεροῖν.
  ἐγὼ δὲ μισῶ μὲν γυναῖκας ἀνοσίους,
πρώτην δὲ θυγατέρ᾽, ἣ πόσιν κατέκτανεν·

520 Ἑλένην τε, τὴν σὴν ἄλοχον, οὔποτ᾽ αἰνέσω
οὐδ᾽ ἂν προσείποιμ᾽, οὐδὲ σὲ ζηλῶ κακῆς
γυναικὸς ἐλθόνθ᾽ οὕνεκ᾽ ἐς Τροίας πέδον.
ἀμυνῶ δ᾽ ὅσονπερ δυνατός εἰμι τῷ νόμῳ,
τὸ θηριῶδες τοῦτο καὶ μιαιφόνον

525 παύων, ὃ καὶ γῆν καὶ πόλεις ὄλλυσ᾽ ἀεί.
  ἐπεὶ τίν᾽ εἶχες, ὦ τάλας, ψυχὴν τότε,
ὅτ᾽ ἐξέβαλλε μαστὸν ἱκετεύουσά σε
μήτηρ; ἐγὼ μὲν οὐκ ἰδὼν τἀκεῖ κακὰ
δακρύοις γέροντ᾽ ὀφθαλμὸν ἐκτήκω τάλας.

530 ἐν γοῦν λόγοισι τοῖς ἐμοῖς ὁμορροθεῖ·
μισῇ γε πρὸς θεῶν καὶ τίνεις μητρὸς δίκας,
μανίαις ἀλαίνων καὶ φόβοις. τί μαρτύρων
ἄλλων ἀκούειν δεῖ μ᾽, ἅ γ᾽ εἰσορᾶν πάρα;
ὡς οὖν ἂν εἰδῆς, Μενέλεως, τοῖσιν θεοῖς

535 μὴ πρᾶσσ᾽ ἐναντί᾽, ὠφελεῖν τοῦτον θέλων,
[ἔα δ᾽ ὑπ᾽ ἀστῶν καταφονευθῆναι πέτροις
ἢ μὴ ᾽πίβαινε Σπαρτιάτιδος χθονός.]
θυγάτηρ δ᾽ ἐμὴ θανοῦσ᾽ ἔπραξεν ἔνδικα·
ἀλλ᾽ οὐχὶ πρὸς τοῦδ᾽ εἰκὸς ἦν αὐτὴν θανεῖν.

540 ἐγὼ δὲ τἄλλα μακάριος πέφυκ᾽ ἀνὴρ
πλὴν ἐς θυγατέρας· τοῦτο δ᾽ οὐκ εὐδαιμονῶ.

530 γοῦν Schaefer: οὖν C: σὺν Willink

was to be restored. Otherwise someone would always be guilty of bloodshed by taking the most recent uncleanness upon his himself.

Now I hate ungodly women, and before all others my daughter who killed her husband. I shall never praise your wife Helen, never speak to her, and I pity you for going to Troy to get back such a wicked creature. But as far as in me lies I will come to the aid of the law by trying to curb sub-human and murderous conduct like this, which always brings countries and cities to ruin.

What was in your mind, hard-hearted wretch, when your own mother supplicated you and bared her breast? Though I was not there to see this calamity, my poor aged eyes run with tears.

One fact, at any rate, supports my argument: you are clearly hated by the gods and are paying the penalty for your mother's death by wandering about in fits of madness and terror. Why should I listen to the witness of others when I can see for myself?

Menelaus, let me make my meaning plain: do not act contrary to the gods by trying to help this man. [Let him be stoned to death by the citizens! Otherwise tread no more on Spartan soil.] My daughter's death was just deserts, but her death at *his* hands was wrong. I am fortunate in all else except my daughters: there I am unlucky.

536–7 [=625–6] del. Brunck

ΧΟΡΟΣ

ΧΟΡΟΣ

ζηλωτὸς ὅστις ηὐτύχησεν ἐς τέκνα
καὶ μὴ 'πισήμους συμφορὰς ἐκτήσατο.

ΟΡΕΣΤΗΣ

ὦ γέρον, ἐγώ τοι πρὸς σὲ δειμαίνω λέγειν
545 [ὅπου σε μέλλω σήν τε λυπήσειν φρένα]·
ἐγᾦδ', ἀνόσιός εἰμι μητέρα κτανών,
ὅσιος δέ γ' ἕτερον ὄνομα, τιμωρῶν πατρί.
ἀπελθέτω δὲ τοῖς λόγοισιν ἐκποδὼν
τὸ γῆρας ἡμῖν τὸ σόν, ὅ μ' ἐκπλήσσει λόγου,
550 καὶ καθ' ὁδὸν εἶμι· νῦν δὲ σὴν ταρβῶ τρίχα.
    τί χρῆν με δρᾶσαι; δύο γὰρ ἀντίθες δυοῖν·
πατὴρ μὲν ἐφύτευσέν με, σὴ δ' ἔτικτε παῖς,
τὸ σπέρμ' ἄρουρα παραλαβοῦσ' ἄλλου πάρα.
[ἄνευ δὲ πατρὸς τέκνον οὐκ εἴη ποτ' ἄν.
555 ἐλογισάμην οὖν τῷ γένους ἀρχηγέτῃ
μᾶλλόν μ' ἀμῦναι τῆς ὑποστάσης τροφάς.]
ἡ σὴ δὲ θυγάτηρ (μητέρ' αἰδοῦμαι λέγειν)
ἰδίοισιν ὑμεναίοισι κοὐχὶ σώφροσιν
ἐς ἀνδρὸς ἤει λέκτρ'· ἐμαυτόν, ἢν λέγω
560 κακῶς ἐκείνην, αἰσχρ' ἐρῶ· λέξω δ' ὅμως·
Αἴγισθος ἦν οἱ κρυπτὸς ἐν δόμοις πόσις.
τοῦτον κατέκτειν', ἐπὶ δ' ἔθυσα μητέρα,
ἀνόσια μὲν δρῶν, ἀλλὰ τιμωρῶν πατρί.
[ἐφ' οἷς δ' ἀπειλεῖς ὡς πετρωθῆναί με χρή,
565 ἄκουσον ὡς ἅπασαν Ἑλλάδ' ὠφελῶ.
εἰ γὰρ γυναῖκες ἐς τόδ' ἥξουσιν θράσους,

CHORUS LEADER

Enviable is the man who has been lucky in his children, not
got ones who are disasters for all to mark!

ORESTES

(*rising to his feet*) Old sir, I am afraid to speak to you
[where I am likely to vex you and your heart]. I realize that
I am unholy since I killed my mother, yet by another de-
scription I am holy for avenging my father. But let your
reverend old age no longer stand in the way of my speech,
and I can go on, though at this moment I stand in awe of
your gray head. (*Tyndareus motions for him to proceed.*)

What should I have done? Set two facts against two
others. My father engendered me, and my mother, plough-
land receiving the seed from another, gave me birth.
[Without a father there could never be a child. I reckoned
that I should come to the defense of the author of my be-
getting rather than of her who gave me nourishment.] But
your daughter (I cannot bring myself to call her mother)
with nuptials private and unchaste went to a man's bed. If I
speak ill of her my words will bring disgrace on myself, but
nonetheless I shall speak: Aegisthus was her secret hus-
band in the house. Him I killed, and after that made a sac-
rifice of my mother, doing an unholy act, to be sure, but
avenging my father. [As for those deeds for which you say I
deserve stoning, hear what a service I am rendering all of
Greece. If women are going to be brazen enough to kill

---

545 del. Paley cl. 608   546 ἐγῷδ’ Hermann: ἐγὼ δ’ C
548 δὲ Paley: δὴ C   554–6 del. Paley (554 iam Nauck)
560 αἴσχρ’ ἐρῶ Kovacs: ἐξερῶ C
561 οἱ Nauck: ὁ C   v. del. Reeve
564–71 del. Kovacs

ἄνδρας φονεύειν, καταφυγὰς ποιούμεναι
ἐς τέκνα, μαστοῖς τὸν ἔλεον θηρώμεναι,
παρ᾽ οὐδὲν αὐταῖς ἦν ἂν ὀλλύναι πόσεις
570 ἐπίκλημ᾽ ἐχούσαις ὅ τι τύχοι. δράσας δ᾽ ἐγὼ
δείν᾽, ὡς σὺ κομπεῖς, τόνδ᾽ ἔπαυσα τὸν νόμον.]
μισῶν δὲ μητέρ᾽ ἐνδίκως ἀπώλεσα,
ἥτις μεθ᾽ ὅπλων ἄνδρ᾽ ἀπόντ᾽ ἐκ δωμάτων
πάσης ὑπὲρ γῆς Ἑλλάδος στρατηλάτην
575 προύδωκε κοὐκ ἔσωσ᾽ ἀκήρατον λέχος·
ἐπεὶ δ᾽ ἁμαρτοῦσ᾽ ᾔσθετ᾽, οὐχ αὑτῇ δίκην
ἐπέθηκεν, ἀλλ᾽, ὡς μὴ δίκην δοίη πόσει,
ἐζημίωσε πατέρα κἀπέκτειν᾽ ἐμόν.
πρὸς θεῶν—ἐν οὐ καλῷ μὲν ἐμνήσθην θεῶν,
580 φόνου δικαστῶν· εἰ δὲ δὴ τὰ μητέρος
σιγῶν ἐπῄνουν, τί μ᾽ ἂν ἔδρασ᾽ ὁ κατθανών;
οὐκ ἄν με μισῶν ἀνεχόρευ᾽ Ἐρινύσιν;
ἢ μητρὶ μὲν πάρεισι σύμμαχοι θεαί,
584 τῷ δ᾽ οὐ πάρεισι, μᾶλλον ἠδικημένῳ;
588 [ὁρᾷς, Ὀδυσσέως ἄλοχον οὐ κατέκτανεν
Τηλέμαχος· οὐ γὰρ ἐπεγάμει πόσει πόσιν,
590 μένει δ᾽ ἐν οἴκοις ὑγιὲς εὐνατήριον.]
ὁρᾷς Ἀπόλλω γ᾽, ὃς μεσομφάλους ἕδρας
ναίων βροτοῖσι στόμα νέμει σαφέστατον
καὶ πειθόμεσθα πάνθ᾽ ὅσ᾽ ἂν κεῖνος λέγῃ·
τούτῳ πιθόμενος τὴν τεκοῦσαν ἔκτανον.
595 ἐκεῖνον ἡγεῖσθ᾽ ἀνόσιον καὶ κτείνετε·
ἐκεῖνος ἥμαρτ᾽, οὐκ ἐγώ. τί χρῆν με δρᾶν;

their husbands, taking refuge with their children, appealing for pity by showing their breasts, it would be a trifle for them to kill their husbands for any grievance whatever. By doing dread deeds, as you proclaim them to be, I put a stop to this practice.] I had just cause to hate my mother and kill her. Her husband was away from home under arms, leading all of Greece. She betrayed him and did not keep the chastity of her bed. And when she realized that she had sinned, she did not lay a penalty on herself but, so that she would not be punished by her husband, she punished my father with death.

In the gods' name—it is untimely of me to mention the gods, who sit in judgment over murder, but still—if I had acquiesced in my mother's actions, what would the dead man have done to me? Would he not hate me, and would not *his* Erinyes be making me leap about? Does my mother have goddesses to fight for her while he, having suffered greater wrongs, has none? [Do you see? Telemachus did not kill Odysseus' wife: she did not take an additional husband but remained a faithful wife.]

Do you see Apollo, who dwells in his sanctuary at the earth's navel[18] and gives utterance most reliable to mortals, and whom we obey in all he says? It was in obedience to him that I killed my mother. Consider *him* unholy, put *him* to death! It was he who acted wrongfully, not I. What

---

[18] See note to line 331 above.

---

580 φόνου δικαστῶν Willink: φόνου δικάζων C: φόνου δικαιῶν Weil   588–90 del. Hartung

591 Ἀπόλλω γ᾽ Willink: -λλων᾽ C

593 καὶ Weil: ᾧ C   v. del. Nauck

ἢ οὐκ ἀξιόχρεως ὁ θεὸς ἀναφέροντί μοι
μίασμα λῦσαι; ποῖ τις οὖν ἔτ’ ἂν φύγοι,
599 εἰ μὴ κελεύσας ῥύσεταί με μὴ θανεῖν;
585 σύ τοι φυτεύσας θυγατέρ’, ὦ γέρον, κακὴν
ἀπώλεσάς με· διὰ τὸ κείνης γὰρ θράσος
587 πατρὸς στερηθεὶς ἐγενόμην μητροκτόνος.
600 ἀλλ’ ὡς μὲν οὐκ εὖ μὴ λέγ’ εἴργασται τάδε,
ἡμῖν δὲ τοῖς δράσασιν οὐκ εὐδαιμόνως.
[γάμοι δ’ ὅσοις μὲν εὖ καθεστᾶσιν βροτῶν,
μακάριος αἰών· οἷς δὲ μὴ πίπτουσιν εὖ,
τά τ’ ἔνδον εἰσὶ τά τε θύραζε δυστυχεῖς.]

605 ἀεὶ γυναῖκες ἐμποδὼν ταῖς συμφοραῖς
ἔφυσαν ἀνδρῶν πρὸς τὸ δυσχερέστερον.

ἐπεὶ θρασύνῃ κοὐχ ὑποστέλλῃ λόγῳ,
οὕτω δ’ ἀμείβῃ μ’ ὥστε μ’ ἀλγῆσαι φρένα,
μᾶλλόν μ’ ἀνάψεις ἐπὶ σὸν ἐξελθεῖν φόνον·
610 καλὸν πάρεργον δ’ αὐτὸ θήσομαι πόνων
ὧν οὕνεκ’ ἦλθον θυγατρὶ κοσμήσων τάφον·
μολὼν γὰρ εἰς ἔκκλητον Ἀργείων ὄχλον
ἑκοῦσαν οὐκ ἄκουσαν ἐπισείσω πόλιν
σοὶ σῇ τ’ ἀδελφῇ, λεύσιμον δοῦναι δίκην.
615 μᾶλλον δ’ ἐκείνη σοῦ θανεῖν ἐστ’ ἀξία,
ἢ τῇ τεκούσῃ σ’ ἠγρίωσ’, ἐς οὖς ἀεὶ
πέμπουσα μύθους ἐπὶ τὸ δυσμενέστερον,

should I have done? Is the god not sufficient to clear my pollution if I cite his authority? Where can anyone take refuge if the god, having given me the order, will not save me from death?

It was you, old sir, who were my undoing since you begot a wicked daughter. Because of her wantonness I was deprived of my father and became a matricide. So say not that this was a bad deed, only that it turned out miserably for the doer. [For mortals whose marriages are established on a good footing, life is blessed. But if marriage does not turn out well, their affairs both within and without are unblest.]

CHORUS LEADER

Women are always an encumbrance to the affairs of men and make life harder to manage.

TYNDAREUS

Since you are brazening it out, not curbing your tongue but answering me so as to wound my heart, you fire me up all the more to go after your death. Here's a fine extra to the task I came here to do, the task of adorning my daughter's tomb: I shall go to the Argive assembly and incite the city to attack you and your sister with all their will, so that you are stoned to death. She deserves to die more than you do. She put you in a mad rage against your mother by always whispering stories in your ear to make you hate her, telling

---

599 μὴ Porson: μὴ ὁ C
585–7 ante 600 trai. Kovacs, post 578 Diggle, del. Reeve
602–4 del. Herwerden
613 οὐχ ἑκοῦσαν Canter

ὄνειδος ἀγγέλλουσα τἀγαμέμνονος
καὶ τοῦθ' ὃ μισήσειαν Αἰγίσθου λέχος

620 οἱ νέρτεροι θεοί (καὶ γὰρ ἐνθάδ' ἦν πικρόν),
ἕως ὑφῆψε δῶμ' ἀνηφαίστῳ πυρί.
   Μενέλαε, σοὶ δὲ τάδε λέγω δράσω τε πρός·
εἰ τοὐμὸν ἔχθος ἐναριθμῇ κῆδός τ' ἐμόν,
μὴ τῷδ' ἀμύνειν φόνον, ἐναντίον θεοῖς,

625 ἔα δ' ὑπ' ἀστῶν καταφονευθῆναι πέτροις,
ἢ μὴ 'πίβαινε Σπαρτιάτιδος χθονός.
τοσαῦτ' ἀκούσας ἴσθι, μηδὲ δυσσεβεῖς
ἕλη, παρώσας εὐσεβεστέρους φίλους·
ἡμᾶς δ' ἀπ' οἴκων ἄγετε τῶνδε, πρόσπολοι.

ΟΡΕΣΤΗΣ

630 στεῖχ', ὡς ἀθορύβως οὑπιὼν ἡμῖν λόγος
πρὸς τόνδ' ἵκηται, γῆρας ἀποφυγὼν τὸ σόν.
   Μενέλαε, ποῖ σὸν πόδ' ἐπὶ συννοίᾳ κυκλεῖς,
διπλῆς μερίμνης διπτύχους ἰὼν ὁδούς;

ΜΕΝΕΛΑΟΣ

ἔασον· ἐν ἐμαυτῷ τι συννοούμενος
635 ὅπῃ τράπωμαι τῆς τύχης ἀμηχανῶ.

ΟΡΕΣΤΗΣ

μή νυν πέραινε τὴν δόκησιν, ἀλλ' ἐμοὺς
λόγους ἀκούσας πρόσθε βουλεύου τότε.

618 ὄνειδος Willink: ὀνείρατ' C
624 ἀμύνων . . . ἐναντίου Broadhead

478

you reproachfully of Agamemnon's fate and Clytaemestra's affair with Aegisthus (may the gods below visit it with their hatred since even up here it was hard to bear) until she set the whole house alight with a fire not of Hephaestus' making.

Menelaus, these are my words to you, and I will make them good: if you set any store by my hostility, the hostility of a father-in-law, do not protect Orestes from death in opposition to the gods. Let him be stoned to death by the citizens! Otherwise, tread no more on Spartan soil. Mark that you have heard this much from me, and do not choose unholy friends and thrust aside godly ones. Servants, lead me away from this house!

Exit TYNDAREUS *with attendants by Eisodos B. Menelaus paces back and forth in thought.*

ORESTES
(*to Tyndareus' retreating back*) Be off! That way my next words to Menelaus can proceed without interruption, freed from your aged presence!

Menelaus, why are you walking back and forth so lost in thought, treading the twofold path of dilemma?

MENELAUS
Let me be: I am pondering something within me and at a loss which path to take in what has happened.

ORESTES
Well don't keep on pondering: first hear what I have to say and then deliberate.

ΜΕΝΕΛΑΟΣ

λέγ'· εὖ γὰρ εἶπας· ἔστιν οὗ σιγὴ λόγου
κρείσσων γένοιτ' ἄν, ἔστι δ' οὗ σιγῆς λόγος.

ΟΡΕΣΤΗΣ

640 λέγοιμ' ἂν ἤδη. τὰ μακρὰ τῶν σμικρῶν λόγων
ἐπίπροσθέν ἐστι καὶ σαφῆ μᾶλλον κλυεῖν.
    ἐμοὶ σὺ τῶν σῶν, Μενέλεως, μηδὲν δίδου,
ἃ δ' ἔλαβες ἀπόδος πατρὸς ἐμοῦ λαβὼν πάρα.
οὐ χρήματ' εἶπον· χρήματ', ἢν ψυχὴν ἐμὴν
645 σώσῃς, ἅπερ μοι φίλτατ' ἐστὶ τῶν ἐμῶν.
    ἀδικῶ· λαβεῖν χρή μ' ἀντὶ τοῦδε τοῦ κακοῦ
ἄδικόν τι παρὰ σοῦ· καὶ γὰρ Ἀγαμέμνων πατὴρ
ἀδίκως ἀθροίσας Ἑλλάδ' ἦλθ' ὑπ' Ἴλιον,
οὐκ ἐξαμαρτὼν αὐτὸς ἀλλ' ἁμαρτίαν
650 τῆς σῆς γυναικὸς ἀδικίαν τ' ἰώμενος.
652 ἀπέδοτο δ', ὡς χρὴ τοῖς φίλοισι τοὺς φίλους,
τὸ σῶμ' ἀληθῶς, σοὶ παρ' ἀσπίδ' ἐκπονῶν,
ὅπως σὺ τὴν σὴν ἀπολάβοις ξυνάορον.
655 ἀπότεισον οὖν μοι ταὐτὸ τοῦτ' ἐκεῖ λαβών,
μίαν πονήσας ἡμέραν, ἡμῶν ὕπερ
657 σωτήριος στάς, μὴ δέκ' ἐκπλήσας ἔτη.
651 ἓν μὲν τόδ' ἡμῖν ἀνθ' ἑνὸς δοῦναί σε χρή.
658 ἃ δ' Αὐλὶς ἔλαβε σφάγι' ἐμῆς ὁμοσπόρου,
ἐῶ σ' ἔχειν ταῦθ'· Ἑρμιόνην μὴ κτεῖνε σύ.
660 δεῖ γάρ σ' ἐμοῦ πράσσοντος ὡς πράσσω τὰ νῦν
πλέον φέρεσθαι κἀμὲ συγγνώμην ἔχειν.
ψυχὴν δ' ἐμὴν δὸς τῷ ταλαιπώρῳ πατρί

MENELAUS

That is good advice. Speak: sometimes speech is better than silence, sometimes silence than speech.

ORESTES

Then I will speak. Long speeches are better than short ones, more convincing to listen to.

Menelaus, do not offer me anything of your own, but merely give back to me what you received from my father. I do not mean possessions: if you save my life, that is the dearest of my possessions.

What I have done is wrong. It is fair that I receive some wrong at your hands in return for this evil. And in fact my father Agamemnon did wrong when he mustered Greece and went to Troy: he did not go astray himself but was trying to put right the straying and wrongdoing of your wife. And he made over his person to you, the way one kinsman should to another, by standing next to your shield in battle so that you might get your wife back. Repay to me the favor you received at Troy by toiling for a single day, not ten years, and standing as champion on my behalf.

This is a gift you must give me in exchange for a gift. As for the victim that Aulis exacted in my sister, I give you leave to keep it: no need to kill Hermione.[19] You are bound to get the better of me in my present circumstances, and I am bound to acquiesce. But grant to my unlucky father the

[19] I. e. Menelaus need not sacrifice his daughter as Agamemnon did his.

---

638 ἔστιν Kirchhoff: ἔστι δ᾽ C   640–1 del. Bothe cl. Σ
644–5 del. Diggle   651 post 657 trai. Paley

[κἀμῆς ἀδελφῆς, παρθένου μακρὸν χρόνον]·
θανὼν γὰρ οἶκον ὀρφανὸν λείψω πατρός.
665 ἐρεῖς· ἀδύνατον. αὐτὸ τοῦτο· τοὺς φίλους
ἐν τοῖς κακοῖς χρὴ τοῖς φίλοισιν ὠφελεῖν·
ὅταν δ' ὁ δαίμων εὖ διδῷ, τί δεῖ φίλων;
ἀρκεῖ γὰρ αὐτὸς ὁ θεὸς ὠφελεῖν θέλων.

φιλεῖν δάμαρτα πᾶσιν Ἕλλησιν δοκεῖς·
670 κοὐχ ὑποτρέχων σε τοῦτο θωπείᾳ λέγω·
ταύτης ἱκνοῦμαί σ'—ὦ μέλεος ἐγώ, κακὸν
ἐς οἷον ἥκω. τί δέ; ταλαιπωρεῖν με δεῖ·
ὑπὲρ γὰρ οἴκου παντὸς ἱκετεύω τάδε.
ὦ πατρὸς ὅμαιμε θεῖε, τὸν κατὰ χθονὸς
675 θανόντ' ἀκούειν τάδε δόκει, ποτωμένην
ψυχὴν ὑπὲρ σοῦ, καὶ λέγειν ἁγὼ λέγω.
[ταῦτ' ἔς τε δάκρυα καὶ γόους καὶ συμφορὰς]
εἴρηκα κἀπήτηκα, τὴν σωτηρίαν
θηρῶν, ὃ πάντες κοὐκ ἐγὼ ζητῶ μόνος.

ΧΟΡΟΣ

680 κἀγώ σ' ἱκνοῦμαι καὶ γυνή περ οὖσ' ὅμως
τοῖς δεομένοισιν ὠφελεῖν· οἷός τε δ' εἶ.

ΜΕΝΕΛΑΟΣ

Ὀρέστ', ἐγώ τοι σὸν καταιδοῦμαι κάρα
καὶ ξυμπονῆσαι σοῖς κακοῖσι βούλομαι.
καὶ χρὴ γὰρ οὕτω τῶν ὁμαιμόνων κακὰ
685 συνεκκομίζειν, δύναμιν ἢν διδῷ θεός
[θνῄσκοντα καὶ κτείνοντα τοὺς ἐναντίους].
τοῦ δ' αὖ δύνασθαι πρὸς θεῶν χρῄζω τυχεῖν·

gift of my life [and that of my sister, so long a maiden]. For if I die, I leave my father's house orphaned.

You will say "Impossible." Precisely: it is in hard times that near and dear should help near and dear. When heaven is blessing you, what need for friends? The god's willingness to help is enough by itself.

All Greece thinks that you love your wife: and I do not say this to wheedle or flatter you. (*kneeling in supplication*) In her name I beg you—O poor me, to what misery I have come! But what of it? I must endure misery and make this supplication for the sake of the whole house. Uncle, my father's own brother, imagine that the dead man beneath the earth hears all this! Imagine him as a soul hovering over you, speaking my words!

[These things for tears and sighs and misfortunes] I have spoken, I have made my plea, trying to save my life, a thing all men, and not I alone, try to win.

CHORUS LEADER

I too beseech you, though I am a woman, to come to the aid of those who ask it: it lies in your power.

MENELAUS

Orestes, of course I respect your claims, and I want to share your misfortunes with you. For that is the way one *should* endure one's relatives' troubles, if heaven gives one the power [by fighting the enemy to the death]. But the power to do so—that I need to get from the gods.

---

663 del. Paley
671 κακὸν Wecklein et Σ: κακῶν C
677 suspectum hab. Wecklein, del. Biehl
686 del. Hermann

ἥκω γὰρ ἀνδρῶν συμμάχων κενὸν δόρυ
ἔχων, πόνοισι μυρίοις ἀλώμενος,
690 σμικρᾷ σὺν ἀλκῇ τῶν λελειμμένων φίλων.
μάχῃ μὲν οὖν ἂν οὐχ ὑπερβαλοίμεθα
Πελασγὸν Ἄργος· εἰ δὲ μαλθακοῖς λόγοις
δυναίμεθ᾽, ἐνταῦθ᾽ ἐλπίδος προήκομεν.
[σμικροῖσι †μὲν γὰρ τὰ† μεγάλα πῶς ἕλοι τις ἂν
695 πόνοισιν; ἀμαθὲς καὶ τὸ βούλεσθαι τάδε.]
ὅταν γὰρ ἡβᾷ δῆμος εἰς ὀργὴν πεσών,
ὅμοιον ὥστε πῦρ κατασβέσαι λάβρον·
εἰ δ᾽ ἡσύχως τις αὐτὸν ἐντείνοντι μὲν
χαλῶν ὑπείκοι καιρὸν εὐλαβούμενος,
700 ἴσως ἂν ἐκπνεύσειεν· ὅτε δ᾽ ἀνῇ πνοάς,
τύχοις ἂν αὐτοῦ ῥᾳδίως ὅσον θέλεις.
[ἔνεστι δ᾽ οἶκτος, ἔνι δὲ καὶ θυμὸς μέγας,
καραδοκοῦντι κτῆμα τιμιώτατον.
ἐλθὼν δὲ Τυνδάρεών τέ σοι πειράσομαι
705 πόλιν τε πεῖσαι τῷ λίαν χρῆσθαι καλῶς.]
καὶ ναῦς γὰρ ἐνταθεῖσα πρὸς βίαν ποδὶ
ἔβαψεν, ἔστη δ᾽ αὖθις ἢν χαλᾷ πόδα.
μισεῖ γὰρ ὁ θεὸς τὰς ἄγαν προθυμίας,
μισοῦσι δ᾽ ἀστοί· δεῖ δέ μ᾽ (οὐκ ἄλλως λέγω)
710 σῴζειν σε σοφίᾳ, μὴ βίᾳ τῶν κρεισσόνων.
ἀλκῇ δέ σ᾽ οὐκ ἄν, ᾗ σὺ δοξάζεις ἴσως,
σώσαιμ᾽ ἄν· οὐ γὰρ ῥᾴδιον λόγχῃ μιᾷ
στῆσαι τροπαῖα τῶν κακῶν ἅ σοι πάρα.
οὐ γάρ ποτ᾽ ⟨ἐκ τ⟩ἄργου γ᾽ ἂν ἐς τὸ μαλθακὸν
715 προσηγόμεσθα· νῦν δ᾽ ἀναγκαίως ἔχει

The spear I came home with lacks allies, and I have but little defense in my few remaining comrades: I have been a wanderer beset with many troubles. So we cannot beat Pelasgian Argos in a fight. Whether we might do so with soothing words—that is as far as my hope extends. [How can one overcome great things by slender efforts? Even to try is foolish.] When the common people fall into a rage and feel their vigor, it is like trying to put out a raging fire. But if in the face of their fury you yourself slacken and give way, watching for the proper moment, their rage may blow itself out, and then when the storm has let up, you can get whatever you want from them. [There is pity there, and there is also towering rage, a most valuable thing for a man who waits. I will go and try to persuade Tyndareus and the city to make good use of their excessiveness.] For a ship too, if its sheet is too vigorously tightened, goes under, but slacken it and the ship will right itself. Heaven hates excessive zeal, and so do the citizens. And I must save you (I cannot deny it) not in the teeth of superior force but by clever words. I cannot save your life by armed might, as you perhaps suppose. It's no easy feat to master by a single spear the woes that are besetting you. I would not be led to adopt such a soft policy ⟨out of⟩ idleness: but as things stand it is

---

694–5 del. Weil (695 iam Brunck)

698 αὐτῷ τις Markland   700 ὅτε Kirchhoff: ὅταν C

702–3 del. Hartung   704–5 del. Kovacs

705 πείσας Hermann

711–3 suspectos habuit Wecklein

714 ⟨ἐκ τ⟩ἀργοῦ Willink (ἀργοῦ γρΣ): Ἄργους C   γ' ἂν Willink: γαῖαν C

485

δούλοισιν εἶναι τοῖς σοφοῖσι τῆς τύχης.

ΟΡΕΣΤΗΣ

ὦ πλὴν γυναικὸς οὕνεκα στρατηλατεῖν
718 τἄλλ᾽ οὐδέν, ὦ κάκιστε, τιμωρεῖν φίλοις,
720 φεύγεις ἀποστραφείς με, τὰ δ᾽ Ἀγαμέμνονος
φροῦδ᾽; ἄφιλος ἦσθ᾽ ἄρ᾽, ὦ πάτερ, πράσσων κακῶς.
οἴμοι, προδέδομαι, κοὐκέτ᾽ εἰσὶν ἐλπίδες
ὅπῃ τραπόμενος θάνατον Ἀργείων φύγω·
οὗτος γὰρ ἦν μοι καταφυγὴ σωτηρίας.
725 ἀλλ᾽ εἰσορῶ γὰρ τόνδε φίλτατον βροτῶν
Πυλάδην δρόμῳ στείχοντα Φωκέων ἄπο,
ἡδεῖαν ὄψιν· πιστὸς ἐν κακοῖς ἀνὴρ
κρείσσων γαλήνης ναυτίλοισιν εἰσορᾶν.

ΠΥΛΑΔΗΣ

θᾶσσον ἤ μ᾽ ἐχρῆν προβαίνων ἱκόμην δι᾽ ἄστεως,
730 σύλλογον πόλεως ἀκούσας ὄντ᾽, ἰδὼν δ᾽ αὐτὸς
σαφῶς,
ἐπὶ σὲ σύγγονόν τε τὴν σήν, ὡς κτενοῦντας αὐτίκα.
τί τάδε; πῶς ἔχεις; τί πράσσεις, φίλταθ᾽ ἡλίκων
ἐμοὶ
καὶ φίλων καὶ συγγενείας; πάντα γὰρ τάδ᾽ εἶ σύ
μοι.

ΟΡΕΣΤΗΣ

οἰχόμεσθ᾽, ὡς ἐν βραχεῖ σοι τἀμὰ δηλώσω κακά.

719 vide ad 499
730 ὄντ᾽ Cron: τὸν δ᾽ C
731 del. Herwerden

486

necessary for the wise to take orders from fortune.

Exit MENELAUS *by Eisodos A, breaking Orestes' suppliant grasp.*

ORESTES
(*rising to his feet*) Coward, no good at defending your kin except by leading an army to get back a woman, are you turning away from me and running? Have Agamemnon's favors to you vanished? So you really are friendless, father, in your misfortune! Oh, I have been abandoned! I have no hope, no place I can turn to escape an Argive death! He was my life-saving refuge.

Enter PYLADES, *running, by Eisodos B.*

But here I see Pylades, my dearest friend, coming at a run from Phocis! A welcome sight he is: when you are in trouble a loyal friend is a fairer sight than clear skies to a sailor.

PYLADES
Exceeding all proper speed I have come through the town. I heard that an assembly of the citizens was taking place— and I saw it with my own eyes—against you and your sister, and that they mean to kill you right away. What is going on? How are you faring, what's your state, dearest of agemates and friends and kinsmen? You are all that to me.

ORESTES
I am done for: you have my plight in brief.

ΠΥΛΑΔΗΣ

735 συγκατασκάπτοις ἂν ἡμᾶς· κοινὰ γὰρ τὰ τῶν
φίλων.

ΟΡΕΣΤΗΣ

Μενέλεως κάκιστος ἐς ἐμὲ καὶ κασιγνήτην ἐμήν . . .

ΠΥΛΑΔΗΣ

εἰκότως, κακῆς γυναικὸς ἄνδρα γίγνεσθαι κακόν.

ΟΡΕΣΤΗΣ

. . . ὥσπερ οὐκ ἐλθὼν ἔμοιγε ταὐτὸν ἀπέδωκεν
μολών.

ΠΥΛΑΔΗΣ

ἦ γάρ ἐστιν ὡς ἀληθῶς τήνδ᾽ ἀφιγμένος χθόνα;

ΟΡΕΣΤΗΣ

740 χρόνιος· ἀλλ᾽ ὅμως τάχιστα κακὸς ἐφωράθη φίλοις.

ΠΥΛΑΔΗΣ

καὶ δάμαρτα τὴν κακίστην ναυστολῶν ἐλήλυθεν;

ΟΡΕΣΤΗΣ

οὐκ ἐκεῖνος· ἀλλ᾽ ἐκείνη κεῖνον ἐνθάδ᾽ ἤγαγεν.

ΠΥΛΑΔΗΣ

ποῦ 'στιν ἢ πλείστους Ἀχαιῶν ὤλεσεν γυνὴ μία;

ΟΡΕΣΤΗΣ

ἐν δόμοις ἐμοῖσιν, εἰ δὴ τούσδ᾽ ἐμοὺς καλεῖν χρεών.

ΠΥΛΑΔΗΣ

745 σὺ δὲ τίνας λόγους ἔλεξας σοῦ κασιγνήτῳ πατρός;

ORESTES

PYLADES

You bring me crashing down as well if that is true: friends
share everything.

ORESTES

Menelaus, cowardly where my sister and I are concerned
. . .

PYLADES

It's only to be expected that a bad woman should have a bad
husband.

ORESTES

. . . has come, but he's done me as little good as if he'd
stayed away.

PYLADES

Has he really arrived in this country?

ORESTES

He was long in coming: but in no time he has been shown
up as disloyal to his kin.

PYLADES

And has he come with his vile wife in tow?

ORESTES

No, not he: it was *she* who brought *him* here.

PYLADES

Where is she, the one woman who killed so many of the
Achaeans?

ORESTES

In my house, if one may call it mine.

PYLADES

What pleas did you make to your father's brother?

EURIPIDES

ΟΡΕΣΤΗΣ

μή μ' ἰδεῖν θανόνθ' ὑπ' ἀστῶν καὶ κασιγνήτην
ἐμήν.

ΠΥΛΑΔΗΣ

πρὸς θεῶν, τί πρὸς τάδ' εἶπε; τόδε γὰρ εἰδέναι
θέλω.

ΟΡΕΣΤΗΣ

ηὐλαβεῖθ', ὃ τοῖς φίλοισι δρῶσιν οἱ κακοὶ φίλοι.

ΠΥΛΑΔΗΣ

σκῆψιν ἐς ποίαν προβαίνων; τοῦτο πάντ' ἔχω
μαθών.

ΟΡΕΣΤΗΣ

750 οὗτος ἦλθ', ὁ τὰς ἀρίστας θυγατέρας σπείρας
πατήρ.

ΠΥΛΑΔΗΣ

Τυνδάρεων λέγεις· ἴσως σοι θυγατέρος θυμούμενος.

ΟΡΕΣΤΗΣ

αἰσθάνῃ. τὸ τοῦδε κῆδος μᾶλλον εἵλετ' ἢ πατρός.

ΠΥΛΑΔΗΣ

κοὐκ ἐτόλμησεν πόνων σῶν ἀντιλάζυσθαι παρών;

ΟΡΕΣΤΗΣ

οὐ γὰρ αἰχμητὴς πέφυκεν, ἐν γυναιξὶ δ' ἄλκιμος.

ΠΥΛΑΔΗΣ

755 ἐν κακοῖς ἄρ' εἶ μεγίστοις· καί σ' ἀναγκαῖον θανεῖν;

ORESTES

Not to look on while my sister and I are put to death by the citizens.

PYLADES

In heaven's name, what did he say to that? I'd like to hear.

ORESTES

He was cautious: that's what the base are like with their friends.

PYLADES

What excuse did he put forward? If I learn this I know the whole story.

ORESTES

That man arrived, he of the peerless daughters.

PYLADES

You mean Tyndareus. Angry no doubt about his daughter.

ORESTES

You've got it. Menelaus preferred his father-in-law to my father.

PYLADES

Did he not have the courage to stand by you and share your troubles?

ORESTES

No, he's no born warrior. A brave man he is—among the ladies.

PYLADES

Then you're in terrible trouble. Is there no escape from death?

ΟΡΕΣΤΗΣ

ψῆφον ἀμφ᾽ ἡμῶν πολίτας ἐπὶ φόνῳ θέσθαι χρεών.

ΠΥΛΑΔΗΣ

ἦ κρινεῖ τί χρῆμα; λέξον· διὰ φόβου γὰρ ἔρχομαι.

ΟΡΕΣΤΗΣ

ἢ θανεῖν ἢ ζῆν· ὁ μῦθος οὐ μακρὸς μακρῶν πέρι.

ΠΥΛΑΔΗΣ

φεῦγέ νυν λιπὼν μέλαθρα σὺν κασιγνήτῃ σέθεν.

ΟΡΕΣΤΗΣ

760 οὐχ ὁρᾷς; φυλασσόμεσθα φρουρίοισι πανταχῇ.

ΠΥΛΑΔΗΣ

εἶδον ἄστεως ἀγυιὰς τεύχεσιν πεφαργμένας.

ΟΡΕΣΤΗΣ

ὡσπερεὶ πόλις πρὸς ἐχθρῶν σῶμα πυργηρούμεθα.

ΠΥΛΑΔΗΣ

κἀμὲ νῦν ὅρα τί πάσχω· καὶ γὰρ αὐτὸς οἴχομαι.

ΟΡΕΣΤΗΣ

πρὸς τίνος; τοῦτ᾽ ἂν προσείη τοῖς ἐμοῖς κακοῖς
κακόν.

ΠΥΛΑΔΗΣ

765 Στρόφιος ἤλασέν μ᾽ ἀπ᾽ οἴκων φυγάδα θυμωθεὶς
πατήρ.

ΟΡΕΣΤΗΣ

ἴδιον ἢ κοινὸν πολίταις ἐπιφέρων ἔγκλημα τί;

ORESTES

The citizens are to try us for murder.

PYLADES

And what will the trial decide? I am rather afraid.

ORESTES

Life or death: small words for large things.

PYLADES

Run for it then with your sister: leave your house.

ORESTES

Don't you see? Guards are on the lookout for us everywhere.

PYLADES

I saw the town's streets closed off with armed men.

ORESTES

Our enemies have put walls about us like a city.

PYLADES

Now see what is happening to me: I too am undone.

ORESTES

By whom? This is trouble to be added to my troubles.

PYLADES

My father Strophius in anger has sent me away from the house in exile.

ORESTES

What was the charge he brought against you, whether on his own or in concert with the citizens?

---

762 δῶμα Wecklein   763–71 del. Grueninger
763 ὅρα Herwerden: ἐροῦ C

ΠΥΛΑΔΗΣ

ὅτι συνηράμην φόνον σοι μητρός, ἀνόσιον λέγων.

ΟΡΕΣΤΗΣ

ὦ τάλας, ἔοικε καὶ σὲ τἀμὰ λυπήσειν κακά.

ΠΥΛΑΔΗΣ

οὐχὶ Μενέλεω τρόποισι χρώμεθ'· οἰστέον τάδε.

ΟΡΕΣΤΗΣ

770 οὐ φοβῇ μή σ' Ἄργος ὥσπερ κἄμ' ἀποκτεῖναι θέλῃ;

ΠΥΛΑΔΗΣ

οὐ προσήκομεν κολάζειν τοῖσδε, Φωκέων δὲ γῇ.

[ΟΡΕΣΤΗΣ

δεινὸν οἱ πολλοί, κακούργους ὅταν ἔχωσι
    προστάτας.

ΠΥΛΑΔΗΣ

ἀλλ' ὅταν χρηστοὺς λάβωσι, χρηστὰ βουλεύουσ'
    ἀεί.]

ΟΡΕΣΤΗΣ

εἶέν. ἐς κοινὸν λέγειν χρή.

ΠΥΛΑΔΗΣ

            τίνος ἀναγκαίου πέρι;

ΟΡΕΣΤΗΣ

775 εἰ λέγοιμ' ἀστοῖσιν ἐλθὼν . . . .

772–3 del. Willink

PYLADES

He calls me unholy since I joined you in killing your mother.

ORESTES

Poor man! It looks as if my troubles are going to vex you as well.

PYLADES

I must put up with it: I don't have Menelaus' character.

ORESTES

Aren't you afraid that Argos will try to kill you just like me?

PYLADES

I do not fall under Argive authority to punish but under Phocian.

[ORESTES

The many are dangerous when they have wicked leaders.

PYLADES

But when they get good ones, their counsels are always good.]

ORESTES

Well then: we must confer.

PYLADES

About what necessary course?

ORESTES

What if I went and told the citizens . . .

ΠΥΛΑΔΗΣ
          … ὡς ἔδρασας ἔνδικα;

ΟΡΕΣΤΗΣ
  … πατρὶ τιμωρῶν ⟨γ᾽⟩ ἐμαυτοῦ;

ΠΥΛΑΔΗΣ
          μὴ ⟨οὐ⟩ λάβωσί σ᾽ ἄσμενοι.

ΟΡΕΣΤΗΣ
ἀλλ᾽ ὑποπτήξας σιωπῇ κατθάνω;

ΠΥΛΑΔΗΣ
                    δειλὸν τόδε.

ΟΡΕΣΤΗΣ
πῶς ἂν οὖν δρῴην;

ΠΥΛΑΔΗΣ
          ἔχεις τιν᾽, ἢν μένῃς, σωτηρίαν;

ΟΡΕΣΤΗΣ
οὐκ ἔχω.

ΠΥΛΑΔΗΣ
          μολόντι δ᾽ ἐλπίς ἐστι σωθῆναι κακῶν;

ΟΡΕΣΤΗΣ
780 εἰ τύχοι, γένοιτ᾽ ἄν.

ΠΥΛΑΔΗΣ
          οὔκουν τοῦτο κρεῖσσον ἢ μένειν;

ΟΡΕΣΤΗΣ
ἀλλὰ δῆτ᾽ ἔλθω;

PYLADES
. . . that your actions were just?

ORESTES
. . . ⟨yes,⟩ when I avenged my father?

PYLADES
I'm afraid they wouldn't be glad to receive you.

ORESTES
So shall I cower here in silence and die?

PYLADES
That would be unmanly.

ORESTES
What should I do then?

PYLADES
If you stay here, do you have any hope of surviving?

ORESTES
None.

PYLADES
But if you go, there is hope you may escape disaster?

ORESTES
It's possible, yes.

PYLADES
Then isn't that better than staying here?

ORESTES
So I should go then?

---

⁷⁷⁶ ⟨γ'⟩ Kirchhoff   ⟨οὐ⟩ Brunck

ΠΥΛΑΔΗΣ

θανὼν γοῦν ὧδε κάλλιον θανῇ.

ΟΡΕΣΤΗΣ

783   εὖ λέγεις· φεύγω τὸ δειλὸν τῇδε.

ΠΥΛΑΔΗΣ

μᾶλλον ἢ μένων.

ΟΡΕΣΤΗΣ

782   καὶ τὸ πρᾶγμά γ' ἔνδικόν μοι.

ΠΥΛΑΔΗΣ

τόδε δοκεῖν εὔχου μόνον.

ΟΡΕΣΤΗΣ

καί τις ἄν γέ μ' οἰκτίσειε . . . .

ΠΥΛΑΔΗΣ

μέγα γὰρ ηὐγένειά σου.

ΟΡΕΣΤΗΣ

785   . . . θάνατον ἀσχάλλων πατρῷον.

ΠΥΛΑΔΗΣ

πάντα ταῦτ' ἐν ὄμμασιν.

ΟΡΕΣΤΗΣ

ἰτέον, ὡς ἄνανδρον ἀκλεῶς κατθανεῖν.

ΠΥΛΑΔΗΣ

αἰνῶ τάδε.

ΟΡΕΣΤΗΣ

ἦ λέγωμεν οὖν ἀδελφῇ ταῦτ' ἐμῇ;

PYLADES

In that case, if you die at least your death will be nobler.

ORESTES

Good advice: I avoid looking like a coward.

PYLADES

More than if you stayed here.

ORESTES

And my case has justice in it.

PYLADES

Just pray that it may seem so!

ORESTES

And someone might take pity on me . . .

PYLADES

Your noble birth is a great advantage there.

ORESTES

. . . indignant at my father's death.

PYLADES

I can see that happening.

ORESTES

I must go: it's cowardly to die ingloriously.

PYLADES

I approve.

ORESTES

Shall we tell my sister?

---

782 post 783 trai. Morell, post 785 Weil
782 τόδε Paley: τὸ vel τῷ C

ΠΥΛΑΔΗΣ

μὴ πρὸς θεῶν.

ΟΡΕΣΤΗΣ

δάκρυα γοῦν γένοιτ' ἄν.

ΠΥΛΑΔΗΣ

οὔκουν οὗτος οἰωνὸς μέγας;

ΟΡΕΣΤΗΣ

δηλαδὴ σιγᾶν ἄμεινον.

ΠΥΛΑΔΗΣ

τῷ χρόνῳ γὰρ κερδανεῖς.

ΟΡΕΣΤΗΣ

790 κεῖνό μοι μόνον πρόσαντες . . .

ΠΥΛΑΔΗΣ

τί τόδε καινὸν αὖ λέγεις;

ΟΡΕΣΤΗΣ

. . . μὴ θεαί μ' οἴστρῳ κατάσχωσ'.

ΠΥΛΑΔΗΣ

ἀλλὰ κηδεύσω σ' ἐγώ.

ΟΡΕΣΤΗΣ

δυσχερὲς ψαύειν νοσοῦντος ἀνδρός.

ΠΥΛΑΔΗΣ

οὐκ ἔμοιγε σοῦ.

ΟΡΕΣΤΗΣ

εὐλαβοῦ λύσσης μετασχεῖν τῆς ἐμῆς.

PYLADES
In heaven's name, no!

ORESTES
Well, she would shed tears for me.

PYLADES
Would this not be a powerful omen of woe?

ORESTES
Clearly better to say nothing.

PYLADES
Yes, it saves us time.

ORESTES
There is only one problem in my way . . .

PYLADES
What new thing are you speaking of?

ORESTES
. . . the fear that the goddesses may seize me with frenzy.

PYLADES
Well, I will take care of you.

ORESTES
It is disgusting to touch a sick man.

PYLADES
Not for me to touch you.

ORESTES
Take care you don't catch my madness.

ΠΥΛΑΔΗΣ

        τόδ᾽ οὖν ἴτω.

ΟΡΕΣΤΗΣ

οὐκ ἄρ᾽ ὀκνήσεις;

ΠΥΛΑΔΗΣ

ὄκνος γὰρ τοῖς φίλοις κακὸν μέγα.

ΟΡΕΣΤΗΣ

795 ἕρπε νυν οἴαξ ποδός μοι . . .

ΠΥΛΑΔΗΣ

      φίλα γ᾽ ἔχων κηδεύματα.

ΟΡΕΣΤΗΣ

. . . καί με πρὸς τύμβον πόρευσον πατρός.

ΠΥΛΑΔΗΣ

      ὡς τί δὴ τόδε;

ΟΡΕΣΤΗΣ

ὥς νιν ἱκετεύσω με σῶσαι.

ΠΥΛΑΔΗΣ

     τό γε δίκαιον ὧδ᾽ ἔχει.

ΟΡΕΣΤΗΣ

μητέρος δὲ μὴ ᾽σίδοιμι μνῆμα.

ΠΥΛΑΔΗΣ

      πολεμία γὰρ ἦν.
ἀλλ᾽ ἔπειγ᾽, ὡς μή σε πρόσθε ψῆφος Ἀργείων
ἕλῃ,
800 περιβαλὼν πλευροῖς ἐμοῖσι πλευρὰ νωχελῆ νόσῳ·

PYLADES

Dismiss the thought!

ORESTES

So, you won't show reluctance?

PYLADES

Friends consider reluctance a great evil.

ORESTES

Be off then, steering oar of my steps . . .

PYLADES

I will, with a dear friend in my care.

ORESTES

. . . and take me to my father's tomb.

PYLADES

Why so?

ORESTES

So that I can entreat him to save my life.

PYLADES

And right it is that he should.

ORESTES

As for my mother's grave, may I never look on it!

PYLADES

No: she was a foe.

But hurry so that you are not convicted by the Argive vote before you get there! Wrap your body, sluggish with

---

798 μὴ 'σίδοιμι F. W. Schmidt: μηδ' ἴδοιμι fere C

ὡς ἐγὼ δι' ἄστεώς σε, σμικρὰ φροντίζων ὄχλου,
οὐδὲν αἰσχυνθεὶς ὀχήσω. ποῦ γὰρ ὢν δείξω φίλος,
εἴ τι μὴ 'ν δειναῖσιν ὄντι συμφοραῖς ἐπαρκέσω;

ΟΡΕΣΤΗΣ

τοῦτ' ἐκεῖνο, κτᾶσθ' ἑταίρους, μὴ τὸ συγγενὲς
μόνον·
805 ὡς ἀνὴρ ὅστις τρόποισι συντακῇ, θυραῖος ὤν,
μυρίων κρείσσων ὁμαίμων ἀνδρὶ κεκτῆσθαι φίλος.

ΧΟΡΟΣ

στρ.

ὁ μέγας ὄλβος ἅ τ' ἀρετὰ
μέγα φρονοῦσ' ἀν' Ἑλλάδα καὶ
παρὰ Σιμουντίοις ὀχετοῖς
810 πάλιν ἀνῆλθ' ἐξ εὐτυχίας Ἀτρείδαις
πάλαι παλαιᾶς ἀπὸ συμφορᾶς δόμων,
ὁπότε χρυσέας ἔρις ἀρ-
νὸς ἦλθε Τανταλίδαις,
οἰκτρότατα θοινάματα καὶ
815 σφάγια γενναίων τεκέων·
ὅθεν πόνῳ πόνος ἐξαμεί-
βων δι' αἵματος οὐ προλεί-
πει δισσοῖσιν Ἀτρείδαις.

803 τι . . . ὄντι Blaydes: σε . . . ὄντα C
811 πάλαι] πάλιν Hartung
813 ἦλθε Hermann: ἤλυθε C
816 πόνῳ πόνος Willink: φόν- φόν- C

your illness, about mine. I will carry you through the city, paying slight attention to the crowd, feeling no embarrassment. Where else could I demonstrate that I am your friend if I do not come to your aid when you are in direst trouble?

ORESTES

This proves it: get comrades, not just blood kin! An outsider whose character fuses with yours is a better friend to have than countless blood relations!

Exit ORESTES *and* PYLADES *by Eisodos B.*

CHORUS

Great wealth and prowess,
thinking proud thoughts throughout Greece
and by Simois' waters,
has now been reversed—their good fortune vanished—for
   the house of Atreus,
because of an age-old woe in the house,
when strife about a golden lamb
came over the Tantalids,
feastings most grim
and slaughtering of high-born children:[20]
from this source trouble in exchange for trouble
runs never failing throughout the bloodline
of the two sons of Atreus.

[20] For the slaughter of Thyestes' children see note on line 1000 below.

ἀντ.

    τὸ καλὸν οὐ καλόν, τοκέων

820 πυριγενεῖ τεμεῖν παλάμᾳ

    χρόα· μελάνδετον δὲ φόνῳ

    ξίφος ἐς αὐγὰς ἀελίοιο δεῖξαι,

    τόδ' αὖ κακούργων ἀσέβεια ποικίλα

    κακοφρόνων τ' ἀνδρῶν παράνοι·

825 Ἅιδα γὰρ ἀμφὶ φόβῳ

    Τυνδαρὶς ἰάχησε τάλαιν'·

    Ἆ, τέκνον, οὐ τολμᾷς ὅσια

    κτείνων σὰν ματέρα· μὴ πατρώ-

    αν τιμῶν χάριν ἐξανά-

830 ψῃ δύσκλειαν ἐς αἰεί.

ἐπῳδ.

    τίς νόσος ἢ τίνα δάκρυα καὶ

    τίς ἔλεος μείζων κατὰ γᾶν

    ἢ ματροκτόνον αἷμα χειρὶ θέσθαι;

    οἷον ἔργον τελέσας

835 βεβάκχευται μανίαις,

    Εὐμενίσι θήραμα, φόβον

    δρομάσι δινεύων βλεφάροις,

    Ἀγαμεμνόνιος παῖς.

    ὦ μέλεος, ματρὸς ὅτ' ἐκ

840 χρυσεοπηνήτων φαρέων

---

820 τεμεῖν Porson: τέμνειν C   823 τόδ' αὖ κακούργων
Weil: τὸ δ' αὖ κακουργεῖν (κακοῦργον γρΣ) C
824–5 παράνοι· Ἅιδα Willink: παράνοια· θανάτου C

That exploit is no exploit, to cut
a parent's flesh with fire-forged violence;
and to display the sword, dark with blood,
to the rays of the sun—
this is the elaborately dressed godlessness of knaves,
and the mad behavior of fools.
For[21] in fear of death
Tyndareus' luckless daughter shrieked
"No, my son: unhallowed is the deed you dare to do,
killing your mother! Do not, by honoring
a father's benefit, fasten on yourself
disgrace for evermore!"

What malady, what tears,
what pitiful fate is greater in the world
than to take a mother's blood upon one's hands?
From doing such a deed
he has been driven wild with fits of madness,
the Eumenides' quarry, his darting eyes
rolling in fear,
he, Agamemnon's son.
Unhappy man: when from his mother's
robes of golden weave he saw

[21] The words of those on the point of death were thought to be inspired, hence Clytaemestra's admonition has probative force here.

826–7 τάλαιν'· ῍Α Willink: τάλαινα C
836 φόβον Koenen dubitanter, Diggle: φόβῳ vel φόνῳ fere C
839 ὅτ᾿ ἐκ Willink: ὅτε C

μαστὸν ὑπερτέλλοντ᾽ ἐσιδὼν
σφάγιον ἔθετο
ματέρα, πατρῴων παθέων ἀμοιβάν.

ΗΛΕΚΤΡΑ
γυναῖκες, ἦ που τῶνδ᾽ ἀφώρμηται δόμων
845 τλήμων Ὀρέστης θεομανεῖ λύσσῃ δαμείς;

ΧΟΡΟΣ
ἥκιστα· πρὸς δ᾽ Ἀργεῖον οἴχεται λεών
[ψυχῆς ἀγῶνα τὸν προκείμενον πέρι
δώσων, ἐν ᾧ ζῆν ἢ θανεῖν ὑμᾶς χρεών].

ΗΛΕΚΤΡΑ
οἴμοι· τί χρῆμ᾽ ἔδρασε; τίς δ᾽ ἔπεισέ νιν;

ΧΟΡΟΣ
850 Πυλάδης· ἔοικε δ᾽ οὐ μακρὰν ὅδ᾽ ἄγγελος
λέξειν τὰ κεῖθεν σοῦ κασιγνήτου πέρι.

ΑΓΓΕΛΟΣ
[ὦ τλῆμον, ὦ δύστηνε τοῦ στρατηλάτου]
Ἀγαμέμνονος παῖ, πότνι᾽ Ἠλέκτρα, λόγους
ἄκουσον οὕς σοι δυστυχεῖς ἥκω φέρων.

ΗΛΕΚΤΡΑ
855 αἰαῖ, διοιχόμεσθα· δῆλος εἶ λόγῳ.
[κακῶν γὰρ ἥκεις, ὡς ἔοικεν, ἄγγελος.]

847–8 del. Willink (848 iam Kirchhoff)
852 del. Paley
856 del. Brunck

the breast rise to his gaze,
he slaughtered his mother,
making requital for his father's woes.

Enter ELECTRA *from the house.*

ELECTRA
Women, has Orestes set out from home, overcome by a fit
of god-sent madness?

CHORUS LEADER
No: he has set off for the Argive assembly [to engage in
the present life struggle in which you two must either live
or die].

ELECTRA
Ah, ah! Why did he do that? Who persuaded him?

CHORUS LEADER
Pylades. But it looks as if this bringer of news will soon tell
what happened there concerning your brother.

Enter by Eisodos B an old man as MESSENGER.

MESSENGER
[Poor woman, unhappy general's child,] Agamemnon's
daughter, lady Electra, hear the unfortunate tale that I
have come to bring you.

ELECTRA
Ah, ah, we are done for! Your words made all plain. [You
come, it seems, as a bearer of bad news.]

EURIPIDES

ΑΓΓΕΛΟΣ

ψήφῳ Πελασγῶν σὸν κασίγνητον θανεῖν
καὶ σ᾽, ὦ τάλαιν᾽, ἔδοξε τῇδ᾽ ἐν ἡμέρᾳ.

ΗΛΕΚΤΡΑ

οἴμοι· προσῆλθεν ἐλπίς, ἣν φοβουμένη
860 πάλαι τὸ μέλλον ἐξετηκόμην γόοις.
ἀτὰρ τίς ἀγών, τίνες ἐν Ἀργείοις λόγοι
καθεῖλον ἡμᾶς κἀπεκύρωσαν θανεῖν;
λέγ᾽, ὦ γεραιέ· πότερα λευσίμῳ χερὶ
ἢ διὰ σιδήρου πνεῦμ᾽ ἀπορρῆξαί με δεῖ,
865 κοινὰς ἀδελφῷ συμφορὰς κεκτημένην;

ΑΓΓΕΛΟΣ

ἐτύγχανον μὲν ἀγρόθεν πυλῶν ἔσω
βαίνων, πυθέσθαι δεόμενος τά τ᾽ ἀμφὶ σοῦ
τά τ᾽ ἀμφ᾽ Ὀρέστου· σῷ γὰρ εὔνοιαν πατρὶ
ἀεί ποτ᾽ εἶχον, καί μ᾽ ἔφερβε σὸς δόμος
870 πένητα μέν, χρῆσθαι δὲ γενναῖον φίλοις.
ὁρῶ δ᾽ ὄχλον στείχοντα καὶ θάσσοντ᾽ ἄκραν,
οὗ φασι πρῶτον Δαναὸν Αἰγύπτῳ δίκας
διδόντ᾽ ἀθροῖσαι λαὸν ἐς κοινὰς ἕδρας.
ἀστῶν δὲ δή τιν᾽ ἠρόμην ἄθροισμ᾽ ἰδών·
875 Τί καινὸν Ἄργει; μῶν τι πολεμίων πάρα
ἄγγελμ᾽ ἀνεπτέρωκε Δαναϊδῶν πόλιν;
ὁ δ᾽ εἶπ᾽· Ὀρέστην κεῖνον οὐχ ὁρᾷς πέλας
στείχοντ᾽, ἀγῶνα θανάσιμον δραμούμενον;
     ὁρῶ δ᾽ ἄελπτον φάσμ᾽, ὃ μήποτ᾽ ὤφελον,
880 Πυλάδην τε καὶ σὸν σύγγονον στείχονθ᾽ ὁμοῦ,

510

MESSENGER

By the vote of the Pelasgians it was resolved that you, poor woman, and your brother must die today.

ELECTRA

Ah, ah! It has come, what I expected! Fear of this made me lament my future! But what was the trial like? What speeches made before the Argives destroyed us and ratified our death sentence? Tell me, old sir: must I breathe my last by stoning or by the sword, sharing in my brother's misfortunes?

MESSENGER

I happened to be making my way from the country to the citadel since I wanted to learn your situation and that of your brother. I always felt good will toward your father: your house gave me sustenance, a poor man, to be sure, but one who treats his friends honorably. I saw a crowd that came and took their seats on the hill where they say that Danaus, prosecuted by Aegyptus, first gathered the people and made them sit together. I saw this gathering and asked one of the townsmen, "What's happening now at Argos? Has some message from enemies set the city of Danaus' sons aflutter?" And he said, "Don't you see Orestes approaching over there? He is about to run a deadly race."

I saw an apparition I did not expect, one I wish I had never seen: Pylades and your brother were walking along

---

863–5 del. Herwerden

τὸν μὲν κατηφῆ καὶ παρειμένον νόσῳ,
τὸν δ' ὥστ' ἀδελφὸν ἶσα φίλῳ λυπούμενον,
νόσημα κηδεύοντα παιδαγωγίᾳ.

ἐπεὶ δὲ πλήρης ἐγένετ' Ἀργείων ὄχλος,
885 κῆρυξ ἀναστὰς εἶπε· Τίς χρῄζει λέγειν,
πότερον Ὀρέστην κατθανεῖν ἢ μὴ χρεών,
μητροκτονοῦντα; κἀπὶ τῷδ' ἀνίσταται
Ταλθύβιος, ὃς σῷ πατρὶ συνεπόρθει Φρύγας.
ἔλεξε δ', ὑπὸ τοῖς δυναμένοισιν ὢν ἀεί,
890 διχόμυθα, πατέρα μὲν σὸν ἐκπαγλούμενος,
σὸν δ' οὐκ ἐπαινῶν σύγγονον, καλοὺς κακοὺς
λόγους ἑλίσσων, ὅτι καθισταίη νόμους
ἐς τοὺς τεκόντας οὐ καλούς· τὸ δ' ὄμμ' ἀεὶ
φαιδρωπὸν ἐδίδου τοῖσιν Αἰγίσθου φίλοις.
895 τὸ γὰρ γένος τοιοῦτον· ἐπὶ τὸν εὐτυχῆ
πηδῶσ' ἀεὶ κήρυκες· ὅδε δ' αὐτοῖς φίλος,
ὃς ἂν δύνηται πόλεος ἔν τ' ἀρχαῖσιν ᾖ.

ἐπὶ τῷδε δ' ἠγόρευε Διομήδης ἄναξ·
οὗτος κτανεῖν μὲν οὔτε σ' οὔτε σύγγονον
900 εἴα, φυγῇ δὲ ζημιοῦντας εὐσεβεῖν.
ἐπερρόθησαν δ' οἱ μὲν ὡς καλῶς λέγοι,
οἱ δ' οὐκ ἐπήνουν.

κἀπὶ τῷδ' ἀνίσταται
ἀνήρ τις ἀθυρόγλωσσος, ἰσχύων θράσει·
[Ἀργεῖος οὐκ Ἀργεῖος, ἠναγκασμένος,
905 θορύβῳ τε πίσυνος κἀμαθεῖ παρρησίᾳ,
πιθανὸς ἔτ' αὐτοὺς περιβαλεῖν κακῷ τινι.
ὅταν γὰρ ἡδύς τις λόγοις φρονῶν κακῶς

together, the latter downcast and slack-limbed with his disease, the former, like a brother, sharing his friend's distress in equal measure and caring for his malady by leading him along as if he were a child.

When the Argive assembly had fully gathered, a herald got up and said, "Who wishes to speak about whether Orestes should die for killing his mother, or be allowed to live?" At this Talthybius got up, who had helped your father destroy the Phrygians. He is subservient to whoever is in power, and so he spoke ambiguously, greatly admiring your father but dispraising your brother by whirling to and fro words fair-seeming and base: Orestes, he said, was establishing a bad precedent toward parents. He kept turning an obsequious face toward Aegisthus' friends. That is what his kind are like. Heralds are always leaping over to join those in prosperity: whoever has power in the city and enjoys high office is their friend.

After him king Diomedes spoke. He was opposed to killing either you or your brother but said that exiling you would satisfy piety's demands. The crowd murmured in response, some saying that the advice was good, others showing disapproval.

Then there stood up a man with no check on his tongue, strong in his brashness; [he was an Argive but no Argive, suborned, relying on noise from the crowd and the obtuse license of his tongue, persuasive enough to involve them in the future in some misfortune. When someone of pleasing speech but without sense persuades the people, it is a great

---

895–7 del. Dindorf   904–13 del. Hartung
906 ἀστοὺς Valckenaer
907 τις Musgrave: τοῖς C

πείθῃ τὸ πλῆθος, τῇ πόλει κακὸν μέγα·
ὅσοι δὲ σὺν νῷ χρηστὰ βουλεύουσ᾽ ἀεί,
910 κἂν μὴ παραυτίκ᾽, αὖθίς εἰσι χρήσιμοι
πόλει. θεᾶσθαι δ᾽ ὧδε χρὴ τὸν προστάτην
ἰδόνθ᾽· ὅμοιον γὰρ τὸ χρῆμα γίγνεται
τῷ τοὺς λόγους λέγοντι καὶ τιμωμένῳ.]
ὃς εἶπ᾽ Ὀρέστην καὶ σ᾽ ἀποκτεῖναι πέτροις
915 βάλλοντας· ὑπὸ δ᾽ ἔτεινε Τυνδάρεως λόγους
[τῷ σφὼ κατακτείνοντι τοιούτους λέγειν].
ἄλλος δ᾽ ἀναστὰς ἔλεγε τῷδ᾽ ἐναντία,
μορφῇ μὲν οὐκ εὐωπός, ἀνδρεῖος δ᾽ ἀνήρ,
ὀλιγάκις ἄστυ κἀγορᾶς χραίνων κύκλον,
920 αὐτουργός, οἵπερ καὶ μόνοι σῴζουσι γῆν,
ξυνετὸς δὲ χωρεῖν ὁμόσε τοῖς λόγοις θέλων,
ἀκέραιον ἀνεπίπληκτον ἠσκηκὼς βίον·
ὃς εἶπ᾽ Ὀρέστην παῖδα τὸν Ἀγαμέμνονος
στεφανοῦν, ὃς ἠθέλησε τιμωρεῖν πατρί,
925 κακὴν γυναῖκα κἄθεον κατακτανών,
ἢ κεῖν᾽ ἀφῄρει, μήθ᾽ ὁπλίζεσθαι χέρα
μήτε στρατεύειν ἐκλιπόντα δώματα,
εἰ τἄνδον οἰκουρήμαθ᾽ οἱ λελειμμένοι
φθεροῦσιν, ἀνδρῶν εὔνιδας λωβώμενοι.
930 καὶ τοῖς γε χρηστοῖς εὖ λέγειν ἐφαίνετο.
κοὐδεὶς ἔτ᾽ εἶπε. σὸς δ᾽ ἐπῆλθε σύγγονος,
ἔλεξε δ᾽· Ὦ γῆν Ἰνάχου κεκτημένοι,
[πάλαι Πελασγοί, Δαναΐδαι δεύτερον,]

913 τῷ τ᾽ ἰωμένῳ Musgrave

misfortune for the city. But those who always give good counsel with intelligence are useful to the city in the long run, if not immediately. One should look at the leader this way: the same thing applies to the public speaker as to the holder of offices;] he proposed putting you and Orestes to death by stoning. But it was Tyndareus who had supplied the arguments [for the man trying to kill you to deliver, like this].

Another man got up and made precisely the opposite proposal. He was not handsome to look at but a brave man, one who rarely had anything to do with the city or the market circle, a man who farmed with his own hands, the sort who alone keep the land from destruction, yet clever enough to grapple in argument when he wanted: he has lived a life of integrity, above reproach. His proposal was that Orestes, son of Agamemnon, should be given a garland[22] for being willing to avenge his father by killing a wicked and godless woman. This woman, he said, was depriving us of all this: there would be no more taking the sword in the hand, no more leaving home to go on campaign if the men left behind would then subvert domestic order by outrageously seducing the soldiers' wives. The better sort of people thought his proposal was good.

No one else spoke. But your brother came forward and said, "You possessors of the land of Inachus, [formerly Pelasgians, later sons of Danaus,] it was in defense of you

---

[22] Like an athletic victor or a public benefactor.

---

916 del. Weil
929 φθεροῦσιν Wecklein: φθείρουσιν C
933 del. Musgrave

ὑμῖν ἀμύνων οὐδὲν ἧσσον ἢ πατρὶ
935 ἔκτεινα μητέρ'. εἰ γὰρ ἀρσένων φόνος
ἔσται γυναιξὶν ὅσιος, οὐ φθάνοιτ' ἔτ' ἂν
θνῄσκοντες, ἢ γυναικὶ δουλεύειν χρεών.
[τοὐναντίον δὲ δράσετ' ἢ δρᾶσαι χρεών·
νῦν μὲν γὰρ ἡ προδοῦσα λέκτρ' ἐμοῦ πατρὸς
940 τέθνηκεν· εἰ δὲ δὴ κατακτενεῖτ' ἐμέ,
ὁ νόμος ἀνεῖται, κοὐ φθάνοι θνῄσκων τις ἄν·
ὡς τῆς γε τόλμης οὐ σπάνις γενήσεται.]
    ἀλλ' οὐκ ἔπειθ' ὅμιλον, εὖ δοκῶν λέγειν·
νικᾷ δ' ἐκεῖνος ὁ κακὸς ἐν πλήθει χερῶν,
945 ὃς ἠγόρευσε σύγγονον σέ τε κτανεῖν.
μόλις δ' ἔπεισε μὴ πετρούμενος θανεῖν
τλήμων Ὀρέστης· αὐτόχειρι δὲ σφαγῇ
ὑπέσχετ' ἐν τῇδ' ἡμέρᾳ λείψειν βίον
σὺν σοί. πορεύει δ' αὐτὸν ἐκκλήτων ἄπο
950 Πυλάδης δακρύων, σὺν δ' ὁμαρτοῦσιν φίλοι
κλαίοντες, οἰκτίροντες· ἔρχεται δέ σοι
πικρὸν θέαμα καὶ πρόσοψις ἀθλία.
    ἀλλ' εὐτρέπιζε φάσγαν' ἢ βρόχον δέρῃ,
ὡς δεῖ λιπεῖν σε φέγγος· ηὐγένεια δὲ
955 οὐδέν σ' ἐπωφέλησεν, οὐδ' ὁ Πύθιος
τρίποδα καθίζων Φοῖβος, ἀλλ' ἀπώλεσεν.

                    [ΧΟΡΟΣ
ὦ δυστάλαινα παρθέν', ὡς ξυνηρεφὲς
πρόσωπον ἐς γῆν σὸν βαλοῦσ' ἄφθογγος εἶ,
ὡς ἐς στεναγμοὺς καὶ γόους δραμουμένη.]

516

no less than of my father that I killed my mother. For if it is allowable for women to kill their menfolk, you had better hurry up and die or you must be slaves to women. [You will be doing the opposite of what you should be doing. For at present she who betrayed my father's bed lies dead. But if you put me to death, established custom is nullified and one might as well be dead: for there will be no lack of this kind of effrontery.]"

Yet he did not persuade the crowd, sensible though his speech seemed. That fellow, the base one, was victorious in the counting of hands, the one who proposed putting you and your brother to death. Poor Orestes barely persuaded them that he should not be stoned to death. He promised to leave his life by his own hand today, and you with him. Pylades, in tears, is bringing him back from the assembly, and his friends are with him weeping and lamenting. It is as an unwelcome spectacle and a vision of misery that he comes to you.

So get the sword ready, or the noose for your neck, since you must leave the daylight behind. Your noble birth has done you no good, nor has Pythian Phoebus who sits on the tripod: instead he has destroyed you.

Exit MESSENGER *by Eisodos B.*

[CHORUS LEADER
O unfortunate maiden, how downcast to earth is your clouded countenance! How silent you are as if about to break forth into wailing and lamentation!]

938–42 del. Wecklein   944 χερῶν Wecklein: λέγων fere C
955 Πύθιον West   957–9 del. Kirchhoff cl. Σ

ΧΟΡΟΣ

στρ.

960 κατάρχομαι στεναγμόν, ὦ Πελασγία,
τιθεῖσα λευκὸν ὄνυχα διὰ παρηίδων,
αἱματηρὸν ἄταν,
κτύπον τε κρατός, ὃν ἔλαχ᾽ ἁ κατὰ χθονὸς
νερτέρων καλλίπαις ἄνασσα.

965 ἰαχείτω δὲ γᾶ Κυκλωπία,
σίδαρον ἐπὶ κάρα τιθεῖσα κούριμον,
πήματ᾽ οἴκων.
ἔλεος ἔλεος ὅδ᾽ ἔρχεται
τῶν θανουμένων ὕπερ,

970 στρατηλατᾶν Ἑλλάδος ποτ᾽ ὄντων.

ἀντ.

βέβακε γὰρ βέβακεν, οἴχεται τέκνων
πρόπασα γέννα Πέλοπος ὅ τ᾽ ἐπὶ μακαρίοις
ζῆλος ὤν ποτ᾽ οἴκοις·
φθόνος νιν εἷλε θεόθεν ἅ τε δυσμενὴς

975 φοινία ψῆφος ἐν πολίταις.
ἰώ, ὦ πανδάκρυτ᾽ ἐφαμέρων
ἔθνη πολύπονα, λεύσσεθ᾽ ὡς παρ᾽ ἐλπίδας
μοῖρα βαίνει.
ἕτερα δ᾽ ἕτερον ἀμείβεται

960n Χο. Weil: Ἠλ. C: Ἠλ. καὶ Χο. Willink
961 λευκᾶν ὄνυχι post Hartung (λευκῶν) Diggle
964 καλλίπαις ἄνασσα Heimsoeth: Περσέφασσα καλλί-
παις θεά C

518

CHORUS

I lead off the lamentation, O Pelasgian land,
drawing my white nails along my cheeks
in bloody disfigurement
and beating my head, an act that falls to the lot of her
below,
the fair-child goddess who rules the dead.[23]
Let the Cylopean land[24] loudly proclaim,
sheering its tresses with iron blade,
the house's woes!
Lamentation, lamentation here comes forth
for those doomed to die,
who once led the hosts of Greece!

Perished, perished and gone
is the whole clan of Pelops and the enviable lot
that once rested on his blessed house.
It was destroyed by the ill will of heaven and the hateful
murderous vote of the citizens.
Ah, ah, you race of mortals, full of tears, trouble-laden,
see how fate
defeats your expectations!
Different woes come by turns to different men

---

[23] Persephone.
[24] The fortifications of Mycenae and Tiryns were thought to
have been built by the Cyclopes.

---

967 πήματ' Musgrave: τῶν Ἀτρειδῶν π- fere C
973 ζῆλος . . . οἴκοις Musgrave: ζηλωτὸς . . . οἶκος C
979 ἕτερον West: ἑτέροις C

980 πήματ' ἐν χρόνῳ μακρῷ,
βροτῶν δ' ὁ πᾶς ἀστάθμητος αἰών.

⟨ΗΛΕΚΤΡΑ⟩

μόλοιμι τὰν οὐρανοῦ
μέσον χθονός ⟨τε⟩ τεταμέναν
αἰωρήμασιν
πέτραν ἁλύσεσιν χρυσέαις,
φερομέναν δίναισι
βῶλον ἐξ Ὀλύμπου,

985 ἵν' ἐν θρήνοισιν ἀναβοάσω
γέροντι πατέρι Ταντάλῳ,
ὃς ἔτεκεν ἔτεκε γενέτορας ἐμέθεν, δόμων
ἃς κατεῖδον ἄτας·
ποτανὸν μὲν δίωγμα πώλων,

990 τεθριπποβάμονι στόλῳ
Πέλοψ ὅτ' ἐπὶ πελάγεσι διε-
δίφρευσε Μυρτίλου φόνον
δικὼν ἐς οἶδμα πόντου,
λευκοκύμοσιν πρὸς Γεραιστίαις
ποντίων σάλων

982n ⟨Ηλ.⟩ Weil
982b ⟨τε⟩ Hermann
984a δίναις ⟨ἀε⟩ί Diggle
988 ἃς Burges: οὗ C
989 ποτανὸν Porson: τὸ πτανὸν C
991a ὅτ' ἐπὶ Burges: ὅτε vel ὁπότε C

over the length of days,
and beyond our power to reckon is the whole course of
   human life.

<ELECTRA>

O that I might go
to the rock hung aloft
between heaven <and> earth
from golden chains,
a rocky mass from Olympus
borne on the heavens' rotation![25]
There in lamentation would I loudly proclaim
to old Tantalus, my ancestor,
who sired, who sired my forefathers,
what ruin I have seen in the house.
First, the flight of winged colts
when with chariot and four
Pelops rode over the waves
and threw Myrtilus to his death
in the swelling deep,
driving his chariot
from the surf

[25] See above, notes to lines 7 and 10. Tantalus' rock (here a
fragment of Olympus) and he himself are held aloft by means
partly poetic and mythical (for the golden chains see *Iliad* 8.19)
and partly redolent of fifth-century science (δίνη, "rotation," was
a favorite word of fifth-century cosmological speculation). To ex-
plain how a rock could hover perpetually over Tantalus' head both
the rock and Tantalus are conceived as rotating about Olympus
like heavenly bodies.

995 ἀιόσιν ἁρματεύσας·
ὅθεν δόμοισι τοῖς ἐμοῖς
ἦλθ᾽ ἀρὰ πολύστονος,
λόχευμα ποιμνίοισι Μαιάδος τόκου,
τὸ χρυσόμαλλον ἀρνὸς ὁπότ᾽
ἐγένετο τέρας ὀλοὸν Ἀτρέος
1000 ⟨ἀγροῖς ἐν⟩ ἱπποβώτα·
ὅθεν Ἔρις τό τε πτερωτὸν
ἀλίου μετέβαλεν ἅρμα
τὰν πρὸς ἑσπέραν κέλευθον
οὐρανοῦ, προσαρμόσασα
χιονόπωλον Ἀῶ,
1005 ἑπταπόρου τε δράμημα
Πλειάδος εἰς ὁδὸν ἄλλαν [Ζεὺς μεταβάλλει].
†τῶνδέ τ᾽† ἀμείβει θανάτους θανάτων
τά τ᾽ ἐπώνυμα δεῖπνα Θυέστου
λέκτρα τε Κρήσσας Ἀερόπας δολί-
1010 ας δολίοισι γάμοις· τὰ πανύστατα δ᾽

1000 ⟨ἀγροῖς ἐν⟩ Diggle (⟨ἐν⟩ iam Willink)
1004 χιονόπωλον West: μονόπωλον ἐς C
1006 Ζεὺς del. Weil, μεταβάλλει del. Biehl
1007 τῷ δ᾽ ἔπ᾽ Willink (τῷ δ᾽ iam Musgrave)

26 In the familiar version Pelops wins his bride from Oenomaus of Elis (in the Peloponnesus, near Olympia), whose custom is to pursue his daughter's suitors in a chariot and kill them if he can overtake them. Pelops bribes Oenomaus' charioteer Myrtilus to sabotage his master's chariot but then cheats him of his reward by throwing him off a cliff. Here Pelops has a winged char-

by the white-waved beach of Geraestus.[26]
From this deed for my house
came a curse laden with groaning,
when, brought to birth in the flocks of the son of Maia,
there came the famous lamb with fleece of gold,
a portent of ruin
⟨in the fields⟩ of horse-pasturing Atreus.[27]
Thereupon Strife changed
the sun's winged car
to a westward course,
yoking to it
Dawn with her snowy horses,
changed the path of the seven-starred
Pleiades onto a different road [Zeus changed it].
And now she brings deaths in requital for deaths,
the feast named for Thyestes,
and the Cretan Aërope's bed of love,
crafty woman in a crafty marriage. Last,

iot, and he appears to be crossing the Aegean and landing at
Geraestus in Euboea. We do not know what role Myrtilus (whose
name suggests Asia Minor or Lesbos) had in this story before his
death in the waves.

[27] The son of Maia is Hermes, who was Myrtilus' father. The
lamb caused strife between Atreus, to whom it belonged, and his
brother Thyestes, who seduced Atreus' wife to win possession of
it, since it marked its possessor as rightful king. In revenge Atreus
killed Thyestes' children and served them to him at a feast. In
some versions of the story, the sun changes course (to its present
east to west path) in horror at these deeds; in others (and perhaps
here) Thyestes says he will not relinquish the lamb unless the sun
changes course, which it proceeds to do, ratifying Atreus' claim to
the throne.

εἰς ἐμὲ συγγενέταν τ᾽ ἐμὸν ἦλθε δόμων
πολυπόνοις ἀνάγκαις.

ΧΟΡΟΣ

καὶ μὴν ὅδε σὸς σύγγονος ἕρπει
ψήφῳ θανάτου κατακυρωθείς,
ὅ τε πιστότατος πάντων Πυλάδης,
1015 ἰσάδελφος ἀνήρ, ⟨δεῦρ᾽⟩ ἰθύνων
νοσερὸν κῶλον,
ποδὶ κηδοσύνῳ παράσειρος.

ΗΛΕΚΤΡΑ

οἲ ᾽γώ· πρὸ τύμβου γάρ σ᾽ ὁρῶσ᾽ ἀναστένω,
ἀδελφέ, καὶ πάροιθε νερτέρου πυρᾶς.
1020 οἲ ᾽γὼ μάλ᾽ αὖθις· ὥς σ᾽ ἰδοῦσ᾽ ἐν ὄμμασιν
παννυστάτην πρόσοψιν ἐξέστην φρενῶν.

ΟΡΕΣΤΗΣ

οὐ σῖγ᾽ ἀφεῖσα τοὺς γυναικείους γόους
στέρξεις τὰ κρανθέντ᾽; οἰκτρὰ μὲν τάδ᾽, ἀλλ᾽ ὅμως
[φέρειν σ᾽ ἀνάγκη τὰς παρεστώσας τύχας].

ΗΛΕΚΤΡΑ

1025 καὶ πῶς σιωπῶ; φέγγος εἰσορᾶν θεοῦ
τόδ᾽ οὐκέθ᾽ ἡμῖν τοῖς ταλαιπώροις μέτα.

ΟΡΕΣΤΗΣ

σὺ μή μ᾽ ἀπόκτειν᾽· ἅλις ὑπ᾽ Ἀργείας χερὸς
τέθνηχ᾽ ὁ τλήμων· τὰ δὲ παρόντ᾽ ἔα κακά.

1011 συγγενέταν τ᾽ Willink: καὶ γενέταν C   ἦλθε Brunck,
Porson: ἤλυθε C

524

against me and my brother has it come
by the toil-laden doom of our house.

Enter by Eisodos B ORESTES *and* PYLADES *supporting him.*

CHORUS LEADER
But look, here comes your brother, a death sentence
passed against him, and loyal Pylades, a man like a brother,
who on caring feet guides Orestes' infirm step ‹toward us›
like a trace horse.

ELECTRA
Ah, ah! I see you in front of your tomb, brother, and before
the pyre of the dead, and I weep! Ah, ah yet again! My eyes
take their last look of you, and I am not right in my mind!

ORESTES
Stop these womanish laments and endure in silence what
has been ordained! To be sure, these things call for tears,
but nevertheless! [You must endure the present misfor-
tunes.]

ELECTRA
How can I keep still? We in our misery can no longer look
on the god's sunlight here.

ORESTES
Don't *you* be the death of me: I am already dead enough at
the hands of the Argives. Let my present woes be.

1015 ‹δεῦρ᾽› Willink
1016 κῶλον unus cod., coni. Elmsley: κ- Ὀρέστου ceteri codd.
1019 νερτέρων πύλης Jacobs
1024 del. Kirchhoff cl. Σ

EURIPIDES

ΗΛΕΚΤΡΑ

ὦ μέλεος ἥβης σῆς, Ὀρέστα, καὶ πότμου
1030 θανάτου τ᾽ ἀώρου. ζῆν ἐχρῆν σ᾽, ὅτ᾽ οὐκέτ᾽ εἶ.

ΟΡΕΣΤΗΣ

μὴ πρὸς θεῶν μοι περιβάλῃς ἀνανδρίαν,
ἐς δάκρυα πορθμεύουσ᾽ ὑπομνήσει κακῶν.

ΗΛΕΚΤΡΑ

θανούμεθ᾽· οὐχ οἷόν τε μὴ στένειν κακά.
πᾶσιν γὰρ οἰκτρὸν ἡ φίλη ψυχὴ βροτοῖς.

ΟΡΕΣΤΗΣ

1035 τόδ᾽ ἦμαρ ἡμῖν κύριον· δεῖ δ᾽ ἢ βρόχους
ἅπτειν κρεμαστοὺς ἢ ξίφος θήγειν χερί.

ΗΛΕΚΤΡΑ

σύ νύν μ᾽, ἀδελφέ, μή τις Ἀργείων κτάνῃ,
ὕβρισμα θέμενος τὸν Ἀγαμέμνονος δόμον.

ΟΡΕΣΤΗΣ

ἅλις τὸ μητρὸς αἷμ᾽· ἐγὼ δέ σ᾽ οὐ κτενῶ,
1040 ἀλλ᾽ αὐτόχειρι θνῇσχ᾽ ὅτῳ βούλῃ τρόπῳ.

ΗΛΕΚΤΡΑ

ἔσται τάδ᾽· οὐδὲν σοῦ ξίφει λελείψομαι.
ἀλλ᾽ ἀμφιθεῖναι σῇ δέρῃ θέλω χέρας.

ΟΡΕΣΤΗΣ

τέρπου κενὴν ὄνησιν, εἰ τερπνὸν τόδε
θανάτου πέλας βεβῶσι περιβαλεῖν χέρας.

1032 ὑπομνήσει Musgrave: ὑπόμνησιν C

526

ELECTRA

How luckless you are, Orestes, for your youth, your fate, and your untimely death! You ought to be living, but you live no more!

ORESTES

Don't cover me with cowardice by making me weep with the recitation of my woes!

ELECTRA

I am about to die and cannot help lamenting my woes. All mortals find their own dear lives a matter for tears.

ORESTES

This is the day fixed for us: our hands must either fasten hanging nooses or sharpen a sword.

ELECTRA

You kill me then, brother, not one of the Argives, which would be an insult to the house of Agamemnon.

ORESTES

My mother's blood is enough. I shall not kill you: rather die by your own hand any way you like.

ELECTRA

It shall be so: I shall ply the sword and follow close after you. But I want to put my arms about your neck.

ORESTES

Enjoy the empty pleasure of an embrace, if pleasure it is to those so close to death.

1041 ξίφει Wecklein: -ους C

ΗΛΕΚΤΡΑ

1045 ὦ φίλτατ᾽, ὦ ποθεινὸν ἥδιστόν τ᾽ ἔχων
τῆς σῆς ἀδελφῆς ὄμμα καὶ ψυχὴ μία.

ΟΡΕΣΤΗΣ

ἔκ τοί μ᾽ ἔτηξας· καί σ᾽ ἀμείψασθαι θέλω
φιλότητι χειρῶν. τί γὰρ ἔτ᾽ αἰδοῦμαι τάλας;
[ὦ στέρν᾽ ἀδελφῆς, ὦ φίλον πρόσπτυγμ᾽ ἐμόν,
1050 τάδ᾽ ἀντὶ παίδων καὶ γαμηλίου λέχους
προσφθέγματ᾽ ἀμφοῖν τοῖς ταλαιπώροις πάρα.]

ΗΛΕΚΤΡΑ

φεῦ·
πῶς ἂν ξίφος νὼ ταὐτόν, εἰ θέμις, κτάνοι
καὶ μνῆμα δέξαιθ᾽ ἕν, κέδρου τεχνάσματα;

ΟΡΕΣΤΗΣ

ἥδιστ᾽ ἂν εἴη ταῦθ᾽· ὁρᾷς δὲ δὴ φίλων
1055 ὡς ἐσπανίσμεθ᾽, ὥστε κοινωνεῖν τάφου.

ΗΛΕΚΤΡΑ

οὐδ᾽ εἶφ᾽ ὑπὲρ σοῦ μὴ θανεῖν σπουδὴν ἔχων
Μενέλαος ὁ κακός, ὁ προδότης τοὐμοῦ πατρός;

ΟΡΕΣΤΗΣ

οὐδ᾽ ὄμμ᾽ ἔδειξεν, ἀλλ᾽ ἐπὶ σκήπτροις ἔχων
τὴν ἐλπίδ᾽ ηὐλαβεῖτο μὴ σῴζειν φίλους.
1060 ἀλλ᾽ εἶ᾽ ὅπως γενναῖα κἀγαμέμνονος
δράσαντε κατθανούμεθ᾽ ἀξιώτατα.

1046 ὄμμα Tyrwhitt: ὄνομα C   ψυχὴ μία Weil: -ην μίαν C
1047 μ᾽ ἔτηξας unus cod., coni. Bothe: με τήξεις ceteri codd.

528

ELECTRA

O dearest one, possessor of your sister's longed-for and dearest joy, one in soul with her!

ORESTES

You have made me melt, you know! I want to return your embrace. Why let myself, poor man that I am, be checked by shame? [O sister's bosom, O dearest of embraces to me, these words for both of us luckless ones take the place of children and the marriage bed.]

They embrace, then separate.

ELECTRA

Ah, how I wish, if it's right to ask, that the same sword could kill us both, and that a single tomb, carved in cedar wood, could receive our bodies!

ORESTES

That would be most welcome! But you see how short we are of kin: there's no one to bury us.

ELECTRA

Did he not even speak on your behalf to prevent your death, Menelaus the base, the betrayer of my father?

ORESTES

He didn't even show his face. His hopes are set on the kingship,[28] and he took care not to save his kin. But come now, see to it that before we die we may do noble deeds worthy

---

[28] Probably he means kingship over Argos as well as Sparta.

1049–51 del. Harberton (1051 iam Nauck, 1050–1 Oeri)

EURIPIDES

κἀγὼ μὲν εὐγένειαν ἀποδείξω πόλει,
παίσας πρὸς ἧπαρ φασγάνῳ· σὲ δ᾽ αὖ χρεὼν
ὅμοια πράσσειν τοῖς ἐμοῖς τολμήμασιν.

1065 Πυλάδη, σὺ δ᾽ ἡμῖν τοῦ φόνου γενοῦ βραβεύς,
καὶ κατθανόντοιν εὖ περίστειλον δέμας
θάψον τε κοινῇ πρὸς πατρὸς τύμβον φέρων.
καὶ χαῖρ᾽· ἐπ᾽ ἔργον δ᾽, ὡς ὁρᾷς, πορεύομαι.

ΠΥΛΑΔΗΣ

ἐπίσχες. ἓν μὲν πρῶτά σοι μομφὴν ἔχω,
1070 εἰ ζῆν με χρῄζειν σοῦ θανόντος ἤλπισας.

ΟΡΕΣΤΗΣ

τί γὰρ προσήκει κατθανεῖν σ᾽ ἐμοῦ μέτα;

ΠΥΛΑΔΗΣ

ἤρου; τί δὲ ζῆν σῆς ἑταιρίας ἄτερ;

ΟΡΕΣΤΗΣ

οὐκ ἔκτανες σὺ μητέρ᾽, ὡς ἐγὼ τάλας.

ΠΥΛΑΔΗΣ

σὺν σοί γε κοινῇ· ταὐτὰ καὶ πάσχειν με δεῖ.

ΟΡΕΣΤΗΣ

1075 ἀπόδος τὸ σῶμα πατρί, μὴ σύνθνῃσκέ μοι.
σοὶ μὲν γάρ ἐστι πόλις, ἐμοὶ δ᾽ οὐκ ἔστι δή,
καὶ δῶμα πατρὸς καὶ μέγας πλούτου λιμήν.
γάμων δὲ τῆς μὲν δυσπότμου τῆσδ᾽ ἐσφάλης,
ἥν σοι κατηγγύησ᾽ ἑταιρίαν σέβων·
1080 σὺ δ᾽ ἄλλο λέκτρον παιδοποίησαι λαβών,
κῆδος δὲ τοὐμὸν καὶ σὸν οὐκέτ᾽ ἔστι δή.

530

of Agamemnon. I will show my nobility to the city by strik-
ing myself to the heart with the sword. Your brave deed
must be just like mine.

Pylades, you must preside over our death: when we
have died, clothe our bodies for burial, take us to our
father's tomb, and bury us together. Farewell! As you see,
I'm headed off to do the deed.

He turns to go indoors.

PYLADES

Stop! First, I have one complaint to make of you, that you
suppose I will want to live when you are dead.

ORESTES

Why on earth must you die along with me?

PYLADES

What a question! Why must I *live* without your friendship?

ORESTES

You have not killed a mother, as I, poor wretch, have done.

PYLADES

Yes I have, together with you. Now I must suffer the same
as you.

ORESTES

Take yourself back to your father, don't die with me. You
have a city, while I have none, you have a father's house and
the great refuge wealth provides. To be sure, you have lost
your marriage to my ill-starred sister here, whom I gave
you to keep in honor of our friendship. But take another
wife and have children! Your marriage tie with me is over.

531

ἀλλ', ὦ ποθεινὸν ὄμμ' ὁμιλίας ἐμῆς,
χαῖρ'· οὐ γὰρ ἡμῖν ἐστι τοῦτο, σοί γε μήν·
οἱ γὰρ θανόντες χαρμάτων τητώμεθα.

ΠΥΛΑΔΗΣ

1085 ἦ πολὺ λέλειψαι τῶν ἐμῶν βουλευμάτων.
μήθ' αἷμά μου δέξαιτο κάρπιμον πέδον,
μὴ λαμπρὸς αἰθήρ, εἴ σ' ἐγὼ προδούς ποτε
ἐλευθερώσας τοὐμὸν ἀπολίποιμι σέ.
καὶ συγκατέκτανον γάρ, οὐκ ἀρνήσομαι,
1090 καὶ πάντ' ἐβούλευσ' ὧν σὺ νῦν τίνεις δίκας·
καὶ ξυνθανεῖν οὖν δεῖ με σοὶ καὶ τῇδ' ὁμοῦ.
ἐμὴν γὰρ αὐτήν, ἧς ⟨γε⟩ λέχος ἐπῄνεσα,
κρίνω δάμαρτα· τί γὰρ ἐρῶ καλόν ποτε
γῆν Δελφίδ' ἐλθών, Φωκέων ἀκρόπολιν,
1095 ὃς πρὶν μὲν ὑμᾶς δυστυχεῖν φίλος παρῆ,
νῦν δ' οὐκέτ' εἰμὶ δυστυχοῦντί σοι φίλος;
οὐκ ἔστιν· ἀλλὰ ταῦτα μὲν κἀμοὶ μέλει·
ἐπεὶ δὲ κατθανούμεθ', ἐς κοινοὺς λόγους
ἔλθωμεν, ὡς ἂν Μενέλεως συνδυστυχῇ.

ΟΡΕΣΤΗΣ

1100 ὦ φίλτατ', εἰ γὰρ τοῦτο κατθάνοιμ' ἰδών.

ΠΥΛΑΔΗΣ

πιθοῦ νυν, ἀνάμεινον δὲ φασγάνου τομάς.

ΟΡΕΣΤΗΣ

μενῶ, τὸν ἐχθρὸν εἴ τι τιμωρήσομαι.

1092 ⟨γε⟩ Porson

So, friend I long to look upon, fare you well: you may fare well, though I cannot, since we who have died are stripped of all joys.

PYLADES

You have badly misjudged my thinking. May the fruitful earth not receive my blood, nor the bright upper air my spirit if I ever betray you and free myself by abandoning you! I joined in the killing and will not deny it, plotted the whole deed for which you are now being punished. So I also ought to die with you and with her. For since I consented to marry her, I consider her my wife. If I came to Delphi, the central city of the Phocians, what could I say to my credit, I who stood by you as a friend before your trouble but now that trouble visits you am your friend no longer? It cannot be: your fate is my concern as well. But since we are going to die, let us plan how Menelaus may suffer with us.

ORESTES

Dearest friend, if only I could see this happen and then die!

PYLADES

Do as I say then: wait a bit for the thrust of the sword.

ORESTES

I will wait if I can take revenge on an enemy.

ΠΥΛΑΔΗΣ

σίγα νυν· ὡς γυναιξὶ πιστεύω βραχύ.

ΟΡΕΣΤΗΣ

μηδὲν τρέσῃς τάσδ᾽· ὡς πάρεισ᾽ ἡμῖν φίλαι.

ΠΥΛΑΔΗΣ

1105 Ἑλένην κτάνωμεν, Μενέλεῳ λύπην πικράν.

ΟΡΕΣΤΗΣ

πῶς; τὸ γὰρ ἕτοιμον ᾔνεσ᾽, εἴ γ᾽ ἔσται καλῶς.

ΠΥΛΑΔΗΣ

σφάξαντες· ἐν δόμοις δὲ κρύπτεται σέθεν.

ΟΡΕΣΤΗΣ

μάλιστα· καὶ δὴ πάντ᾽ ἀποσφραγίζεται.

ΠΥΛΑΔΗΣ

ἀλλ᾽ οὐκέθ᾽, Ἅιδην νυμφίον κεκτημένη.

ΟΡΕΣΤΗΣ

1110 καὶ πῶς; ἔχει γὰρ βαρβάρους ὀπάονας.

ΠΥΛΑΔΗΣ

τίνας; Φρυγῶν γὰρ οὐδέν᾽ ἂν τρέσαιμ᾽ ἐγώ.

ΟΡΕΣΤΗΣ

οἵους ἐνόπτρων καὶ μύρων ἐπιστάτας.

ΠΥΛΑΔΗΣ

τρυφὰς γὰρ ἥκει δεῦρ᾽ ἔχουσα Τρωικάς;

ΟΡΕΣΤΗΣ

ὡς Ἑλλὰς αὐτῇ σμικρὸν οἰκητήριον.

PYLADES

Softly then: I have little confidence in women.

ORESTES

Have no fear of these women: they are here as my friends.

PYLADES

Let's kill Helen and cause Menelaus sharp grief.

ORESTES

How? I approve your eagerness provided the outcome is successful.

PYLADES

Cut her throat. She is hiding in your house.

ORESTES

Yes. In fact she is putting the whole house under her seal.

PYLADES

She won't do that any longer: her new husband is Hades.

ORESTES

How can that be? She has foreign slaves.

PYLADES

What slaves? I'm not afraid of anyone from Phrygia.

ORESTES

Men fit to hold her mirror and myrrh bottles.

PYLADES

What? Has she brought luxuries with her from Troy?

ORESTES

Know this: Greece is too small an abode for her.

1106 ἤνεσ᾽ Willink: ἔστιν C

EURIPIDES

ΠΥΛΑΔΗΣ

1115 οὐδὲν τὸ δοῦλον πρὸς τὸ μὴ δοῦλον γένος.

ΟΡΕΣΤΗΣ

καὶ μὴν τόδ᾽ ἔρξας δὶς θανεῖν οὐχ ἅζομαι.

ΠΥΛΑΔΗΣ

ἀλλ᾽ οὐδ᾽ ἐγὼ μήν, σοί γε τιμωρούμενος.

ΟΡΕΣΤΗΣ

τὸ πρᾶγμα δήλου καὶ πέραιν᾽, ὅπως λέγεις.

ΠΥΛΑΔΗΣ

εἴσιμεν ἐς οἴκους δῆθεν ὡς θανούμενοι.

ΟΡΕΣΤΗΣ

1120 ἔχω τοσοῦτον, τἀπίλοιπα δ᾽ οὐκ ἔχω.

ΠΥΛΑΔΗΣ

γόους πρὸς αὐτὴν θησόμεσθ᾽ ἃ πάσχομεν.

ΟΡΕΣΤΗΣ

ὥστ᾽ ἐκδακρῦσαί γ᾽ ἔνδοθεν κεχαρμένην.

ΠΥΛΑΔΗΣ

καὶ νῷν παρέσται ταῦθ᾽ ἅπερ κείνῃ τότε.

ΟΡΕΣΤΗΣ

ἔπειτ᾽ ἀγῶνα πῶς ἀγωνιούμεθα;

ΠΥΛΑΔΗΣ

1125 κρύπτ᾽ ἐν πέπλοισι τοισίδ᾽ ἕξομεν ξίφη.

ΟΡΕΣΤΗΣ

πρόσθεν δ᾽ ὀπαδῶν τίς ὄλεθρος γενήσεται;

PYLADES

Slaves are nothing in comparison to free men.

ORESTES

Well, when I have done this, I do not shrink from dying
twice.

PYLADES

Nor do I, provided I can avenge you.

ORESTES

Carry on and explain the deed: what do you mean?

PYLADES

We enter the house as if about to die.

ORESTES

That much I understand, the rest not.

PYLADES

We bewail our plight to her.

ORESTES

Yes, so that she will weep while inwardly being glad.

PYLADES

The same will be true for us as for her.

ORESTES

And how do we then fight our fight?

PYLADES

We'll have swords hidden in these garments of ours.

ORESTES

How will the attendants be got rid of first?

ΠΥΛΑΔΗΣ
ἐκκλήσομέν σφας ἄλλον ἄλλοσε στέγης.

ΟΡΕΣΤΗΣ
καὶ τόν γε μὴ σιγῶντ᾽ ἀποκτείνειν χρεών.

ΠΥΛΑΔΗΣ
εἶτ᾽ αὐτὸ δηλοῖ τοὔργον οἷ τείνειν χρεών.

ΟΡΕΣΤΗΣ
1130   Ἑλένην φονεύειν· μανθάνω τὸ σύμβολον.

ΠΥΛΑΔΗΣ
ἔγνως· ἄκουσον δ᾽ ὡς καλῶς βουλεύομαι.
εἰ μὲν γὰρ ἐς γυναῖκα σωφρονεστέραν
ξίφος μεθεῖμεν, δυσκλεὴς ἂν ἦν φόνος·
νῦν δ᾽ ὑπὲρ ἀπάσης Ἑλλάδος δώσει δίκην,
1135   ὧν πατέρας ἔκτειν᾽, ὧν δ᾽ ἀπώλεσεν τέκνα,
νύμφας τ᾽ ἔθηκεν ὀρφανὰς ξυναόρων·
ὀλολυγμὸς ἔσται, πῦρ τ᾽ ἀνάψουσιν θεοῖς,
σοὶ πολλὰ κἀμοὶ κέδν᾽ ἀρώμενοι τυχεῖν,
κακῆς γυναικὸς οὕνεχ᾽ αἷμ᾽ ἐπράξαμεν.
1140   ὁ μητροφόντης δ᾽ οὐ καλῇ ταύτην κτανών,
ἀλλ᾽ ἀπολιπὼν τοῦτ᾽ ἐπὶ τὸ βέλτιον πεσῇ,
Ἑλένης λεγόμενος τῆς πολυκτόνου φονεύς.
οὐ δεῖ ποτ᾽, οὐ δεῖ Μενέλεων μὲν εὐτυχεῖν,
τὸν σὸν δὲ πατέρα καὶ σὲ κἀδελφὴν θανεῖν,
1145   μητέρα τ᾽ . . . ἐῶ τοῦτ᾽· οὐ γὰρ εὐπρεπὲς λέγειν·
δόμους δ᾽ ἔχειν σοὺς δι᾽ Ἀγαμέμνονος δόρυ
λαβόντα νύμφην· μὴ γὰρ οὖν ζῴην ἔτι,
εἰ μὴ ᾽π᾽ ἐκείνῃ φάσγανον σπάσω μέλαν.

PYLADES

We'll lock them up in various rooms of the palace.

ORESTES

Yes, and any who won't keep quiet we must kill.

PYLADES

Thereafter the task itself makes plain where we must go.

ORESTES

Yes, killing Helen. I understand what your words imply.

PYLADES

You take my meaning. But hear what a good plan I am concocting. If we were to take the sword to a woman of greater virtue, the bloodletting would bring disgrace on us. As things are, she'll be paying for her crimes against all of Hellas, those whose fathers she slew and whose sons she destroyed while depriving brides of their husbands. There will be shouts of joy, they will light altar fires for the gods and pray many blessings on your head and mine for killing a wicked woman! You won't be known as "the matricide" once you kill her: you'll leave all that behind for a better lot and be called "the killer of deadly Helen." It is not right, no it is not, that Menelaus should prosper while your father, your sister, and you perish, and your mother—but I leave that topic alone since it is a disgrace to speak of it—and that he should have your house, having got his wife back through Agamemnon's spear. May I live no longer if I don't draw my dark sword against her! Well, if we don't succeed

EURIPIDES

ἢν δ' οὖν τὸν Ἑλένης μὴ κατάσχωμεν φόνον,
1150 πρήσαντες οἴκους τούσδε κατθανούμεθα.
ἑνὸς γὰρ οὐ σφαλέντες ἕξομεν κλέος,
καλῶς θανόντες ἢ καλῶς σεσωμένοι.

ΧΟΡΟΣ

πάσαις γυναιξὶν ἀξία στυγεῖν ἔφυ
ἡ Τυνδαρὶς παῖς, ἢ κατήσχυνεν γένος.

ΟΡΕΣΤΗΣ
1155 φεῦ·
οὐκ ἔστιν οὐδὲν κρεῖσσον ἢ φίλος σαφής,
οὐ πλοῦτος, οὐ τυραννίς· ἀλόγιστον δέ τοι
τὸ πλῆθος ἀντάλλαγμα γενναίου φίλου.
σὺ γὰρ τά τ' εἰς Αἴγισθον ἐξηῦρες κακὰ
καὶ πλησίον παρῆσθα κινδύνων ἐμοί,
1160 νῦν τ' αὖ δίδως μοι πολεμίων τιμωρίαν
κοὐκ ἐκποδὼν εἶ· παύσομαί σ' αἰνῶν, ἐπεὶ
βάρος τι κἀν τῷδ' ἐστίν, αἰνεῖσθαι λίαν.
ἐγὼ δὲ πάντως ἐκπνέων ψυχὴν ἐμὴν
δράσας τι χρῄζω τοὺς ἐμοὺς ἐχθροὺς θανεῖν,
1165 ἵν' ἀνταναλώσω μὲν οἵ με προύδοσαν,
στένωσι δ' οἵπερ κἄμ' ἔθηκαν ἄθλιον.
Ἀγαμέμνονός τοι παῖς πέφυχ', ὃς Ἑλλάδος
ἦρξ' ἀξιωθείς, οὐ τύραννος, ἀλλ' ὅμως
ῥώμην θεοῦ τιν' ἔσχ'· ὃν οὐ καταισχυνῶ
1170 δοῦλον παρασχὼν θάνατον, ἀλλ' ἐλευθέρως
ψυχὴν ἀφήσω, Μενέλεων δὲ τείσομαι.
ἑνὸς γὰρ εἰ λαβοίμεθ', εὐτυχοῖμεν ἄν·

540

in killing Helen, we'll set fire to this house and then perish. We will be successful at one or the other of these and win renown either by gloriously dying or by gloriously saving our lives.

Tyndareus' daughter deserves the hatred of all women. She has disgraced her sex.

Ah ah! There is nothing greater than a firm friend, not money, not kingly power! The value of a true friend is incalculably great![29] It was you who devised death for Aegisthus and stood by me when danger was near, and here again you provide me with vengeance against my enemies: you won't run for cover. But I must stop praising you since excess in praise, as in other things, is irksome.

Now since I am in any case going to breathe out my life, I want to do something to my enemies before I die so that I can repay with destruction those who have betrayed me and so that those who have made me miserable may smart for it. I am, after all, the son of Agamemnon, who ruled Greece not by right of kingship but because he was thought deserving (though he did acquire a certain god-like might). I shall not bring disgrace on him by dying a slavish death. Rather I shall expend my life like a free man and punish Menelaus. For if I can grasp one of my goals, I

[29] Or "It would be a fool's bargain to take the favor of the crowd in exchange for a single true friend."

1161 fort. παύσομαι δ᾽ αἰνῶν σ᾽

κεἴ ποθεν ἄελπτος παραπέσοι σωτηρία
κτανοῦσι μὴ θανοῦσιν, εὔχομαι τάδε.
1175 ὃ βούλομαι γάρ, ἡδὺ καὶ διὰ στόμα
πτηνοῖσι μύθοις ἀδαπάνως τέρψαι φρένα.

ΗΛΕΚΤΡΑ
ἐγώ, κασίγνητ᾽, αὐτὸ τοῦτ᾽ ἔχειν δοκῶ,
σωτηρίαν σοι τῷδέ τ᾽ ἐκ τρίτων τ᾽ ἐμοί.

ΟΡΕΣΤΗΣ
θεοῦ λέγεις πρόνοιαν. ἀλλὰ ποῦ τόδε;
1180 ἐπεὶ τὸ συνετόν γ᾽ οἶδα σῇ ψυχῇ παρόν.

ΗΛΕΚΤΡΑ
ἄκουε δή νυν, καὶ σὺ δεῦρο νοῦν ἔχε.

ΟΡΕΣΤΗΣ
λέγ᾽· ὡς τὸ μέλλειν ἀγάθ᾽ ἔχει τίν᾽ ἡδονήν;

ΗΛΕΚΤΡΑ
Ἑλένης κάτοισθα θυγατέρ᾽; εἰδότ᾽ ἠρόμην.

ΟΡΕΣΤΗΣ
οἶδ᾽, ἥν ⟨γ᾽⟩ ἔθρεψεν Ἑρμιόνην μήτηρ ἐμή.

ΗΛΕΚΤΡΑ
1185 αὕτη βέβηκε πρὸς Κλυταιμήστρας τάφον.

ΟΡΕΣΤΗΣ
τί χρῆμα δράσουσ᾽; ὑποτίθης τίν᾽ ἐλπίδα;

1173 κεἴ Willink: εἰ C
1175 ὃ] οὐ Σ, unde οὐ Willink
1184 ⟨γ᾽⟩ West

will be a lucky man. And if somehow I receive my life unexpectedly as a bonus and can kill without being killed—well, that is my prayer. Where wishing is concerned it is sweet to gratify the mind by winged words that cost nothing to utter.

ELECTRA
Dear brother, I think I have the very thing you speak of, rescue from death for you, for him, and thirdly for me.

ORESTES
Divine providence, you mean. But where is that to be found? I ask you since I know that you have good brains in your head.

ELECTRA
Hear me then. (*to Pylades*) And you listen as well.

ORESTES
Speak then: what pleasure is there in delaying our blessings?

ELECTRA
You know Helen's daughter? How could you not?

ORESTES
‹Yes,› Hermione, whom my mother raised.

ELECTRA
She has gone off to Clytaemestra's tomb.

ORESTES
To do what? What hope are you holding out?

ΗΛΕΚΤΡΑ

χοὰς κατασπείσουσ᾽ ὑπὲρ μητρὸς τάφῳ.

ΟΡΕΣΤΗΣ

καὶ δὴ τί μοι τοῦτ᾽ εἶπας ἐς σωτηρίαν;

ΗΛΕΚΤΡΑ

ξυλλάβεθ᾽ ὅμηρον τήνδ᾽, ὅταν στείχῃ πάλιν.

ΟΡΕΣΤΗΣ

1190   τίνος τόδ᾽ εἶπας φάρμακον τρισσοῖς φίλοις;

ΗΛΕΚΤΡΑ

Ἑλένης θανούσης ἤν τι Μενέλεώς σε δρᾷ
ἢ τόνδε κἀμέ (πᾶν γὰρ ἓν φίλον τόδε),
λέγ᾽ ὡς φονεύσεις Ἑρμιόνην· ξίφος δὲ χρὴ
δέρῃ πρὸς αὐτῇ παρθένου σπάσαντ᾽ ἔχειν.
1195   κἂν μέν σε σῴζῃ μὴ θανεῖν χρῄζων κόρην
[Μενέλαος Ἑλένης πτῶμ᾽ ἰδὼν ἐν αἵματι],
μέθες πεπᾶσθαι πατρὶ παρθένου δέμας·
ἢν δ᾽ ὀξυθύμου μὴ κρατῶν φρονήματος
κτείνῃ σε, καὶ σὺ σφάζε παρθένου δέρην.
1200   καί νιν δοκῶ, τὸ πρῶτον ἢν πολὺς παρῇ,
χρόνῳ μαλάξειν σπλάγχνον· οὔτε γὰρ θρασὺς
οὔτ᾽ ἄλκιμος πέφυκε. τήνδ᾽ ἡμῖν ἔχω
σωτηρίας ἔπαλξιν· εἴρηται λόγος.

ΟΡΕΣΤΗΣ

ὦ τὰς φρένας μὲν ἄρσενας κεκτημένη,
1205   τὸ σῶμα δ᾽ ἐν γυναιξὶ θηλείαις πρέπον,
ὡς ἀξία ζῆν μᾶλλον ἢ θανεῖν ἔφυς.

ELECTRA

To pour libations on the tomb on her mother's behalf.

ORESTES

And how does what you are saying relate to our survival?

ELECTRA

You must seize her as a hostage when she returns.

ORESTES

Your words—what cure do they effect for us three kinsmen?

ELECTRA

If Menelaus, after Helen's death, tries to do anything to you, him, or me (we're all one in kinship here), threaten to kill Hermione: you must hold your drawn sword right up against the girl's neck. And if he saves your life for love of the girl, [Menelaus having seen Helen's dead body lying in blood,] give him back his daughter to keep. But if he fails to conquer his pride and anger and tries to kill you, you must proceed to the cutting of the girl's throat. If he comes on violent at first, I think he will calm down in time. He's not a bold or brave man. That is the means of survival I have thought of. That is all I have to say.

ORESTES

O woman with the heart of a man, yet with a beauty of body outstanding among women, how richly you deserve to live

---

1196 del. Nauck

Πυλάδη, τοιαύτης ἆρ᾽ ἁμαρτήσῃ τάλας
γυναικὸς ἢ ζῶν μακάριον κτήσῃ λέχος.

ΠΥΛΑΔΗΣ

εἰ γὰρ γένοιτο, Φωκέων δ᾽ ἔλθοι πόλιν
1210 καλοῖσιν ὑμεναίοισιν ἀξιουμένη.

ΟΡΕΣΤΗΣ

ἥξει δ᾽ ἐς οἴκους Ἑρμιόνη τίνος χρόνου;
ὡς τἄλλα γ᾽ εἶπας, εἴπερ εὐτυχήσομεν,
κάλλισθ᾽, ἑλόντες σκύμνον ἀνοσίου πατρός.

ΗΛΕΚΤΡΑ

καὶ δὴ πέλας νιν δωμάτων εἶναι δοκῶ·
1215 τοῦ γὰρ χρόνου τὸ μῆκος αὐτὸ συντρέχει.

ΟΡΕΣΤΗΣ

καλῶς· σὺ μέν νυν, σύγγον᾽ Ἠλέκτρα, δόμων
πάρος μένουσα παρθένου δέχου πόδα,
φύλασσε δ᾽ ἤν τις, πρὶν τελευτηθῇ φόνος,
[ἢ ξύμμαχός τις ἢ κασίγνητος πατρός,]
1220 ἐλθὼν ἐς οἴκους φθῇ, γέγωνέ τ᾽ ἐς δόμους,
ἢ σανίδα παίσασ᾽ ἢ λόγους πέμψασ᾽ ἔσω·
ἡμεῖς δ᾽ ἔσω στείχοντες ἐπὶ τὸν ἔσχατον
ἀγῶν᾽ ὁπλιζώμεσθα φασγάνῳ χέρας
[Πυλάδη· σὺ γὰρ δὴ συμπονεῖς ἐμοὶ πόνους].
1225 ὦ δῶμα ναίων Νυκτὸς ὀρφναίας πάτερ,
καλῶ σ᾽ Ὀρέστης παῖς σὸς ἐπίκουρον μολεῖν
[τοῖς δεομένοισι· διὰ σὲ γὰρ πάσχω τάλας
ἀδίκως, προδέδομαι δ᾽ ὑπὸ κασιγνήτου σέθεν,
δίκαια πράξας· οὗ θέλω δάμαρθ᾽ ἑλὼν

rather than to die! Poor Pylades, such is the wife whom you will be bereft of—or whose bed, should you survive, will make you blessed!

PYLADES
I pray that may happen and that she may come to the land of Phocis, celebrated by lovely bridal songs!

ORESTES
But when will Hermione return? All else you have said is excellent provided we can succeed in catching this whelp of a godless sire.

ELECTRA
Well, I suppose she is quite near the house. The length of her absence in itself supports this.

ORESTES
Good! Therefore, Electra my sister, you must stay in front of the house and await the girl's arrival. And be on guard in case someone [either an ally or a brother of your father] should come to the house before the murder is complete, and let us know inside, either by pounding on the door or by sending word. As for us, since we are going in to face our final struggle, let us put swords in our hands [Pylades, since you are joining me in the work].

O father, dwelling in the halls of dark Night, I your son Orestes call on you to come to my aid [to those who need you. For it is on your account that I suffer misery unjustly, and I have been abandoned by your brother though I acted

---

1219 del. Herwerden
1224 del. Hermann
1226 καλῶ Herwerden: -εῖ C
1227–30 del. Nauck cl. Σ

1230 κτεῖναι· σὺ δ᾽ ἡμῖν τοῦδε συλλήπτωρ γενοῦ].

ΗΛΕΚΤΡΑ
ὦ πάτερ, ἱκοῦ δῆτ᾽, εἰ κλύεις ἔσω χθονὸς
τέκνων καλούντων, οἳ σέθεν θνήσκουσ᾽ ὕπερ.

ΠΥΛΑΔΗΣ
ὦ συγγένεια πατρὸς ἐμοῦ, κἀμὰς λιτάς,
Ἀγάμεμνον, εἰσάκουσον· ἔκσωσον τέκνα.

ΟΡΕΣΤΗΣ
1235 ἔκτεινα μητέρ᾽ . . .

ΗΛΕΚΤΡΑ
ἠψάμην δ᾽ ἐγὼ ξίφους.

ΠΥΛΑΔΗΣ
ἐγὼ δέ γ᾽ ἐπεκέλευσα κἀπέλυσ᾽ ὄκνου.

ΟΡΕΣΤΗΣ
. . . σοί, πάτερ, ἀρήγων.

ΗΛΕΚΤΡΑ
οὐδ᾽ ἐγὼ προύδωκά σε.

ΠΥΛΑΔΗΣ
οὔκουν ὀνείδη τάδε κλυὼν ῥύσῃ τέκνα;

ΟΡΕΣΤΗΣ
δακρύοις κατασπένδω σ᾽.

ΗΛΕΚΤΡΑ
ἐγὼ δ᾽ οἴκτοισί γε.

ΠΥΛΑΔΗΣ
1240 παύσασθε, καὶ πρὸς ἔργον ἐξορμώμεθα.

548

justly. I want to take his wife and kill her. But you be my
helper]!

ELECTRA

Father, come, if you hear deep in earth the voices of your
children calling you, children who are being killed because
of you!

PYLADES

Agamemnon, kinsman of my father, hear my prayer as
well: save your children!

ORESTES

I killed my mother . . .

ELECTRA

And I put my hand to the sword.

PYLADES

And I urged him on and overcame his hesitation.

ORESTES

. . . in aid of you, father.

ELECTRA

I did not abandon you either.

PYLADES

Will you not listen to these reproaches and save your
children?

ORESTES

To you I pour a libation of my tears.

ELECTRA

And I of my laments.

PYLADES

Stop now and let us set off for our work. If prayers reach

εἴπερ γὰρ εἴσω γῆς ἀκοντίζουσ᾽ ἀραί,
κλύει. σὺ δ᾽, ὦ Ζεῦ πρόγονε καὶ Δίκης σέβας,
δότ᾽ εὐτυχῆσαι τῷδ᾽ ἐμοί τε τῇδέ τε·
τρισσοῖς φίλοις γὰρ εἷς ἀγών, δίκη μία.
1245 [ἢ ζῆν ἅπασιν ἢ θανεῖν ὀφείλεται.]
στρ.

ΗΛΕΚΤΡΑ

Μυκηνίδες ὦ φίλιαι,
τὰ πρῶτα κατὰ Πελασγὸν ἕδος Ἀργείων . . .

ΧΟΡΟΣ

τίνα θροεῖς αὐδάν, πότνια; παραμένει
1250 γὰρ ἔτι σοι τόδ᾽ ἐν Δαναϊδᾶν πόλει.

ΗΛΕΚΤΡΑ

. . . στῆθ᾽ αἱ μὲν ὑμῶν τόνδ᾽ ἁμαξήρη τρίβον,
αἱ δ᾽ ἐνθάδ᾽ ἄλλον οἶμον ἐς φρουρὰν δόμων.

ΧΟΡΟΣ

τί δέ με τόδε χρέος ἀπύεις;
ἔνεπέ μοι, φίλα.

ΗΛΕΚΤΡΑ

1255 φόβος ἔχει με μή τις ἐπιδὼν κάσιν
σταθέντ᾽ ἐπὶ φοίνιον αἷμα
πήματα πήμασιν ἐξεύρῃ.

ΧΟΡΟΣ Α

χωρεῖτ᾽, ἐπειγώμεσθ᾽· ἐγὼ μὲν οὖν τρίβον
τόνδ᾽ ἐκφυλάξω τὸν πρὸς ἡλίου βολάς.

within the earth, he hears us. But, Zeus our progenitor and
holy Justice, grant good fortune to this man, to this woman,
and to me. For we three kinsmen face a single trial and a
single judgment. [All of us must either live or die.]

Exit ORESTES *and* PYLADES *into the house.*

ELECTRA

Dear women of Mycenae,
who rank high in the Pelasgian land of the Argives . . .

CHORUS

What are you saying, my lady? For that
is still your title in the city of the sons of Danaus.

ELECTRA

. . . stand, some of you, on the carriage road here,
and the rest on this other path, to guard the house.

CHORUS

Why this cry, this task for me?
Tell me, dear friend.

ELECTRA

I am afraid that someone might see my brother
poised for the bloody deed
and invent new woes on top of old.

LEADER OF CHORUS A

Come on now, let's hurry! I shall guard
this path here, the one toward the sun's rays.

1245 del. Nauck
1246 φίλιαι Hermann: φίλαι C
1255–6 ἐπιδὼν κάσιν / σταθέντ᾽ Willink: ἐπὶ δώμασι / σταθεὶς
fere C

ΧΟΡΟΣ Β

1260 καὶ μὴν ἐγὼ τόνδ᾽, ὃς πρὸς ἑσπέραν φέρει.

ΗΛΕΚΤΡΑ

δόχμιά νυν κόρας διάφερ᾽ ὀμμάτων.

ΧΟΡΟΣ

ἐκεῖθεν ἐνθάδ᾽ εἶτα πάλιν σκοπιὰν
1265 ἔχομεν, ὡς θροεῖς.

ἀντ.

ΗΛΕΚΤΡΑ

ἑλίσσετέ νυν βλέφαρον,
κόρας διάδοτε πάντᾳ διὰ βοστρύχων.

ΧΟΡΟΣ Α

ὅδε τις ἐν τρίβῳ, πρόσεχε· τίς ὅδ᾽ ἄρ᾽ ἀμ-
1270 φὶ μέλαθρον πολεῖ σὸν ἀγρότας ἀνήρ;

ΗΛΕΚΤΡΑ

ἀπωλόμεσθ᾽ ἄρ᾽, ὦ φίλαι· κεκρυμμένας
θήρας ξιφήρεις αὐτίκ᾽ ἐχθροῖσιν φανεῖ.

ΧΟΡΟΣ Α

ἄφοβος ἔχε· κενός, ὦ φίλα,
στίβος ὃν οὐ δοκεῖς.

ΗΛΕΚΤΡΑ

1275 τί δέ; τὸ σὸν βέβαιον ἔτι μοι μένει;
δὸς ἀγγελίαν ἀγαθάν τιν᾽,
εἰ τάδ᾽ ἔρημα τὰ πρόσθ᾽ αὐλᾶς.

1267 κόρας διάδοτε Canter cl. *Pho.* 1371: κόραισι δίδοτε C

LEADER OF CHORUS B

And I this westward one.

ELECTRA

Sideways turn the glance of your eyes.

CHORUS

From that side to this and then back again
we turn our watchful gaze, as you command.

ELECTRA

Wheel your eyes about,
turn your glance in all directions through the locks of your
   hair.

CHORUS A

Here is someone in the path, take heed! What rustic is this
who comes to your palace?

ELECTRA

We are done for then, my friends: he will reveal
to our enemies the stealthy sword hunt.

CHORUS A

Have no fear: the path is empty,
though you thought it was not.

ELECTRA

And you? Is your side still secure?
Give a report, a good one,
say whether all is empty before the house.

1268–9 πρόσεχε Seidler: προσέρχεται C

ΧΟΡΟΣ Β

καλῶς τά γ᾽ ἐνθένδ᾽. ἀλλὰ τἀπὸ σοῦ σκόπει·
ὡς οὔτις ἡμῖν Δαναϊδῶν πελάζεται.

ΧΟΡΟΣ Α

1280 ἐς ταὐτὸν ἥκεις· καὶ γὰρ οὐδὲ τῇδ᾽ ὄχλος.

ΗΛΕΚΤΡΑ

φέρε νυν ἐν πύλαισιν ἀκοὰν βάλω.

ΧΟΡΟΣ

τί μέλλεθ᾽ οἱ κατ᾽ οἶκον ἐν ἡσυχίᾳ
1285 σφάγια φοινίσσειν;
ἐπῳδ.

ΗΛΕΚΤΡΑ

οὐκ εἰσακούουσ᾽· ὦ τάλαιν᾽ ἐγὼ κακῶν.
ἆρ᾽ ἐς τὸ κάλλος ἐκκεκώφηται ξίφη;

ΧΟΡΟΣ

τάχα τις Ἀργείων ἔνοπλος ὁρμάσας
1290 ποδὶ βοηδρόμῳ μέλαθρα προσμείξει.

ΗΛΕΚΤΡΑ

σκέψασθέ νυν ἄμεινον· οὐχ ἕδρας ἀγών·
ἀλλ᾽ αἱ μὲν ἐνθάδ᾽, αἱ δ᾽ ἐκεῖσ᾽ ἑλίσσετε.

ΧΟΡΟΣ

1295 ἀμείβω κέλευθον σκοπεύουσα πάντα.

1278 τἀπὸ Blomfield: τἀπὶ fere C
1293 ἐκεῖσε λεύσσετε van Gent
1294–5 σκοπεύουσα Nauck: σκοποῦσα C

554

LEADER OF CHORUS B

All is well here. But take a look at your side:
no sons of Danaus are approaching me.

LEADER OF CHORUS A

I have nothing different to report: no crowd comes this
  way either.

ELECTRA

Come, let me listen at the gates.

CHORUS

You in the house, why are you so slow, when all is quiet,
to stain your victims red?

There is a pause as all listen.

ELECTRA

They do not hear us! O misery for me!
Have their swords been blunted by her beauty?

CHORUS

Soon some Argive in full armor
will rush on rescuing feet and approach the house.

ELECTRA

Keep better watch, then. This is no time to sit around:
some of you wheel about in this direction, others in that.

The two semichoruses change positions.

CHORUS

I move along the path, spying in all directions.

ΕΛΕΝΗ

(ἔσωθεν)
ἰὼ Πελασγὸν Ἄργος, ὄλλυμαι κακῶς.

ΗΛΕΚΤΡΑ

ἠκούσαθ'; ἄνδρες χεῖρ' ἔχουσιν ἐν φόνῳ·
Ἑλένης τὸ κώκυμ' ἐστίν, ὡς ἀπεικάσαι.

ΧΟΡΟΣ

ὦ Διὸς ὦ Διὸς ἀέναον κράτος,
1300   ἔλθ' ἐπίκουρος ἐμοῖσι φίλοισι πάντως.

ΕΛΕΝΗ

(ἔσωθεν)
Μενέλαε, θνῄσκω· σὺ δὲ παρών μ' οὐκ ὠφελεῖς.

ΧΟΡΟΣ

καίνετε, καίνετε, θείνετ' ἀπόλλυτε,
δίπτυχα δίστομα φάσγαν' ἐκ χερὸς ἱέμενοι
1305   τὰν λιποπάτριδα λιπογάμετον, ἃ πλείστους
ἔκανεν Ἑλλάνων
δορὶ παρὰ ποταμὸν ὀλομένους,
ὅθι δάκρυα δάκρυσι πέσε σιδαρέοις
1310   βέλεσιν ἀμφὶ τὰς Σκαμάνδρου δίνας.

ΧΟΡΟΣ

σιγᾶτε σιγᾶτ'· ᾐσθόμην κτύπου τινὸς
κέλευθον ἐσπεσόντος ἀμφὶ δώματα.

1302n Ηλ. καὶ Χο. Di Benedetto cl. 1314
1302 καίνετε καίνετε unus cod.: φονεύετε κ- fere ceteri codd.
ἀπόλλυτε Wecklein: ὄλλυτε C

HELEN

(*within*) Help, Pelasgian Argos! Foul murder!

ELECTRA

Did you hear? The men have their hands in blood!
That was Helen's cry, I think.

CHORUS

O unfailing power of Zeus, Zeus,
come by all means to help my friends!

HELEN

(*within*) They're murdering me, Menelaus! You are not
here to help me!

CHORUS

Slay, slay, smite, destroy her,
plying at close range your twin double-edged swords,
slay the betrayer of country and husband, who killed
so many Greeks
by the spear at the river's edge,
where iron weapons made tears fall on tears
by Scamander's eddies!

CHORUS LEADER

Silence, silence! I heard someone's footfall, someone coming along the path near the palace!

Enter by Eisodos A HERMIONE.

1305 λιποπάτριδα Herwerden: -πάτορα fere C   λιπο-
γάμετον West: λιπόγαμον fere C

1309 πέσε Willink: ἔπεσε vel συνέπεσε(ν) vel συνέπεσεν
ἔπεσε C

ΗΛΕΚΤΡΑ

ὦ φίλταται γυναῖκες, ἐς μέσον φόνον
ἥδ᾽ Ἑρμιόνη πάρεστι· παύσωμεν βοήν.
1315 στείχει γὰρ ἐσπεσοῦσα δικτύων βρόχους.
καλὸν τὸ θήραμ᾽, ἢν ἁλῷ, γενήσεται.
πάλιν κατάστηθ᾽ ἡσύχῳ μὲν ὄμματι,
χροιᾷ δ᾽ ἀδήλῳ τῶν δεδραμένων πέρι·
κἀγὼ σκυθρωποὺς ὀμμάτων ἔξω κόρας,
1320 ὡς δῆθεν οὐκ εἰδυῖα τἀξειργασμένα.
    ὦ παρθέν᾽, ἥκεις τὸν Κλυταιμήστρας τάφον
στέψασα καὶ σπείσασα νερτέροις χοάς;

ΕΡΜΙΟΝΗ

ἥκω, λαβοῦσα πρευμένειαν. ἀλλά μοι
φόβος τις εἰσελήλυθ᾽, ἥντιν᾽ ἐν δόμοις
1325 τηλουρὸς οὖσα δωμάτων κλύω βοήν.

ΗΛΕΚΤΡΑ

τί δ᾽; ἄξι᾽ ἡμῖν τυγχάνει στεναγμάτων.

ΕΡΜΙΟΝΗ

εὔφημος ἴσθι· τί δὲ νεώτερον λέγεις;

ΗΛΕΚΤΡΑ

θανεῖν Ὀρέστην κἄμ᾽ ἔδοξε τῇδε γῇ.

ΕΡΜΙΟΝΗ

μὴ δῆτ᾽, ἐμοῦ γε συγγενεῖς πεφυκότας.

ΗΛΕΚΤΡΑ

1330 ἄραρ᾽· ἀνάγκης δ᾽ ἐς ζυγὸν καθέσταμεν.

ELECTRA

Dearest women, here comes Hermione into the middle of
the slaughter. We must stop our shouting: she has fallen
right into the toils of our net and is approaching! She'll be a
fine catch if catch her we can.[30] Compose yourselves: make
your expressions calm and let your color betray nothing of
what has happened. And I shall put on a crestfallen look
and not let on that I know what has happened.

Hermione, have you come from garlanding Clytae-
mestra's grave and making a libation to the dead?

HERMIONE

I have: I have won her good will. But I am frightened at the
shouting I heard in the palace when I was far off.

ELECTRA

Well, things that call for tears have befallen us.

HERMIONE

Speak no ill-omened word! But what new thing do you
mean?

ELECTRA

This land has decreed that Orestes and I must die.

HERMIONE

Say not so: you are my kinsmen!

ELECTRA

It is fixed: we find ourselves in necessity's yoke.

---

[30] An animal might be in the nets but still escape capture.

1315–6 in suspicionem voc. Diggle
1315 ἐσπαίσουσα Wecklein cl. *Rh.* 560

ΕΡΜΙΟΝΗ

ἦ τοῦδ' ἕκατι καὶ βοὴ κατὰ στέγας;

ΗΛΕΚΤΡΑ

ἱκέτης γὰρ Ἑλένης γόνασι προσπεσὼν βοᾷ . . .

ΕΡΜΙΟΝΗ

τίς; οὐδὲν οἶδα μᾶλλον, ἢν σὺ μὴ λέγῃς.

ΗΛΕΚΤΡΑ

. . . τλήμων Ὀρέστης, μὴ θανεῖν, ἐμοῦ θ' ὕπερ.

ΕΡΜΙΟΝΗ

1335   ἐπ' ἀξίοισί τἄρ' ἀνευφημεῖ δόμος.

ΗΛΕΚΤΡΑ

περὶ τοῦ γὰρ ἄλλου μᾶλλον ἂν φθέγξαιτό τις;
ἀλλ' ἐλθὲ καὶ μετάσχες ἱκεσίας φίλοις,
σῇ μητρὶ προσπεσοῦσα τῇ μέγ' ὀλβίᾳ,
Μενέλαον ἡμᾶς μὴ θανόντας εἰσιδεῖν.
1340   ἄγ', ὦ τραφεῖσα μητρὸς ἐν χεροῖν ἐμῆς,
οἴκτιρον ἡμᾶς κἀπικούφισον κακῶν.
ἴθ' εἰς ἀγῶνα δεῦρ', ἐγὼ δ' ἡγήσομαι·
σωτηρίας γὰρ τέρμ' ἔχεις ἡμῖν μόνη.

ΕΡΜΙΟΝΗ

ἰδού, διώκω τὸν ἐμὸν ἐς δόμους πόδα.
1345   σώθηθ' ὅσον γε τοὐπ' ἔμ'.

ΗΛΕΚΤΡΑ

                    ὦ κατὰ στέγας
φίλοι ξιφήρεις, οὐχὶ συλλήψεσθ' ἄγραν;

560

HERMIONE

Is that why there was shouting in the house?

ELECTRA

Yes: falling as suppliant before Helen's knees and crying out . . .

HERMIONE

Was who? I know nothing more unless you tell me.

ELECTRA

. . . was poor Orestes: his plea was that he not die, and for me he pled as well.

HERMIONE

So there is good reason for the house to wail aloud.

ELECTRA

Yes: what better reason to cry out? But come and take part with your kin in the entreaty, falling at the feet of your most prosperous mother, begging that Menelaus not watch us be put to death. Come, you who were brought up by my mother, take pity on us and relieve us from trouble. Come to the contest: I shall lead the way. You alone are our final salvation.

HERMIONE

There, I am going quickly into the house! Be rescued—as far as depends on me!

Exit HERMIONE *into the house. Electra stands just outside the door looking in.*

ELECTRA

My sword-bearing friends within the house, seize your prey!

ΕΡΜΙΟΝΗ

οἲ 'γώ· τίνας τούσδ' εἰσορῶ;

ΗΛΕΚΤΡΑ

σιγᾶν χρεών·
ἡμῖν γὰρ ἥκεις, οὐχὶ σοί, σωτηρία.
ἔχεσθ' ἔχεσθε· φάσγανον δὲ πρὸς δέρῃ
1350 βαλόντες ἡσυχάζεθ', ὡς εἰδῇ τόδε
Μενέλαος, οὕνεκ' ἄνδρας, οὐ Φρύγας κακούς,
εὑρὼν ἔπραξεν οἷα χρὴ πράσσειν κακούς.

ΧΟΡΟΣ

στρ.

ἰὼ ἰὼ φίλαι,
κτύπον ἐγείρετε, κτύπον καὶ βοὰν
πρὸ μελάθρων, ὅπως ὁ πραχθεὶς φόνος
1355 μὴ δεινὸν Ἀργείοισιν ἐμβάλῃ φόβον,
βοηδρομῆσαι πρὸς δόμους τυραννικούς,
πρὶν ἐτύμως ἴδω τὸν Ἑλένας φόνον
καθαιμακτὸν ἐν δόμοις κείμενον,
ἢ καὶ λόγον του προσπόλων πυθώμεθα·
1360 τὰ μὲν γὰρ οἶδα συμφοράς, τὰ δ' οὐ σαφῶς.
διὰ δίκας ἔβα θεῶν
νέμεσις ἐς Ἑλέναν.
δακρύοισι γὰρ Ἑλλάδ' ἅπασαν ἐπλήρωσεν
διὰ τὸν ὀλόμενον ὀλόμενον Ἰδαῖον
1365 Πάριν, ὃς ἄγαγ' Ἑλλάδ' εἰς Ἴλιον.

1347n Ἠλ. Π, u. v., coni. Lachmann: Ορ. C
1363 ἐπλήρωσεν Diggle: ἔπλησε C

HERMIONE

(*within*) Ah, ah, who are these men I see?

ELECTRA

No more talk! You have come to save our lives, not yours!
Take hold, take hold of her! Place the sword against her
neck and bide your time, so that Menelaus may see that he
has met with real men, not cowardly Phrygians, and has
fared as a coward ought to fare!

Exit ELECTRA *into the house.*

CHORUS

Come, come, my friends,
stamp your feet, your feet, and raise a shout
before the house so that the Argives
may not take dreadful fright at murder just done
and come to the palace to help her
before I see for sure Helen's murdered body
lying bloodied in the palace,
or hear some report from a servant:
part of what has happened I know well, part not well.
By the justice of the gods has come
retribution upon Helen:
she filled all Hellas with weeping
because of that accursed, accursed man of Ida,
Paris, who brought Hellas to Troy.

Enter from the skene *a* PHRYGIAN, *one of Helen's retinue.*

—ἀλλὰ κτυπεῖ γὰρ κλῇθρα βασιλείων δόμων·
σιγήσατ᾽, ἔξω γάρ τις ἐκβαίνει Φρυγῶν,
οὗ πευσόμεσθα τὰν δόμοις ὅπως ἔχει.

ΦΡΥΞ

Ἀργεῖον ξίφος ἐκ θανάτου
πέφευγα βαρβάροις ἐν εὐ-
1370   μάρισιν κεδρωτὰ πα-
στάδων ὑπὲρ τέραμνα
Δωρικάς τε τριγλύφους,
φροῦδα φροῦδα, Γᾶ Γᾶ,
βαρβάροισι δρασμοῖς.
1375   αἰαῖ· πᾷ φύγω, ξέναι, πολιὸν αἰ-
θέρ᾽ ἀμπτάμενος ἢ
πόντον, Ὠκεανὸς ὃν
ταυρόκρανος ἀγκάλαις
ἑλίσσων κυκλοῖ χθόνα;

ΧΟΡΟΣ

1380   τί δ᾽ ἔστιν, Ἑλένης πρόσπολ᾽, Ἰδαῖον κάρα;

ΦΡΥΞ

Ἴλιον Ἴλιον, ὤμοι μοι,
Φρύγιον ἄστυ καὶ καλλίβωλον Ἴ-
δας ὄρος ἱερόν, ὥς σ᾽ ὀλόμενον στένω
[ἁρμάτειον ἁρμάτειον μέλος]
1385   βαρβάρῳ βοᾷ δι᾽ ὀρνιθόγονον
ὄμμα κυκνοπτέρου καλλοσύνας, Λήδας
σκύμνον Δυσελέναν Δυσελέναν,

1366–8 histrionibus imputat Σ

564

CHORUS LEADER

But the bars of the palace gate are clanging. Hush, here
comes one of the Phrygians, from whom we shall learn
how matters stand indoors.

PHRYGIAN

From the realm of death I have escaped
the Argive sword in my barbarian slippers,
passing beyond the bedchamber's
cedar timbers
and their Doric triglyphs,
gone, gone, O Lady Earth, Earth,
in my barbarian flight!
Ah, ah! Where shall I run, foreign ladies? Shall I fly
up to the white upper air
or to the sea, which Ocean,
the bull-headed river god, encircles
in his arms as he goes around the earth?

CHORUS LEADER

What is it, worthy Idaean, Helen's servant?

PHRYGIAN

Ilium, Ilium, ah me, ah me,
the Phrygian citadel and the lovely ground
of Ida's holy mount, how I lament
[the chariot, chariot melody]
with barbarian cry your destruction through the bird-
     begotten
vision of swan-plumed loveliness, Leda's
whelp Ill-helen, Ill-helen, Erinys

1384 om. t, del. Murray cl. Σ   1385 δι᾽ Porson: διὰ τὸ τᾶς C
1386 κυκνοπτέρου Scaliger: κυκνόπτερον C
1387 Δυσελέναν bis Kirchhoff: -νας bis fere C

ξεστῶν περγάμων Ἀπολ-
λωνίων Ἐρινύν.
ὀτοτοτοῖ·
1390 ἰαλέμων ἰαλέμων
Δαρδανία τλάμων,
Γανυμήδεος ἱπποσύνα, Διὸς εὐνάτα.

ΧΟΡΟΣ

σαφῶς λέγ' ἡμῖν αὖθ' ἕκαστα τὰν δόμοις.
[τὰ γὰρ πρὶν οὐκ εὔγνωστα συμβαλοῦσ' ἔχω.]

ΦΡΥΞ

1395 αἴλινον αἴλινον ἀρχὰν θρήνου
βάρβαροι λέγουσιν,
αἰαῖ, Ἀσιάδι φωνᾷ, βασιλέων
ὅταν αἷμα χυθῇ κατὰ γᾶν ξίφεσιν
σιδαρέοισιν Ἅιδα.
1400 ἦλθον ⟨ἦλθον⟩ ἐς δόμους,
ἵν' αὖθ' ἕκαστά σοι λέγω,
λέοντες Ἕλλανες
δύο διδύμω ⟨ῥυθμῷ⟩·
τῷ μὲν ὁ στρατηλάτας
ἐκλῄζετο πατήρ,
ὁ δὲ παῖς Στροφίου, κακόμητις ἀνὴρ
οἷος Ὀδυσσεύς, σιγᾷ δόλιος,
1405 πιστὸς δὲ φίλοις, θρασὺς εἰς ἀλκάν,

1394 om Π, iam del. Kirchhoff cl. Σ
1395 θρήνου Hartung: θανάτου C
1400a ⟨ἦλθον⟩ Willink

of the adze-smoothed towers
built by Apollo!
Ah, ah!
Luckless the land of Troy
in its dirges, dirges,
riding place of Ganymede, Zeus's bedmate![31]

Tell us exactly what happened indoors. [For your previous
words were not clear, and I could not interpret them.]

Ailinon, ailinon the outlanders say
at the beginning of their lament,
ah me, in Asian accents, when kings' blood
is shed on the ground by the murderous
sword of iron.
There came, ⟨there came⟩, into the house—
I tell you all exactly—
Greek lions
two of them with twofold ⟨motion⟩.
One was said
to have the general for his father,
the other was the son of Strophius, a guileful fellow
like Odysseus, silently crafty,
but loyal to friends, bold for the fight,

---

[31] For Ganymede, a beautiful Trojan prince taken up to Olympus to serve as the gods' cupbearer and male concubine, see *Trojan Women* 820–4.

1401b ⟨ῥυθμῷ⟩ Diggle
1402b ἐκλῄζετο πατήρ Willink: π- ἐ- C

ξυνετὸς πολέμου, φόνιός τε δράκων·
ἔρροι τᾶς ἡσύχου
προνοίας κακοῦργος ὤν.
οἱ δὲ πρὸς θρόνους ἔσω
μολόντες ἃς ἔγημ' ὁ το-
1410 ξότας Πάρις γυναικός, ὄμ-
μα δακρύοις πεφυρμένοι,
ταπείν' ἔζονθ', ὁ μὲν
τὸ κεῖθεν, ὁ δὲ τὸ κεῖθεν, ἄλ-
λος ἄλλοθεν δεδραγμένοι.
περὶ δὲ γόνυ χέρας ἱκεσίους
1415 ἔβαλον ἔβαλον Ἑλένας ἄμφω.
ἀνὰ δὲ δρομάδες ἔθορον ἔθορον
ἀμφίπολοι Φρύγες·
προσεῖπεν δ' ἄλλος ἄλ-
λον πεσὼν ἐν φόβῳ,
1420 μή τις εἴη δόλος·
κἀδόκει τοῖς μὲν οὔ,
τοῖς δ' ἐς ἀρκυστάτων
μηχανὰν ἐμπλέκειν
παῖδα τὰν Τυνδαρίδ' ὁ
ματροφόντας δράκων.

ΧΟΡΟΣ
1425 σὺ δ' ἦσθα ποῦ τότ'; ἢ πάλαι φεύγεις φόβῳ;

ΦΡΥΞ
Φρυγίοις ἔτυχον Φρυγίοισι νόμοις

skilled in war, and a deadly snake:
a curse on his cool planning,
that villain!
Once inside they went to the throne
of the woman who was bride
of the archer Paris,
and their faces were smeared with weeping:
all lowly they sat, the one
on this side, the other on the other,
grasping her from this side and that,
the both of them casting, casting
their suppliant hands about her knees.
They came on a run, leaping, leaping,
the Phrygian slaves,
and one would speak to another,
as he grew afraid
that there was some guile.
Some thought there was not,
but others suspected
that Tyndareus' daughter
was being entwined in the crafty hunting net
by that matricidal snake.

CHORUS LEADER

Where were you at that time? Or were you already taking
to your heels in fear?

PHRYGIAN

I happened in Phrygian, Phrygian style

1412a ταπείν' Willink: ταπεινοὶ C
1413 δεδραγμένοι Shilleto: πεφραγμένοι C
1422 ἀρκυστάτων Blomfield: -ταν C

παρὰ βόστρυχον αὔραν αὔραν
Ἑλένας Ἑλένας εὐπᾶγι κύκλῳ
πτερίνῳ πρὸ παρῆδος ἀίσσων
1430 βαρβάροις νόμοισιν.
ἁ δὲ λίνε᾽ ἠλάκατα
δακτύλοις ἕλισσε, νῆ-
μα δ᾽ ἵετο πέδῳ,
σκύλων Φρυγίων ἐπὶ τύμβον ἀγάλ-
1435 ματα συστολίσαι χρῄζουσα λίνῳ,
φάρεα πορφύρεα, δῶρα Κλυταιμήστρᾳ.
προσεῖπεν δ᾽ Ὀρέστας
Λάκαιναν κόραν· Ὦ Διὸς παῖ,
θὲς ἴχνος πέδῳ δεῦρ᾽
1440 ἀποστᾶσα κλισμοῦ,
Πέλοπος ἐπὶ προπάτορος ἕδρανα
παλαιᾶς ἑστίας,
ἵν᾽ εἰδῇς λόγους ἐμούς.
ἄγει δ᾽ ἄγει νιν· ἁ δ᾽ ἐφείπετ᾽,
1445 οὐ πρόμαντις ὢν ἔμελ-
λεν· ὁ δὲ συνεργὸς ἄλλ᾽ ἔπρασσ᾽
ἰαχῶν κακὸς
Φωκεύς· Οὐκ ἐκποδών;
ἴτ᾽ ἄλλα, κακοὶ Φρύγες.
ἔκλησεν δ᾽ ἄλλον ἄλ-
λοσε στέγας, τοὺς μὲν ἐν

1428 εὐπᾶγι Hermann: εὐπαγεῖ fere C
1430 del. Hartung

to be wafting a breeze, a breeze toward the locks
of Helen, Helen with a disk of well-set plumes,
wafting them past her cheek
in outland fashion.
And she in her fingers twirled
the linen distaff strands,
and the thread sank down to the floor.
From the Phrygian spoils she wanted to stitch with her
   thread
adornments for burial,
robes of purple as a gift to Clytaemestra.
But Orestes addressed
the woman of Sparta: "Zeus's daughter,
put your feet on the ground and come here,
leaving your couch behind,
to the seat by the ancient hearth
of Pelops my ancestor,
so you may learn what I have to say."
And he led her, led her, and she followed,
with no foreknowledge of what was to be.
But his accomplice was tending to other business,
the wicked Phocian, shouting,
"Clear off, won't you?
Go elsewhere, you cowardly Phrygians!"
And he locked them up, in this part of the house
and in that, some

1431 λίνε᾽ ἠλάκατα Willink: λίνον ἠλακάτᾳ C

1446b ἰαχῶν Diggle: ἰὼν C

1447b ἄλλᾳ unus cod., u. v. (coni. Scaliger): ἀλλ᾽ αἰεὶ ceteri
codd.

σταθμοῖσιν ἱππικοῖσι, τοὺς δ'
1450 ἐν ἐξέδραισι, τοὺς δ' ἐκεῖσ'
ἐκεῖθεν [ἄλλον ἄλλοσε] διαρμόσας
ἀποπρὸ δεσποίνας.

ΧΟΡΟΣ
τί τοὐπὶ τῷδε συμφορᾶς ἐγίγνετο;

ΦΡΥΞ
Ἰδαία μᾶτερ μᾶτερ,
ὀβρίμα ὀβρίμα, αἰαῖ ‹αἰαῖ›
1455 φονίων παθέων ἀνόμων τε κακῶν
ἅπερ ἔδρακον ἔδρακον ἐν δόμοις τυράννων.
ἀμφιπορφύρων πέπλων
ὑπὸ σκότου ξίφη σπάσαν-
τες ἐν χεροῖν ἄλλοσ' ἄλ-
λοθεν δίνευον ὄμ-
μα, μή τις παρὼν τύχοι.
1460 ὡς κάπροι δ' ὀρέστεροι
γυναικὸς ἀντίοι σταθέν-
τες ἐννέπουσι· Κατθανῇ κατθανῇ·
κακός σ' ἀποκτείνει πόσις,
κασιγνήτου προδοὺς
ἐν Ἄργει θανεῖν γόνον.
1465 ἁ δ' ἀνίαχεν ἴαχεν· Ὤμοι μοι.
λευκὸν δ' ἐμβαλοῦσα πῆχυν στέρνα
κτύπησεν κάρα ‹τε› μέλεον πλαγάν,

1451 ἄλλον ἄλλοσε del. Burges
1454b ‹αἰαῖ› Hartung

572

in the stables, some
in the arcades, while others he moved
from here to there [each severally], keeping them
far from their mistress.

CHORUS LEADER

And what happened after that?

PHRYGIAN

Mother, mother of Ida,
mighty, mighty goddess, alas ⟨alas⟩
for the murderous sufferings, the lawless woes
I have seen, have seen in the royal palace!
From beneath the concealment
of purple-bordered robes
they took swords in their hands
and whirled their glances from one side to the other
to see that no one was there.
Like wild boars of the mountain
they halted before the woman
and said, "You will die, you will die!
Your slayer is your cowardly husband,
who abandoned his brother's son
to death in Argos."
And she cried out, cried out, "Ah, ah me!"
And plying her pale forearm she made
her chest ⟨and⟩ head resound with a pitiable blow,

1458–9a ἄλλοσ᾽ ἄλλοθεν Burges: ἄλλος ἄλλοσε C

1466 στέρνα Weil: -οις C

1467 κάρα ⟨τε⟩ Willink (⟨τε⟩ iam Weil): κρᾶτα C

573

φυγάδι δὲ ποδὶ τὸ χρυσεοσάμβαλον ἴχνος
ἔφερεν ἔφερεν· ἐς κόμας δὲ δακτύλους
1470 δικὼν Ὀρέστας, Μυκηνίδ᾽ ἀρβύλαν
προβάς, ὤμοις ἀρι-
στεροῖσιν ἀνακλάσας δέραν,
παίειν λαιμῶν ἔμελ-
λεν εἴσω μέλαν ξίφος.

ΧΟΡΟΣ

ποῦ δ᾽ ἦτ᾽ ἀμύνειν οἱ κατὰ στέγας Φρύγες;

ΦΡΥΞ

ἰαχᾷ δόμων θύρετρα καὶ σταθμοὺς
1475 μοχλοῖσιν ἐκβαλόντες, ἔνθ᾽ ἐμίμνομεν,
βοηδρομοῦμεν ἄλλος ἄλλοθεν στέγας,
ὁ μὲν πέτρους, ὁ δ᾽ ἀγκύλας,
ὁ δὲ ξίφος πρόκωπον ἐν χεροῖν ἔχων.
ἔναντα δ᾽ ἦλθεν Πυλάδας ἀλίαστος,
1480 οἷος οἷος Ἕκτωρ
ὁ Φρύγιος ἢ ⟨καὶ⟩ τρικόρυθος Αἴας,
ὃν εἶδον εἶδον ἐν πύλαις Πριαμίσι· φασ-
γάνων δ᾽ ἀκμὰς συνήψαμεν.
τότε δὴ τότε διαπρεπεῖς
Φρύγες ὅσσον Ἄρεως ἀλκὰν ⟨ἀλκὰν⟩
1485 ἥσσονες Ἑλλάδος ἐγενόμεθ᾽ αἰχμᾶς,
ὁ μὲν οἰχόμενος φυγάς, ὁ δὲ νέκυς ὤν,
ὁ δὲ τραῦμα φέρων, ὁ δὲ λισσόμενος,

1468 φυγάδι Facius: φυγᾷ fere C
1481 ⟨καὶ⟩ Diggle metri causa

then with fleeing foot her gold-sandaled step
she bore away, away. But Orestes
darted his fingers to her hair,
putting his Mycenean boot ahead,
and yanking her neck back to his left shoulder
meant to thrust his dark
sword into her throat.

CHORUS LEADER
And where were you to defend her, you Phrygian house
slaves?

PHRYGIAN
As the house reechoed the sound we with crowbars
forced out the doorposts and frames where we were being
    held
and ran to her aid from here and there in the palace,
one man carrying stones, another a curved bow,
another a drawn sword in his hand.
But to meet us there came Pylades, unyielding
as Hector, Hector
the Phrygian or <even> triple-helmeted Ajax,
whom I saw, I saw, at Priam's gates.
We joined sword points.
And then, then it was clear
how much, in the fight, <the fight> of Ares,
the Phrygians were born inferior to Greek war might:
one of us fled away, one lay dead,
one was wounded, and another fell to entreaty

1484 Φρύγες post Herwerden Diggle: ἐγένοντο Φρύγες C
<ἀλκὰν> West

θανάτου προβολάν·
ὑπὸ σκότον δ' ἐφεύγομεν.
[νεκροὶ δ' ἔπιπτον, οἱ δ' ἔμελλον, οἱ δ' ἔκειντ'.]
1490 ἔμολε δ' ἁ τάλαιν' Ἑρμιόνα δόμους
ἐπὶ φόνῳ χαμαιπετεῖ ματρὸς ἅ
νιν ἔτεκεν τλάμων.
ἄθυρσοι δ' οἷά νιν
Βάκχαι σκύμνον ἐν χεροῖν
ὀρείαν ξυνήρπασαν·
πάλιν δὲ τᾶς Διὸς κόρας
ἐπὶ σφαγὰν ἔτεινον· ἁ δ'
1495 ἐγένετο διαπρὸ δωμάτων ἄφαντος,
ὦ Ζεῦ καὶ Γᾶ καὶ Φῶς καὶ Νύξ,
ἤτοι φαρμάκοις
ἢ μάγων τέχναις ἢ θεῶν κλοπαῖς.
τὰ δ' ὕστερ' οὐκέτ' οἶδα· δραπέταν γὰρ ἐξ-
έκλεπτον ἐκ δόμων πόδα.
1500 πολύπονα δὲ πολύπονα πάθεα Μενέλας
ἀνσχόμενος Τροίαθεν ἀνόνατ' ἔλαβε
τὸν Ἑλένας γάμον.

ΧΟΡΟΣ

καὶ μὴν ἀμείβει καινὸν ἐκ καινῶν τόδε·
ξιφηφόρον γὰρ εἰσορῶ πρὸ δωμάτων
1505 βαίνοντ' Ὀρέστην ἐπτοημένῳ ποδί.

1489 del. Willink
1493a Βάκχαι Willink: δραμόντε(ς) B- C
1494a τᾶς ... κόρας Paley: τὰν ... κόραν C

576

to save his life.
We fled into the shadows.
[Some were falling dead, others were about to, and others
    lay dead.]
But poor Hermione came into the house
just as the luckless mother who bore her
was being killed and sinking to earth.
Like bacchants without thyrsoi
falling upon a mountain whelp
they rushed and seized her in their grasp.
Then back they turned to the slaying
of Zeus's daughter. But she
was nowhere to be seen throughout the house—
O Zeus and Earth, O Daylight and Dark Night—
either because of drugs
or magicians' contrivance or stolen away by the gods.
What happened thereafter I do not know: I stole
my feet from the house and ran.
Though Menelaus has endured trouble and toil, toil,
it was all in vain that from Troy he brought home
Helen his wife.

Enter ORESTES, *sword in hand, from the house.*

CHORUS LEADER
But see, one strange thing succeeds another: I see Orestes,
armed with a sword, coming out in front of the house with
agitation in his step.

1494b ἁ δ' Wilamowitz: ἁ δ' ἐκ θαλάμων C
1500 Μενέλας Willink: Μενέλαος C
1501 Τροίαθεν ἀνόνατ' Willink: ἀνόνητον ἀπὸ Τροίας C

ΟΡΕΣΤΗΣ

ποῦ 'στιν οὗτος ὃς πέφευγε τοὐμὸν ἐκ δόμων ξίφος;

ΦΡΥΞ

προσκυνῶ σ', ἄναξ, νόμοισι βαρβάροισι
προσπίτνων.

ΟΡΕΣΤΗΣ

οὐκ ἐν Ἰλίῳ τάδ' ἐστὶν ἀλλ' ἐν Ἀργείᾳ χθονί.

ΦΡΥΞ

πανταχοῦ ζῆν ἡδὺ μᾶλλον ἢ θανεῖν τοῖς σώφροσιν.

ΟΡΕΣΤΗΣ

1510   οὔτι που κραυγὴν ἔθηκας, Μενέλεῳ βοηδρομεῖν;

ΦΡΥΞ

σοὶ μὲν οὖν ἔγωγ' ἀμύνειν· ἀξιώτερος γὰρ εἶ.

ΟΡΕΣΤΗΣ

ἐνδίκως ἡ Τυνδάρειος ἆρα παῖς διώλετο;

ΦΡΥΞ

ἐνδικώτατ', εἴ γε λαιμοὺς εἶχε τριπτύχους τεμεῖν.

ΟΡΕΣΤΗΣ

δειλίᾳ γλώσσῃ χαρίζῃ, τἄνδον οὐχ οὕτω φρονῶν.

ΦΡΥΞ

1515   οὐ γάρ, ἥτις Ἑλλάδ' αὐτοῖς Φρυξὶ διελυμήνατο;

ΟΡΕΣΤΗΣ

ὄμοσον (εἰ δὲ μή, κτενῶ σε) μὴ λέγειν ἐμὴν χάριν.

1512 διώλλυτο West: -ώλετ' ἄν Herwerden
1513 τεμεῖν post F. W. Schmidt (θενεῖν) Kovacs: θανεῖν C

578

ORESTES

Where is the man who fled from the house before my
sword?

PHRYGIAN

(*bowing down before him*) I prostrate myself before you,
my lord, bowing down in Asian fashion.

ORESTES

We're not in Ilium now: this is Argos.

PHRYGIAN

Everywhere the prudent find it sweeter to live than to die.

ORESTES

Were you by chance trying to raise help for Menelaus?

PHRYGIAN

Oh no, help for you! You deserve it more!

ORESTES

So it was just that Tyndareus' daughter perished?

PHRYGIAN

Oh, most just, even if she had three throats to cut!

ORESTES

You're a coward, trying to curry favor with your tongue:
this is not what you really think.

PHRYGIAN

No? When she has ruined Greece—and the Phrygians
too?

ORESTES

Swear an oath (or I'll kill you) that you're not just saying so
to please me.

ΦΡΥΞ

τὴν ἐμὴν ψυχὴν κατώμοσ’, ἣν ἂν εὐορκοῖμ’ ἐγώ.

ΟΡΕΣΤΗΣ

ὧδε κἀν Τροίᾳ σίδηρος πᾶσι Φρυξὶν ἦν φόβος;

ΦΡΥΞ

ἄπεχε φάσγανον· πέλας γὰρ δεινὸν ἀνταυγεῖ φόνον.

ΟΡΕΣΤΗΣ

1520   μὴ πέτρος γένῃ δέδοικας ὥστε Γοργόν’ εἰσιδών;

ΦΡΥΞ

μὴ μὲν οὖν νεκρός· τὸ Γοργοῦς δ’ οὐ κάτοιδ’ ἐγὼ
κάρα.

ΟΡΕΣΤΗΣ

δοῦλος ὢν φοβῇ τὸν Ἅιδην, ὅς σ’ ἀπαλλάξει
κακῶν;

ΦΡΥΞ

πᾶς ἀνήρ, κἂν δοῦλος ᾖ τις, ἥδεται τὸ φῶς ὁρῶν.

ΟΡΕΣΤΗΣ

εὖ λέγεις· σῴζει σε σύνεσις. ἀλλὰ βαῖν’ ἔσω
δόμων.

ΦΡΥΞ

1525   οὐκ ἄρα κτενεῖς μ’;

ΟΡΕΣΤΗΣ

ἀφεῖσαι.

ΦΡΥΞ

καλὸν ἔπος λέγεις τόδε.

PHRYGIAN

I swear by my life—and I'd not swear falsely by that!

ORESTES

Were you Phrygians so afraid of the sword even in Troy?

PHRYGIAN

Move your sword away from me: close up it has grim death in its gleam.

ORESTES

Afraid that you'll turn to stone, like one who has seen a Gorgon?

PHRYGIAN

No, that I'll turn to a corpse: I know nothing about this Gorgon person.

ORESTES

Do you fear death, slave that you are, a death that will release you from misery?

PHRYGIAN

Everyone, even a slave, takes pleasure in looking on the light.

ORESTES

Well said! Your good sense is your salvation. But go into the house.

PHRYGIAN

So you won't kill me?

ORESTES

You have been spared.

PHRYGIAN

What you say is good news.

ΟΡΕΣΤΗΣ

ἀλλὰ μεταβουλευσόμεσθα.

ΦΡΥΞ

τοῦτο δ᾽ οὐ καλῶς λέγεις.

ΟΡΕΣΤΗΣ

μῶρος, εἰ δοκεῖς με τλῆναί σ᾽ ἂν καθαιμάξαι δέρην·
οὔτε γὰρ γυνὴ πέφυκας οὔτ᾽ ἐν ἀνδράσιν σύ γ᾽ εἶ.
τοῦ δὲ μὴ στῆσαί σε κραυγὴν οὕνεκ᾽ ἐξῆλθον
    δόμων·

1530 ὀξὺ γὰρ βοῆς ἀκούσαν Ἄργος ἐξεγείρεται.
Μενέλεων δ᾽ οὐ τάρβος ἡμῖν ἀναλαβεῖν ἔσω ξίφους.
ἀλλ᾽ ἴτω ξανθοῖς ἐπ᾽ ὤμων βοστρύχοις
    γαυρούμενος.
εἰ δέ γ᾽ Ἀργείους ἐπάξει τοῖσδε δώμασιν λαβών,
τὸν Ἑλένης φόνον διώκων, κἀμὲ μὴ σώει θανεῖν

1535 σύγγονόν τ᾽ ἐμὴν φίλον τε τὸν τάδε ξυνδρῶντά μοι,
παρθένον τε καὶ δάμαρτα δύο νεκρὼ κατόψεται.

ἀντ.

ΧΟΡΟΣ

ἰὼ ἰὼ τύχα·
ἕτερον εἰς ἀγῶν᾽ ἕτερον αὖ δόμος
φοβερὸν ἀμφὶ τοὺς Ἀτρείδας πίτνει.
τί δρῶμεν; ἀγγέλλωμεν ἐς πόλιν τάδε;

1540 ἢ σῖγ᾽ ἔχωμεν; ἀσφαλέστερον, φίλαι.
ἴδε πρὸ δωμάτων ἴδε προκηρύσσει

1526 fort. μεταβουλευόμεσθα   1527 σ᾽ ἂν Monk: σὴν C

ORESTES

But I shall adopt a new plan.

PHRYGIAN

That's not good news.

ORESTES

Fool, do you think that I would deign to bloody your neck?
You're not a woman by birth nor yet do you count as a man.
But it was to stop you raising a cry that I came out of the
house: Argos is keen when roused, once it has heard a
shout. Yet after all I'm not afraid of catching Menelaus at
sword range. Let him come in all his pride over his shoul-
der-length golden locks! But if he brings Argives against
this house, intent upon avenging Helen's murder, and
won't save me, my sister, and my friend and accomplice
from death, he will see both his daughter and his wife lying
dead.

Exit the PHRYGIAN *by Eisodos A,* ORESTES *into the* skene.

CHORUS

Ah, ah, fate!
Into another fearful trial, another, concerning the Atridae
the house again falls.
What shall we do? Shall we bear this news to the city
or keep silent? Silence is safer, my friends.
See, before the house, see, leaping high into the air

1533–6 del. Seidensticker dubitanter (1535 iam Paley)
1533 δέ γ' Willink: γὰρ C
1534 σώσει θανεῖν Blaydes: σώσῃ θ- a: σῴζειν θέλῃ ceteri
codd.   1535 φίλον Weil: Πυλάδην C

θοάζων ὅδ' αἰθέρος ἄνω καπνός.
ἅπτουσι πεύκας, ὡς πυρώσοντες δόμους
τοὺς Τανταλείους οὐδ' ἀφίστανται πόνου.
1545 τέλος ἔχει δαίμων βροτοῖς,
τέλος ὅπᾳ θέλῃ.
μεγάλα δέ τις ἁ δύναμις καὶ ἀλαστόρων·
ἔπεσ' ἔπεσε μέλαθρα τάδε δι' αἱμάτων
διὰ τὸ Μυρτίλου πέσημ' ἐκ δίφρου.

—ἀλλὰ μὴν καὶ τόνδε λεύσσω Μενέλεων δόμων πέλας
1550 ὀξύπουν, ᾐσθημένον που τὴν τύχην ἢ νῦν πάρα.
οὐκέτ' ἂν φθάνοιτε κλῇθρα συμπεραίνοντες μοχλοῖς,
ὦ κατὰ στέγας Ἀτρεῖδαι. δεινὸν εὐτυχῶν ἀνὴρ
πρὸς κακῶς πράσσοντας, ὡς σὺ νῦν, Ὀρέστα,
δυστυχεῖς.

МЕΝΕΛΑΟΣ
ἥκω κλυὼν τὰ δεινὰ καὶ δραστήρια
1555 δισσοῖν λεόντοιν· οὐ γὰρ ἄνδρ' αὐτὼ καλῶ.
ἤκουσα μὲν γὰρ τὴν ἐμὴν ξυνάορον
ὡς οὐ τέθνηκεν, ἀλλ' ἄφαντος οἴχεται,
κενὴν ἀκούσας βάξιν, ἣν φόβῳ σφαλεὶς
ἤγγειλέ μοί τις. ἀλλὰ τοῦ μητροκτόνου
1560 τεχνάσματ' ἐστὶ ταῦτα καὶ πολὺς γέλως.
ἀνοιγέτω τις δῶμα· προσπόλοις λέγω
ὠθεῖν πύλας τάσδ', ὡς ἂν ἀλλὰ παῖδ' ἐμὴν
ῥυσώμεθ' ἀνδρῶν ἐκ χερῶν μιαιφόνων

---

¹⁵⁴⁴ πόνου a: φόνου b   ¹⁵⁴⁷ καὶ West: δι' C

smoke is bringing a first message.
They are lighting torches in order to set fire
to the house of Tantalus, they do not rest from toil.
The outcome for mortals is sent by God,
the outcome as he wishes.
But great too is the power of avenging spirits.
This house has been thrown, been thrown into the midst
    of blood
by Myrtilus' fall from the chariot.

Enter MENELAUS *with retinue by Eisodos A.*

CHORUS LEADER
But here I see Menelaus approaching the house with hurried step: he must have heard about what has happened. You in the house, Atreus' descendants, it's high time you finished bolting the doors with bars! A prospering man is a dangerous thing when he comes against those with misfortunes like yours, Orestes!

MENELAUS
I have come here because I have heard of the terrible and violent deeds of these twin lions: I do not call them "men." To be sure, what I have heard is that my wife has disappeared, not been killed. That was an idle tale, reported to me by someone confused by fear. In reality this is a piece of the matricide's trickery, and an absurd story it is.

    Open up the house, someone! Attendants, I order you to push in these gates so that at least I may rescue my daughter from the hands of the murderers [and so that I

1550 del. Nauck   1556 μὲν γὰρ Kirchhoff: γὰρ δὴ C

[καὶ τὴν τάλαιναν ἀθλίαν δάμαρτ᾽ ἐμὴν
1565 λάβωμεν, ᾗ δεῖ ξυνθανεῖν ἐμῇ χερὶ
τοὺς διολέσαντας τὴν ἐμὴν ξυνάορον].

ΟΡΕΣΤΗΣ

οὗτος σύ, κλῄθρων τῶνδε μὴ ψαύσῃς χερί·
Μενέλαον εἶπον, ὃς πεπύργωσαι θράσει·
ἢ τῷδε θριγκῷ κρᾶτα συνθραύσω σέθεν,
1570 ῥήξας παλαιὰ γεῖσα, τεκτόνων πόνον.
μοχλοῖς δ᾽ ἄραρε κλῇθρα, σῆς βοηδρόμου
σπουδῆς ἅ σ᾽ εἴρξει, μὴ δόμων ἔσω περᾶν.

ΜΕΝΕΛΑΟΣ

ἔα, τί χρῆμα; λαμπάδων ὁρῶ σέλας,
δόμων δ᾽ ἐπ᾽ ἄκρων τούσδε πυργηρουμένους,
1575 ξίφος δ᾽ ἐμῆς θυγατρὸς ἐπίφρουρον δέρῃ.

ΟΡΕΣΤΗΣ

πότερον ἐρωτᾶν ἢ κλύειν ἐμοῦ θέλεις;

ΜΕΝΕΛΑΟΣ

οὐδέτερ᾽· ἀνάγκη δ᾽, ὡς ἔοικε, σου κλύειν.

ΟΡΕΣΤΗΣ

μέλλω κτανεῖν σου θυγατέρ᾽, εἰ βούλῃ μαθεῖν.

ΜΕΝΕΛΑΟΣ

Ἑλένην φονεύσας ἐπὶ φόνῳ πράσσεις φόνον;

1564–6 suspectos habuit Wecklein, del. Harberton

might get hold of my poor suffering wife, who must be joined in death by those who destroyed my wife]!

Menelaus' servants are approaching the gates when ORESTES, *Electra, Pylades, and Hermione appear on the roof of the* skene. *Orestes holds a sword to the throat of Hermione, and Pylades and Electra hold smoking torches.*

ORESTES

You there, keep your hands off those doors! I mean you, Menelaus, so towering in your pride! Or with this coping stone, broken off from the ancient cornice masons have made, I shall smash your head! The doors are made fast with bars, and they will keep you from going in and trying to rescue anyone.

MENELAUS

Ah, ah, what is this? I see the gleam of torches, these men besieged on the top of the house, and a sword standing guard at my daughter's neck!

ORESTES

Do you want to ask questions or listen to me?

MENELAUS

Neither, but it seems I must listen to you.

ORESTES

If you'd like to know, I am about to kill your daughter.

MENELAUS

Having murdered Helen are you compounding murder with murder?

ΟΡΕΣΤΗΣ

1580 εἰ γὰρ κατέσχον μὴ θεῶν κλεφθεὶς ὕπο.

ΜΕΝΕΛΑΟΣ

ἀρνῇ κατακτὰς κἀφ' ὕβρει λέγεις τάδε;

ΟΡΕΣΤΗΣ

λυπράν γε τὴν ἄρνησιν· εἰ γὰρ ὤφελον . . .

ΜΕΝΕΛΑΟΣ

τί χρῆμα δρᾶσαι; παρακαλεῖς γὰρ †ἐς φόβον†.

ΟΡΕΣΤΗΣ

τὴν Ἑλλάδος μιάστορ' εἰς Ἅιδου βαλεῖν.

ΜΕΝΕΛΑΟΣ

1585 ἀπόδος δάμαρτος νέκυν, ὅπως χώσω τάφῳ.

ΟΡΕΣΤΗΣ

θεοὺς ἀπαίτει. παῖδα δὲ κτενῶ σέθεν.

ΜΕΝΕΛΑΟΣ

ὁ μητροφόντης †ἐπὶ φόνῳ πράσσεις φόνον†;

ΟΡΕΣΤΗΣ

ὁ πατρὸς ἀμύντωρ, ὃν σὺ προύδωκας θανεῖν.

ΜΕΝΕΛΑΟΣ

οὐκ ἤρκεσέν σοι τὸ παρὸν αἷμα μητέρος;

1583 fort. ἐς στόνον vel ἐκ φόβου

1587-8 suspectos habuit Wecklein, del. Wilamowitz, propter
1579: sed fort. ex 1579 huc irrepserunt verba ἐπὶ . . . φόνον,
extrusis quae antiquitus hic steterunt, e.g. συγγενεῖς κτείνεις ἀεί

1589-90 ante 1585 trai. West

ORESTES
How I wish I had accomplished that and not been robbed of it by the gods!

MENELAUS
Are you denying you killed her and saying this to mock me?

ORESTES
Yes, and an unwelcome denial it is: if only I had managed . . .

MENELAUS
To do what? Your words make me weep.

ORESTES
. . . to cast that defiler of Hellas into Hades!

MENELAUS
Give me back my wife's body so that I may pile a grave mound on it!

ORESTES
Ask the gods for her. But I shall kill your daughter.

MENELAUS
Will you, the mother killer, keep on killing?

ORESTES
Yes, I the father avenger, whom you abandoned to his death!

MENELAUS
Your mother's blood already on your hands was not enough for you?

ΟΡΕΣΤΗΣ

1590 οὐκ ἂν κάμοιμι τὰς κακὰς κτείνων ἀεί.

ΜΕΝΕΛΑΟΣ

ἦ καὶ σύ, Πυλάδη, τοῦδε κοινωνεῖς φόνου;

ΟΡΕΣΤΗΣ

φησὶν σιωπῶν· ἀρκέσω δ' ἐγὼ λέγων.

ΜΕΝΕΛΑΟΣ

ἀλλ' οὔτι χαίρων, ἤν γε μὴ φύγῃς πτεροῖς.

ΟΡΕΣΤΗΣ

οὐ φευξόμεσθα· πυρὶ δ' ἀνάψομεν δόμους.

ΜΕΝΕΛΑΟΣ

1595 ἦ γὰρ πατρῷον δῶμα πορθήσεις τόδε;

ΟΡΕΣΤΗΣ

ὡς μή γ' ἔχῃς σύ, τήνδ' ἐπισφάξας πυρί.

ΜΕΝΕΛΑΟΣ

κτεῖν'· ὡς κτανών γε τῶνδέ μοι δώσεις δίκην.

[ΟΡΕΣΤΗΣ

ἔσται τάδε.

ΜΕΝΕΛΑΟΣ

ἆ ἆ, μηδαμῶς δράσῃς τάδε.]

ΟΡΕΣΤΗΣ

1599 σίγα νυν, ἀνέχου δ' ἐνδίκως πράσσων κακῶς.

ΜΕΝΕΛΑΟΣ

1608 ἄπαιρε θυγατρὸς φάσγανον.

ORESTES

ORESTES
I won't grow weary of always killing wicked women.

MENELAUS
Pylades, are you also taking part in this murder?

ORESTES
By his silence he says yes. It is enough that I do the talking.

MENELAUS
But you'll pay for your crime unless you escape on wings.

ORESTES
We will not escape: we're going to set fire to the house.

MENELAUS
Will you really sack this house that was your father's?

ORESTES
Yes, to keep you from getting it! And I'll cut her throat over the flames!

MENELAUS
Kill away! You'll pay the penalty for her murder to me!

[**ORESTES**
I'll do it.

MENELAUS
Ah, ah, don't!]

ORESTES
Say no more then and endure the bad fortune you have deserved!

MENELAUS
Remove the sword from my daughter!

1598 del. Heiland   1608–12 post 1599 trai. Willink

ΟΡΕΣΤΗΣ
ψευδὴς ἔφυς.

ΜΕΝΕΛΑΟΣ
1609 ἀλλὰ κτενεῖς μου θυγατέρ';

ΟΡΕΣΤΗΣ
οὐ ψευδὴς ἔτ' εἶ.

ΜΕΝΕΛΑΟΣ
1610 οἴμοι, τί δράσω;

ΟΡΕΣΤΗΣ
πεῖθ' ἐς Ἀργείους μολὼν . . .

ΜΕΝΕΛΑΟΣ
1611 πειθὼ τίν';

ΟΡΕΣΤΗΣ
ἡμᾶς μὴ θανεῖν αἰτοῦ πόλιν.

ΜΕΝΕΛΑΟΣ
1612 ἢ παῖδά μου φονεύσεθ';

ΟΡΕΣΤΗΣ
ὧδ' ἔχει τάδε.

ΜΕΝΕΛΑΟΣ
1600 ἦ γὰρ δίκαιον ζῆν σε;

ΟΡΕΣΤΗΣ
καὶ κρατεῖν γε γῆς.

ΜΕΝΕΛΑΟΣ
ποίας;

ORESTES

Ah, so you were dissembling.

MENELAUS

But will you kill my daughter?

ORESTES

Now you're being truthful.

MENELAUS

Ah, ah, what am I to do?

ORESTES

Go and persuade the Argives . . .

MENELAUS

Persuade them of what?

ORESTES

Ask the city that we not be killed.

MENELAUS

Or you'll kill my daughter?

ORESTES

That's the way things stand.

MENELAUS

Can it be right for you to live?

ORESTES

Yes, and to rule the country.

MENELAUS

What country?

ΟΡΕΣΤΗΣ
ἐν Ἄργει τῷδε τῷ Πελασγικῷ.

ΜΕΝΕΛΑΟΣ
εὖ γοῦν θίγοις ἂν χερνίβων . . .

ΟΡΕΣΤΗΣ
τί δὴ γὰρ οὔ;

ΜΕΝΕΛΑΟΣ
. . . καὶ σφάγια πρὸ δορὸς καταβάλοις.

ΟΡΕΣΤΗΣ
σὺ δ᾽ ἂν καλῶς;

ΜΕΝΕΛΑΟΣ
ἁγνὸς γάρ εἰμι χεῖρας.

ΟΡΕΣΤΗΣ
ἀλλ᾽ οὐ τὰς φρένας.

ΜΕΝΕΛΑΟΣ
1605   τίς δ᾽ ἂν προσείποι σ᾽;

ΟΡΕΣΤΗΣ
ὅστις ἐστὶ φιλοπάτωρ.

ΜΕΝΕΛΑΟΣ
ὅστις δὲ τιμᾷ μητέρ᾽;

ΟΡΕΣΤΗΣ
εὐδαίμων ἔφυ.

ΜΕΝΕΛΑΟΣ
1607   οὔκουν σύ γ᾽.

ORESTES

Pelasgian Argos here.

MENELAUS

You would be just the man to handle the lustral basin . . .

ORESTES

Well, why not?

MENELAUS

. . . and make sacrifices before battle!

ORESTES

But *you* would be better?

MENELAUS

Yes: my hands are pure.

ORESTES

But your heart is not.

MENELAUS

But who would speak to you?

ORESTES

Anyone who loves his father.

MENELAUS

And anyone who honors his mother?

ORESTES

He's a lucky man.

MENELAUS

Which *you* at any rate are not.

ΟΡΕΣΤΗΣ
οὐ γὰρ ἁνδάνουσιν αἱ κακαί.

ΜΕΝΕΛΑΟΣ
1613 ὦ τλῆμον Ἑλένη ...

ΟΡΕΣΤΗΣ
τἀμὰ δ᾽ οὐχὶ τλήμονα;

ΜΕΝΕΛΑΟΣ
... σφάγιον ἐκόμισά σ᾽ ἐκ Φρυγῶν ...

ΟΡΕΣΤΗΣ
εἰ γὰρ τόδ᾽ ἦν.

ΜΕΝΕΛΑΟΣ
1615 ... πόνους πονήσας μυρίους.

ΟΡΕΣΤΗΣ
πλήν γ᾽ εἰς ἐμέ.

ΜΕΝΕΛΑΟΣ
πέπονθα δεινά.

ΟΡΕΣΤΗΣ
τότε γὰρ ἦσθ᾽ ἀνωφελής.

ΜΕΝΕΛΑΟΣ
ἔχεις με.

ΟΡΕΣΤΗΣ
σαυτὸν σύ γ᾽ ἔλαβες κακὸς γεγώς.
ἀλλ᾽ εἶ᾽, ὕφαπτε δώματ᾽, Ἠλέκτρα, τάδε·
σύ τ᾽, ὦ φίλων μοι τῶν ἐμῶν σαφέστατε,
1620 Πυλάδη, κάταιθε γεῖσα τειχέων τάδε.

ORESTES

No: I don't like wicked women.

MENELAUS

O my luckless Helen . . .

ORESTES

Am I not luckless?

MENELAUS

. . . I brought you home from Troy only to have your throat cut . . .

ORESTES

I wish it were so!

MENELAUS

. . . after toiling without measure!

ORESTES

But no toiling on my behalf.

MENELAUS

I have suffered terribly.

ORESTES

Yes: because you would not help us.

MENELAUS

You have captured me.

ORESTES

You captured yourself by your own cowardice.

Come then, Electra, set this house on fire! And you, Pylades, most faithful of friends to me, set alight these battlements!

1617 fort. εἶλές με

ΜΕΝΕΛΑΟΣ

ὦ γαῖα Δαναῶν ἱππίου τ᾽ Ἄργους κτίται,
οὐχ εἶ᾽ ἐνόπλῳ ποδὶ βοηδρομήσετε;
πᾶσαν γὰρ ὑμῶν ὅδε βιάζεται πόλιν
ζῆν, αἷμα μητρὸς μυσαρὸν ἐξειργασμένος.

ΑΠΟΛΛΩΝ

1625 Μενέλαε, παῦσαι λῆμ᾽ ἔχων τεθηγμένον·
Φοῖβός σ᾽ ὁ Λητοῦς παῖς ὅδ᾽ ἐγγὺς ὢν καλῶ·
σύ θ᾽ ὃς ξιφήρης τῇδ᾽ ἐφεδρεύεις κόρῃ,
Ὀρέσθ᾽, ἵν᾽ εἰδῇς οὓς φέρων ἥκω λόγους.
Ἑλένην μέν, ἣν σὺ διολέσαι πρόθυμος ὢν
1630 ἥμαρτες, ὀργὴν Μενέλεῳ ποιούμενος,
[ἥδ᾽ ἐστίν, ἣν ὁρᾶτ᾽ ἐν αἰθέρος πτυχαῖς,
σεσωμένη τε κοὐ θανοῦσα πρὸς σέθεν.]
ἐγώ νιν ἐξέσωσα χὐπὸ φασγάνου
τοῦ σοῦ κελευσθεὶς ἥρπασ᾽ ἐκ Διὸς πατρός.
1635 Ζηνὸς γὰρ οὖσαν ζῆν νιν ἄφθιτον χρεών,
Κάστορί τε Πολυδεύκει τ᾽ ἐν αἰθέρος πτυχαῖς
σύνθακος ἔσται, ναυτίλοις σωτήριος·
[ἄλλην δὲ νύμφην ἐς δόμους κτῆσαι λαβών.]
ἐπεὶ θεοὶ τῷ τῆσδε καλλιστεύματι
1640 Ἕλληνας εἰς ἓν καὶ Φρύγας συνήγαγον
θανάτους τ᾽ ἔθηκαν, ὡς ἀπαντλοῖεν χθονὸς
ὕβρισμα θνητῶν ἀφθόνου πληρώματος.

1631–2 suspectos habuit Paley, del. Murray
1638 del. Wilamowitz

MENELAUS

Ho, land of the Danaans! Ho, settlers in horse-loving Argos! Arm yourselves and come on the run to help! This man, who has committed the abominable murder of his mother, is winning his life by violence against your whole community!

Enter by Eisodos B armed Argive citizens on the run. APOLLO appears with Helen on the mechane. *His first words cause the running citizens to halt in their tracks.*

APOLLO

Menelaus, blunt the keen edge of your heart's anger! I am Apollo, son of Leto, and I am calling you from nearby. And you, Orestes, who menace this girl, sword in hand, do likewise so that you can hear the message I am bringing.

As for Helen, whom you were eager to kill in your anger at Menelaus but could not: [here she is, she whom you see in heaven's recesses, not killed by you but safe and sound:] I saved her from under your very sword and spirited her away. Those were the orders of Zeus my father. For she is Zeus's daughter and so must live[32] an imperishable life, and with Castor and Polydeuces in heaven's recesses she will be enthroned as a savior to seafarers.[33] [Take another wife into your house.] For it was by her beauty that the gods brought Greeks and Phrygians to one place and caused deaths, in order to relieve the earth of the rank growth of mortals' boundless population.[34]

[32] There is a wordplay between *Zenos* (genitive of Zeus) and *zen*, "to live."   [33] This was Castor and Polydeuces' role: cf. *Electra* 1347–55. Giving this role to Helen is apparently an innovation of Euripides.   [34] See note on *Helen* 41.

τὰ μὲν καθ᾽ Ἑλένην ὧδ᾽ ἔχει· σὲ δ᾽ αὖ χρεών,
Ὀρέστα, γαίας τῆσδ᾽ ὑπερβαλόνθ᾽ ὅρους

1645 Παρράσιον οἰκεῖν δάπεδον ἐνιαυτοῦ κύκλον.
κεκλήσεται δὲ σῆς φυγῆς ἐπώνυμον
[Ἀζᾶσιν Ἀρκάσιν τ᾽ Ὀρέστειον καλεῖν].
ἐνθένδε δ᾽ ἐλθὼν τὴν Ἀθηναίων πόλιν
δίκην ὑπόσχες αἵματος μητροκτόνου

1650 Εὐμενίσι τρισσαῖς· θεοὶ δέ σοι δίκης βραβῆς
πάγοισιν ἐν Ἀρείοισιν εὐσεβεστάτην
ψῆφον διοίσουσ᾽, ἔνθα νικῆσαί σε χρή.

ἐφ᾽ ἧς δ᾽ ἔχεις, Ὀρέστα, φάσγανον δέρῃ,
γῆμαι πέπρωταί σ᾽ Ἑρμιόνην· ὃς δ᾽ οἴεται

1655 Νεοπτόλεμος γαμεῖν νιν, οὐ γαμεῖ ποτε.
θανεῖν γὰρ αὐτῷ μοῖρα Δελφικῷ ξίφει,
δίκας Ἀχιλλέως πατρὸς ἐξαιτοῦντά με.
Πυλάδῃ δ᾽ ἀδελφῆς λέκτρον, ᾧ ποτ᾽ ᾔνεσας,
δός· ὁ δ᾽ ἐπιών νιν βίοτος εὐδαίμων μένει.

1660 Ἄργους δ᾽ Ὀρέστην, Μενέλεως, ἔα κρατεῖν,
ἐλθὼν δ᾽ ἄνασσε Σπαρτιάτιδος χθονός,
φερνὰς ἔχων δάμαρτος, ἥ σε μυρίοις
πόνοις διδοῦσα δεῦρ᾽ ἀεὶ διήνυσεν.
τὰ πρὸς πόλιν δὲ τῷδ᾽ ἐγὼ θήσω καλῶς,

1665 ὅς νιν φονεῦσαι μητέρ᾽ ἐξηνάγκασα.

ΟΡΕΣΤΗΣ

ὦ Λοξία μαντεῖε, σῶν θεσπισμάτων
οὐ ψευδόμαντις ἦσθ᾽ ἄρ᾽, ἀλλ᾽ ἐτήτυμος.

1647 del. Paley

600

That is how things stand with Helen. But you, Orestes, must cross this land's frontier and for the circuit of a year live in the plain of Parrhasia. It will receive a name from your exile there [for the Azanes and Arcadians to call it Oresteum].[35] From there go to the city of Athens and allow yourself to be prosecuted for matricide by the three Eumenides. On the Areopagus the gods as judges in the case will cast their votes most piously for either side, and there you are fated to be victorious.

Orestes, you are destined to marry Hermione, the woman at whose neck you are holding a sword: Neoptolemus, the man who thinks he will marry her, will never do so. He is fated to perish by a Delphian sword when he demands satisfaction from me for the death of his father Achilles. Give your sister in marriage to Pylades, the man to whom you promised her. The life that awaits him will be a blessed one.

Menelaus, in Argos allow Orestes to be king, and go rule the land of Sparta, enjoying it as a dowry from your wife, who to this present hour has constantly presented you with trouble. This man's relations with the city I shall set to rights, since it was I who compelled him to kill his mother.

ORESTES

O prophetic Loxias, you are not after all false in your prophecies but truthful! Yet at the time I was worried that

[35] In Parrhasia, in southern Arcadia, there was a town called Orestheion or Oresthasion. The similarity to Orestes' name gave rise to the legend of his exile there. Euripides, here and at *Electra* 1275, alludes to the city without giving its name, and it was an interpolator who supplied 1647.

καίτοι μ᾽ ἐσῄει δεῖμα, μή τινος κλύων
ἀλαστόρων δόξαιμι σὴν κλύειν ὄπα.
1670 ἀλλ᾽ εὖ τελεῖται, πείσομαι δὲ σοῖς λόγοις.
ἰδού, μεθίημ᾽ Ἑρμιόνην ἀπὸ σφαγῆς,
καὶ λέκτρ᾽ ἐπῄνεσ᾽, ἡνίκ᾽ ἂν διδῷ πατήρ.

ΜΕΝΕΛΑΟΣ

ὦ Ζηνὸς Ἑλένη χαῖρε παῖ· ζηλῶ δέ σε
θεῶν κατοικήσουσαν ὄλβιον δόμον.
1675 Ὀρέστα, σοὶ δὲ παῖδ᾽ ἐγὼ κατεγγυῶ,
Φοίβου λέγοντος· εὐγενὴς δ᾽ ἀπ᾽ εὐγενοῦς
γήμας ὄναιο καὶ σὺ χὠ διδοὺς ἐγώ.

ΑΠΟΛΛΩΝ

χωρεῖτέ νυν ἕκαστος οἷ προστάσσομεν,
νείκους τε διαλύεσθε.

ΜΕΝΕΛΑΟΣ

πείθεσθαι χρεών.

ΟΡΕΣΤΗΣ

1680 κἀγὼ τοιοῦτος· σπένδομαι δὲ συμφοραῖς,
Μενέλαε, καὶ σοῖς, Λοξία, θεσπίσμασιν.

ΑΠΟΛΛΩΝ

ἴτε νυν καθ᾽ ὁδόν, τὴν καλλίστην
θεῶν Εἰρήνην τιμῶντες· ἐγὼ δ᾽
Ἑλένην Διὸς μελάθροις πελάσω,
1685 λαμπρῶν ἄστρων πόλον ἐξανύσας,
ἔνθα παρ᾽ Ἥρᾳ τῇ θ᾽ Ἡρακλέους

1674 κατοικήσουσαν Weil: -σασαν C

I heard the voice of some avenging spirit and thought I was hearing yours. Still, it is turning out well, and I will do as you say.

See, I am releasing Hermione from slaughter. And I accept marriage with her whenever her father shall give her.

MENELAUS
Helen, daughter of Zeus, I wish you joy! And I count you blessed that you will go to live in the gods' blessed home.

Orestes, I give my daughter to you at Phoebus' command. Nobleman that you are, marrying into a noble house, may you have joy of it, both you and I who give her!

APOLLO
Go, each of you, where I have told you to go, and end your quarrel.

MENELAUS
We must obey.

ORESTES
That is my view too. I make peace with what has happened and with your oracles, Loxias.

The characters on the roof descend into the skene *and emerge from its door.*

APOLLO
Go your ways, then, holding Peace, loveliest of the gods, in honor. I shall bring Helen to the halls of Zeus, journeying to the bright starry sky. There by the side of Hera and

---

1684 Δίοις Nauck: Ζηνὸς vel Διὸς C

Ἥβῃ πάρεδρος θεὸς ἀνθρώποις
ἔσται σπονδαῖς ἔντιμος ἀεὶ
σὺν Τυνδαρίδαις τοῖς Διός, ὑγρᾶς
1690   ναύταις μεδέουσα θαλάσσης.

[ΧΟΡΟΣ
ὦ μέγα σεμνὴ Νίκη, τὸν ἐμὸν
βίοτον κατέχοις
καὶ μὴ λήγοις στεφανοῦσα.]

1691–3 del. Blomfield

Heracles' bride Hebe she will sit enthroned as a goddess for men, always worshiped with libations together with Zeus's sons, the Tyndarids, and will rule over the sea waves to the benefit of sailors!

[CHORUS LEADER
Victory, may you have my life in your charge and never cease garlanding my head!]

Exit APOLLO *and Helen by the* mechane, ORESTES, *Hermione,* MENELAUS *and retinue by Eisodos A, and Electra, Pylades, and* CHORUS *by Eisodos B.*

605

*Composed in ZephGreek and ZephText by
Technologies 'N Typography, Merrimac, Massachusetts.
Printed in Great Britain by St Edmundsbury Press Ltd,
Bury St Edmunds, Suffolk, on acid-free paper.
Bound by Hunter & Foulis Ltd, Edinburgh, Scotland.*